Microsoft® Works Suite 2000 For Dummies®

Cheat Sheet

Quick Formatting in Word

To Do This . . .	Press This . . .
Add or remove space	Ctrl+0 (zero) before paragraph
Indent	Ctrl+M
Un-indent	Ctrl+Shift+M
Bullet on/off	Click bullets button on toolbar
Format subscript	Ctrl+Equal sign (=)
Format superscript	Ctrl+Shift+Plus sign (+)

D0746418

Quick Spreadsheet Tricks

To Do This . . .	Do This . . .
Sum at end of column or row	Press Ctrl+M, or click Σ in the toolbar
Change column width	Drag edge to the right of column letter
Change row height	Drag edge below row number
Insert row above	Choose Insert⇨Row
Insert column to left	Choose Insert⇨Column

Number Formats in Spreadsheets and Databases

To Do This . . .	Press This . . .
Dollars	Ctrl+4 ($ key)
Percent	Ctrl+5 (% key)
Comma at thousands	Ctrl+, (comma)

Quick Formatting Almost Everywhere

To Do This . . .	Press This . . .
Undo edits	Ctrl+Z
Bold	Ctrl+B, or click B button on toolbar
Italic	Ctrl+I, or click *I* button on toolbar
Underline	Ctrl+U, or click U button on toolbar
Center	Ctrl+E, or click center-align button on toolbar
Left-align	Ctrl+L, or click left-align button on toolbar
Right-align	Ctrl+Shift+R, or click right-align button on toolbar
Remove font styles	Ctrl+spacebar
Insert page break	Ctrl+Enter
Change page margins	Choose File⇨Page Setup

For Dummies®: Bestselling Book Series for Beginners

Microsoft® Works Suite 2000 For Dummies®

Cheat Sheet

Navigating in Almost Any Document

To Do This . . .	Do This . . .
Scroll up/down	Use vertical scroll bar
Scroll sideways	Use horizontal scroll bar
Move right, left, up, down	Press arrow key
End of column/next paragraph	Press Ctrl+↓
Start of column, paragraph	Press Ctrl+↑
One screen up/down	Press PgUp/PgDn keys
Beginning/end of line or row	Press Home/End keys
Beginning/end of document	Press Ctrl+Home/Ctrl+End keys

Controlling Programs, Windows, and Documents Almost Everywhere

To Do This . . .	Do This . . .
Start Program	Double-click program icon
Start Program	Choose Start⇨Programs⇨ *your program*
Exit program	Choose File⇨Exit, or press Alt+F4
Start a new document	Choose File⇨New
Save a document	Press Ctrl+S
Open a document	Press Ctrl+O
Close a document	Press Ctrl+W
Choose an open window	Choose Window⇨1 *or* 2 *or* 3. . .
Print Preview	Choose File⇨Print Preview
Print	Press Ctrl+P
Get Help	Press F1

Editing Almost Everywhere

To Do This . . .	Do This . . .
Select something	Click it or drag across it
Select everything	Press Ctrl+A
Select with keys	Press Shift+*navigation key*
Delete	Press Delete key or Backspace key
Cut selection to Clipboard	Press Ctrl+X
Copy selection to Clipboard	Press Ctrl+C
Paste from Clipboard	Press Ctrl+V
Move	Select, drag to position
Copy	Select, Ctrl+drag to position
Insert file into document	Drag file from My Computer window

For Dummies®: Bestselling Book Series for Beginners

Microsoft® Works Suite 2000
FOR DUMMIES®

by David Kay

IDG Books Worldwide, Inc.
An International Data Group Company

Foster City, CA ◆ Chicago, IL ◆ Indianapolis, IN ◆ New York, NY

Microsoft® Works Suite 2000 For Dummies®

Published by
IDG Books Worldwide, Inc.
An International Data Group Company
919 E. Hillsdale Blvd.
Suite 400
Foster City, CA 94404
www.idgbooks.com (IDG Books Worldwide Web site)
www.dummies.com (Dummies Press Web site)

Library of Congress Catalog Card No.: 99-69373

ISBN: 0-7645-0685-4

Printed in the United States of America

10 9 8 7 6 5 4 3

1B/RY/QU/QQ/IN

Distributed in the United States by IDG Books Worldwide, Inc.

Distributed by CDG Books Canada Inc. for Canada; by Transworld Publishers Limited in the United Kingdom; by IDG Norge Books for Norway; by IDG Sweden Books for Sweden; by IDG Books Australia Publishing Corporation Pty. Ltd. for Australia and New Zealand; by TransQuest Publishers Pte Ltd. for Singapore, Malaysia, Thailand, Indonesia, and Hong Kong; by Gotop Information Inc. for Taiwan; by ICG Muse, Inc. for Japan; by Intersoft for South Africa; by Eyrolles for France; by International Thomson Publishing for Germany, Austria and Switzerland; by Distribuidora Cuspide for Argentina; by LR International for Brazil; by Galileo Libros for Chile; by Ediciones ZETA S.C.R. Ltda. for Peru; by WS Computer Publishing Corporation, Inc., for the Philippines; by Contemporanea de Ediciones for Venezuela; by Express Computer Distributors for the Caribbean and West Indies; by Micronesia Media Distributor, Inc. for Micronesia; by Chips Computadoras S.A. de C.V. for Mexico; by Editorial Norma de Panama S.A. for Panama; by American Bookshops for Finland.

For general information on IDG Books Worldwide's books in the U.S., please call our Consumer Customer Service department at 800-762-2974. For reseller information, including discounts and premium sales, please call our Reseller Customer Service department at 800-434-3422.

For information on where to purchase IDG Books Worldwide's books outside the U.S., please contact our International Sales department at 317-596-5530 or fax 317-572-4002.

For consumer information on foreign language translations, please contact our Customer Service department at 1-800-434-3422, fax 317-572-4002, or e-mail rights@idgbooks.com.

For information on licensing foreign or domestic rights, please phone +1-650-653-7098.

For sales inquiries and special prices for bulk quantities, please contact our Sales department at 800-762-2974 or write to the address above.

For information on using IDG Books Worldwide's books in the classroom or for ordering examination copies, please contact our Educational Sales department at 800-434-2086 or fax 317-572-4005.

For press review copies, author interviews, or other publicity information, please contact our Public Relations department at 650-653-7000 or fax 650-653-7500.

For authorization to photocopy items for corporate, personal, or educational use, please contact Copyright Clearance Center, 222 Rosewood Drive, Danvers, MA 01923, or fax 978-750-4470.

is a registered trademark under exclusive license to IDG Books Worldwide, Inc. from International Data Group, Inc.

About the Author

Dave Kay is a writer, engineer, wildlife tracker, and aspiring artist, combining professions with the same effectiveness as his favorite business establishment, Acton Muffler, Brake, and Ice Cream (now defunct). Dave's computer book contributions include IDG Books Worldwide, Inc., *For Dummies* titles on Microsoft Works, WordPerfect, Web publishing, and Dragon NaturallySpeaking, and McGraw-Hill titles *Internet: The Complete Reference*, and *Graphics File Formats*.

In his other life, Dave is the poo-bah of BrightLeaf Communications, where he writes and teaches. He spends his spare time in the woods, playing with molten glass, designing stage scenery, and singing Gilbert and Sullivan choruses in public. He lives in the boondocks of Massachusetts with his wife Katy and golden retriever, Alex.

ABOUT IDG BOOKS WORLDWIDE

Welcome to the world of IDG Books Worldwide.

IDG Books Worldwide, Inc., is a subsidiary of International Data Group, the world's largest publisher of computer-related information and the leading global provider of information services on information technology. IDG was founded more than 30 years ago by Patrick J. McGovern and now employs more than 9,000 people worldwide. IDG publishes more than 290 computer publications in over 75 countries. More than 90 million people read one or more IDG publications each month.

Launched in 1990, IDG Books Worldwide is today the #1 publisher of best-selling computer books in the United States. We are proud to have received eight awards from the Computer Press Association in recognition of editorial excellence and three from Computer Currents' First Annual Readers' Choice Awards. Our best-selling ...*For Dummies®* series has more than 50 million copies in print with translations in 31 languages. IDG Books Worldwide, through a joint venture with IDG's Hi-Tech Beijing, became the first U.S. publisher to publish a computer book in the People's Republic of China. In record time, IDG Books Worldwide has become the first choice for millions of readers around the world who want to learn how to better manage their businesses.

Our mission is simple: Every one of our books is designed to bring extra value and skill-building instructions to the reader. Our books are written by experts who understand and care about our readers. The knowledge base of our editorial staff comes from years of experience in publishing, education, and journalism — experience we use to produce books to carry us into the new millennium. In short, we care about books, so we attract the best people. We devote special attention to details such as audience, interior design, use of icons, and illustrations. And because we use an efficient process of authoring, editing, and desktop publishing our books electronically, we can spend more time ensuring superior content and less time on the technicalities of making books.

You can count on our commitment to deliver high-quality books at competitive prices on topics you want to read about. At IDG Books Worldwide, we continue in the IDG tradition of delivering quality for more than 30 years. You'll find no better book on a subject than one from IDG Books Worldwide.

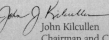

John Kilcullen
Chairman and CEO
IDG Books Worldwide, Inc.

Eighth Annual Computer Press Awards ≥ 1992

Ninth Annual Computer Press Awards ≥ 1993

WINNER

Tenth Annual Computer Press Awards ≥ 1994

WINNER

Eleventh Annual Computer Press Awards ≥ 1995

Dedication

This book is dedicated to Yankee Golden Retriever Rescue (www.ygrr.org) who made possible our blissful lives with wonderful adopted dogs: Teddy, Rusty (the Wonder Dog), and now, Alex.

Author's Acknowledgments

I would like to acknowledge the support of my wife Katy and my friends and family, from whose company I am sadly removed while writing these books. Special thanks for their help with this book go to the following folks:

- Richard Mansfield, author of *Visual Basic 6 Database Programming For Dummies* and *Visual Studio 6 For Dummies,* for his invaluable assistance in updating this book.

- Matt Wagner and the rest of the folks at Waterside Productions.

- The congenial editors employed by IDG Books Worldwide, including:

  - Project editor Paul (I only call if there's trouble) Levesque and the project editor for the previous edition of this book, Brian Kramer. They fainted not, though the hour drew nigh.

  - Copy editor Kim Darosett, for tolerating my tormented sentence structure and curmudgeonly ways.

  - Polymath technical editor Allen Wyatt, for his breadth of expertise, including his deep knowledge of seasonal employment patterns among house painters. (Allen offers his WordTips wisdom, free, at www.VitalNews.com/WordTips/).

Publisher's Acknowledgments

We're proud of this book; please register your comments through our IDG Books Worldwide Online Registration Form located at http://my2cents.dummies.com.

Some of the people who helped bring this book to market include the following:

Acquisitions, Editorial, and Media Development

Project Editor: Paul Levesque

Acquisitions Editor: Laura Moss

Copy Editors: Kim Darosett, William Barton

Technical Editor: Allen Wyatt

Editorial Manager: Leah Cameron

Editorial Assistant: Beth Parlon

Production

Project Coordinator: E. Shawn Aylsworth

Layout and Graphics: Amy Adrian, Kelly Hardesty, Tracy K. Oliver, Jill Piscitelli, Brent Savage, Brian Torwelle, Dan Whetstine, Erin Zeltner

Proofreaders: Laura Albert, Corey Bowen, John Greenough, Marianne Santy, Ethel Winslow, Vickie Broyles

Indexer: Sherry Massey

Special Help:
Amanda Foxworth, Sarah Shupert

General and Administrative

IDG Books Worldwide, Inc.: John Kilcullen, CEO

IDG Books Technology Publishing Group: Richard Swadley, Senior Vice President and Publisher; Walter R. Bruce III, Vice President and Publisher; Joseph Wikert, Vice President and Publisher; Mary Bednarek, Vice President and Director, Product Development; Andy Cummings, Publishing Director, General User Group; Mary C. Corder, Editorial Director; Barry Pruett, Publishing Director

IDG Books Consumer Publishing Group: Roland Elgey, Senior Vice President and Publisher; Kathleen A. Welton, Vice President and Publisher; Kevin Thornton, Acquisitions Manager; Kristin A. Cocks, Editorial Director

IDG Books Internet Publishing Group: Brenda McLaughlin, Senior Vice President and Publisher; Sofia Marchant, Online Marketing Manager

IDG Books Production for Branded Press: Debbie Stailey, Director of Production; Cindy L. Phipps, Manager of Project Coordination, Production Proofreading, and Indexing; Tony Augsburger, Manager of Prepress, Reprints, and Systems; Laura Carpenter, Production Control Manager; Shelley Lea, Supervisor of Graphics and Design; Debbie J. Gates, Production Systems Specialist; Robert Springer, Supervisor of Proofreading; Kathie Schutte, Production Supervisor

Packaging and Book Design: Patty Page, Manager, Promotions Marketing

◆

The publisher would like to give special thanks to Patrick J. McGovern, without whom this book would not have been possible.

◆

Contents at a Glance

Cartoons at a Glance

By Rich Tennant

Fax: 978-546-7747
E-mail: richtennant@the5thwave.com
World Wide Web: www.the5thwave.com

Table of Contents

· ·

Introduction

· ·

Congratulations! You have already proven your superior intelligence. Rather than blowing several hundred bucks on the latest and most muscle-bound software you can find, you're using Microsoft Works Suite 2000 — a bunch of software that can do probably everything you need for a lot less trouble and money. Heck, you're so smart that maybe you bought a PC with Works Suite already installed.

So then why, exactly, should you be reading a book for Dummies? Because Dummies are an underground group of people smart enough to say, "Okay, so I'm not a computer wizard. So sue me. Call me a dummy if you will. I still want to use this stuff." The *For Dummies* books are for people who

- ✔ Want to find out more about their software without being bored silly.

- ✔ Feel there should be a manual to explain the software manual.

- ✔ Actually want to get some work done. Soon. Like today.

- ✔ Don't want to wade through a lot of technical gibberish.

- ✔ Don't think like computer software engineers seem to think.

What's in This Book

This book describes how to use the software and tools of Microsoft Suite 2000, separately and together (for better or for worse, in sickness and in health, 'til an upgrade do you part). This book also includes an extensive appendix, which reveals all those Windows basics that most other books assume you already know. Specifically, in this book, you can find out about the following topics:

- ✔ Windows basics (opening, closing, and painting them shut)

- ✔ Word processing (like food processing, only messier) in Word

- ✔ Spreadsheets (for soft, comfortable naps on your spreadbed) in Works

- ✔ Databases (for storing all your baseless data) in Works

- ✔ Graphics (for charting and general doodling) in Word and Works

- ✔ Managing money (for your personal interest) with Microsoft Money

- ✔ Web browsing in Internet Explorer

✔ E-mail and newsgroup communications in Outlook Express

✔ Researching in the Encarta computerized encyclopedia

✔ Creating your own greeting cards, banners, and what-have-you in Microsoft Home Publishing

✔ Getting un-lost with Microsoft Streets and Trips

Who Do I Think You Are, Anyway?

Apart from thinking that you are a brilliant and highly literate person (evidenced by the fact that you bought or are considering buying this book), here's what I assume about you, the esteemed reader:

✔ Your PC has Microsoft Works Suite 2000 installed on it.

✔ You're more or less a beginner on the PC. You are not necessarily familiar with Works Suite, Windows, PC screens, keyboards, or mice.

✔ Speaking of mice, you don't really give a mouse's eyelash about Windows or PCs except for what you absolutely need to do your work.

✔ Heck, you may even have thought that Works Suite was part of Windows, if it came with your PC. (It's not.)

✔ If you're on a private computer network, you have a computer and network *guru* available — an expert whom you can pay off in cookies or pizza to solve network problems.

Apart from that, you could be darn near anybody. I know of mathematicians, computer scientists, business people, computer book authors, and day care center managers who use the Works Suite programs quite happily.

How to Use This Book

Nobody wants to sit down and read a book before they use their software. So don't. Instead, just look something up in the Index or Table of Contents and "go to it."

The only sane way to use this book is to follow along on your PC, using this book as a tour guide or road map — don't just read. I use pictures sometimes, but I don't throw in a picture of everything because you have the pictures right there on your PC screen. Those pictures are even in color!

This is mainly a reference book, so you don't have to read it from front to back. In fact, if you're new to PCs, start at the back: Read the appendix first. Within each part, the earlier chapters cover the more fundamental stuff. So if you want, you can just read the chapters in order (in each part) to get from the fundamentals to the more advanced tasks.

How This Book Is Organized

This book breaks things down into the following useful parts, including one part for each piece of Works Suite. Each part has something for everyone, whether you've never used a similar tool before or you're an old hand who just needs to figure out how a particular program works.

Part I: Crunching Numbers, Organizing Information

Two things that computers are traditionally good at (besides frustrating users) are crunching numbers and organizing information. A PC that didn't do those tasks would be stripped of its epaulets and drummed out of the ranks. Works Suite equips you with two general-purpose tools for doing all kinds of crunching and organizing: a spreadsheet program for analyzing and charting numbers, and a database program for organizing lists and inventories. Because these programs are general-purpose, and you need more information in order to bend them to your will, Part I is one of the larger sections of this book.

Part II: Putting Words in Word

In Part II, discover how to create documents of all kinds on one of the world's most commonly used word processors, Microsoft Word. Part II covers word processing starting with really basic basics, such as typing, deleting, moving, and copying, to subtle and elusive facts, such as where paragraph formatting hides. Later chapters introduce editing techniques and important adornments like page numbers, tables, borders, lines, headers, footers, graphics, and footnotes.

Part III: Learning to Love Money

You're probably already fond of money, but Part III helps you feel warmly about Microsoft Money. Find out how to track your income and expenses, create and stick to a budget, print checks, report your taxables and tax-deductibles, and create graphs and reports that make understanding your finances as easy as pie (charts).You can even track your investment values with price data downloaded from the Internet.

Part IV: 'Netting Ventured, 'Netting Gained

There's an information highway out there, all right, but it winds through a vast digital wilderness called the Internet. This part covers how to get connected to the Internet and use Microsoft's Internet Explorer to read information and download free stuff from the World Wide Web. Part IV also tells you how to start sending and receiving e-mail and joining in newsgroup discussions by using Outlook Express.

Part V: Entertaining Enlightenment

All work and no play makes PC users fall asleep on their keyboards. Microsoft, to help software users avoid such embarrassment, includes fun — and even enlightening — *infotainment* in Works Suite. In Part V, discover how Microsoft Encarta encyclopedia lets you explore a topic in half the time it would take in a printed encyclopedia. Part V also shows you how to create, print, and electronically send greeting cards, posters, banners, and other colorful projects with Microsoft Home Publishing. And if that's not entertainment or enlightenment enough — get lost! And then use Expedia Streets and Trips to get found again.

Part VI: The Part of Tens

The Part of Tens? Why not the part of twelves? Who knows, but thanks to the perfectly random act of fate that gave humans ten fingers, every *For Dummies* book has a Part of Tens. Here are Ten Nifty Tricks and Ten Things Not to Do, providing recommendations that make your PC a better place to live.

Appendix: Clues for the Clueless: PC Basics

Some software books leave beginners without a clue about the basics of PCs and Windows. Not this one. If you're new to Windows, files, directories, mice, or disks, the appendix is the place to turn. Here's how to start programs, make your various windows behave, and get basic keyboard and mouse skills that apply to nearly all programs.

Icons Used in This Book

You'd think we were in Czarist Russia from the popularity of icons in the computer world. Not to be left behind, this book uses icons, too. Here's what they mean:

For an easier or faster way to do something, or to check out something really cool, look for these pictures in the margin.

Looking for a hot tip? Look no further than the Tip icon, sprinkled liberally throughout the book.

This icon reminds you that you shouldn't forget to remember something — something that was said earlier but is easily forgotten.

This icon cheerfully tells you of something that may go wrong, with consequences ranging from mild indigestion to weeping, wailing, and gnashing of teeth.

You won't see too much of Mr. Science (alias the Dummies guy) in this book. When he does appear, he indicates a little inside information on how things work. But, if you ignore him, you won't be much worse off.

Sometimes more details about a subject are located elsewhere in the book. This icon highlights references to those other sections or chapters.

The One Shortcut Used in This Book

This book always uses genuine English words to describe how things work! Well, almost always. (Sorry.) There's one important exception. When you see an instruction that looks something like this,

> Choose Blah⇨Fooey from the menu bar

it means: Click Blah in the menu bar, and then click Fooey in the menu that drops down. (If you don't know what *click, menu bar,* or *menu* mean, that's okay — see the appendix.)

This sort of instruction crops up so often that, if I didn't use that shortcut, you'd be bored silly by Chapter 3 — and IDG Books would have to slaughter another forest worth of trees to get the extra paper to print the book!

(You may also notice another very minor typographic habit of this book. This book capitalizes all the first letters of certain features, even though the software itself doesn't. That habit makes sentences like "Select the Center Across Selection check box" at least slightly readable, whereas, "Select the Center across selection check box" is utter gibberish.)

Where to Go from Here

You've probably already tried to do something with Works Suite and are perplexed, annoyed, or intrigued by something you've seen. If so, go to the Table of Contents or the Index and see what this book has to say about it.

Here's another place to go! After you go online to the Internet with Internet Explorer as Part IV describes, you can fill out the online registration form at www.dummies.com/register.html on the World Wide Web!

Part I

Crunching Numbers, Organizing Information

The 5th Wave   By Rich Tennant

In this part . . .

Software comes in two varieties: Some are specialists, like money management programs or street atlases. Others are generalists that you can bend to any purpose you like. Works Suite comes with two such generalists, one for number crunching of all kinds, and the other for data storage and management. Those two programs are the following:

- ✔ The spreadsheet program, which performs calculations, numerical analyses, and charts.

- ✔ The database program, which organizes and helps you sort through large quantities of information, such as inventories, names and addresses, or purchase orders.

This part of the book deals mainly with these spreadsheet and database programs. These programs are simpler relatives of muscle-bound programs for which you can pay a *lot* more money, such as Microsoft Excel and Access, but may be just fine for what you want to do. In addition, this part tells you how to use Works Calendar to organize your schedule, whether for work or home.

Chapter 1

Starting Your Suite Programs

● ●

In This Chapter

▶ Starting the Works Task Launcher

▶ Starting programs without the Task Launcher

▶ Using and getting rid of the Task Launcher window

▶ Creating new documents by using Tasks

▶ Reopening existing documents

● ●

*E*veryone — and every program — has to start somewhere. If you already have a general idea of how to use a mouse, a keyboard, and windows, you're starting in the right place. This chapter shows you different ways of starting the programs in Microsoft Works Suite, depending on whether you want to start with a clean, blank slate or with a partly prefabricated document, spreadsheet, or database — or just want to work on something you've created previously in Works Suite.

If you're completely new to computing, however, you may first want to find out more about the basics: how to use the mouse and keyboard; what icons, files, disks, and folders are; and how to print things. If you're fuzzy about these concepts, take a look at the appendix. Otherwise, read on boldly.

Finding and Starting the Works Task Launcher

First things first — you need to wake Works up and get it running. Finding and starting Works is very easy if, when it was installed, a *shortcut* icon was placed on your PC screen (called the Windows *desktop*).

Look on your screen for an *icon* (a tiny picture) labeled *Microsoft Works* and then double-click that icon. Figure 1-1 shows that icon and some of the other things that are probably on your screen.

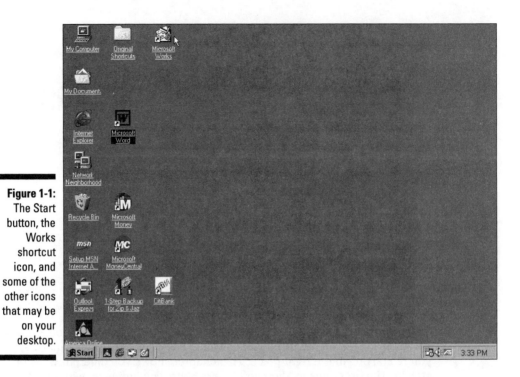

Figure 1-1:
The Start
button, the
Works
shortcut
icon, and
some of the
other icons
that may be
on your
desktop.

Double-clicking the icon launches something called the Works Task Launcher, a kind of centralized location from which you can go to any of the Works Suite programs. The Task Launcher also provides predesigned *Tasks* that automatically build specific kinds of documents for you by using those programs. See the section "Using and Losing the Task Launcher," coming up soon.

If you *can't* find a Microsoft Works icon on your screen, here's how to find and start Works:

1. **Click the Start button (shown in the lower-left corner of Figure 1-1).**

   The Start button is on a bar called the Windows *taskbar*. It's normally at the bottom of your screen, but it can be dragged to another side of your screen.

2. **On the menu that springs up (sometimes called a *submenu*), point with your mouse pointer to Programs and pause (or click) there.**

   Another menu appears next to the first one.

3. Move your pointer horizontally until it's on the new menu.

Look for an icon labeled Microsoft Works. In the next step, you're going to move your pointer vertically to point to it and then click it. However, depending on how Works was installed, you may find two icons labeled Microsoft Works: one a picture of a folder and the other, well . . . *not* a folder. Figure 1-2 points out the two types.

4. Click the cluttered-looking Microsoft Works Task Launcher icon (*not* a folder icon).

In the rest of this book, I summarize a series of steps like the preceding one by saying something like choose Start⇨Programs⇨Microsoft Works. It saves trees and time, too.

Hey, you did it! You got Works running, and the Works window appears on your screen, looking something like Figure 1-3. You know that the window is the Works window if the title *Microsoft Works* appears on the top line. (All windows have a top line like this one, called the *title bar* of the window, that gives the name of the program or file that appears in that window.)

Other individual Suite programs   Folder containing individual Suite programs

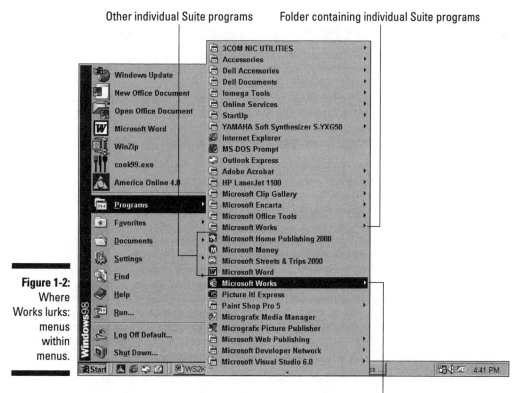

Figure 1-2:
Where
Works lurks:
menus
within
menus.

Cluttered-looking icon for Task Launcher

Starting Works Suite Programs from the Start Menu

For some direct types — who know what they want and like to take the fastest route — launching the various Works programs from the Windows Start menu may be the way to go. If you just want to open Money or Word or some other Works program, try choosing Start⇨Programs.

From this point, the Works Suite programs are sprinkled around the menu. If you see a *folder* icon labeled Microsoft Works (as Figure 1-2 shows) and click it, a submenu pops out. On that submenu, you can choose Address Book, Calendar, Getting Started Manual, Database, and Spreadsheet. Click one to launch that program.

Microsoft Encarta, Word, Money, and the other Works Suite programs are (usually) *not* in the Microsoft Works folder. You see them listed on the first menu that appears when you choose Start⇨Programs, as Figure 1-2 shows.

Using and Losing the Task Launcher

When you first start Works, it displays a window titled Microsoft Works, as shown in Figure 1-3. This window is called the Task Launcher because it helps you get going. Specifically, it can find files you've worked on recently, start up the program that you need to create or work on a document, or create a new document by using something called a *Task* (something that does a lot of the groundwork for you in starting a new document).

A shortcut for menu-haters

Pressing Ctrl+Alt+*Shortcut key* (where the *shortcut key* is a key on your keyboard that you choose) is the quickest way in Windows 98 to start nearly *any* application — including most of the Works Suite programs. You can press the key combination at any time and launch that program (any program, not just Works programs).

Here's how to do it, using Microsoft Money as an example. Choose Start⇨Programs and then right-click on Microsoft Money. Then choose

Properties from the menu that appears. Click in the Shortcut Key text box to select it and then press the M key. This defines Ctrl+Alt+M as the key combination that launches Money. Now click the Close button to shut the dialog box. Try pressing Ctrl+Alt+M and watch Money launch itself. (Unfortunately, this trick does not work for the version of Word 2000 that comes with Works Suite. Go figure!)

Click History to see a list of your previous documents

Click Tasks to see the tasks

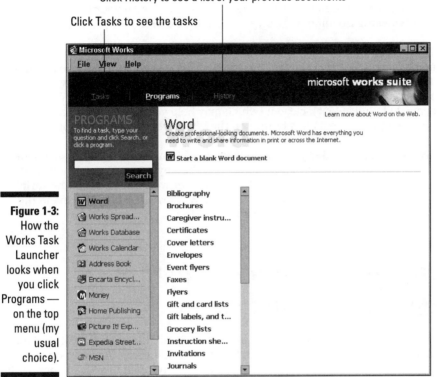

Figure 1-3:
How the
Works Task
Launcher
looks when
you click
Programs —
on the top
menu (my
usual
choice).

You can call up the Task Launcher at any time while you're using one of the three main Works programs (Word — the word processor — or Works Spreadsheet, or Works Database). Choose File⇨New from the menu bar at the top of the Works window you're using. (If you're using Word, you must choose File⇨New⇨Works Task Launcher.)

The Works Task Launcher gives you three ways to get going, represented as three *options,* whose names you see in Figure 1-3. The Programs option is displayed in this figure. The other options that you can select are Tasks and History. Click an option name to see what it can do. Specifically, here's what option to choose, depending on what you want to do:

✔ **The Programs option:** Go directly to one of the Works Suite Programs, where you can start a completely new document or work on an existing one. (I usually choose this approach. If you go this way, too, page ahead in the chapter to the section, "Starting by Choosing a Program from the Task Launcher.")

✔ **The Task option:** Have Microsoft create a new document for you with a lot of stuff already filled in and prettied up. (See "Starting with a Task.")

> ✔ **The History option:** Select a document from a list of recently worked-on documents or find any existing document that's on your PC. (See "Opening Documents You've Worked On Before.")

The Task Launcher is like a separate program whose only function in life is to help you find files and start up the programs you need. It doesn't do much on its own. After you have started working in a Works program window, you probably don't need the Task Launcher. You can leave it on your screen (clutter-some, but convenient), close it (which may help your PC run a bit faster), or reduce it (minimize it) to a button on the Windows taskbar (a compromise).

My suggestion is (after you are done using it) to minimize the Task Launcher to a button on the Windows taskbar. Click the tiny minus sign (–) button at the far upper-right corner of the Task Launcher window. The window shrinks to a button labeled *Microsoft Works* on the Windows taskbar. To expand the Task Launcher window again, click that button.

Starting by Choosing a Program from the Task Launcher

Some of us simpler-minded types prefer to skip all this helpful Task stuff and just start by choosing the program that we want. If that's the way you work, too, just click Programs on the Task Launcher. (To open the Task Launcher if it's not on your screen already, choose File➪New from the Works menu bar.)

Works has several programs, listed down the left side of the Programs screen. Click a program to see a brief description of what it does and a list of the Tasks that use that program. For instance, in Figure 1-3, I have clicked Word, and the right panel of the window now shows a screen of stuff for Word.

To start a new, blank document in a program, click the colored text, `Start a Blank Word Document` (or `Spreadsheet` or `Database`). Underneath that text is a list of Tasks (Bibliography through Journals in Figure 1-3) that run in Word. If you want to start Word (or whatever program you've chosen) with one of those Tasks, click the Task instead.

For more details on each program, see that program's section in this book.

Some programs listed on this page aren't really Works programs! They come with Works, and the Works Task Launcher links you up to them, but they are their own separate programs. (I cover most of them in this book, anyway.)

The Calendar is a program that keeps track of your appointments. MSN is *The Microsoft Network,* Microsoft's entry into the very competitive Internet ser-vice provider industry of businesses that connect you to the Internet. The

Address Book is an accessory program that comes with Windows, and Microsoft hopes that you will use it to store your addresses. Internet Explorer is Microsoft's Web browser for viewing the World Wide Web.

Starting with a Task

Tasks (also sometimes called *TaskWizards,* or just plain *wizards,* and sometimes *templates*) are automated programs that automatically build (or at least begin to build) the document that you need. Tasks are great for keeping things simple, if you don't mind Works making some of your decisions for you.

You can begin a Task only from the Works Task Launcher. So if you're using one of the Works programs and you want to see the Task Launcher, choose File⇨New from the Works program's menu bar (or in Word, choose File⇨ New⇨Works Task Launcher). This brings up the Task Launcher. Or, if you have previously minimized the Task Launcher window to a button labeled *Microsoft Works* on the Windows taskbar, click that button.

In the Task Launcher, click the Tasks option near the upper left of the window. Lots of Tasks, in several categories, are waiting to do your bidding. Categories include Letters and Labels, Newsletters and Flyers, Household Management, and more, listed down the left side of the Task Launcher window. Take these steps to select and launch a Task:

1. **To see what Tasks are in a category (in the column at the left of the Launcher window), click the category.**

   The various Tasks appear in a list near the center of the window.

2. **To see a description of any task listed, click its name in the center of the window.**

   A description appears on the right of the window, with a Start button.

3. **To start the Task, click the Start button that appears on the right side of the window.**

A Task starts up a Works program and builds a document in that program. For instance, the Tasks for letters create documents in Word, the word processor program. After you start a Task, a screen appears on top of the program window and shows you various alternative document styles that you can select. Click one and — *poof!* — you have a document.

Tasks generally just get you started — you still have to customize the document. Making changes can sometimes be tricky, so you may need to refer to the chapter on the particular program that you find yourself in.

You can also start tasks by choosing a program (click Program at the top of the Works window) and clicking one of the tasks listed for that program. Figure 1-3 shows the task listing in the Program view.

Opening Documents You've Worked On Before

If you have recently used the Task Launcher to create or work on a document, it remembers.

When you get the urge to return to one of your recently created or recently worked-on documents, click the History option in the Works Task Launcher. You see a list, which is similar to Figure 1-4.

To select a document from this list, just click the document name. The document then opens in its own window. If you see the same document listed more than once, you can click any of the listings. By listing the document several times, Works is just trying to help you remember your history of working on that document.

Database document

Word processor documents | Spreadsheet document

Microsoft Works

File   View   Help

microsoft **works suite**

Tasks | Programs | **History**

HISTORY

To open a file you worked on before, click its name in the list, or click Find Files or Folders.

Find Files or Folders...

Using History...
- The History area is the easiest way to find documents you worked on before.
- To open a document, just click the row that lists the document you want.
- To arrange documents in a different order, click the arrow beside the column name. Works sorts documents in ascending or decending order.
- Or click with the right mouse button within a row to delete an entry from the list.

Name	Date ▼	Task	Program
funds	11/24/1999	Fundraising	Works Spreadsh...
library	11/24/1999	Home inventory wo...	Works Database
tebus	11/24/1999	Cover letters	Word
WS2K19	11/24/1999	Unavailable	Word
WS2K09	11/24/1999	Unavailable	Word
ws2k01	11/24/1999	Unavailable	Word
WS2K14	11/24/1999	Unavailable	Word
Ws2k01old	11/24/1999	Unavailable	Word
MSW01final	11/24/1999	Unavailable	Word
WS2KA@^	11/23/1999	Unavailable	Word
WS2KA	11/23/1999	Unavailable	Word
WS2K02	11/22/1999	Unavailable	Word
WS2K22	11/22/1999	Unavailable	Word
WS2K25	11/22/1999	Unavailable	Word
WS2KA	11/22/1999	Unavailable	Word
WS2K25	11/22/1999	Unavailable	Word
WS2K24	11/22/1999	Unavailable	Word
WS2K20	11/22/1999	Unavailable	Word

Figure 1-4: Works lists what documents you have recently used and when you worked on them.

If you are working in a Works Suite program, not the Task Launcher, you can find a short list of documents most recently worked on by that program. Click File in the program's menu bar. Click one of the documents listed at the bottom of the menu to open it.

Opening Documents Not Listed under History

It is possible to have a document stored on your PC's hard drive but not have it show up on the History option of the Task Launcher. This happens when you haven't used the document in a while, or your copy of Works has never seen the document before, so Works doesn't know about it.

For example, the document may have been created by another program or the document may have been created before you installed your current version of Works.

If the Task Launcher doesn't show your file, you need another way to open it. This section tells you how you can open a document from within a Works program.

You can also open a document directly from Windows. First, you open a window on the folder where your document file is, and then you double-click that file. For instance, double-click the My Computer icon to see the various disk drives; then double-click the C disk drive icon to look in the hard drive, and so on. Look for files that say *Microsoft Works* in the Type column. Double-click your file when you see it, and the correct Works program then launches, displaying your file.

If you are already using one of the three main programs in Works (Word, Works Spreadsheet, or Works Database), choose File⇨Open from the menu bar of that program's window or press Ctrl+O (that's the letter *O,* not the number 0). This procedure takes you to the Open dialog box. If you don't know how to use this dialog box, see the appendix.

Finding Documents with the Task Launcher

It doesn't take too long before you're knee-deep in documents and folders and need a little help finding the document that you want. Your buddy, the Task Launcher, can come to your rescue. With the Task Launcher on your screen, click the History option and then click Find Files or Folders.

The Find: All Files dialog box springs into view. The Find dialog box may look familiar to you if you have used the Find program in Windows 98 — they're the same program! (You get the Find dialog box directly from Windows by choosing Start⇨Find⇨Files or Folders from the Windows taskbar.) For the full, juicy details of using the Find dialog box, see the appendix.

Chapter 2

Spreading Your First Sheets

. . . .

In This Chapter

▶ Understanding spreadsheets

▶ Creating a new, blank spreadsheet

▶ Examining the spreadsheet window and toolbar

▶ Using cells and ranges

▶ Typing text and numbers

▶ Changing column widths and row heights

▶ Inserting and deleting rows and columns

▶ Entering sequential headings and data automatically

. . . .

So you're ready to set sail into the uncharted seas of calculation? With the Works spreadsheet hoisted squarely to the wind, you can sail to exotic lands where budgets, business plans, alphabetized lists, expense analyses, profit-and-loss statements, scientific experiments, and sales forecasts live.

If you've never used spreadsheets before, however, you need to know a few basics first, which is where this chapter comes in. Here you find out what you can do with a spreadsheet, what's what in the spreadsheet window, how to navigate around in spreadsheets, and how to enter text and numbers. To perform calculations and tackle the more exciting stuff, page ahead to Chapter 3.

Understanding and Appreciating Spreadsheets

Truth be told, you can't fully appreciate a spreadsheet until you use one (sort of like using an electric toothbrush but even more fun — if you can imagine that). But to understand a spreadsheet, try to think of it as a table of numbers and calculations where the results of the calculations change to reflect any changes you make in the numbers. A simple form of spreadsheet, for example, is one that automatically sums up rows and columns of numbers and adjusts the sums whenever you change a number.

Some of the main reasons spreadsheets are so popular follow:

- ✔ Because spreadsheets automatically recalculate every time you change a value, they enable you to carry out what-if analyses — for example, what if inflation goes from 4 to 8 percent? When can *we* retire?

- ✔ Spreadsheets include built-in formulas to perform the complex calculations you need for such analyses as mortgages, retirement plans, and statistics.

- ✔ You can also use spreadsheets for simple lists and collections of data — for example, the names of students in your class and their grades. Spreadsheets overlap with databases in this role. Spreadsheets are more useful for small lists that perhaps require a calculation for every item, whereas databases are more useful for ever-expanding collections of data (such as mailing lists) or those requiring summary reports (such as inventories).

- ✔ After you have data in a spreadsheet, you can turn that data into a chart in minutes. We look at this process in more detail in Chapter 5.

Starting Out

To review how to start Works and the different ways of starting a spreadsheet document, check out Chapter 1. If you're starting a new spreadsheet, a wizard or a template can do a lot of the work for you. Or, to start by creating a blank document, click the Programs button at the top of the Task Launcher and then click the Works Spreadsheet item in the list box on the left side. Then click Start a Blank Spreadsheet just above the list of available templates. You're now gazing at a window like the one shown in Figure 2-1.

What's what in a spreadsheet window

Figure 2-1 shows you what's what in your spreadsheet window. Near the top of the Works window is the usual Works menu bar with all the commands, and underneath that menu bar is the spreadsheet toolbar with all its buttons and icons.

The spreadsheet toolbar

A popular way to give commands to Works (other than traditional shouting methods) is by using the toolbar — the thing with all the pictures (see Figure 2-2). The toolbar is just a faster way than the menu bar to do some of the same things. You click a button and stuff happens.

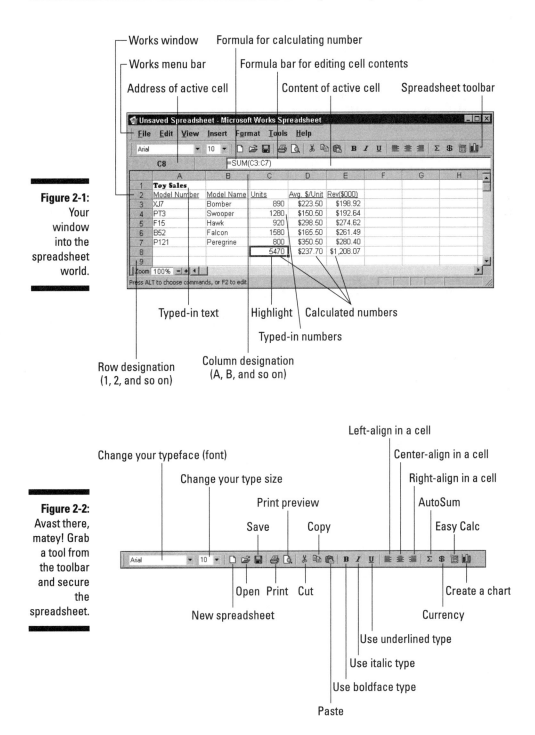

Figure 2-1:
Your
window
into the
spreadsheet
world.

Works window
Works menu bar
Address of active cell
Formula for calculating number
Formula bar for editing cell contents
Content of active cell
Spreadsheet toolbar

Typed-in text
Highlight
Calculated numbers
Typed-in numbers

Row designation
(1, 2, and so on)
Column designation
(A, B, and so on)

Figure 2-2:
Avast there,
matey! Grab
a tool from
the toolbar
and secure
the
spreadsheet.

Change your typeface (font)
Change your type size
Print preview
Save
Copy
Left-align in a cell
Center-align in a cell
Right-align in a cell
AutoSum
Easy Calc

Open Print Cut
New spreadsheet
Create a chart
Currency
Use underlined type
Use italic type
Use boldface type
Paste

As you discover in the other chapters of this part of the book, much of the spreadsheet toolbar is similar to the toolbars in other Works programs.

I don't go into detail about any of the toolbar buttons here, but I discuss them as I go along. Here's where to go to read about the buttons that are particularly interesting for working with spreadsheets:

- ✔ **Left-, center-, and right-align:** See the section in Chapter 4 on changing alignment of your information.

- ✔ **Currency (format a number as dollars and cents):** See the section in Chapter 4 on formatting numbers.

- ✔ **AutoSum:** See the section in Chapter 3 on shortcuts for creating formulas.

- ✔ **Create a chart:** See Chapter 5.

The spreadsheet document

The spreadsheet document looks like a big table of figures, which is gratifying, because that's what a spreadsheet is. Here are two important points to note:

- ✔ Each horizontal row in this table has a number (at the far left), and each vertical column has a letter (at the top) in tasteful battleship gray.

- ✔ A spreadsheet has no pages (until you print it); it's one vast table. To see spreadsheet stuff beyond your screen limits, scroll the document up or down, left or right, by using the gray scroll bars along the right and bottom sides. (See the appendix if scroll bars are new to you.)

Cells

A *cell* is one of those little rectangles on the spreadsheet shown in Figure 2-1; it's the intersection of a row and a column. Everything that you type into a spreadsheet goes in cells.

Each cell has an address so that you can talk to Works about it in your calculations, graphs, and other activities. A cell address is made up of the column letter and row number, smashed together as, for example, B12, which is the cell at column B and row 12.

Entering and Editing Data in Cells

As you can in most Windows programs, if you make a mistake, you can press Ctrl+Z or choose Edit➪Undo *Something* to undo your most recent action (which is the *Something* that appears after the word Undo on the Edit menu).

Moving from cell to cell

The cell you're about to type in, edit, format, or otherwise muck around with is called the *active cell.* It's surrounded by a rectangular halo called the *highlight.* (In computer heaven, the halos are rectangular.) The address of the active cell (cell C8 in Figure 2-1) appears near the upper left of the Works window, under the font window of the toolbar.

The easiest way to choose a new active cell is to move your mouse so that the mouse cursor — a big, fat plus sign (+) — hovers over the new cell and then click. Of course, you can't click what you can't see. To view various areas of your spreadsheet, use the scroll bars on the right side and bottom of the document window.

You can also move the highlight by using the navigation keys on your keyboard. See the section "Navigating in Almost Any Document," on the Cheat Sheet inside the front cover of this book, for information on using these keys.

If you know the address of the cell that you want but it's nowhere nearby, press the F5 key. An itsy-bitsy Go To dialog box appears. Type the cell address — **Q200** for example — and click the OK button to access that cell.

People often type headings on top of columns or to the left of rows to identify what data the row or column contains. After you create column and/or row headings, you can *freeze* those headings in place on-screen for convenience while you move around in the rest of the spreadsheet. In the row just under the topmost row (where you have entered headings for your columns), click the cell just to the right of the leftmost column (where you have entered headings for your rows). Then choose Format➪Freeze Titles. Repeat to unfreeze.

Typing stuff in cells

Typing something into a cell involves the following simple procedure:

1. **Click a cell.**

   You can also move your highlight to it by using an arrow key or other navigation keys.

2. **Type what you want in the cell.**

   Use the Backspace key to delete any mistakes. If you decide not to save what you type, press the Esc key.

3. **After the text, number, or formula is the way you want it, press the Enter key or move to another cell by using the mouse, the Tab key, or a navigation key.**

Typing more stuff than can fit into a cell's width is okay. You can always increase the cell width later. Don't worry if the stuff appears to overlap the empty cell to the right.

If you type more text than you can display in a cell, or if you type a number that turns into a bunch of ##### characters, your column is too skinny. See the following section, "Changing column widths and row heights."

Changing column widths and row heights

Following are several ways to set the column widths and row heights.

To quickly set a column's width, double-click the column letter at the top of the column. Works sizes the column to fit the largest entry in that column. (What about row height? Works sizes row height automatically to the largest font size you use.)

An intuitive way to change the width of a column (or height of a row) is to *drag* its edge by using your mouse. In the gray area where the column letters (or row numbers) are, position your cursor over the right edge of the column (or bottom edge of the row) until the cursor reads Adjust. Click and drag to adjust.

A more precise way to change the width of a column or row is to first click anywhere in that column or row. To adjust several adjacent columns (or rows), drag across them (highlight them) with your mouse at any row (or column). Then choose Format⇨Column Width (or Row Height).

The Format Column Width (or Format Row Height) dialog box springs into action. Type a new width number into the Column Width (or Row Height) text box and then click OK. If you're setting column width, the width number specifies approximately how many characters wide the column is, using 10-point type. For row height, the number is in *points* (as in a 12-point font). (A point is roughly ½ of an inch.)

To put multiple lines of text in a single cell, you need to increase row height and enable the line-wrapping feature. To enable line wrapping, choose Format⇨Alignment. On the Alignment card of the Format Cells dialog box that appears, click in the Wrap Text check box to select it. Text now wraps automatically to a second line if the length exceeds the column width.

Entering different kinds of cell contents

A spreadsheet can contain three different kinds of contents, each of which is treated differently. (A single cell, though, can contain only one kind of content at a time.) The three kinds of cell content are as follows:

- ✔ **Text.** In Figure 2-3, the model names are text.

- ✔ **A typed number.** In Figure 2-3, the revenues are typed numbers.

- ✔ **A calculation, which displays its result.** In Figure 2-3, the totals in the last row and column are the results of calculations.

Dates in the spreadsheet program appear to be a fourth kind of content, but they are actually numbers! See the discussion of number formatting in Chapter 4.

Text   Typed-in numbers

Figure 2-3:
Contents of a
few example
cells in the
Toy Sales
spreadsheet.

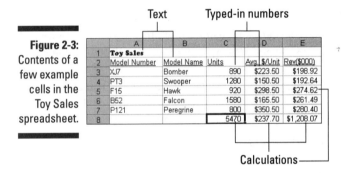

	A	B	C	D	E
1	Toy Sales				
2	Model Number	Model Name	Units	Avg. $/Unit	Rev($000)
3	XJ7	Bomber	890	$223.50	$198.92
4	PT3	Swooper	1280	$150.50	$192.64
5	F15	Hawk	920	$298.50	$274.62
6	B52	Falcon	1580	$165.50	$261.49
7	P121	Peregrine	800	$350.50	$280.40
8			5470	$237.70	$1,208.07

Calculations ——————

The following sections explain how to enter the first two kinds of cell contents: text and typed numbers. We explain calculations in Chapter 3.

Unless you tell Works otherwise, it aligns text entries against the left side of their cells and numeric entries against the right side. I tell you how to tell Works otherwise in the section on cell alignment in Chapter 4.

Typing text

To simply enter some text, such as a column heading or title — something that you don't use in a calculation — just click the cell and type the text. Press the Enter key after you finish typing. Works recognizes any entry containing letters as being a text entry.

After you type your text and press Enter, you may notice that up in the formula bar, Works sticks a quote character in front of what you typed. The quote mark doesn't appear in the cell, just in the bar. This character is Works' subtle way of saying that it interprets the contents of this cell as text, not as a number or calculation.

Sometimes you must enter that quotation mark yourself: before zip codes (or any all-numeral code or identifier beginning with zero); before any text beginning with =, +, or –; and before any text that already begins with a quotation mark (in other words, you must enter two quotation marks to start).

Note: Text entries require only the opening quotation marks (no ending quotation marks) for reasons lost in the dim mists of spreadsheet history.

Typing numbers

Entering numbers into a cell is as simple as entering text into a cell. Just click a cell and type the numbers. Here are a few of the most popular options you have for entering numbers, some of which Figure 2-4 illustrates:

- ✔ You can precede a number with a minus sign (–) if it's negative, or you can use a dollar sign ($) if it's money. Use –$ or parentheses for negative money amounts. Use as many decimal places as you need, but Works rounds off the numbers to two decimal places if you use the dollar sign or parentheses.

- ✔ For percentages, add a percent sign (%) immediately after the number. Just as mathematics dictates, if you type **100%**, Works understands it to mean 1.00.

- ✔ If you're a scientific type, you can use scientific notation: You can type 1,253,000,000 as **1.253e9**, for example, or as **1.253E+09**. In fact, if you type a big number, Works automatically displays it in this format.

What actually happens after you type a number a certain way is that Works automatically chooses a *number format* for that cell. If you begin with a $ symbol, for example, Works chooses *currency* format. For more information on number formats, see Chapter 4.

If a number has units, such as *fathoms,* enter the units as text in the next cell to the right. Don't type *36 fathoms* all in a single cell, or Works thinks that the entry is text, not a number, and can't perform calculations with the entry at all.

Editing the contents of a cell

You may notice something a bit odd as you type things into cells. Works is normally set up so that as you type things into cells, you're actually typing in two places at once! Works (as it comes out of the box) is set up to enable you to edit cell contents in either of the following places:

- ✔ In the formula bar
- ✔ In the cell itself

A number, but too wide for the column.

Figure 2-4:
A few
popular
formats in
which you
can write
numbers
(and one in
which you
can't).
Chapter 4
gives
you more
number
formats.

These are all valid numbers.

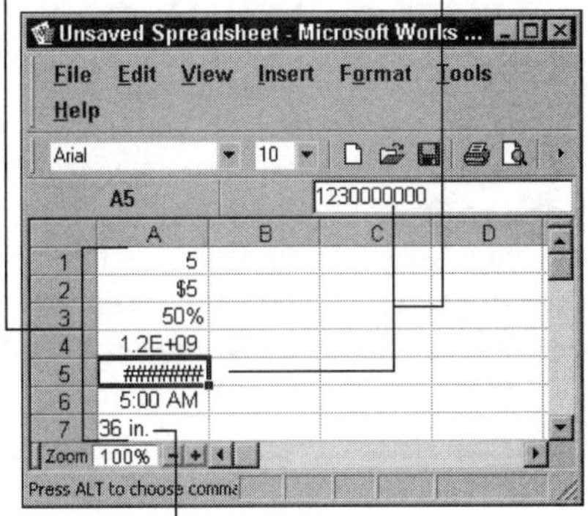

Unsaved Spreadsheet - Microsoft Works ...

File   Edit   View   Insert   Format   Tools
Help

Arial   10

A5   1230000000

	A	B	C	D
1	5			
2	$5			
3	50%			
4	1.2E+09			
5	#######			
6	5:00 AM			
7	36 in.			

Zoom 100%

Press ALT to choose comma

Adding *in.* made this number into text.

Here's how to edit the contents of a cell, either in the formula bar or in a cell:

1. **Click the cell you want to edit.**

   The cell shows its little rectangular halo and displays the contents of the cell in the formula bar.

2. **Click the formula bar to edit in the formula bar or double-click the cell to edit in the cell.**

   Alternatively, you can press F2.

3. **Edit the contents of the cell just as you edit text in a Windows dialog box.**

   Type new text, use the Backspace key to fix errors, and so on. See the appendix for details on editing in dialog boxes.

4. **To enter your changes into the cell, press the Enter key or click the check mark button on the formula bar.**

   If you decide that you don't want to change the cell contents after all, press the Esc key. If you're editing in the formula bar, you can click the X button on the formula bar.

If the data you're editing is too long to fit in the editing area of the formula bar, the navigation keys (the left- and right-arrow keys, Home, and End) are an easier way to move the insertion point than the mouse.

TIP

$!@($?)&$!!! What's all this #########?

If you're typing a number that's too wide for the column, you often get a distressing result. You get a bunch of pound (or "score") symbols, ####, in the cell, which is a message from Works saying, "I can't display this number here; make the column wider, will ya?" (Refer to Figure 2-4.) Sometimes this situation occurs because the cell in question has the wrong number format — some formats are wider than others. If you use the default format for numbers, the *General* format, Works simply switches to nice, compact scientific notation if a number gets too large. You may or may not approve of this switch. For details on number formats, see the section on formatting numbers in Chapter 4.

Trying Out a Sample Spreadsheet

One of the fastest ways to understand spreadsheets is to create one yourself. Figure 2-5 shows an example of a spreadsheet with the first week of a diet plan for an anonymous, but very earnest, calorie-counting person.

Here's how to duplicate this spreadsheet (18 quick steps to weight control!):

1. **Start a fresh spreadsheet: With the spreadsheet program open, press Ctrl+N.**

   A fresh, new spreadsheet appears on-screen. The current active cell (where the highlight is) is A1.

2. **Type** My Diet **in the active cell and press the Enter key.**

3. **Click cell B2 (column B, row 2), type** Calories, **and press the Enter key.**

4. **Press the right-arrow key and then the up-arrow key to highlight cell C2. Then type** Weight **and press the Enter key.**

5. **Click cell A3 and type** Monday.

6. **Press the down-arrow key and type** Tuesday; **keep pressing the down-arrow key and entering days of the week through** Sunday.

   On the seventh day, rest.

   TIP

   To avoid manually typing the days of the week, you can try out Autofill here, instead. See the section, "Entering Sequential Headings and Data Automatically by Using Autofill," later in this chapter.

7. **Click cell B3 and type** 3250.

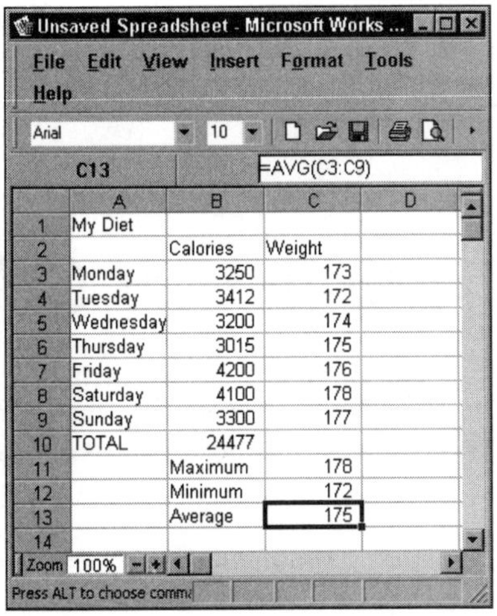

Figure 2-5:
A typical
first-week
diet, with
typical
first-week
results.

8. **Press the down-arrow key and type** 3412; **refer to Figure 2-5 for the other calories and continue this through** Sunday.

9. **Click cell C3 and type** 173; **refer to Figure 2-5 for the other weights and continue this through** Sunday.

10. **Click cell A10 and type** TOTAL.

    This text is simply a label.

11. **Press the right-arrow key to highlight cell B10, type** =SUM(B3:B9), **and press Enter.**

    Wow! Magic! The total calories for the week.

12. **Your highlight is now on cell B11; type** Maximum.

13. **Press the down-arrow key to highlight cell B12 and type** Minimum.

14. **Press the down-arrow key to highlight cell B13 and type** Average.

15. **Click cell C11 and type** =MAX(C3:C9).

16. **Press the down-arrow key to highlight cell C12 and type** =MIN(C3:C9).

17. **Press the down-arrow key to highlight cell C13, type** =AVG(C3:C9), **and press Enter.**

    If you followed these steps, you're looking at an exact duplicate of Figure 2-5.

Notice that you save some effort by not pressing Enter every time you type something (although you may press Enter if you want). All you need to do to enter what you just typed is to move the highlight to a new cell by using the arrow keys.

Try changing some of the calorie or weight values to see what happens to the calculated values at the bottom. The value labeled Minimum is the lowest weight in cells C3 to C9; the Maximum is the highest, and the Average is the average.

Working with Ranges: Groups of Cells

One essential feature of spreadsheets is the ability to perform calculations and other operations on groups of cells. You can move a group of cells, for example, copy it, format it, sum a column of numbers, or average all the data in a group.

Any rectangular block of cells is a *range*. A range can be a large, small, skinny, or wide rectangle of cells anywhere in your spreadsheet. A range can consist of just two adjacent cells, a column, a row — and even the entire spreadsheet. The following sections tell you how to work with ranges.

Selecting a range of cells

The easiest way to specify a range of cells to Works — either because you're about to format all of them in some way or because you're referring to them in a calculation — is to select them. (The other way is to refer to them by their range address, as I describe in the following section.)

To select any group of cells (any row, column, or rectangular area), click one end or corner of the group and drag the mouse cursor across the cells you want to select. Release the mouse button when you're done.

To select an entire row or column, click the column letter or row number (in the gray area of the spreadsheet). To select the entire spreadsheet, click the unmarked button where the row-number and column-letter areas intersect (at the upper-left corner).

To select a columnar group of only those cells that have data in them (as opposed to selecting the entire column, from row 1 to row 16384), click the top cell of the group and then press Ctrl+Shift+↓. To select a row of filled cells, click the left-most cell and then press Ctrl+Shift+→. The selection stops at the first blank cell in the column or row, or where a data type changes, such as text shifting to numbers.

Referring to a range by its address

The way Works describes a range in its formulas (calculations) and in various dialog boxes is by using the range's *address.* You need to understand range addresses to use these formulas (discussed in the next chapter) and dialog boxes. A range's address combines the addresses of the two cells in opposite corners of the range, with a colon (:) in between. Which cell address comes first doesn't matter. To refer to two separate ranges at once, use a comma between them.

Here are the addresses of a few of the ranges in Figure 2-3, which appears earlier in this chapter:

Contents of Spreadsheet in Figure 2-3	*Range of Content*
All the model names	B3:B7 or B7:B3
Everything concerning the XJ7	A3:E3 or E3:A3
Revenues for all models	E3:E7 or E7:E3
Unit sales for every model but Hawk	C3:C4, C6:C7

Copying, Moving, and Deleting

Works provides a variety of features that enable you to copy, move, and delete chunks of your spreadsheet. These features work pretty much the same way in every program in Works. Here's how these things work in your spreadsheet:

✔ To delete a cell or range, select it and then press the Delete or Backspace key.

✔ To move a cell or range, select it and then slowly move your mouse cursor across the thick frame that appears around the selected area, until the cursor changes to an arrow labeled *drag.* At that point, click the mouse and drag the copy of the frame that appears to the new location. Release the mouse button, and the cells are moved.

✔ To copy, carry out the same actions as you do for moving cells but hold down the Ctrl key while you drag.

✔ Another way to copy is to use the Windows Clipboard. Select the cell or range that you want to copy and then press Ctrl+C. Click the cell where you want the copy to appear and press Ctrl+V to paste. If you're pasting a range of cells, click where you want the upper-left-corner cell of that range to go and then press Ctrl+V.

✔ To cut out the contents of a cell or range and paste it elsewhere in the spreadsheet, select the cell or range to be cut and then press Ctrl+X; then click the cell where you want to paste and press Ctrl+V. (If you're pasting a range, click where you want the upper-left corner of the range to go.)

✔ To make multiple copies of a single cell, click the cell to copy and press Ctrl+C. Then highlight a range and press Ctrl+V. All the cells in the range are filled with a copy of the original cell's contents.

✔ To *fill* a row or column of cells with copies of an adjacent cell, click the cell, position the mouse cursor over the cell's lower-right corner so that the cursor reads Fill and then drag across adjacent cells.

You have three alternatives to using the Ctrl key combinations for copy, cut, and paste. You can use the Copy, Paste, and Cut buttons on the toolbar (refer to Figure 2-2); you can right-click on a selection with your mouse and then choose Copy, Cut, or Paste from the menu that appears; or you can choose Edit⇨Copy, Cut, or Paste from the Works menu bar.

Following are a few things to remember while moving and copying things:

✔ If you move or copy something to already occupied cells, you wipe out the earlier contents of those cells.

✔ If you move a cell (say, you're moving what's in A1 to B5) that contains data that you use in a formula anywhere in the spreadsheet (say, =A1/3), the formula changes to follow its data. (In this example, it changes to =B5/3.) See Chapter 3 if you're not familiar with formulas.

✔ If you copy a formula, the addresses in it change. See the section on the mysteries of copying formulas in Chapter 3.

Inserting and Deleting Rows and Columns

Imagine that you're a high-priced lifestyle consultant, typing up your monthly invoice for September. You have a row for each day that you worked. You've made it to September 30, and suddenly you remember that you taught your client swing dancing on Saturday the 18th. Swell — what do you do now?

Well, you can select everything after the 18th and move it down a row, but how tedious and pedestrian! No, no, — a with-it, turn-of-the-millennium kind of person such as you should be inserting rows. Or columns — whatever. To do so, follow these steps:

1. **To insert a new row *above* an existing row, click anywhere in the existing row.**

   To insert a row *above* row 5, for example, click row 5.

2. **To insert a new column *to the left of* an existing column, click anywhere in the existing column.**

   To insert a column *to the left of* column D, for example, click column D.

3. **Choose Insert⇨Insert Row or Insert Column.**

   You can also right-click on the existing column or row with your mouse and choose Insert Row or Insert Column from the menu that appears.

Deleting a row or column (as opposed to just deleting its contents and leaving the row or column blank) is a similar procedure: Click anywhere in the row or column you want to delete and then choose Insert⇨Delete Row *or* Delete Column. Using the Insert menu to delete may seem odd, but that's the way it is.

If you insert a row or a column (say, a new row 5) into the middle of a range that you use in a formula (say, =SUM(A1:A10)), the formula now includes the new row or column. If, however, you insert a new row or column *on the edge* of a range of numbers (say, a new row 1 or row 11), the formula does *not* include the new row or column. So if you have an alphabetical list and add an Aaron or a Zykowski, you may want to double-check that your totals are still correct. If they are not, you must edit your formulas, as Chapter 3 describes.

Entering Sequential Headings and Data Automatically by Using Autofill

Sometimes the entries in a row or column — especially row and column headings — follow some predictable sequence. That sequence may be 1, 2, 3; or Monday, Tuesday, Wednesday (refer to Figure 2-5) where an equal interval lies between each entry. Unfortunately, typing in these predictable sequences can become really boring. After a while, you find yourself thinking, "This sequence is so predictable. This thing I'm typing on is a computer. Couldn't the computer, like, *predict* or something?" The answer is yes: by using Autofill. Follow these steps:

1. **Type the first two items from the sequence in adjacent cells.**

   In Figure 2-5, for example, you'd type **Monday** in A3 and **Tuesday** in A4.

2. **Select the two cells in which you just typed. (Drag across them.)**

3. **Move your mouse cursor to the lower-right corner of the two-cell block that you just selected, until the word Fill appears under your cursor.**

4. **Click and drag over all the cells that you want Works to fill automatically.**

    In the example in Figure 2-5, you drag until the highlighted area includes the two cells that you typed, plus the next five in the same column.

5. **Release the mouse button.**

Presto! Works extends the sequence to fill the selected cells. Was figuring out all this stuff worth the effort just to avoid typing the names of five days? Maybe . . . maybe not. But if you ever need to type all the days of a *year* into a row or column, you may come to think very fondly of the Autofill feature.

Chapter 3

Making Calculations

*M*any people have discovered how much fun they can have with *spread sheets*. (Sailors, mostly). Spreadsheets aren't bad, either, if your idea of fun is doing calculations. Works gives you the following two nifty ways to perform the amazing variety of calculations that a spreadsheet can do:

✔ **Easy Calc:** An automated take-you-by-the-hand approach to performing calculations.

✔ **The traditional write-it-yourself approach:** You can also use this approach for editing calculations.

This chapter explores both techniques. It also gives you labor-saving tricks, tips, and insights into the way spreadsheets work.

Never try to write while you're thinking about sheets.

Basic Ideas behind Spreadsheet Calculations

You need to understand a few basic concepts in order to do calculations in spreadsheets. Here are the biggies:

✔ You do calculations by putting *formulas* in cells. Those formulas compute their results by using data from various other cells in the spreadsheet.

✔ You put the formula *in the cell where you want the answer.* The cell displays the *result,* not the formula itself.

✔ If you change any of the numbers on which the formula works, the formula immediately recalculates a new result.

✔ You can use a formula cell as data for another formula. You can sum a row of sums, for example.

✔ You can often save time by copying a formula from one row or column to another.

Using Easy Calc in Works

The designers of Works created a special program called Easy Calc that builds a formula for you. Of course, you need to know what sort of data the calculation requires. If you're computing Net Present Value, for example, Works expects you to give it a value for the Rate of Return.

I designed the spreadsheet in Figure 3-1 to compute the average cost per night for lodging during my family's vacation in Canada (where the sheets are always nice and clean). I've entered the data, including an exchange rate for how many Canadian dollars we get for our American dollars. I'm now ready to enter my calculations.

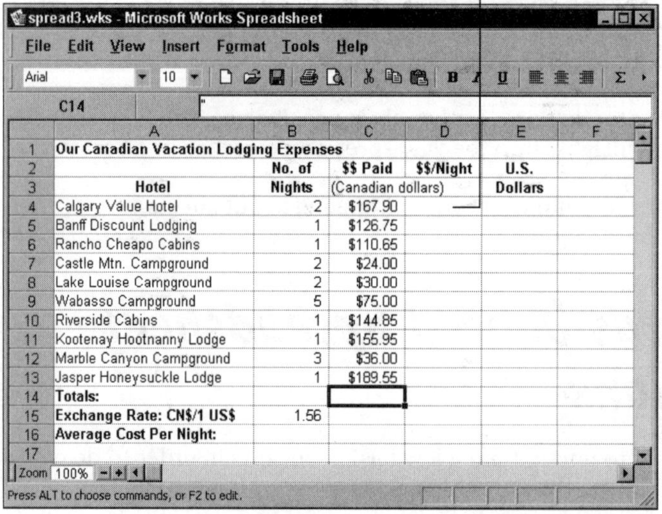

I will add my first formula here.

Figure 3-1:
A spread-sheet, ready to add formulas.

Here's how to use Easy Calc to perform basic calculations on data that you enter in your spreadsheet:

1. **Choose Tools⇨Easy Calc from the Works menu bar or click the Easy Calc button (the calculator with a gleam) near the right end of the toolbar.**

   The Easy Calc dialog box appears, as shown in Figure 3-2.

2. **Click the button for the kind of calculation you want to do.**

   If you don't see the calculation you want among the buttons shown in the dialog box, click the Other button. (See the sidebar "Doing *other* calculations in Easy Calc," later in this chapter.)

   In the example shown in Figure 3-1, I first want to compute the dollars per night for each lodging place, which means that I click the Divide button to divide the total dollars in column C by the number of nights in column B.

   A different Easy Calc dialog box now appears, as shown in Figure 3-3.

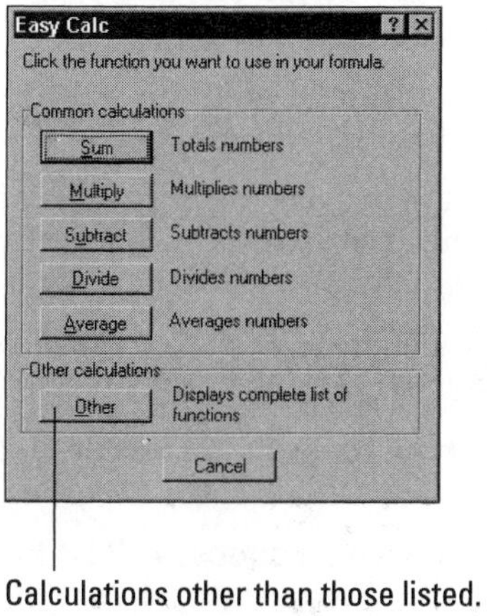

Figure 3-2: Choose your calculation in Easy Calc.

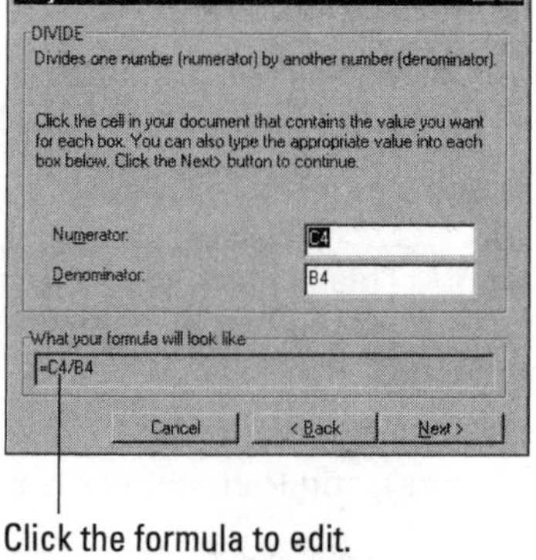

Calculations other than those listed.

Figure 3-3: Telling Easy Calc how to divide one cell's contents by another's.

Click the formula to edit.

3. **Enter the values (numbers used in the calculation) or cell addresses containing those values.**

   You can type the actual values into the text boxes, or if the value appears in a cell of your spreadsheet, you can type its cell address (such as B12 for column B, row 12) or click that cell. (To click a cell, you may need to drag the Easy Calc dialog box to one side, or use the vertical or horizontal scroll boxes on the right or bottom side of your spreadsheet window to see the portion of the spreadsheet that you need.)

   If Easy Calc prompts you for a range (as it does for Sum and Average), you can either type the range (such as **B1:D20**) or click and drag your cursor across the range to highlight it.

   See Chapter 2 if you don't understand cell addresses or ranges.

   If you make a mistake, click the text box containing the mistake and try again. If you made a mistake in a previous step, click the Back button.

   At the bottom of the Easy Calc dialog box, as the callout for Figure 3-3 shows, Works displays the formula it constructs for you. This display is a good example of how to write formulas. You can also click this display and edit the formula if you need to.

4. **Click the Next button and enter additional numbers, text, ranges, or cell addresses, as the Easy Calc dialog box prompts you.**

   Depending on the sort of calculation you ask for, Easy Calc may need additional information. You may need to go through one or two more dialog boxes, clicking Next each time to proceed.

   The final piece of information for which Easy Calc asks is the cell address where you want the result to appear.

5. **In the Result At text box, either type the cell address or click that cell; then click the Finish button.**

   In the example shown in Figure 3-1, I would choose cell D4 for our result and then click the Finish button.

Here are some of the other calculations I can do for the spreadsheet in Figure 3-1:

- ✔ **Compute American dollars from Canadian.** This calculation involves dividing the Canadian dollars in column D (beginning with D4) by the currency exchange rate in cell B15 and putting the results in column E (beginning with E4).

- ✔ **Compute the total number of nights.** This is just a check to make sure that I didn't miss any. This calculation would involve summing the range B4:B13 and putting the result in cell B14.

- ✔ **Compute the total cost.** You do this by summing C4:C13, placing the result in cell C14 (for Canadian dollars), and then doing the same for the American dollars in column D.

Doing *other* calculations in Easy Calc

If basic arithmetic and averaging can't do the job that you have in mind, Works can carry out lots of other calculations, known as *functions*, which you can access by clicking the Other button in the initial Easy Calc dialog box. (See the section "You're Invited to a Function," later in this chapter, for more details about these mathematical marvels.)

If you choose Tools⇨Easy Calc and click the Other button, the Insert Function dialog box swings into action. For instructions on using this dialog box, see Figure 3-5 and the numbered steps in the section "Shortcuts for Creating Formulas," later in this chapter.

After you click the Insert button in the Insert Function dialog box, Easy Calc resumes its helpful dialog, as I note in Step 3 in "Using Easy Calc in Works."

✔ **Compute the average cost per night for lodging in American dollars.** You can perform this calculation by averaging the range E4:E13 and putting the result in cell B16. Or you can do it by dividing the total cost in cell D14 by the total number of nights in cell B14.

Some of this calculation work is easier if you copy formulas. You can copy from cell C14 the formula that summed Canadian dollars, for example, and can paste it in cell E14, where it sums American dollars.

The same trick, however, doesn't work well for copying the formula for computing American dollars in cell E4 to the other cells in column E. The copied formulas fail to refer to the exchange rate in cell B15. If I copy the formula for each of the nine rows, the copies refer instead to cells B16, B17, and so on, through B24. To understand why this error occurs and how to prevent it, see "The Joys and Mysteries of Copying Formulas," later in this chapter.

Writing Formulas: Beyond Easy Calc

Writing your own formulas (as opposed to using Easy Calc to write them for you) enables you to make more powerful calculations in a single cell. To do a calculation, you type a formula into a cell. You can design a formula to do a lot of work all at once, as does the following example:

```
=(SUM(B1:B8))/(SUM(C9:C17))*A17-3.7
```

Believe it or not, this formula is not a random collection of symbols. It means something — or at least it does to the Works Spreadsheet program. This section helps you write formulas like that one (or simpler ones).

Works doesn't care whether you write formulas, cell addresses, or ranges in uppercase or lowercase letters. Works may convert some of the lowercase letters to uppercase letters, but that's its business.

Entering a formula

To enter a formula into a cell (whether you type directly into the cell or into the formula bar), follow these steps:

1. **Click the cell where you want the formula to go.**

   Or use the navigation keys to move the highlight to that cell. Use a blank cell; don't try to put the formula in the same cell that holds the numbers that you're using in the calculation.

2. **Type an equal sign (=) and then a mathematical expression.**

   Spreadsheet formulas are mathematical expressions, which look something like the following example:

   ```
   =5.24+3.93
   ```

   Starting Works formulas with an = sign tells Works that you're doing a calculation and not entering text or a number.

3. **Press Enter.**

   Or click the check mark button on the formula bar . . . or move the highlight by clicking another cell . . . or press a navigation key.

   These actions enter the formula into the cell, which then displays the result. The formula remains in the cell, but only the result appears.

If you type **=5.24+3.93** into a cell and press the Enter key, the cell shows the answer: 9.17. Isn't that exciting! This is why people spend thousands of dollars on computers and software. Well, maybe not; you may have been able to do that more easily on a $5 calculator. What you can't do on a $5 calculator, however, is type something like the following example:

```
=5.24+B1
```

Hmmm. Shades of algebra. What this formula really means is "Show me the sum of 5.24 and whatever is in cell B1." If B1 has the number 3.93 in it, you get 9.17. If B1 has the number 6 in it, you get 11.24. You can keep plugging new numbers into cell B1 and watch the answer change in the cell that contains this formula.

Okay, this stuff is amusing — but wait! There's more! What if you want a formula to add up a bunch of cells? You can type the following:

```
=B1+B2+B3+B4+B5+B6+B7+B8
```

Pretty boring. You can see why this type of thing may drive you back to your calculator. So to avoid losing your business, the software folks came up with a way to tell Works to "sum up the range B1 through B8." You do so by entering the following:

```
=SUM(B1:B8)
```

You don't even need to type **B1:B8** while you're entering the formula! You can stop typing for a moment, select that range with your mouse, and then type the final parenthesis. See the section "Shortcuts for Creating Formulas," later in this chapter, for more information on this technique. See Chapter 2 for more information on ranges and range addresses such as B1:B8.

SUM and other built-in calculations are known as *functions*. And, if you use them correctly, they do — function, that is. Works includes a whole passel of other functions for doing all kinds of things. (You can find more information about those functions in the section "You're Invited to a Function," later in this chapter.)

All calculations, no matter how complex, are performed this way in the spreadsheet: by mixing together numbers, mathematical operations (such as addition and subtraction), and functions to make formulas.

Seeing and editing formulas

The spreadsheet displays only the result of a formula, although the formula actually remains in the cell. "So," you may well ask, "how can we see my formula?"

You can see an individual formula at any time by clicking its cell (or by using the navigation keys to place your highlight on the cell) and looking in the formula bar.

You edit a formula the same way that you edit any other contents of a cell: To edit by using the formula bar, click the cell and then click the formula bar. To edit directly in the cell, double-click the cell or press F2. (See the section on editing inside a cell in Chapter 2.)

To see all the formulas in your spreadsheet, choose <u>V</u>iew⇨<u>F</u>ormulas. This command turns on a Formula view that's pretty ugly but does show all your formulas. You can work using this view, if you want. To turn off the Formula view, do the same thing you did to turn it on.

Hello, operator?: Mathematical operations

In the earlier section, "Entering a formula," I use the plus (+) symbol to represent addition in a formula. Among the common operators (math actions) that you can use to create your mathematical formulas are + (add), – (subtract), / (divide), * (multiply), and ^ (raise to the power of . . .).

In a formula that uses several operators, put the expressions you want to compute first in parentheses to make sure that Works computes things in the order you want. Works evaluates the expression (2+3)*4, for example, as 5*4, giving 20 as the result. Without the parentheses, the expression is 2+3*4. Works does multiplication first, creating 2+12; then it does addition, giving 14 as the result, not 20! Without parentheses, Works evaluates expressions according to the operator that you use, in the following order of priority: ^, *, or /; then + or –. To break any ties (if the formula uses, say, both * and / operators), Works evaluates the formula from left to right. But rather than memorize all this order-of-priority stuff, it's easier to just use parentheses to indicate what you want evaluated first.

You're Invited to a Function

Works has quite a few convenient built-in functions, such as SUM, which are very inviting. Functions produce some sort of value, which you can, in turn, use within a formula, for instance SUM(A2:A22)/B4. Here are some functions, in addition to SUM, that you often use:

AVG(*cells*)	The average of the values in the cells
MAX(*cells*)	The maximum value among the cells
MIN(*cells*)	The minimum value among the cells
ROUND(*cell, # of digits*)	The value in the cell rounded off to some number of digits

The word *cell* in italics in the preceding minitable means that you type in a single, specific cell address (such as **B1**), not the word *cell*. And the word *cells* means that you type in a range, such as **B1:B8** or a set of ranges, such as **B1:B8, D5:D13, F256**. (Microsoft uses the term *range reference* instead of *cells*.) You can also use actual numbers in formulas instead of addresses containing numbers.

The phrase *# of digits* in the minitable means to use a specific number, such as 2 or 3. Alternatively, *# of digits* may be the address of a cell that contains the number of digits, but that's getting complicated.

If a function uses its own result, you're in trouble. The formula =SUM(A1:A10), for example, better not appear in any of the cells A1 through A10. If you're lucky, Works tells you that you've got a *circular reference.* If you're not lucky, Works just merrily calculates something bizarre and doesn't tell you why.

So many functions are available that even a short list is more than this book can handle. Two places describe these functions: the spreadsheet program itself and the Works Help feature. We discuss the spreadsheet program's listing in the section "Shortcuts for Creating Formulas," later in this chapter. To read about functions by using the Help feature, follow these steps:

1. **Choose <u>H</u>elp⇨<u>I</u>ndex to display the Index card of the Help Topics window.**

2. **Type** functions **in the top text box.**

3. **Click the Use Spreadsheet Functions folder in the Topics Found list box.**

   A list appears with each item, starting with the word *Use.* If you want a function that calculates averages, for example, click Use Statistical Functions, which gives you a list of documents describing all the functions of this type.

4. **Click the document (they all begin with "Use . . .") describing any function. To see the function for averages, click Use AVG.**

   Help appears in a window on the right side of the screen.

5. **In the Help window, click the <u>What is the Ave function?</u> link to read a description of the function.**

Shortcuts for Creating Formulas

As you create formulas, Works provides several typing shortcuts, as the following list describes:

✔ **Don't type the range address.** When you reach the point where you need a range address — say, for example, that you just typed =**SUM()** — take your mouse in hand and drag across the range you want or click the cell that you want in the function. Then type the closing parenthesis and any subsequent parts of the formula you need.

✔ **When summing a row or column, don't bother to type the** SUM **function.** Whenever you have a column (or row) of numbers that you want to add up, just select the empty cell at the bottom of the column (or at the end of the row) and click the AutoSum button — the button on the toolbar with the Greek letter sigma on it (Σ). The sum formula then appears in the empty cell with the column or row range address automatically entered.

✔ **Don't type the function you want to use.** Instead, Works provides you with a feature for inserting the function itself, as the remainder of this section describes.

To insert a function without typing it, follow these steps:

1. **Click a cell and start typing your formula.**

   At the point where you need a function, move to Step 2.

2. **Choose Insert⇨Function.**

   The Insert Function dialog box swings into action, as shown in Figure 3-4. At this point, the big Choose a Function list box shows all the functions that Works offers. Scroll down the list to find the function that you want.

Put this function in your formula.

See specific categories of functions.

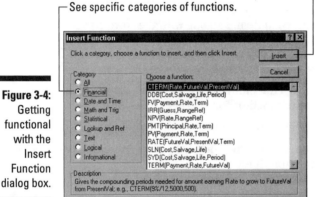

Figure 3-4:
Getting
functional
with the
Insert
Function
dialog box.

3. **If you don't see what you want on the main list, click a button in the Category area to reduce the display of functions to a specific type.**

   To see only mathematical and trigonometric functions in the Choose a Function list box, for example, click the Math and Trig radio button. (Oddly, to my mind, the SUM function is in the Statistical collection, not the Math collection.)

4. **Click a function in the Choose a Function list box.**

   You can see a brief description of what the selected function does at the bottom of the Insert Function dialog box.

5. **Click the Insert button.**

   The dialog box goes away, leaving your chosen function in the formula bar. Works doesn't yet know what cell or cells you want the function to apply to, however, so it leaves text (such as RangeRef) as a placeholder in the places where cell addresses go.

For a detailed explanation of the function from Works Help files, turn on Help by choosing <u>H</u>elp⇨<u>I</u>ndex and then follow the instructions in the section titled "You're Invited to a Function," earlier in this chapter. Also see Chapter 1 for information on using other Help controls.

6. Edit the formula to add cell addresses.

You can do so two ways: You can type the cell addresses you need and delete any extraneous text, or you can drag across the placeholder text to highlight it and then use your mouse to click a cell or drag across a range in your spreadsheet. As you do so, their addresses replace any highlighted placeholder text.

7. Press Enter after you finish entering the entire formula.

The Joys and Mysteries of Copying Formulas

Spreadsheets usually contain tables, which are rows and columns of numbers. In these tables, you often use essentially the same formula over and over again. If you're summing columns, for example, the only difference from column to column is the range you're summing.

If you're doing calculations on columns or rows of a table, you can often save yourself work by copying the formula instead of retyping it — especially if the formula is complex. Works automatically takes care of changing the range in the formula from, say, A1:A10 to B1:B10.

In fact, in a table, you can successfully copy *any* formula (not just a sum) to another column (or row), as long as the formula doesn't use data from outside its own column (or row). The column (or row) of data must be the same size as the original.

Copy a formula just as you'd copy a number or text or anything else — for example, copy by pressing Ctrl+C and paste by pressing Ctrl+V. Remember that by selecting (highlighting) several cells before pasting, you can make several copies at once (one copy in each selected cell). See Chapter 2 for various ways of copying stuff.

For formula copying to work without special tricks, one condition must be true: The location of a formula relative to its data must be the same for all copies as for the original. If the original formula uses a cell that's three columns over and one row down from its address, you must provide each copy with data three columns over and one row down from *its* address.

What happens if you copy formulas?

The best way to explain what happens if you copy a formula is to show you an example: Figure 3-5 shows part of a spreadsheet just after I finished copying a bunch of formulas in column D. The task before me was to calculate the D column (average price per unit sold) from the C (unit sales) and E (total sales revenues) columns. Instead of entering a formula for each cell of the D column, I typed the formula only once, for the total in cell D8, and then I copied it to the other five cells, D3 through D7 (shown highlighted in Figure 3-5).

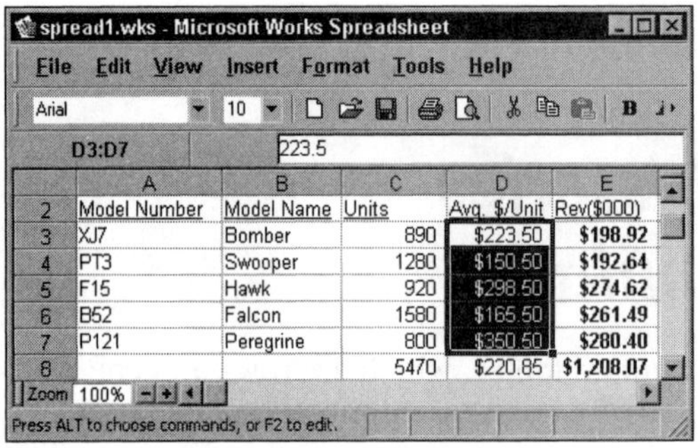

Figure 3-5:
Copying
formulas
can save
you a lot of
typing time.

As I began, column D had no formulas in it. My procedure for adding the formulas is described in these following steps:

1. **Enter the formula** =1000*E8/C8 **into cell D8 and press Enter.**

   (The 1000 is there because we express the revenues in column E in terms of thousands of dollars.) Wouldn't this formula be a pain to type five more times just to put it in rows 3 through 7?

2. **Click the Copy button on the toolbar to copy the formula in D8.**

3. **Select the range D3:D7.**

4. **Click the Paste button on the toolbar to paste copies of the formula into cells D3 through D7.**

Notice that each copy of the formula uses only cells in its own row. You can see the formula in the formula bar after you click those cells. The formula in cell D5, for example, is =1000*E5/C5; in cell D6, it's =1000*E6/C6; and so on. Pretty neat, huh?

Here's what happens to cell addresses if you copy formulas:

✔ **After you copy a formula to a new column, the letter (column) portion of the cell address changes.** If you copy something one column to the right and you have an address of A1 in your formula, it changes to B1; Q17 changes to R17; and so on.

✔ **After you copy a formula to a new row, the number (row) portion of the cell address changes.** If you copy something one row down and you have an address of A1 in your formula, A1 changes to A2; Q17 changes to Q18; and so on.

(If you copy a formula to a new row *and* column, *both* the row and column change in any cell addresses in that formula.)

Note: If you *move* a formula (by dragging it) or cut and paste the formula, the addresses in the formula don't change. Addresses change only if you *copy* something — either by dragging it or by using the Copy and Paste commands (Ctrl+C and Ctrl+V).

Fixing formulas that don't copy correctly

You can often still copy formulas that don't copy correctly if you tweak them a bit beforehand. Following is a simple example that you can generalize to fix many of your formula-copying problems.

A typical formula-copying problem is that the formula you want to copy refers to a single cell containing a key value or fudge factor. Back in Figure 3-1, for example, the formula in cell E4 (American dollars) depends on the exchange rate in cell B15. If you copy the formula in cell E4 to the other rows (E5, E6, and so on), the reference to B15 changes rows — to B16, B17, and so on — and is wrong.

The solution is to keep the reference to that one cell from changing as you copy. To keep a reference from changing, put a dollar sign in front of the column letter and/or row number in the formula. In cell E4 of Figure 3-1, for example, you'd type **=D4/B15** instead of **=D4/B15**. After you copy that formula to the next row, the E4 changes to E5, but B15 remains the same. This trick is called *absolute addressing*.

If, instead of typing your cell addresses into a formula, you prefer to point to them with the mouse, press the F4 key after you point to create an absolute address such as B15. Press F4 again to get B$15 and again to get $B15. This trick also works if you enter cell addresses in Easy Calc.

The dollar sign here has *absolutely nothing* to do with dollars (U.S. or Canadian) *or* currency formatting; use of the dollar sign is just an ancient convention in spreadsheets, probably started by Dan Bricklin when he created VisiCalc or by one of the other spreadsheet pioneers.

Chapter 4

Formatting and Printing Your Spreadsheets

. . . .

In This Chapter

▶ Formatting the entire spreadsheet by using AutoFormat

▶ Formatting characters and numbers

▶ Aligning within a cell

▶ Entering and formatting dates and times

▶ Doing basic arithmetic on dates and times

▶ Using borders and gridlines

▶ Making and sorting lists

▶ Printing your spreadsheet

. . . .

Making a spreadsheet is one thing. Getting the spreadsheet ready for prime time — formatting its numbers and dates correctly, giving it a face lift, and, finally, printing it out — is another.

Dates are a particular challenge (as many unmarried people understand), as are times. This chapter helps you deal with dates, times, and basic date-and-time arithmetic. (You can read this chapter while you're waiting for your date to arrive, which should impress him or her with your intellectual capacity.)

Feeling out of sorts (possibly because your date is late)? This chapter shows you how to sort lists and data into alphabetical or numerical order.

Finally, this chapter delves into the unique opportunities that spreadsheets present for really messing things up as you print. Why, this chapter even provides some solutions!

Formatting in One Swell Foop!

Back when disco ruled and quiche was the trendy food of the day, spreadsheets were dull, boring grids. No more! Today's spreadsheets sport designer colors, shading, lines, borders, and fancy fonts in different sizes and styles.

You can apply all these fancy formats individually if you want. But Works also combines a bunch of formatting into various stylish ensembles, which Works refers to as *automatic formatting*. Automatic formatting, or *autoformatting*, is truly a great idea (unless you don't want all those particular changes).

If you copy a cell, you also *copy all its formatting*. Formatting includes number formatting, alignment, borders, and shading.

Figure 4-1 shows what happens to the toy sales spreadsheet from Chapter 3 after you deck it out in an automatic format called *3-D Effects 2*. All kinds of stuff has changed here — even the formats of some of the numbers. Zowie! All these changes result from a few mouse clicks.

Figure 4-1:
Auto-
formatting:
Just a few
clicks can
get you
a whole
new look.

	A	B	C	D	E
1	**Toy Sales**				
2	Model Number	**Model Name**	**Units**	**Avg. $/Unit**	**Rev($000)**
3	XJ7	Bomber	890	223.505618	$198.92
4	PT3	Swooper	1280	$150.50	$192.64
5	F15	Hawk	920	$298.50	$274.62
6	B52	Falcon	1580	$165.50	$261.49
7	P121	Peregrine	800	$350.50	$280.40
8			5470	220.853748	$1,208.07

The AutoFormat feature presumes that you have a fairly classic table structure: rows, columns, and maybe (although not necessarily) totals. If you meet these standards, AutoFormat away by following these steps:

1. **Make sure that you have column and row headings.**

   Or, if you don't have 'em, at least have a blank row above and a blank column to the left of your table. (Use these "empties" for your title row and column in Step 2.)

2. **Select all the rows and columns of your table, including the title row and column and the total row and/or column.**

   If you have a title for the entire spreadsheet, you can include or exclude it, as you want. I excluded the *Toy Sales* line in Figure 4-1.

3. **Choose Format⇨AutoFormat.**

   The AutoFormat dialog box leaps into action, as shown in Figure 4-2.

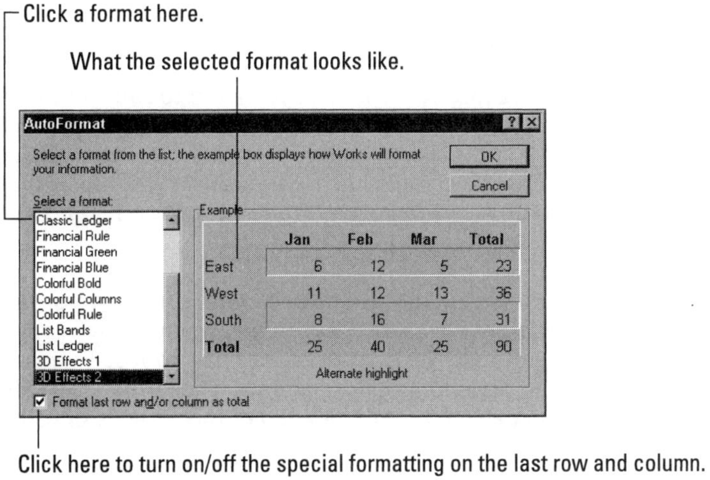

Click a format here.

What the selected format looks like.

Figure 4-2:
The
AutoFormat
dialog box.
If only
reformatting
my auto was
this easy.

AutoFormat	? X

Select a format from the list; the example box displays how Works will format your information.

OK

Cancel

Select a format:

Classic Ledger
Financial Rule
Financial Green
Financial Blue
Colorful Bold
Colorful Columns
Colorful Rule
List Bands
List Ledger
3D Effects 1
3D Effects 2

Example

	Jan	Feb	Mar	Total
East	6	12	5	23
West	11	12	13	36
South	8	16	7	31
Total	25	40	25	90

Alternate highlight

☑ Format last row and/or column as total

Click here to turn on/off the special formatting on the last row and column.

4. Select any interesting-sounding format in the Select a Format list box.

The Example area shows you how the format looks. If you don't like this format, select another format. If you don't like any of 'em, press the Esc key.

5. Examine the Format Last Row and/or Column as Total check box.

If you're not using a total row or column or if you have your total somewhere other than at the end of the range, make sure that this check box is blank (deselected). If you do have a total row or column, click in the check box to add a check mark but look at the example to see whether this particular format puts the total in the same place that you did.

In the toy sales example, I chose to deselect the check box because cell D8 is an average, not a total.

6. Click the OK button.

Foop! A brief flurry of activity takes place, and suddenly, your spreadsheet looks like the inside pages of a quarterly report. If you don't like the results, press Ctrl+Z immediately to undo the formatting — before you make any other changes to the spreadsheet — and try again.

7. Throw in some finishing touches if you want.

In Figure 4-1, for example, I'd probably do something to get rid of all those digits after the decimal point in D3 and D8, either by using the ROUND function or by selecting column D and changing to currency format. (See the section "Formatting Numbers," later in this chapter.)

Formatting Cells Yourself

If AutoFormat doesn't ring your chimes, you need to ring your own chimes. The basics of font, font size, colors, and text alignment all work the same way for all the programs in the Works Suite. Press Ctrl+R to right-align, for example, or press Ctrl+E to center-align text. See Chapter 1 for instructions on using the Works toolbar, the keyboard, and the Font and Style dialog box to change characters and their alignments.

For a greater variety of cell formatting, select the cells that you want to format; then either right-click with your mouse and choose Format on the context menu that appears or, from the menu bar, choose Format➪Number, Alignment, Font and Style, Border, or Shading. The Format Cells dialog box appears, where you can click a tab for each of those types of cell formatting.

This chapter deals mainly with formatting options on the Number and Border tabs. The Shading feature is pretty self-explanatory.

The Alignment tab offers a few other choices besides the toolbar's standard left, right, and center options. To use one, select the cells that you want to align and then choose Format➪Alignment.

For *vertical alignment,* select Top, Center, or Bottom to position your cell contents at the top, center, or bottom of a cell. Row height must exceed text height to see any effect! To have *multiple lines of text* in your cell, select the Wrap Text check box.

Additional interesting *horizontal alignment* tricks exist. To *fill* a cell that contains a single character with copies of that character (useful for making horizontal lines out of hyphens or equal signs), select Fill. To *center a title across several cells,* select Center Across Selection as your horizontal alignment. To restore usual text and number alignments for Works, select General.

Formatting Numbers

Formatting numbers is not quite the same as formatting text. If you format numbers, the actual characters and punctuation change to different characters and punctuation, adding dollar signs or parentheses, for example. The number itself doesn't change, but it puts on a radically different face. Sometimes it doesn't even look like a number anymore.

If, for example, you enter the number **3284.2515** in a cell and use your formatting options (which Table 4-1 lists), you can make that number look like any of the stuff in the How It Looks column of Table 4-1.

Table 4-1	Different Formatting for the Number 3284.2515	
How It Looks	**Format Name**	**About That Format and Options You Can Specify**
3284.25	General	As precise as possible for the column width; this style is how Works formats numbers unless you tell it otherwise.
3284.252	Fixed	Specifies decimal places (in this example, *three*).
$3,284.25	Currency	Dollar sign, comma, specifies decimal places; negative numbers appear in parentheses. *Optional:* Negative numbers also in red.
3,284.25	Comma	Similar to Currency but no dollar sign.
328425.15 %	Percent	Displays number multiplied by 100, adds percent symbol; specify your decimal places.
3.28 E+03	Exponential	Single-digit number with power of ten; specify your decimal places (in this example, *two*).
03284	Leading Zeros	No fraction; displays as many digits as you specify (in this example, *five*); adds zeros or trims leading digits to do so. Good for zip codes.
3248 3/10	Fraction	Expresses fractional part as fraction: Choose halves, thirds, quarters, eighths, tenths, and so on (in this example, *tenths*).
TRUE	True/False	If zero, displays FALSE; if not zero, displays TRUE.
November 21, 1908	Date	Interprets number as number of days since midnight December 31, 1899; Works uses this format if you enter a date.
6:02 AM	Time	Interprets fractional part of number as fraction of one day; displays fraction as hour of that day. Works uses this format if you enter a time.
3284.2515	Text	If you apply format *before* entering a number, turns number into text. Useful for serial numbers or other numeric codes.

Date and time formats are among the weirder ones in this list because they make numbers look like text. For more information on how the Works spreadsheet application handles the passage of time, see the section "Working with Dates and Times," later in this chapter.

The Currency format is the easiest to apply: Select the cell or cells to format and click the toolbar button with the $ icon on it.

Note: You don't actually format a number in the spreadsheet program; you format *cells.* The cell can be empty as you format it, and after you type a number in that cell, the number takes on the formatting you applied to the cell. If you type text in that cell, the formatting doesn't affect the text. If you delete an entry from a cell, the number format remains.

Works starts with every cell in the General format. To change the format of specific cells, follow these steps:

1. **Select a cell or bunch of cells.**

   Click the cell or highlight the bunch of cells.

2. **Choose Format➪Number.**

   The Number tab of the Format Cells dialog box presents itself for duty, as shown in Figure 4-3.

Choose a format first.   Choose options second.

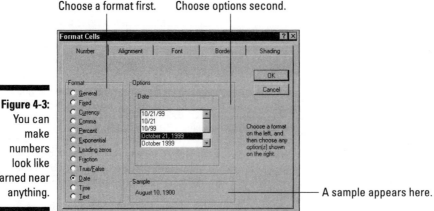

Figure 4-3:
You can make numbers look like darned near anything.

A sample appears here.

3. **Select any format in the Format area of the dialog box.**

   As Figure 4-3 shows, Works displays a sample in the Sample area. If a number is already in the cell, Works uses that number in the sample. If you don't like what you see, select another format. Refer to Table 4-1 for notes about these formats.

Some formats enable you to specify precision: How many digits are to the right (or left, in the case of the Leading Zeros format) of the decimal point? Normally, Works uses two digits here. To change the precision, type a number in the Decimal Places text box (which appears only for formats that use decimal places).

The Currency and Comma formats enable you to optionally put negative numbers in red; just select the Negative Numbers in Red check box (which appears if you select these formats).

The Fractions format normally rounds numbers to a fraction that you specify and reduces them to the lowest possible denominator. *Reduction* means, for instance, that if you choose ½₂ for Round To (which appears for fractions format), and your number ends in .125, that fraction displays as ⅛. If you really want that fraction to appear as ⁴⁄₃₂ or whatever fraction you've chosen, select the Do Not Reduce check box.

4. Click OK.

Changing formatting doesn't change what's really in the cell — it changes only the appearance of what's there.

Working with Dates and Times

The secret of using dates and times successfully in a spreadsheet is to realize that, to a spreadsheet, dates and times are numbers! Works just formats the numbers to *look like* dates or times. You don't usually need to understand the details of how Works represents time, but if you want to understand it, see the accompanying sidebar, "The clockwork behind dates and times in Works."

Ever heard of a "year 2079 bug?" Works (Release 5, anyway) can't handle dates later than June 3, 2079, so don't make any hundred-year plans.

Typing dates and times

If you want to do calculations based on your dates and times, you must type them in valid Works date and time formats. Table 4-2 shows valid formats for entering dates and times.

If you enter a date or time in a format that Works doesn't recognize, your entry may end up simply as text, not a number, and you can't use it for calculations.

The clockwork behind dates and times in Works

Here's what's behind the scenes: Works keeps track of time by giving every day a number; Works starts the sequence at 12 AM, January 1, 1900, which is represented as 1.00. Days are whole numbers. Hours and minutes in that day are represented by a fractional portion. So 8 AM on January 1, 1900 is 1.333333333. Just plain 8 AM is 0.33333.

If you type in a date or a time, Works shows it to you as a date or a time, which is nice. But Works secretly changes the entry to a number. If you type **8 AM**, for example, Works enters 0.33333 and selects a *time format* for the number. If you type in a date, Works enters the number for midnight on that date and applies a *date format* that duplicates the format in which you typed the number.

Table 4-2	Valid Formats for Entering Dates and Times
Dates	*Times*
August 28, 1945	2:30 PM
8/28/45	14:30
8/28/1945	2:00
August	2 AM
August 2	2:00 AM
8/2	2:00 am

You can enter times *without* using AM or PM, but Works interprets them all as *a.m.* unless they're in 24-hour time format (for example, *14:00*). Works interprets dates (such as *August 28, 1945*) as *12 a.m.* on that date. You can enter dates without adding a year designation (for example, *8/28*), but Works actually assumes that they're in the current year. Likewise, you can enter months alone (*August,* for example), and Works translates them as 12 a.m. (midnight) on the first of that month, the current year.

To enter today's date, press Ctrl+; (that's Ctrl and the semicolon key). To enter the current time, press Ctrl+Shift+; (that's Ctrl+Shift+semicolon)..

To enter a date that's current all the time, such as on a day/date watch, type in the function =**NOW()** and format the cell by using a date format. The date updates every time you change a cell or press the F9 (recalculate) key. To display a time that's always current, format the same cell with a *time format.*

Formatting dates and times

Working with dates and times in a spreadsheet often produces weird numbers, such as 16679 or 0.33333, that don't resemble a date or time. No problem. Really. What you get is the number that Works secretly uses for handling dates or times: the number (and any fractional portion) of days between the date in question and January 1, 1900. For more info, see the sidebar, "The clockwork behind dates and times in Works," a bit earlier in this chapter.

If your date or time appears in such an un-date-and-time-like format, you need to format this number as a date or time yourself. (Unless, of course, you don't care how the date looks.) Choose Format⇨Number and, on the Number tab of the Format Numbers dialog box that appears, select Date or Time. For details, see the section, "Formatting Numbers," earlier in this chapter.

Doing basic date and time arithmetic

The Works spreadsheet program enables you to do calculations based on time, but you need to be a little careful. Works secretly uses numbers to represent dates and makes them look "date-ish" by using a date *format*. If you do calculations, the results may come out as funny numbers instead of the date, number of days, or number of hours that you were hoping for. The following instructions generally keep things working well.

Subtracting dates and adding days to dates

If you have two dates, you can easily calculate the time between them by subtracting exactly how much time elapses between them.

Calculating intervals between dates can be depressing if you're single and your social life is less than satisfactory.

You subtract dates just as you subtract regular numbers. To type a date directly into a formula, however, you must enclose it in single quote marks and use the slash-date format, as in **=B4 – '4/14/95'**. The result is the number of days between the dates, so use a regular number format, not a date format, for the cell containing this formula.

Adding dates is silly. (December 25 plus July 4 equals . . . what?) But adding *days* to dates is quite reasonable in a Works formula. For example, *= '9/15'* + *35* adds 35 days to September 15. You format this formula by using a date format, because the result is a date.

Subtracting and adding times

You subtract and add time in much the same way that you subtract and add dates. For example, enter **=B4-'0:15'** to subtract 15 minutes from the time in cell B4. As in that example, if you type a time value directly into a formula, you must enclose it in single quotes.

If you add or subtract times, the result may need some mathematical correction and time formatting. If, for example, you're paid by the hour and you keep time records, whenever you subtract, say, 10:17 a.m. from 10:32 a.m., the result is 0.0104167! You have two problems: 0.0104167 doesn't look like 15 minutes, and (even if you format it correctly) if you multiply that number by your hourly rate (say, $100), you end up billing for only $1.04!

Works keeps track of hours as fractions of a day. One hour is ¹⁄₂₄ of a day, so to fix the problem in this example, multiply by 24 in your billing formula. (If the time is in cell B4, type **=B4*100*24** — where the asterisks are times symbols.) To convert the result of time subtraction to hours, multiply by 24; to convert the result of time subtraction to minutes, multiply by 24*60.

To fix the appearance problem, use a time format. (See the section "Formatting Numbers," earlier in this chapter.)

Adding Borders, Viewing Gridlines

Works takes much of the pain and strain out of prettying up spreadsheets with its AutoFormat feature. (See the section "Formatting in One Swell Foop!" earlier in this chapter.) Alas, sometimes you still need a few lines to dress things up further.

Borders are lines that you add along the top, bottom, or sides of a cell. Some borders are so thin that the *gridlines* that normally cover a spreadsheet mask them. To turn off the gridlines, choose <u>V</u>iew⇨Gridlines. The same action turns the gridlines back on. The highlight that appears around selected cells can also mask your borders. Click elsewhere to move the highlight.

Select (highlight) the cell or block of cells to which you want to apply borders and then choose F<u>o</u>rmat⇨<u>B</u>order. The Border tab of the Format Cells dialog box materializes, as shown in Figure 4-4.

To create a border, select one first (Outline, Top, Bottom, Left, or Right). Then select any of the Line Style examples shown in the dialog box. Select a color, if you want, too. Click OK when you're done.

Select a border first. No border.

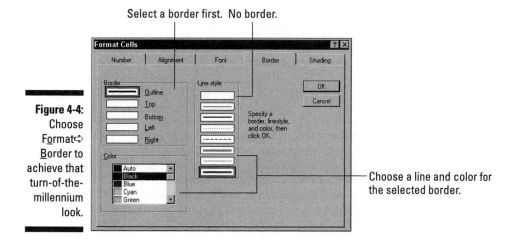

Figure 4-4:
Choose
Format⇨
Border to
achieve that
turn-of-the-
millennium
look.

Choose a line and color for
the selected border.

Following are a few tips for using the Border controls of this dialog box:

✔ To create a single horizontal or vertical line in your spreadsheet, simply apply a top, bottom, left, or right border to a row or column.

✔ In applying borders to a range (block) of cells, the Outline option in the Border area refers to the entire range; Top, Bottom, Left, and Right refer to the borders of each and every cell in that range.

✔ To change or clear (remove) a border, repeatedly click its selection box in the Border area. Clicking cycles the border through two states (and, if a border already exists on some of the selected cells, but not others, possibly three states). Click once to set the border to the currently selected line style; click again to clear it. If a border already exists in some of the cells that you have selected, click a third time to leave it unchanged, signified by shading in the box.

✔ To remove an outline border, you must clear all individual borders.

Sorting Your Data

One of the nice things that the Works spreadsheet program can do for you is to sort your data. If, for example, you're keeping a spreadsheet that lists students and computes their grades, you may want to alphabetize the list by name or sort by class rank. Works can sort alphabetically or numerically. It can also sort by *primary, secondary,* and *tertiary* considerations, such as last name, first name, and middle initial. Such sorting groups all the Smiths together, sorting them by first names, and then sorts any John Smiths by middle initial. The procedure for sorting follows:

1. **Save your spreadsheet as a file (by pressing Ctrl+S), in case anything goes wrong.**

   If anything *does* go terribly wrong and pressing Ctrl+Z doesn't undo the error, close the spreadsheet without saving it and then reopen the original file.

2. **Select (highlight) only the rows and columns that contain the data you want to sort.**

   You may include or not include a row of column heads if you have one.

3. **Choose Tools➪Sort.**

   If this is your first attempt at sorting, the First-Time Help dialog box appears. If you want to be stepped-through the process, Wizard-style, or see a demo, click one of the two buttons. For the purposes of this example, just click the OK button. (You'll always be able to see the First-Time Help demos in the future, as long as you *don't* select the check box labeled Don't display this message in the future.)

   After you click the OK button, the Sort dialog box appears. Go along with its suggestion: to sort only the columns selected.

4. **Click OK.**

   This action opens the second Sort dialog box, shown in Figure 4-5, which asks which column to sort on and whether to sort in ascending or descending order.

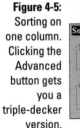

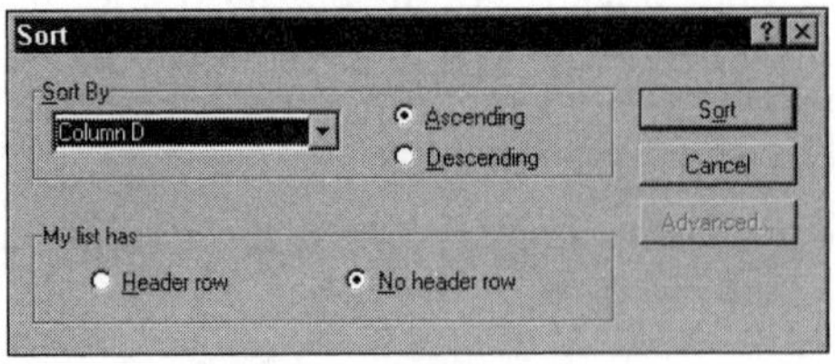

Figure 4-5: Sorting on one column. Clicking the Advanced button gets you a triple-decker version.

5. **In the Sort By drop-down list box, select the column by which you want to sort.**

6. **Select either the Ascending or Descending radio button.**

   Ascending means that, reading from top to bottom, numbers or letters go from low to high (such as A to Z). *Descending* means, well, the opposite.

7. **Select either the Header Row or No Header Row radio button.**

   If the cells you highlighted in Step 2 include a header row, select Header Row. Otherwise, select No Header Row.

8. **If you want secondary or tertiary sorting (say, sorting multiple Smiths by their first names and middle initials), click the Advanced button.**

   A sort of triple-decker version of the Sort dialog box appears. The top deck contains the column and sort order that you just specified. The second and third decks are available for you to specify additional columns for Works to sort on in the event of identical entries in the primary sort column.

9. **Click the Sort button.**

   Works sorts your list (that is, it shuffles your rows around in the order that you specified). To return to the original order, you can press Ctrl+Z as long as you haven't made any other changes.

If you're clever and created a column in which you give each record (row) a serial number, you can always sort by selecting that column in the Sort By drop-down list box and restore the original order.

You can dress up your list by using the AutoFormat feature, just as you can any other spreadsheet. A couple of formats are even made especially for lists: List Bands and List Ledger. See the section "Formatting in One Swell Foop!" earlier in this chapter.

Dealing with Printing Peculiarities

Printing spreadsheets is pretty much like printing anything else in Works, so for the general picture, see Chapter 1. Following, however, are a few peculiarities about printing spreadsheets:

 ✔ To print only a portion of the spreadsheet, not the entire spreadsheet, select a range and use the Set Print Area command: Choose Format⇨Set Print Area. To go back to printing the entire spreadsheet, select the entire spreadsheet (Ctrl+A) and repeat the Set Print Area command.

 ✔ Works splits up your spreadsheet to make it fit on a printed page. If the spreadsheet is bigger than the page, you literally must cut and paste paper pages together to re-create the original layout. Use the Print Preview feature (by choosing File⇨Print Preview) to see how your spreadsheet will print.

Calculating in sorted areas

By sorting, you can unintentionally change the data to which your formulas refer! Here's how to avoid problems: You can safely use a formula that refers to a range of the sorted area only if that range covers an *entire column* of data (as a sum or average does). If a formula refers to *specific cells in the sorted area,* it should refer only to *cells in the same row* as that formula. You must include the column containing the formula in the sort. Otherwise, after you sort the rows, the range address that the formula specifies remains unchanged, but it now refers to different data.

If you add rows to the list, do so by inserting a new row, not by moving other rows. Check your formulas after inserting new rows to make sure that the formulas include the new data rows.

To control page breaks yourself, you can split up the document horizontally and/or vertically and create page-sized pieces. Follow these steps:

1. **For a horizontal break, click the row below where you want the break; for a vertical break, click the column to the right of the break.**

2. **Choose Insert⇨Page Break.**

   A tiny Insert Page Break dialog box appears.

3. **In the Insert Page Break dialog box, select Column for a vertical break or Row for a horizontal one, and then click OK.**

If you repeat the process — keeping your highlight at the same cell that you used in Step 1 — Works automatically assumes that you want the new break to run in the opposite orientation (vertical if the existing one is horizontal, for example). It doesn't open an Insert Page Break dialog box to ask you.

To get rid of a page break, put your cursor to the right of the page break (for vertical) or under the page break (for horizontal); then choose Insert⇨ Delete Page Break.

Chapter 5

Creating Charts from Spreadsheets

● ●

● ●

*F*or a multi-program package with plenty of other things on its mind, Works offers a rather nice selection of chart types and variations and makes the job of charting a breeze. Or is it a snap? Whatever. A snapping breeze perhaps. Very easy, in any event.

You produce charts from data in your spreadsheets. You can print the charts or copy them to other documents that you create in Word and many other Windows programs. This chapter tells you how to make the jump from dry rows and columns of numbers to graphical "eye scream" that delights the soul and satisfies the intellect.

A Gallery of Chart Types and Variations

Works has more kinds of charts than Ben & Jerry's has kinds of ice cream. Works displays the array of possibilities whenever you create a chart, as shown in Figure 5-1. The following list describes how each chart relates to the cells of your spreadsheet:

✔ **Bar:** If you make a bar chart, each cell inspires a separate bar on the chart; the cell's value determines the height of its bar. For multiple rows or columns of data, bars appear differently colored (like popsicles) and can sit side by side or stacked to show the sum.

✔ **Pie:** If you make a pie chart, each cell determines the size of pie slice. By using the *variations* in Works, you can display your pie charts whole, with one slice partially removed, or exploded into separate slices (a microwaved pie). *À la mode* is not an option.

✔ **Line:** In a line chart, each cell determines the height of a dot, and the dots run horizontally, connected by lines. Variations include lines alone, dots alone, or high/low/close (for tracking your *Ben & Jerry's* stock values).

✔ **Stacked line:** Stacked-line charts are for multiple sets *(series)* of data that you want to display together but in a way that reveals what portion of the total comes from each set. A stacked-line chart can show how ice-cream sales from your eastern, western, northern, and southern sales divisions contribute to your total sales. The divisional sales *stack* on top of each other to show the total.

✔ **Area:** An area chart is like a stacked-line chart but filled in with color underneath the lines.

✔ **Scatter:** A scatter plot enables you to compare two sets of data. If your data is in two columns, each row gives the X,Y coordinates of a point. To the extent that the dots appear to form a straight line, the two sets correlate (as do, for example, daily ice-cream consumption and cholesterol level).

✔ **Radar:** A radar chart is kind of like a line chart that's going around in a circle: Instead of the line's height varying, its radius from a center point varies. Radar plots are useful for showing variations in cyclical events — for example, consumption of ice cream by month. See Figure 5-1; radar charts are kind of hard to describe.

✔ **Combination:** A combination chart enables you to mix lines and bars in a single chart. A Neapolitan ice cream kind of chart!

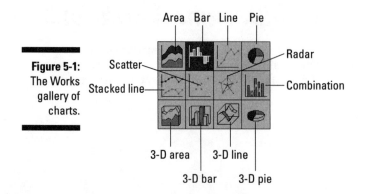

Figure 5-1:
The Works gallery of charts.

I'm not going to get into all of these chart types here. After you know about the basic types, you can pick up the others pretty easily.

You can get the basic types of charts in several *variations* and with various features. (Not including chocolate sprinkles.) See the section "Changing Chart Types and Variations," later in this chapter.

You can also size the charts to any size you need; put a border around them; and change the fonts, colors, shading, gridlines, and even the shapes of the data points. I don't discuss all these variations here, but you should be aware of what's possible.

Creating Any Chart, Step-by-Step

To create a new chart, start with a spreadsheet — preferably, one that's laid out with row and column headings, although you can chart any spreadsheet that you want. Just follow these steps:

1. **Select a range containing the data that you want to chart.**

   Select only the data that you want to plot; if you don't want to plot a column or row, leave it out. If headings are immediately adjacent to the row or column that you want to plot, include them in your selection; otherwise leave them out. See Figure 5-2.

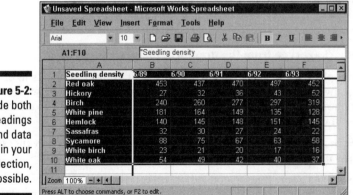

Figure 5-2:
Include both headings and data in your selection, if possible.

For a pie chart, select just the one column (or row) containing the numbers you want to chart; if headings are in an adjacent column, include them.

2. **Choose Tools⇨Create New Chart or click the New Chart button (which looks like a tiny bar chart) on the toolbar.**

   (If this is your first time creating a chart — or you've selected no cells — you'll see a dialog box asking if you want to take a Quick Tour of Charting. Instead of that option, click the other button — the one labeled To Create a Chart. If you haven't selected any data, do so.) The New Chart dialog box swings into action, as shown in Figure 5-3. It shows you a sample of a bar chart based on the data you selected. It also tries to figure out whether you included line and column headings; if so, it uses them as labels in the chart.

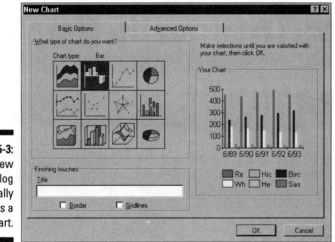

Figure 5-3:
The New Chart dialog box initially suggests a bar chart.

3. **Select a chart type from the graphical picture gallery.**

   The sample area on the right shows you what your chart looks like. Works always starts out by showing you a bar chart. To review your other choices, see the section "A Gallery of Chart Types and Variations," earlier in this chapter.

4. **If the chart in the sample area looks incorrect, click the Advanced Options tab to see various options that you can change.**

   Works makes some guesses based on what it finds. Works may have misinterpreted your spreadsheet data, for example, by reading your data series across instead of down or vice versa.

   • If necessary, change selection 1, Which Way Do Your Series Go?

     Remember that a series is a column or row of data that you want to chart in a single color. If your data is in columns, select Down. I often find thinking about this too confusing. If the chart looks wrong, I just choose the alternative: either Across or Down. For more help, see the sidebar, "What the heck are series and categories?"

- If necessary, change the settings for First Column Contains and First Row Contains.

  If you have numbers in the first row or column that you actually intend to be *labels* for your data, not the data to chart, click Legend Text.

- If you have dates or times in the first row or column and you actually intend them to be data and not labels, click the A value (Y) series button.

- All better now? Click the Basic Options tab to return to the other tab in this dialog box.

5. **Enter a title for the chart in the Title text box at the bottom of the Basic Options tab.**

   Click in the Title text box and type something descriptive, such as **Sales by Quarter**. The sample chart in the dialog box reflects your choice.

6. **If you want a border around the whole chart, select the Border check box; if you want gridlines, select the Gridlines check box.**

7. **Click OK.**

A chart window appears with your lovely work of numeric art in spunky primary colors. To enhance or change your chart, see the section "Changing Chart Types and Variations," later in this chapter.

What the heck are series and categories?

Works keeps yammering about series and categories. What the heck are these things anyway?

A *series* is the group of numbers that you're plotting — a single row or column of data. A series always appears in a single color.

A *category* is a name for each of the numbers in the series. January, February, and March, for example, are separate categories in a series of 12 monthly sales figures. If your series are in columns, your categories are the rows.

A *series label* is a description of what the numbers represent, such as Sales or Rainfall. Usually Works copies labels from the headings on your columns or rows of data. If you include any headings in your initial selection of cells, the labels appear automatically in the legend. The legend identifies what series a particular color represents.

Using the Chart Window, Menu, and Toolbar

After you finish creating a new chart, Works creates a chart window, as shown in Figure 5-4. Even though the chart appears in a separate window, it's part of your spreadsheet and is saved with the spreadsheet file. (By default the chart's window fills the entire Works Spreadsheet application's window — see the following Tip paragraph to learn how to resize the chart window.)

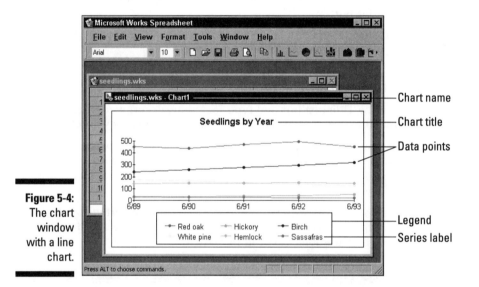

Figure 5-4: The chart window with a line chart.

Notice that the menu bar has changed a little, and the toolbar has changed a lot. That's because, as long as the chart window is active, you're in the *chart tool* — the thing this chapter has been talking about. If you switch to the spreadsheet (by, say, clicking its title bar), you're in the *spreadsheet tool,* where you make spreadsheets.

Another way to switch between your chart and its spreadsheet is to choose View⇨Chart or View⇨Spreadsheet. A View Chart dialog box appears, displaying the list of available charts. Double-click the one you want to use. (You can also select a chart or spreadsheet on the Window menu.)

If the chart looks rather squished and crowded and the words appear chopped off, don't panic. That's just how Works deals with a too-small chart window. Click and drag a side or corner of the chart window to make it bigger.

To reduce a spreadsheet or chart window so that it looks like Figure 5-4 (it doesn't fill the entire Works Spreadsheet application), click the middle button in the upper-right corner of the chart's or spreadsheet's window. This button reduces a *maximized* window to a *normal* window. Windows contained within larger windows are called *child windows,* and sometimes *document* windows. You can see two child windows in Figure 5-4, contained within the larger Works Spreadsheet program's window.

The chart menu bar

The chart menu bar looks and works like menu bars everywhere, but it contains some commands that don't appear in any other Works program, as the following list describes:

- ✔ The Edit menu of the chart tool gives you not only the usual cut-and-paste stuff, but also everything that you need for changing the range of data (the series) in the spreadsheet that you're charting. It also allows you to edit the titles and labels in the chart.

- ✔ The View menu of the chart tool enables you to switch between the spreadsheet and any of the charts that you may attach to it.

- ✔ Choosing Format➪Chart Type displays the Chart Type dialog box (shown in Figure 5-5) and enables you to change the type and variation of the chart. See the section "Changing Chart Types and Variations," later in this chapter. The toolbar buttons also enable you to do the same thing.

- ✔ The Format menu also gives you commands that control the chart's appearance: its fonts, patterns, colors, axes, borders, legends, and 3-D-osity.

- ✔ The Tools menu gives you commands to create, name, and delete charts that attach to the spreadsheet.

I cover the most important menu choices in more detail in the remainder of this chapter.

The chart toolbar

The toolbar, as always, is just another vehicle for giving commands to Works (instead of the traditional semaphore flags). About half the buttons (the ones on the left side) are identical to the buttons on the spreadsheet toolbar, covering options such as font, size, saving, printing, and copying.

You can always discover the purpose of a toolbar button by placing your mouse cursor over it (but don't click!). A tiny tag appears with actual English words on it, telling you what the button is or does.

The buttons on the right half of the toolbar are, for the most part, WYSIWYG (*What You See Is What You Get*) — that is, they have pictures of charts on 'em. (Really! Just get out your magnifying glass.) Click 'em, and your chart can look something like what you see on the icon, only bigger and prettier. See the following section, "Changing Chart Types and Variations," for more information.

The rightmost button (not visible in Figure 5-4, but displaying the white arrow and the number 1) is a secret passage to the spreadsheet — specifically, to the first data series in the spreadsheet. If you have a big spreadsheet and are charting just a portion of it, clicking this button is a quick way to get to the right place.

Changing Chart Types and Variations

To change the chart's *type* or *variation,* either choose Format⇨Chart Type from the chart menu bar or click a toolbar button. Either way, you get a lovely graphical display of various ways to show off your data.

If, for example, you click the button that looks like downtown Chicago (the 3-D Bar Chart button), you open the Chart Type dialog box, shown in Figure 5-5.

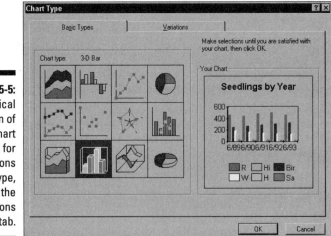

Figure 5-5:
A graphical selection of basic chart types; for variations on a type, click the Variations tab.

The top tab in the Chart Type dialog box shows you the basic types of charts available, such as bar, line, or 3-D bar. (If you click a toolbar button to get here, your chosen chart type is already selected.) Select a different type of chart by clicking one of the pictures.

Click the Variations tab, the second tab in this dialog box, to explore different versions of the basic chart type that you choose. Browse through the variations by clicking them and carefully watching the changes in the example chart shown on this tab.

If you change your chart type or variation, do so before you apply finishing touches, such as data labels (which I discuss later in this chapter). Changing the chart type or variation may remove these niceties if the new type of chart doesn't use them. Even if you change back to the old type, your finishing touches are still gone.

Click OK to close the dialog box and select the variation at which you're looking. The following list describes some of the variations from which you may choose:

✔ **3-D bar, line, and pie charts:** Works doesn't really mean 3-D; it means that the chart appears to have thickness and shading, as if it were made of chunks of plastic. Very trendy.

✔ **Titles:** You can have two lines in a title that identifies the chart.

✔ **Labels:** You can add *data labels,* which label the top of each bar or each point along a line with text or numbers (the cell values). You can also add *category labels* (such as text that identifies each bar in a bar chart).

✔ **Legends:** A *legend* is a box that identifies what sets of data the various colors or shades represent. Sales figures, for example, may appear in blue and costs in green.

✔ **Axes:** You can have two Y axes if you plot two different kinds of data, such as temperature and weight, on the same chart.

Naming, Saving, and Managing Multiple Charts

Creative artist that you are, you're probably not content with a single chart of your spreadsheet. No, you want two charts — maybe a line chart to compare annual sales by region and then a bar chart to show total sales by product.

Works enables you to create multiple new charts and keeps them as part of the spreadsheet file. You don't save charts as separate files. If you save your spreadsheet (by choosing File⇨Save), you save all the charts associated with it. If a chart is utterly wrong and you don't want to bother trying to rehabilitate it, delete it by choosing Tools⇨Delete Chart, as I describe in the following list.

To create, name, delete, or duplicate a chart, choose Tools and then one of the following selections from the Tools menu:

- **Create New Chart:** This command performs the customary routine with the New Chart dialog box, as I describe earlier in this chapter.

- **Rename Chart:** To keep your charts straight and to buttress their self-esteem, give your charts names. Choosing the Rename Chart command opens the Rename Chart dialog box. Click the chart that you want to rename in the Select a Chart list. Click in the Type a Name Below text box at the bottom of the dialog box and then type a name for the current chart. Click the Rename button. The new chart name now appears in the chart's title bar. Click OK.

- **Delete Chart:** This command opens the Delete Chart dialog box (surprise). Click the chart that you want to delete in the list of charts and then click the Delete button. Click OK.

- **Duplicate Chart:** This command is handy for creating a slightly different version of an existing chart. In the Duplicate Chart dialog box that appears, click the chart that you want to duplicate and then click in the Name text box. Type a new name, click the Duplicate button, and then click OK.

To switch among charts, just choose View⇨Chart. A humble View Chart dialog box appears, displaying a list of charts by name. Double-click a name to open that chart window.

Customizing Axes and Other Lines

All those spiffy types and styles of charts, such as 3-D area charts, are artistic as all heck — but without lines going across them, the charts may occasionally leave your viewers wondering exactly what values they're looking at: "Is that bar 10, 12, or 15 units high?"

Unless you've already done a lot of customizing of your chart, the simplest way to get horizontal or vertical lines across your chart is to select a style that gives the lines to you. (Choose the Format⇨Chart Type command or click the buttons on the toolbar that depict various chart types.) The other way to add lines is by formatting the axes of your chart, as I describe in the following two sections.

Figure 5-6 shows some options for a 3-D bar chart. Lines that run across the chart horizontally (at intervals along the vertical, or *Y,* axis) are perhaps most in demand. To get these lines, see the following section, "Customizing the Y axis." For lines that run up the chart vertically (at intervals along the horizontal, or *X,* axis), see the section "Customizing the X axis," later in this chapter.

Figure 5-6:
Horizontal
lines at
intervals of
100 along
the Y axis
improve this
chart.

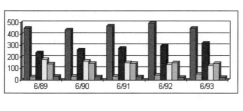

Customizing the Y axis

The Y axis is the axis that goes up toward the heavens. An axis with such lofty ambitions deserves a bit of dressing up. To extend horizontal lines out from the Y axis or to otherwise fool around with the Y axis, choose Format➪ Vertical (Y) Axis. The Format Vertical Axis dialog box appears, looking like the example shown in Figure 5-7.

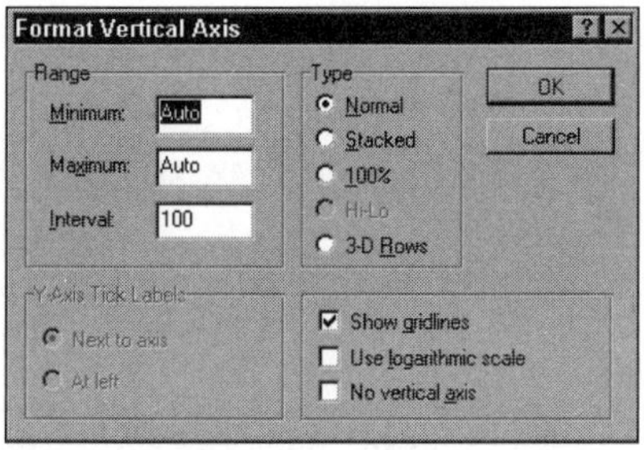

Figure 5-7:
The place
to go for
a more
refined axis.

Following is a rundown of what you can accomplish in the Format Vertical Axis dialog box:

✔ For gridlines at each interval along the axis, select the Show Gridlines check box.

✔ For more or fewer intervals along the axis, click in the Interval text box and type a new value. For a numbered tick mark along the axis every $50 (or 50 ducks or 50 inches of rain or whatever), for example, enter **50**.

✔ To start or end the axis at a different value, edit the values in the Minimum or Maximum text boxes, respectively. This option is good if you have several extreme values that you're embarrassed about and don't care to present.

✔ If you have values over a very wide range (for example, over several powers of 10 — say, from 1 to 1,000), select the Use Logarithmic Scale check box. (This option isn't available for area charts.)

✔ To eliminate the vertical axis altogether (economists and PR folks, take note), select the No Vertical Axis check box. Hey, if you let folks see actual numbers, you just get a lot of picky debate.

✔ You can fool around with what I call the chart's variation by clicking one of the (non–grayed out) entries in the Type area. Sometimes you find variations here that aren't available if you use the Format⇨Chart Type command or the toolbar buttons (such as line charts expressing themselves as percent fractions).

Customizing the X axis

The X axis is the one that goes across the bottom of the chart. To extend vertical lines up from the X axis or otherwise fool around with the X axis, choose Format⇨Horizontal (X) Axis. The Horizontal Axis dialog box appears.

Following are some of the things that you can accomplish in the Horizontal Axis dialog box:

✔ Select the Show Gridlines check box to, well, show gridlines — the vertical-line thingies at every interval.

✔ In an area-type chart, where gridlines disappear behind the curve, you can also select the Show Droplines check box: Works superimposes these lines on the area curve.

✔ To eliminate the horizontal axis altogether, click the No Horizontal Axis check box.

✔ To trim out some of the category labels along a crowded X axis, type a larger value in the Label Frequency text box. Type **3**, for example, to show every third label.

Customizing Charts: Text and Numbers

Works enables you to put text — including titles, series labels, and data labels (the very numbers that you're charting) — in several places in your chart.

Font and style

Charts use a single font and style for all text. You can change the chart font and style in the charting tool just as you do in any other Works program: by using the toolbar, keyboard shortcuts (such as Ctrl+B for bold), or the Format➪Font and Style menu command. See Chapter 1 for details.

You can also change the font and style by double-clicking any tick mark along an axis or a data label. Or right-click on any text and choose Font and Style from the context menu that appears. The Font and Style dialog box then appears.

Don't be too quick to reduce font size. If the text seems too large, you may simply be looking at the chart in a rather small window. Check your chart by using the Print Preview command before you assume that the type is too large (by choosing File➪Print Preview).

Number formats

If your numbers need dollar signs, a different number of decimal places, or any of the other number formatting with which you're familiar from spreadsheets, this problem is not your chart's problem! No, it's your spreadsheet's problem.

Return to your spreadsheet window (by pressing F3, for example) and change the number formatting of your data. See Chapter 4 for details on number formatting.

Chart and axis titles

Titles are important. I once had a cartooning teacher who said that if you can't draw a rabbit, make sure the title says rabbit somewhere. So if you create an incomprehensible chart, at least give it a good title.

Remember the following points about titles:

- *Chart titles* are the one or two lines at the top of the chart.
- *Axis titles* go along an axis and tell you what the axis represents: months, furlongs, doughnuts, and so on.

To create chart or axis titles, choose Edit➪Titles. The Titles dialog box moves regally into view. (Regally because — after all — you're conferring a title!) Just click the appropriate text box and type your title, as the following list describes:

- You can enter two lines of title for the chart in two separate text boxes: Chart Title and Subtitle.
- To type an identifier (text) that prints alongside the X or Y axis, click Horizontal (X) Axis or Vertical (Y) Axis and type the identifier.
- Some charts use the right vertical axis for the second of two things being plotted (say, coffee and doughnut consumption by month). Enter an identifier for Right Vertical Axis if you have a second Y axis (say, Doughnuts).

Click OK after you finish titling your chart.

If your titles don't look very good in the chart window, remember that they don't really look like that after you print them. To see how the chart really looks, use the Print Preview feature (by choosing File➪Print Preview).

Data labels

Data labels display actual data values (such as the number *181*) in the chart. (The values may appear along the line, atop the bars, or alongside the pie slices — depending on what kind of chart you choose.) Take a look at the example shown in Figure 5-8, which includes data labels.

Figure 5-8:
Data labels
leave no
doubt about
what the
numbers
are.

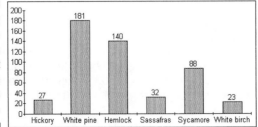

Data labels for all points

To simply print the numbers corresponding to all the points on the chart for every data series, follow these steps:

1. **Choose Edit⇨Data Labels.**

   The Data Labels dialog box puts in an appearance.

2. **Select the Use Series Data check box.**

3. **Click OK.**

Data labels are great, but they can become confusing if you have several data series on the chart at once. The example in Figure 5-8 displays only one data series, so it's pretty easy to read. The trouble with the procedure I just gave you is that it puts numbers on every point of the chart; if you have many points or several data series, the numbers may overlap or crowd each other. If that problem arises, see the following section, "Data labels for a select few points."

Text may look crowded in the Works chart window but appear okay on the printout. Use the Print Preview feature (by choosing File⇨Print Preview) to see how your chart will look after you print it. If your text still looks crowded after you print the chart, another alternative is simply to select a smaller font size from the toolbar.

Data labels for a select few points

To put data labels on a particular data series (one line of a line chart, or one set of bars in a bar chart, for example), I suggest that you use the following copy-and-paste approach:

1. **Choose Window⇨Tile so that you can see both the spreadsheet and the chart.**

2. **In the spreadsheet window, select (highlight) the range of cells that you want to use as data labels and then press Ctrl+C to copy the range of cells to the Windows Clipboard.**

   (You usually want to choose the same range that you use for the series, but you can choose a completely different range, too, as long as it contains the same number of cells.)

3. **Click anywhere in the chart window and then choose Edit⇨Data Labels.**

   The Data Labels dialog box appears.

4. **If a check mark appears in the Use Series Data check box, click the check box to clear the mark.**

5. **Click in the text box for the series that you want to label (Series 1 or Series 2, and so on) and click the Paste button to paste the range address.**

Don't press Ctrl+V, the usual way to paste.

6. Click OK.

7. Repeat Steps 2 through 6 for each series that you want to label.

Leave a series box blank if you want no data labels on that series.

Printing a Chart

A great piece of industrial art such as your chart deserves to appear proudly on canvas. Because your printer probably doesn't do canvas very well, however, you must settle for printing your chart on paper (and proudly displaying it on the refrigerator door perhaps?).

First make sure that the chart window is open and active (by choosing View⇨Chart). Then choose whichever of Works printing commands or buttons you normally prefer to set up, preview, and print documents.

Following are a few tips for printing charts, all concerning the Page Setup dialog box:

✔ Many, if not most, charts fit better if you print them sideways (in *landscape* mode). Choose File⇨Page Setup; click the Source, Size and Orientation tab; and select Landscape. Click OK.

✔ To proportion the chart just as it appears in the chart window, open the Page Setup dialog box (by choosing File⇨Page Setup), click the Other Options tab, and choose Screen Size. Click OK. The graphics keep the same proportion; the text is whatever point size you select.

✔ Other options (not surprisingly) also appear on the Other Options tab of the Page Setup dialog box. The Full Page, Keep Proportions option keeps the same proportions as the chart window, but fills the paper page either to the side margins or to the top and bottom margins. Full Page expands the height and width to the margins and doesn't worry about proportions.

✔ To set the dimensions more precisely by using the Page Setup dialog box, select either of the two Full Page options on the Other Options tab and then set the page margins on the Margins tab.

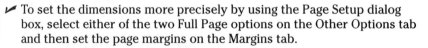

To see how a chart will look on your printer, choose View⇨Display as Printed.

To put your chart in another document (say, a Word document), see Chapter 13.

Chapter 6

Organizing Your Data with a Database

*T*he time has come to give your data a little discipline. Have your scraggly lists of names and addresses, inventory lists, and sales or inventory records report for duty at the database and give them the Works. Anything that you currently do using paper forms, or about which you've thought, "I'd like to computerize that," is a possible candidate for becoming a Works database. In this chapter, you find out how to create a database and enlist your data in electronic form.

Using a Database

If you've ever used a library-card index, a Rolodex file, a dictionary, or a phone book, you've used a database. A *database* is just a collection of information that has some organization to it. (Every card in a Rolodex, for example, has the same structure: a line for a name, usually last name first; a couple of lines for an address; a line for the phone number; and so on.)

If you put a database on a computer, a *database manager* or *database program* is the software that you use to read the database and to put information into the database. Because database programs always accompany databases, people get lazy and lump the terms together, calling the whole ball of wax a *database.*

What does the Works database do for you?

The most basic benefit of computerizing your data in a database is tidy record keeping and the capability of neatly printing your forms, receipts, invoices, or reports. The bigger deal with computer databases, however, is that they help you find, group, and sort things quickly and also help you analyze and summarize your records. Following are the three main functions that the Works database program can perform for you:

- **Sorting** enables you to organize *records* alphabetically (by last name, for example) or numerically. (See the following section for an explanation of records.) Sorting your database records also groups similar records together. If you sort based on zip code, for example, the database groups all the records sharing a common zip code together.

- **Filtering** reveals certain records in your database. You can, for example, create a filter that — by using the Age and Town *fields* of your student database — screens out say, every child except the 12-year-olds from Mudville. (See the following section for an explanation of fields.) You can then create mailings specifically for that group or any other group.

- **Reporting** neatly prints the results of filtering. It can also provide mathematical summaries of certain fields. You can, for example, create a report of your customers in the state of California that you group by zip code, with total sales by month.

A Works database can also serve as an address book from which you, too, can do your very own junk mailing! Yes — you, too, *Mr. Smith* of *345 Smithtown Road,* may already be a wiener. See Chapter 8 for the exciting details!

Fields and records: How Works stores information

Works talks a lot about fields and records, so you need to understand what they are. The Rolodex file metaphor is great for understanding fields and records, which are part of every database program.

Each card in your Rolodex file is like a *record* in a database. (If you don't have a Rolodex file, think of a recipe card file; each recipe card is a record.)

Each card has the same blank areas to fill out: name, telephone number, and address, at the very least. These blank areas are known as *fields* in computer databases. Each field has a name, similar to the *Address* field in a Rolodex file (or *Cooking Time* if you're thinking of recipe cards). Each record has different entries in those fields, which typically describe a person (as in the Rolodex), a transaction (such as a sale or a phone call), an object, or a location.

The Database Window

Figure 6-1 shows what the Works database program looks like after you create or open a database.

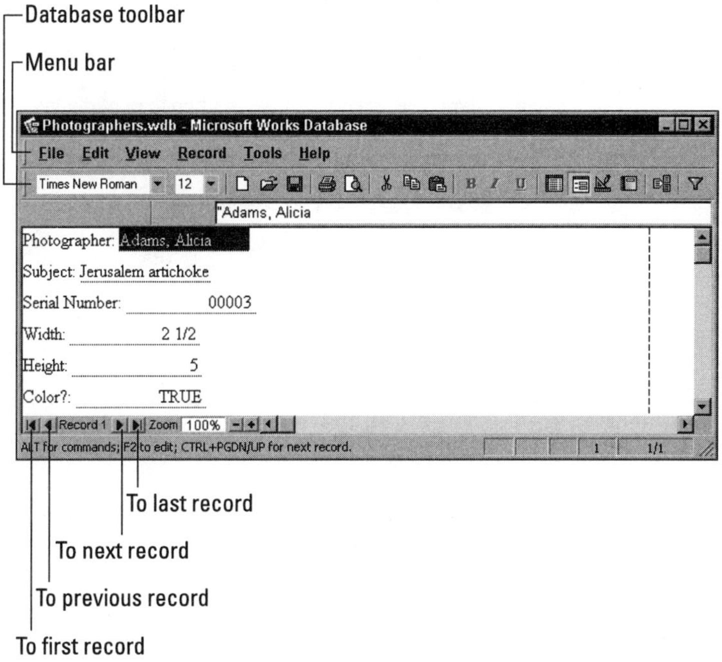

Database toolbar

Menu bar

Figure 6-1:
A Works
database in
Form view,
which
shows one
data record
at a time.

To last record

To next record

To previous record

To first record

Make a mental note that Figure 6-1 shows you only one of two main *views* of a database. The view shown here is known as *Form* view, and the other view, which looks like a spreadsheet, is known as *List* view. (A third view, *Form Design* view, looks like Form view but is actually an editing feature to enable you to change how Form view looks.)

The basic file and edit menu commands work as they do in all Works programs. Be aware, however, that in this database program certain menu commands and toolbar buttons change between Form view, List view, and Form Design view. See Figure 6-2 for the database toolbar.

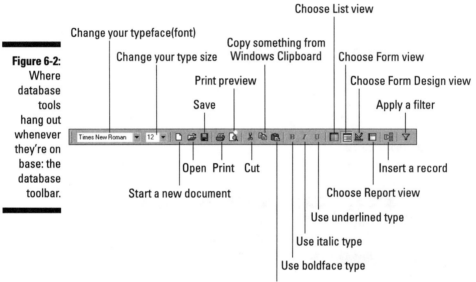

Figure 6-2: Where database tools hang out whenever they're on base: the database toolbar.

Don't try to memorize all the stuff in these figures. Stick a pencil here, or an unused stick of gum, or turn back the corner of the page and come back whenever you need to refresh your memory.

The buttons nearer the right-hand end of the toolbar are specific to data-bases. Here's where to go for a discussion of what each of these buttons (starting at the far right) refers to:

- ✔ **Filters:** See Chapter 7.
- ✔ **Insert record:** See the section "Adding, Inserting, and Deleting Records," later in this chapter.
- ✔ **Report View:** See Chapter 7.
- ✔ **List, Form, and Form Design view:** See the section "Viewing Your Database," later in this chapter.

To quickly see what a button on the toolbar does, place your mouse cursor over the button (don't click) and wait half a second. A tiny sign appears and gives you a tiny description.

Starting the Database Program

You can start a new document in the database program as you do in any other Works program. Start the Task Launcher and click Programs, near the top of the Works Suite window. From the Works Programs list box on the left side of the Task Launcher, select Works Database. (See Chapter 1 if you're unfamiliar with the Task Launcher.) Then either select one of the template (sample) databases or click Start a Blank Database. Chapter 8 discusses templates in more detail. If you're a new PC user and commands, menus, and dialog boxes are still new to you, see the appendix.

The first time that you start a database document, you may see a First-Time Help dialog box, as shown in Figure 6-3. If so, please refer to Chapter 1, where I discuss First-Time Help.

Works now displays the Create Database dialog box, described in the next section.

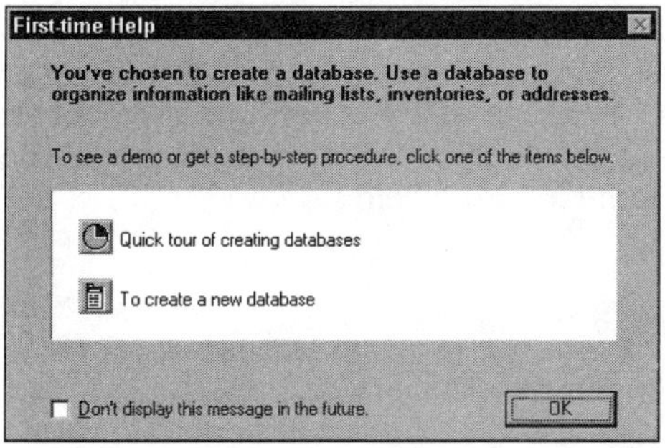

Figure 6-3:
Ever helpful,
Works
enables you
to either
take a tour
or get down
to business.

> **First-time Help**
>
> You've chosen to create a database. Use a database to organize information like mailing lists, inventories, or addresses.
>
> To see a demo or get a step-by-step procedure, click one of the items below.
>
> 🔘 Quick tour of creating databases
>
> 📄 To create a new database
>
> ☐ Don't display this message in the future.   [OK]

Creating New Database Fields

Whenever you create a new database without using a task or template (a pre-designed database supplied by Works and displayed in the Task Launcher), your principal job is entering fields. Here, in New England, we wear our rubber boots and watch where we step whenever we enter fields. No such precautions are necessary for entering fields into your database. Following, however, are some guidelines for creating fields:

✔ Create a field for anything you may want to search for, report on, or print on a form, an envelope, or a label — such as a date, manufacturer, color, price, vendor, nickname, neck size, zip code, and so on. If in doubt, create a field.

✔ Use a separate field for anything that's separable. For example, the names of many people in your database may begin with Mr., Ms., Mrs., or Dr.; keep this information in a separate field.

✔ Always create a serial-number field, which contains a unique number for each record of the database. Doing so ensures that each record has something unique by which to identify it, in case the descriptions are otherwise identical (two people named Smith, for instance). A serial-number field also ensures that you can later reconstruct the original order in which you entered the data. Reconstruction helps in various ways. You may want to check your entries against data copied on paper forms, for instance, and want to reconstruct the original (haphazard) order for easier reference.

Following is the procedure for creating new fields by using the Create Database dialog box, shown in Figure 6-4. Repeat the following procedure for each field that you think you need:

1. In the Field Name text box, enter a name for a field.

The field's name must be shorter than 15 characters. In Figure 6-4, for example, I'm starting to create a database of photographs that I use in my business. The first field that I want is one for the photographer's name. (Don't append the colon that you see in Figure 6-1 at the end of the field name; Works adds one for you in Form view, as a way of visually separating the field name from the field's data.)

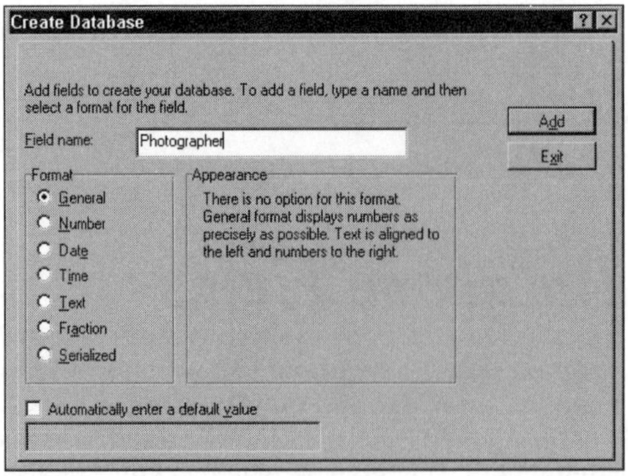

Figure 6-4:
Enter fields
one at a
time in the
Create
Database
dialog box.

2. **In the Format area of the dialog box, select a format for the field by clicking the appropriate radio button.**

The following formats are very much like the number formats for spreadsheets. Refer to the section on formatting numbers in Chapter 4 of this book. You can change formats later, so don't worry too much about your choice now. (See the section "Applying and Changing Formats," later in this chapter, for more information.) Here are the different formats available:

- **General:** You can use the General format for most fields, but you run across a few special circumstances — such as fields containing dates, dollars, or fractions — where you may want to select something other than General.

- **Number:** Select this format if you want dollar signs, commas, percentages, or scientific notation to appear without your needing to type them. Number formats also include TRUE/FALSE for fields such as the Color? field displayed in Figure 6-1, where you can enter **1** for TRUE or **0** for FALSE.

- **Date** *and* **Time:** Use these formats for date or time fields. These formats give you flexibility to change the way dates or times appear in your database, and enable you to summarize your data in reports, such as in calculating total labor time.

- **Text:** Use this format to enter certain data, such as zip codes that begin with zero. Otherwise, the zip code 01776 turns into 1776.

- **Fraction:** Use this format and Works automatically rounds off data that you enter in decimal form, such as 2.125, into mixed-number fractional form, such as 2⅛. Choose what fraction you want the number to round off to from the list that appears. This format is useful for listing things in nonmetric dimensions, such as inches. Works reduces a fraction such as ⅘ to ½ unless you select the Do Not Reduce check box.

- **Serialized:** Most databases benefit from having a unique number for each record, which a serial-number field provides. Select the Serialized format to create such a field, and you don't even need to enter the numbers yourself: Works does it for you automatically each time you enter a new record. In the Next Value text box that has now appeared, enter the number with which you want the next record to start. If you want the number to increase by increments of something other than 1, enter that increment in the Increment text box.

3. **Specify a default value for the field (if this field is often going to contain the same value).**

At the bottom of the Create Database dialog box, select the Automatically Enter a Default Value check box and then type the value in the box at the very bottom. A *default value* is data that appears automatically whenever you create a new record, and it saves you time. If, for example, most of the photographs in my photography database are by the same person — say, Johnson — I can make *Johnson* my default value. Then, whenever I record a new photograph in my database, Johnson automatically appears in the Photographer field. (I can replace the default with another name if the photographer is someone other than Johnson.)

Fields that use default values behave a little oddly as you enter data into a record: *The default value doesn't appear until you enter data in at least one other field.*

4. Click the Add button.

This action adds the field that you just specified to the database, and it enables you to move on to the next field. If you're done creating fields, go to Step 5. Otherwise, return to Step 1 and keep adding fields until you have all that you need — and then go to Step 5.

5. Click the Done button to exit the Create Database dialog box.

After you finish, your database is ready for you to add some data. But wait! How come it looks just like a spreadsheet? Well, the odd thing about databases is that they can look like darned near anything. The following section gives you the details on viewing your database.

Viewing Your Database

One reason people sometimes get a bit confused by using the Works database program is that the program can show your data in different ways, known as *views*. Figures 6-5 and 6-6, for example, show the same database in two different views.

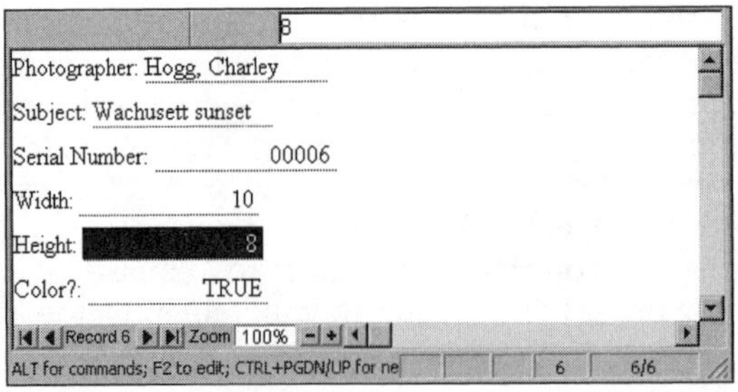

Figure 6-5:
My database for cataloging photographs in Form view, showing record 6.

Photographer: Hogg, Charley
Subject: Wachusett sunset
Serial Number: 00006
Width: 10
Height: 8
Color?:   TRUE

Record 6 ▶ ▶| Zoom 100% – + ◀
ALT for commands; F2 to edit; CTRL+PGDN/UP for ne| 6   6/6

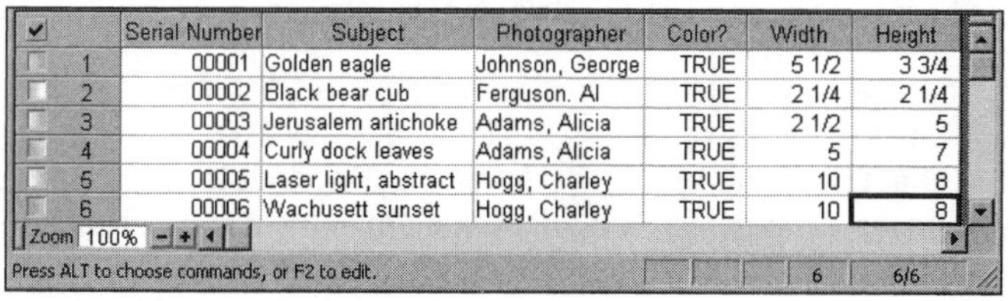

Figure 6-6:
The same
database as
shown in
Figure 6-5,
but now in
List view
showing
records 1–6.

✓		Serial Number	Subject	Photographer	Color?	Width	Height	
☐	1	00001	Golden eagle	Johnson, George	TRUE	5 1/2	3 3/4	
☐	2	00002	Black bear cub	Ferguson. Al	TRUE	2 1/4	2 1/4	
☐	3	00003	Jerusalem artichoke	Adams, Alicia	TRUE	2 1/2	5	
☐	4	00004	Curly dock leaves	Adams, Alicia	TRUE	5	7	
☐	5	00005	Laser light, abstract	Hogg, Charley	TRUE	10	8	
☐	6	00006	Wachusett sunset	Hogg, Charley	TRUE	10	8	

Zoom 100% − + ◄

Press ALT to choose commands, or F2 to edit.   6   6/6

Here are the different views of Works and what they do for you:

- **Form view** enables you to enter, look at, and print data as if you entered it on a paper form. Figure 6-5 shows a database in Form view. A blank line, where you enter data, follows the field names (Photographer, Subject, Serial Number, Width, Height, and Color? in Figure 6-5).

- **List view** looks like a pad of lined paper on which you copied all the information from your Rolodex, using columns for the fields of, say, Name, Address, and Phone Number. You can see several records at once. Figure 6-6 shows the same database that Figure 6-5 does but in List view. (I did rearrange the fields by clicking the field name and then dragging it to a different position.)

  In this view, your database is a big spreadsheet-like table of rows and columns. The rows, which Works numbers along the left side, are individual records. (Blank rows are records in which you haven't yet entered data.) The columns are your fields.

- **Form Design view** enables you to design the form you see in Form view. In this view, you can move, resize, reformat, or otherwise change how the fields are going to look in Form view. You can also use Form Design view to add text, such as headings or explanations, or even add illustrations to your forms (say, a logo, if you're printing invoices).

- **Report view** is complicated. In principal, it enables you to create printed summary reports. In fact, it's too complicated for most Works users. Fortunately, you can create useful reports without using it.

To switch among views, take any of the following actions:

- Choose View⇨List, View⇨Form, or View⇨Form Design.

- Click the List View, Form View, or Form Design button on the toolbar (see Figure 6-2).

- Press the F9 key to go to Form view, press Shift+F9 to go to List view, or press Ctrl+F9 to go to Form Design view.

The spreadsheet connection

In List view, the Works database program has a great deal in common with the Works spreadsheet program, except that the database program performs calculations differently. You cannot sum columns in List view, nor can you put a formula in any old cell, as you can in a spreadsheet. Nonetheless, the List view of a Works database looks very much like a spreadsheet, and you can control it very much like you do a spreadsheet. You can easily cut and paste data between the List view of a database and a spreadsheet without too much confusion. You may want to find out more about spreadsheets at some point to pick up some tricks for working with databases in List view. Take a look at Chapters 2 through 4 for more information on spreadsheets.

Navigating in Different Views

An important part of your basic training at the database is navigation. You don't want your metaphoric half-tracks wandering all over your metaphoric field. Here's how to get around with minimal casualties and good gas mileage.

If you apply a filter, some records are hidden as you navigate your database. To see them all, choose Record⇨Show⇨1 All Records from the menu bar. See Chapter 7 for more information on using filters.

Navigating in Form view or Form Design view

In Form or Form Design view, you're looking at a representation of a page that's 8½ x 11 inches, unless you fooled with the Page Setup commands. You can look at any part of the page or (in Form Design view) type anywhere on the page. The dashed lines indicate page boundaries.

To scroll around vertically or horizontally, use the scroll bars on the right side and bottom of the document window. (See the appendix if you don't know how to use scroll bars.) To move around vertically on the page, you can also use your keyboard's arrows and other navigation keys.

To advance from one field to the next, press the Tab key. Press Shift+Tab to move in the opposite direction.

To move between records, use one of the following methods:

✔ To advance one record, press Ctrl+PgDn. To back up, press Ctrl+PgUp. Pressing the Tab key after making the last entry on the page (record) also advances you to the next record.

✔ Another way to advance or go back one record is to click the inner left or right arrow in the following gadget, which you find in the bottom-left border of your document window:

|◄| |◄| Record 3 |►| |►|

✔ To go to the first or last record in your database, click the outer left or right arrow in that gadget.

✔ Or, to go to the first record, press Ctrl+Home; to go to the last record, press Ctrl+End.

Navigating in List view

Navigating a database in List view is almost exactly like navigating a spreadsheet, which I describe in Chapter 2. Following is a short review.

To select a cell (the intersection of a row and column) to type in or to format, simply click that cell. Click and drag to select several cells at once. Click the field name (in gray) at the top of a column or the record number (in gray) of a row to select the entire column or row. An alternative way to move the rectangular highlight around a cell is by using the navigation keys on your keyboard. To look around your database in List view, use the scroll bars on the right side and bottom of the document window.

Entering Data

To enter data into your database, you generally fill out one record at a time, starting with the first record. Form view is usually the best choice for conventional, one-record-at-a-time data entry. In a nutshell, the procedure is just to click a field in Form view (or click a cell in List view) and then type.

Use any of the techniques mentioned in the preceding section ("Navigating in Different Views") to move from one field or record to the next. A popular method is to press the Tab key to advance from one field to the next (press Shift+Tab to go backward) and to advance to the next record after one is complete.

Following are a few tips for entering data:

- To put a new record into your database, just add it at the end: Press Ctrl+End in Form view; in List view, press Ctrl+End and then press Tab.

- For fields that you format as TRUE/FALSE fields, you can enter the number **1** for TRUE or **0** for FALSE, or you can type the words **TRUE** or **FALSE**.

- If the symbol ######## appears after you enter some data, the field isn't wide enough to display the data. A quick fix, if you're in List view, is to double-click the field name in the top cell of the column. See the section "Moving and Resizing Fields," later in this chapter, for other techniques.

Creating a Sample Database

Show time! Here's an example of how to create a database. (The example is a very simple, five-field database for cataloging photographs.)

The Rule of This Design, as dictated by its omnipotent creator (me), is that you shall have five fields: Photographer, Subject, Width, Height, and Color?. (The Color? field has a question mark because it has only a yes/no answer.)

I like having *standards* for data, as illustrated by the following Rules: The Photographer field shall contain the last name first, a comma, and then the first name; the Subject field shall contain a short description of what's in the photo; the Width and Height fields shall give the dimension in inches and ⅛ fractions of an inch; and the Color? field shall be a TRUE/FALSE field indicating whether the photo is in color (TRUE) or black and white (FALSE).

To go ahead and create this example of a database, just follow these steps:

1. **In the Works Task Launcher, click the Programs option at the top of the Task Launcher window.**

2. **Click Start a Blank Database.**

   A First-Time Help dialog box may appear. If so, click the To Create a New Database button. The Create Database dialog box appears.

3. **Type** Photographer **into the Field Name box, and click the Add button or press the Enter key.**

   Every time that you click Add from now on, a new, blank field form appears in the Create Database dialog box.

4. **Type** Subject **in the Field Name text box and click the Add button.**

5. **Type** Serial **into the Field Name text box; then, in the Format area, select the Serialized radio button and click the Add button.**

6. Type Width **in the Field Name text box; then, in the Format area, select the Fraction radio button; from the Appearance list box, select ⅛; and click the Add button.**

7. Type Height **in the Field Name text box; then, in the Format area, select the Fraction radio button; from the Appearance list box, select ⅛; and click Add.**

8. Type Color? **in the Field Name box; then, in the Format area, select the Number radio button; in the Appearance list box, scroll to the bottom and select True/False; click the Add button and then click the Done button.**

You created a database! Well, the structure of it, at least. But your database still needs some data.

Now start entering data. You can do so in either List view (which is what you're looking at) or Form view. Simply click a cell (in List view) or a field (in Form view) and start typing. Press the Tab key to advance to the next field.

Moving and Resizing Fields

If you don't like the position or size of your fields, changes are a simple matter. You can make the changes in either Form Design view or List view.

Moving fields in Form Design view

To move the position of a field as it appears in Form and Form Design view, perform the following steps:

1. **Switch to Form Design view, if you're not there already.**

   To switch to Form Design view, click the Form Design button on the toolbar, or choose View⇨Form Design, or press Ctrl+F9.

2. **Click and then drag the field where you want it.**

   To move a bunch of fields at once, press and hold down the Ctrl key and click each field that you want to move. Release the Ctrl key and then click and drag the entire group of fields.

Moving fields in List view

To move a field (column) in List view, follow these steps:

1. **Click the top cell of the column — the one containing the field name.**

   This action selects the field/column.

2. **Click the top cell of the column again and then drag the column to the left or the right.**

   The dark vertical line that appears between columns indicates where the column appears after you release the mouse button.

Resizing fields in Form Design view

If a field is too small to display your data in Form or Form Design view, you can resize the field. (You may need to move adjoining fields to allow for the change in size.) Follow these steps:

1. **Switch to Form Design view, if you're not there already.**

   To switch to Form Design view, click the Form Design button on the toolbar, or choose View⇨Form Design, or press Ctrl+F9.

2. **Click the underlined area to the right of the field name.**

   This action highlights the field, and three tiny, gray squares (known as *handles*) appear in the highlight. Figure 6-7 shows a blown-up view of the highlighted area.

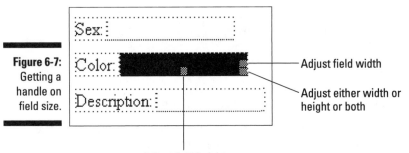

Figure 6-7: Getting a handle on field size.

Adjust field width

Adjust either width or height or both

Adjust field height

3. **Adjust the field size by dragging the handles.**

   To make a field wider, drag the handle at the center of the right edge to the right. To make the field higher (to add lines), drag the handle at the center of the bottom edge down. The handle at the corner enables you to drag both width and height at the same time.

   To adjust field size more precisely, click the underlined area next to the field name; then choose Format⇨Field Size to open the Field Size dialog box. Enter a width (how many characters) in the Width text box, and a height (how many rows) in the Height text box for the data entry.

Resizing fields in List view

To resize a field (change column width) in List view, you can either drag a column edge or use the Field Width dialog box, as the following paragraphs describe:

- ✔ **To change the width of the column by dragging:** Move your cursor to the gray row at the top of the columns, where the field names appear. In this row, slowly move your mouse pointer across the right-hand edge of the column that you want to change. After the pointer changes to a double-headed-arrow-sort-of-deal with the attached word *Adjust,* click and drag the column edge left or right.

- ✔ **To set the width of a column more precisely:** Use the Field Width dialog box. First click any cell in that column to select the column. Then choose Format➪Field Width. After the Field Width dialog box appears, type a number slightly larger than the maximum number of characters that you expect for data in this field and then press Enter.

To make your field size just large enough to hold the longest entry in your database, double-click the field name (in the top cell of the column).

Editing Data and Field Names

If you need to change some data or a field name in your database, the tool that you can rely on in Form, List, or Report views is the *formula bar.* (You cannot change data while in Form Design view.) The formula bar works just the same as the formula bar in the Works spreadsheet program, which I describe in Chapter 2. You can see the formula bar located just under the toolbar in Figure 6-8.

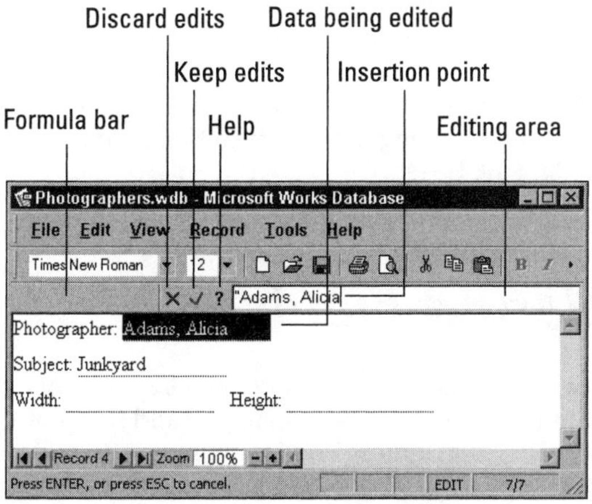

Figure 6-8:
Using the
formula bar.

Click a field name or data and then make your changes in the editing area of the formula bar (refer to Figure 6-8). Click the check mark button or press Enter on your keyboard to make the change permanent. Click the button displaying the X or press the Esc key to abandon your edits and leave whatever you were editing in its original state.

If the data you're editing is too long to fit entirely in the editing area of the formula bar, the navigation keys (left and right arrow keys, Home, and End) offer an easier way to move the insertion point than does the mouse.

In List view, just as in spreadsheets, you can edit data right in its cell: Just double-click the cell, and the insertion point you need for editing appears in the cell.

Surviving (or Using) the Protection Racket

If you find that Works complains (or prevents you) when you try to edit some data, the complaint probably arises because Works is protecting the field in which you're working against data changes. This situation arises if you use certain templates or a Serialized field. Here's what to do to defeat this protection scheme:

1. **Switch to either List view or Form Design view.**
2. **Click the protected field.**
3. **Choose Format➪Protection to open a Format Protection dialog box.**
4. **If you find a check mark in the Protect Field check box, click that check box to clear it and then click OK.**

On the other hand, you may want to use this protection racket yourself. By protecting a field, you can help avoid accidental changes to important data. This protection is especially valuable if you're working with another person who may not realize how important some data is. To protect a field, follow the same four steps in the preceding list, but turn the check mark *on* by clicking in the Protect Field check box.

Adding and Deleting Fields

As any general knows, sometimes you advance on a field and sometimes you retreat from a field. Similarly, in database work, you add fields at certain times and remove them at other times. The following sections describe how to add or remove a field.

Adding new fields

You can add new fields in either List view or Form Design view. The advantage of using List view is that the process is very simple. The advantage of using Form Design view is that, after you add a field, you're then conveniently in the correct view for positioning or sizing the field. The choice is yours!

Adding new fields in List view

In List view, the fields are columns. New fields are columns that go to the right or left of existing columns. Follow these steps to create new fields in List view:

1. **Click the column next to where you want to add a new column.**

2. **Choose Record⇨Insert Field; then select 1 Before (to put a new field to the left of your chosen column) or select 2 After (to put a new field to the right of your chosen column).**

   An Insert Field dialog box appears to grace your screen, bearing a familiar face: It looks and works just like the Create Database dialog box that you use to create your database. See the section "Creating New Database Fields," earlier in this chapter, if you need instructions on how to use the Insert Field dialog box.

3. **Type in a name for the field (and choose a special format if you need to) and then click the Add button.**

4. **For additional fields, repeat Step 3.**

5. **After you finish adding fields, click the Done button, which now appears in the Insert Field dialog box.**

Adding new fields in Form Design view

Here's how to add fields in Form Design view:

1. **Click the place on the page where you want the field to appear.**

   Don't click to the right or below any dashed line that you see at edges of the window. That dashed line is the page margin area, which is visible if your Works window is sufficiently large.

   A set of coordinates tells you where you are on the page, if you care. Look in the upper-left corner of the Works window, just under the Font box in the text bar. The number after X gives the horizontal position from the left edge of the page; the number after Y gives the vertical position from the bottom edge.

2. **Choose Insert⇨Field.**

   The Insert Field dialog box appears, asking for a field name and format, just as a similar dialog box appears when you first create your database.

3. **Type a field name of fewer than 15 characters (and select a special format if you need it) and then click the OK button.**

   The dialog box closes and your new field appears.

Deleting (removing) fields

If you remove a field, you also remove all the data that's in it — data that may well represent a lot of work on somebody's part. If you think that you may want to access the field and its data again sometime, do the following: Before you delete the field, save your unmodified database under a new name by using the File⇨Save As command.

Removing a field in List view is a little safer than is removing a field in Form Design view because you can undo the removal in List view by pressing Ctrl+Z.

Here's how to remove a field in both views:

- ✔ **In Form Design view:** Just click the field name and press the Delete key. A warning box appears to ask whether you want to Delete this field and all of its contents? and warns that you can't undo this delete. If you really do want to delete the field, click OK.

- ✔ **In List view:** First, click anywhere in that field's column; then choose Record⇨Delete Field. A warning box appears, asking whether you in fact want to Permanently delete this information?. If you really do want to delete the field, click OK.

Zap! It's dead, Jim.

Adding, Inserting, and Deleting Records

Many unprincipled people have wished, over the years, that they could add or delete certain records in their files. If only they knew how easily you can add or delete records in a Works database.

Adding a record

After you acquire yet another antique popsicle stick for your collection, you undoubtedly want to add another record to your popsicle stick database. Remember that a record is an entire screen or row of related data, not just one piece of data. The easiest way to add a record is to add it to the end of your database. To get to the end, take one of the following actions:

  ✔ In Form view, press Ctrl+End.

  ✔ In List view, press Ctrl+↓ and then press the down arrow (without the Ctrl key).

Either way, a blank, new record appears. (If you're of the pre–compact disc, or *vinyl,* generation, think of these records as albums, not singles.)

Inserting or deleting a record

To add a record at a particular point in your database, you *insert* it. First, indicate to Works where you want to insert the new record. In Form view, just navigate to that record. In List view, click that row. Then take one of the following actions, as appropriate:

  ✔ **To insert a record:** Choose Record⇨Insert or click the Insert Record button. (Refer to Figure 6-2, the toolbar illustration at the beginning of this chapter, or slowly move your mouse pointer across the buttons and read the pop-up labels that appear.) A blank record appears for you to fill in.

  ✔ **To delete a record:** Choose Record⇨Delete. Works then deletes the record, and you're left gazing at the next higher record in the database.

You can alternatively delete just the contents of a record rather than the record itself. This trick is useful if you're replacing an item in your database (say, a deceased computer in your inventory). In List view, click the row number (in the gray area on the left) to highlight the entire row — or highlight just as much as you want to delete — and then press the Delete key. The record is now blank (except for serialized fields), and you can enter new data into it.

Applying and Changing Formats

Just as your mother said, appearances are important. You can take a number of actions to change the way your field names and data appear in a Works database. The following list describes the formats you can change.

  ✔ **Field:** How Works interprets and displays your data: as a number, time, or text.

  ✔ **Alignment:** Whether data or a field name is left- or right-justified or centered, for example.

  ✔ **Font:** What typeface and style the data or field name appears in.

✔ **Border:** For borders around data or field names.

✔ **Shading:** To apply a background color or shade to data or field names.

Fonts, borders, and shading that you apply in one view don't apply to the other view. Field and alignment formats do apply to all views.

To format the data of a particular field, first click that field. Then choose Format➪Field, Format➪Alignment, Format➪Font, Format➪Border, or Format➪Shading. The Format dialog box appears, as shown in Figure 6-9.

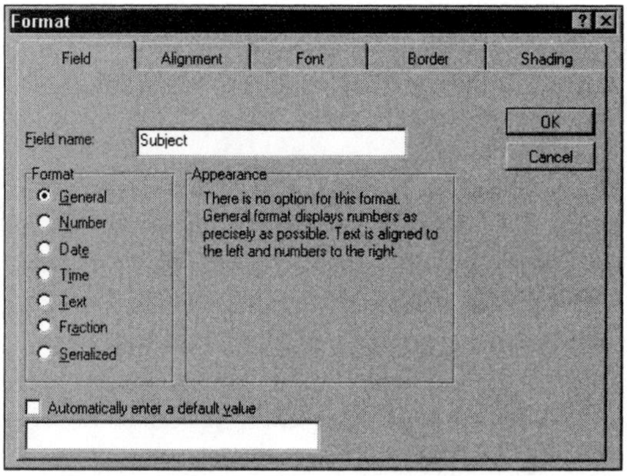

Figure 6-9:
The Format
dialog box,
where
appearance
is
everything.

Following is the executive summary of what you can accomplish on each tab of the Format dialog box:

✔ **Field tab:** Enables you to modify the same elements that you specified when you first created the field, changing the field name or telling Works to display the value as, for example, a date, a fraction, or a dollar amount. (For a discussion of field formats, see the section, "Creating New Database Fields," earlier in this chapter.) Changes to Field formats affect all views.

If you change a field from General or Text to a Date or Time format, you may need to reenter the data in that field.

✔ **Alignment tab:** Enables you to click Left, Right, or Center respectively to left-justify, right-justify, or center text in its field. Selecting General aligns text to the left and numbers to the right. If you're using List view, you can choose to make text wrap within a cell in List view by selecting the Wrap Text check box. If, in List view, your rows are higher than a single character height, you can also align text vertically. To do so, click Top, Center, or Bottom.

✔ **Font tab:** Works just as it does elsewhere in Works. See Chapter 1 for more information.

✔ **Border tab:** Enables you to put an outline around a field or data for emphasis. Click a line style from the list of style boxes on the tab, and then click on one or more edges in the Border section of the dialog box. Click the top line-style box (containing no line) to turn off a border.

✔ **Shading tab:** Enables you to apply a background color or pattern. Select a pattern from the Pattern selection box; patterns are made up of two colors, taken from your selection of foreground and background colors. Unless you have a color printer or don't intend to print at all, sticking to Auto for both colors is best.

If you print from Form view, as you may want to for address labels, you probably don't want a big gap between the city and the state. As you design the form, however, you must use a City field wide enough for, say, "Lake Memphremagog," which pushes your State field way over to the right. Then, if the name of a city in a different record is short — such as Big Sky, Montana — a lot of open space would appear before Montana. (As it does in real life, come to think of it.) Works provides a trick to get rid of this excess space during printing. Using Form Design view, click either the field name or data area of the field on the right (the State field, for example). Choose Format➪Alignment. Click the Alignment tab and then select the Slide to Left check box. Use Print Preview to check the result.

Printing Your Database

How and what you print depends on what you need. To print address labels, you may want to print out your entire address database in Form view or only certain addresses that you select by *filtering.* To print a sales invoice, you probably want to print only the record that's currently on-screen, in Form view. To print an inventory report, you generally print from Report view. The basic procedure for printing databases is pretty much the same as the procedure for printing anything else in Works, so for procedural details, see Chapter 1. Following, however, are a few peculiarities about printing databases.

✔ To print only certain groups of records, you first need to hide the other records. Works hides records that you filter out or that you specifically select for hiding. See Chapter 7 for details on hiding and filtering. To print only the record that you're currently viewing in Form view, choose File➪Print; then, in the Print dialog box, select Current Record Only.

✔ If you print in Form view, you normally print one record on a page. To print multiple records on a page, as you would do for mailing labels, choose File➪Page Setup, click the Other Options tab in the Page Setup dialog box, and then deselect the Page Breaks Between Records check box. Adjust the spacing between records by clicking the up or down arrows in the Space Between Records box.

✔ Printing from List view normally prints data only — no headings and no gridlines. To change this situation, choose File➪Page Setup to open the Page Setup dialog box. Click the Other Options tab in this dialog box. Select the appropriate check box: Print Gridlines and/or Print Record and Field Labels.

✔ To force a page break prior to a particular row or column in the List view, click the column or row header (the cell that's gray) and then choose Format➪Insert Page Break.

Chapter 7

Getting Answers from Your Database

. . . .

In This Chapter

▶ Finding data

▶ Hiding and showing records

▶ Creating, applying, and deleting a filter

▶ Using multiple criteria

▶ Using math in filtering

▶ Sorting data

▶ Creating standard reports

▶ Viewing your report

▶ Modifying your report

. . . .

As Chapter 6 notes, the real value in a database is not that it enables you to amass an army of data on your computer or print out rank upon rank of uniformly typed and regimented data. The real value is that a database helps you interrogate your data: to find, display, print, and compute meaningful answers from legions of data. *Finding, filtering, sorting,* and *reporting* are the biggest features for getting results in Works.

Finding Specific Records

To locate records that contain a specific word, phrase, or number, the simplest thing you can do is to use the *Find* command. You can tell Works to find either the *first* example of that word, phrase, or number, or to show you *all* examples. Here's how to do it:

1. Press Ctrl+Home.

This action is not mandatory, but it takes you to the top of the document so that Works begins its search with the first record of the database.

2. **Choose Edit⇨Find (or press Ctrl+F).**

   A small but helpful Find dialog box appears.

3. **Type the word, number, or phrase for which you're searching in the Find What text box.**

   You must specify lowercase or uppercase letters. Searching for *Copy Paper* doesn't find records containing *copy paper*.

   Type only as much as you remember or need. To find copy paper, printer paper, or any kind of paper, type **paper**. The symbol *?* can substitute for a single character and help you find a broad range of records. If searching for zip codes, for example, typing **0792?** finds all the zip codes beginning with 0792. The symbol * can substitute for one or more characters as long as you precede the * by at least one other character. Typing **M*.**, for example, finds *Mr., Mrs.,* and *Ms.* (but not Miss — because this particular search specifies that a period must come at the end).

4. **To find only the next matching record, select Next Record in the Match area of the Find dialog box. To find all matching records (and hide the other records), select All Records.**

5. **Click OK.**

   In Form view, Works displays the next record it finds that matches what you're searching for. In List view, Works moves the rectangular "active cell" highlight to the next matching record and field.

   Note: If you choose to find All Records in Step 4, Works hides the records that don't match your search text! (See the following section for details on showing and hiding records.) To unhide (or show) those records again, choose Record⇨Show⇨1 All Records.

Using Selected Records: Marking, Showing, and Hiding

Often you ask Works to display or make use of only certain records: to print mailing labels for one zip code only, for example, or show only the employees you hired this month. To accomplish your command, Works *shows* certain data and *hides* the other data. Works automagically hides data if you ask it to *find all records* that match certain criteria, or to *filter* your data (which I describe in a minute). In addition, you can manually specify which records Works hides and which ones it shows.

The following list describes the operations involved in showing and hiding data, whether Works does the job automatically or you do it manually:

- ✔ **Hiding** is a way to make records invisible in List or Form view or to omit them from printouts or reports.

- ✔ **Showing** is the opposite of hiding. Works initially shows all records.

- ✔ **Marking** is a convenient way to identify a group of records for manual hiding or showing.

To hide an individual record, either click the record in List view or display it in Form view; then choose Record⇨Hide Record.

To show or hide a specific group of records, mark them first: In List view, select the check box in the leftmost column (the *marking column*) of each row that you want to hide. To mark a group that's all together, click and drag down the marking column (the check boxes only, not the numbers next to them). (In Form view, choose Record⇨Mark Record for each record.)

Then, to show the marked records (and hide the rest), choose Record⇨Show⇨2 Marked Records. To hide the marked records instead, choose Record⇨Show⇨3 Unmarked Records.

To reverse the logic and make the currently hidden records the shown ones, choose Record⇨Show⇨4 Hidden Records.

To undo all this hiding stuff and show all records, choose Record⇨ Show⇨1 All Records.

To clear all your marks, go to List view and click the check mark at the very top of the marking column.

Filtering Your Data

Sometimes the Find command isn't enough. You may need Works to look for a certain range of values or for combinations of data in multiple fields. To print address labels for a letter targeting potential big donors to your organization, for example, you may want to select people in your donor database who either contributed $100 or more in the past *or* who live in a wealthy community. The Find command can find only records containing *one* specific hunk o' text or a specific number.

To find records based on more complex criteria, you need to *filter* your data. When Works filters your data, it goes through your database, record by record, comparing what's in those records to certain criteria that you give it and hiding those records that don't meet the criteria.

The gadget that you use for applying a filter is the Filter dialog box, shown in Figure 7-1. To access one of these little gems, perform either of the following actions:

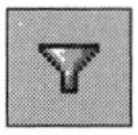

- ✔ Choose Tools⇨Filters.
- ✔ Click the Filters button on the toolbar.

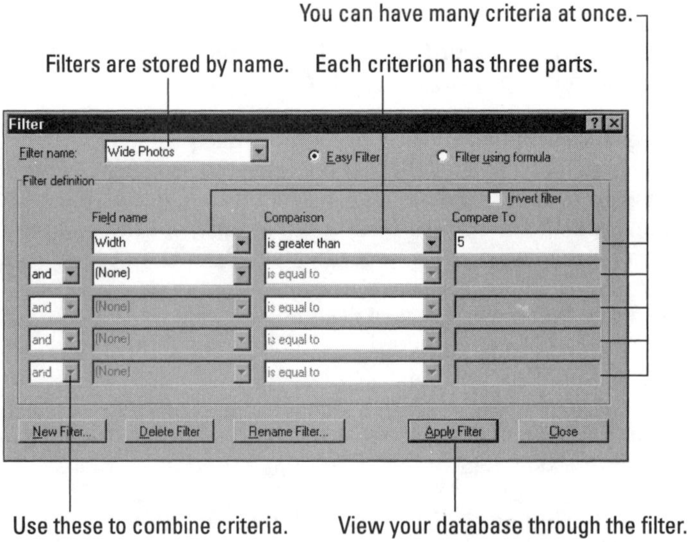

You can have many criteria at once.

Filters are stored by name.   Each criterion has three parts.

Figure 7-1:
Use this
dialog box
to tell Works
your criteria
for picking
out certain
records.

Filter			? ✕
Filter name:	Wide Photos ▾	⦿ Easy Filter	○ Filter using formula
Filter definition			☐ Invert filter
	Field name	Comparison	Compare To
	Width ▾	is greater than ▾	5
and ▾	[None] ▾	is equal to ▾	
and ▾	[None] ▾	is equal to ▾	
and ▾	[None] ▾	is equal to ▾	
and ▾	[None] ▾	is equal to ▾	
New Filter...	Delete Filter	Rename Filter...	Apply Filter Close

Use these to combine criteria.   View your database through the filter.

The first time you create a filter, Works displays a First-Time Help dialog box. See Chapter 1 for notes on such help boxes. Click OK to proceed.

If your database currently has no filters, a Filter Name dialog box appears; enter a descriptive name no longer than 15 characters, such as **Big Contributor**. If your database currently has filters, you can choose a filter to edit by clicking in the Filter Name drop-down list box in the Filter dialog box. To create a new, additional filter, click the New Filter button. Click OK when done.

To specify which records you want, you must enter three pieces of information into the following text boxes of the Filter dialog box:

- ✔ **Field Name:** Click to select the name of the field where you want Works to look. Choose the *No. of Children* field, for example, if you have such a field and want to find families based on the number of children they have.

- ✔ **Comparison:** Click to select the way you want Works to test the data in the field. You may, for example, test that the data in the No. of Children field is greater than some value. For purposes of comparison, later dates and times are greater than earlier ones. Letters that fall later in the alphabet are greater than earlier ones.

> ✔ **Compare To:** Type whatever value (text or a number) that you want Works to compare the data to — such as **2** for two kids. In filters (unlike in finds), Works doesn't take note of capitalization. The words *Potato* and *potato* are identical to Works. You can use the *?* and * characters just as you do in a Find command, if you want. See the section "Finding Specific Records," earlier in this chapter, for more information on using these characters.

The following list offers some examples of the records for which you may filter in different databases. (The terms you'd select in the Filter dialog box are in italics.)

> ✔ In a Families database, you may want those records in which the *No. of Children* field *is equal to 2.*
>
> ✔ In a Members database, you may want those records in which a *Town* field *is not Mudville.*
>
> ✔ In a mailing list, you may want those records in which an *Age* field *is greater than or equal to 21.*

Press the Enter key or click the Apply Filter button to execute the filtering. For the clearest view of your results, use List view (press Shift+F9).

You're done! In List view, Works shows you only those records that meet your criterion. The other records are hidden. After you finish looking over your success, choose Record⇨Show⇨1 All Records to make the other records reappear.

Applying, changing, and deleting filters

Creating a filter takes a bit of work; so, for your future convenience, Works saves your filter, under the name that you give it, as part of your database file.

Because Works saves filters, you can fool around with them until they're correct, and you can easily switch from one to the other, applying them to your database whenever you need them. The idea is that you're likely to want a few standard filters that you apply to your database regularly. One Works quirk, however, is that you can't have more than eight saved filters in any one database.

To apply the filter you used most recently, just press F3. To apply any other filter to your database, choose Record⇨Apply Filter and then select a filter from the Filter drop-down list. List view (press Shift+F9) now shows you all the records that match your filter criteria. To restore all the hidden records, choose Record⇨Show⇨1 All Records.

To change or delete a filter, choose Tools⇨Filters (or click the Filters button on the toolbar). After the Filter dialog box appears, click in the Filter Name box and select the filter on which you want to work. Then you can perform any of the following actions:

> ✔ To edit an existing filter, choose new criteria. (See the preceding section, "Filtering Your Data," for information.)
>
> ✔ To change the name of the filter, click the Rename Filter button. Enter a new name in the Filter Name dialog box that appears and click OK.
>
> ✔ To delete a filter, click the Delete Filter button. Click the Yes button in the warning dialog box that appears, to make sure that you want to delete this filter. (If the Filter Name dialog box appears now, click its Cancel button.)

Click the Close button of the Filter dialog box after you finish changing or deleting a filter.

Using more than one criterion

You can have Works use up to five criteria at one time in a filter, which is why the Filter dialog box contains five rows. This five-criteria feature enables you to narrow down or expand your search.

If, for example, you want only the families in your database that have more than two kids and that also live out of town, you create one row for the kids' criterion and a second row for the Town field. You specify that the town Works selects should not equal your town of Mudville. Figure 7-2 shows such a two-part filter, using a different example.

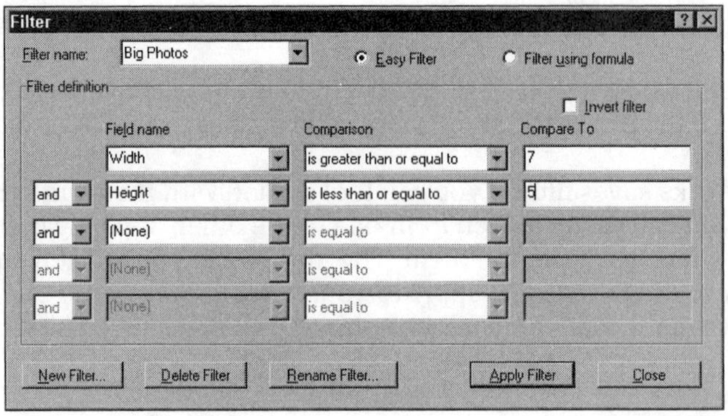

Figure 7-2: Using two criteria for a query.

To use more than one criterion, just select and fill in the first one as usual. Select either *and* or *or* from the drop-down list box that begins the next line; then select and fill in the second criterion in a similar fashion. Do the same for any other criteria that you need.

In the example shown in Figure 7-2, you tell Works that it must meet both of the following criteria on each record that it finds:

The photograph's *Width is greater than or equal to 7* inches.

AND

The photograph's *Height is less than or equal to 5* inches.

So you click the *and* selection from the drop-down list on the second line.

You use the *or* selection to specify that a record can meet either criterion. If you change *and* to *or* in Figure 7-2, the search results include photographs that are less than or equal to 5 inches high (but can be any width) as well as photographs that are at least 7 inches wide (but any height).

You can also have multiple criteria lines using the same field, one on each line — for example, *width is greater than or equal to 7* on the first line and *width is less than or equal to 14* on the second line. This search finds all photos with a width between 7 and 14 inches.

If you set your logic up incorrectly and end up filtering *out* things that you want to filter *in,* select the Invert Filter check box in the Filter dialog box. (It filters things *in* that you had filtered *out.*) This method is also a good way to look at the filtered-out crowd and make sure that the filter is working correctly.

Trickier filtering using formulas

Sometimes you need to filter on something that just isn't in your database. My Photographs database, for example, has a *width* and a *height,* and I can create a filter for a certain range of those dimensions. But if I want a photograph that fits a certain ratio of height to width, I can't make a filter by using straightforward criteria. No field for *ratio* is available.

One solution to this sort of problem is to use formulas. In a formula, you can combine field names, mathematical expressions, and Works functions to describe the filter that you want. If I want to filter for all photographs where the height is 80 percent or less of the width, for example, I enter the criteria shown in Figure 7-3.

Figure 7-3:
By using a
field name
and some
math, I can
filter for
height-
to-width
ratio.

Note: Works functions for databases are the same as for spreadsheets. For a complete listing of functions by type, choose Help⇨Index and type **functions:** (note the colon). Select Use Database Functions in the Topics Found list box and then click whichever category you're interested in (Date, Financial, Math, and so on) from the list that appears.

Sorting

Sorting is useful for grouping similar records together for your viewing or printing convenience. Are you printing mailing labels from an address database? You may want to sort by zip code to make bulk mailing easier. Do you want to sort your inventory records alphabetically by location or numerically by dollar value? Either way, the choice is yours.

The database sorting process is very similar to the spreadsheet sorting process. For background information on sorting, see Chapter 4.

Works enables you to sort by up to three fields. This capability, in turn, enables you to sort your records into categories (say, by the zip code field), subcategories (say, by street name within each zip code), and sub-subcategories (say, the last names of people living on the street).

List view gives you the clearest picture of your results, so if you're currently in Form view, I suggest that you switch to List view (by pressing Shift+F9). Now, here's how to sort:

1. **Choose Record⇨Sort Records.**

   The Sort Records dialog box jumps gaily into your lap (so to speak), as shown in Figure 7-4. (The first time you sort, Works displays a First-Time Help dialog box, as I describe in Chapter 1. Click OK to continue.)

2. **Click the Sort By drop-down box to select the principal field to sort by.**

Figure 7-4: Choosing what fields to sort by in the Sort Records dialog box.

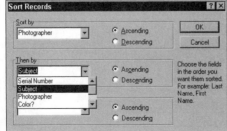

3. Select a sorting direction for that field by clicking the appropriate radio button.

Ascending is the order A, B, C or 1, 2, 3. *Descending* is the opposite.

4. Optionally, follow the same steps for a second field (your subcategory) and a third field (sub-subcategory).

If your principal field is, say, zip code, the Then By field enables you to sort the identically zip-coded records in, perhaps, alphabetical order by street name. If you don't fill out this information, the records don't sort in any particular order within each zip code. Similarly, the final Then By field provides sorting among any duplicate entries in the second field (for example, several people on the same street).

5. Click OK.

If you're in List view, you now see your database with its records shuffled around in the order you specified. Records don't keep their original record numbers (the number at the far left of each row in List view) after you sort them, which is one reason why having a serial number field is important (as I mention in Chapter 6). The serial number field enables you to reconstruct the original order by sorting by that field.

Figure 7-5 shows the result of sorting a database by photographer's name and then subject.

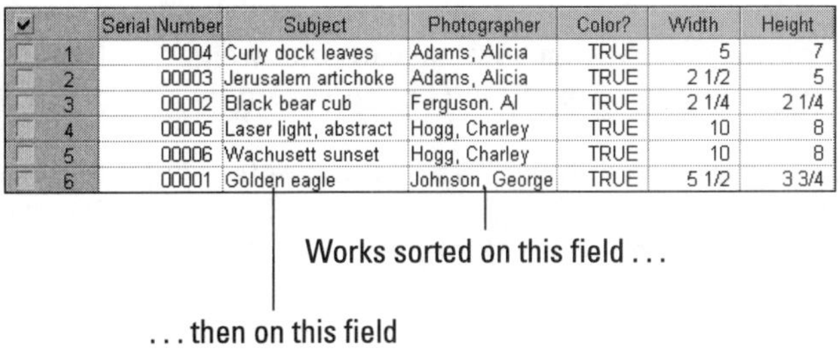

Figure 7-5:
Sorting
groups of
records with
identical
data.

✔	Serial Number	Subject	Photographer	Color?	Width	Height
1	00004	Curly dock leaves	Adams, Alicia	TRUE	5	7
2	00003	Jerusalem artichoke	Adams, Alicia	TRUE	2 1/2	5
3	00002	Black bear cub	Ferguson, Al	TRUE	2 1/4	2 1/4
4	00005	Laser light, abstract	Hogg, Charley	TRUE	10	8
5	00006	Wachusett sunset	Hogg, Charley	TRUE	10	8
6	00001	Golden eagle	Johnson, George	TRUE	5 1/2	3 3/4

Works sorted on this field . . .

. . . then on this field

Reporting

The Works report feature provides nifty summaries of the data in your database. I need to make sure that you know what I'm talking about when I say *report,* however, because it's a vague term.

A Works report is something for you to print, not view on your PC screen (although you can see it in Print Preview). A Works report shows the following two kinds of information:

- ✔ A list of records very much like that of List view, typically sorted into categories
- ✔ A summary based on your records

A mailroom, for example, may have a database consisting of the packages that it's shipped, the date of shipping, the destination zip codes, the package weights, the shipper, and the cost of shipping.

From this shipping database, management may want reports on how cost-effective various shippers are; how much product is being shipped by weight every month; how much is shipping to each zip code; the average weight shipped; and other typical, nosy management requests. All these reports require either a summary of some sort, or a list, or both.

What's a standard report?

To make creating a report easier for you, Microsoft's *ReportCreator* steps you through the creation process. The result of using ReportCreator is what I call a *standard report*. You could make a custom report by using Report view, but that process is too complicated for many users.

A standard report from the shipping department's database may show all the packages sent, together with a summary of total weight and total cost. Such a standard report may look something like the example shown in Figure 7-6.

The report in Figure 7-6 contains lists of shipments grouped by shipper, with total weight and average weight shipped for each group, and total and average weight at the bottom. Not bad for a little database program!

Creating a standard report

Works makes creating a standard report fairly simple, but you must play your cards right! The ReportCreator dialog box deals you six different tabs that you need to fill out.

You may not need to create a report at all if you make your database by using a Works template. Such databases include very nice, formatted reports for special purposes such as business inventory or accounts payable. If you create your database by using a template, you need only to choose the report that you want by choosing View⇨Report.

shipping.wdb - Wt. by Shipper

Shipper	Weight		
CityZIP	0.73		
CityZIP	0.94		
CityZIP	0.21		
CityZIP	0.67		
CityZIP	0.75		
CityZIP	0.95		
CityZIP	0.18		
CityZIP	0.82		
GROUP TOTAL Weight:		5.26	
AVERAGE Weight:		0.66	
DinEx	0.80		
DinEx	0.44		
DinEx	0.63		
GROUP TOTAL Weight:		1.86	
AVERAGE Weight:		0.62	
Hercules	0.05		
Hercules	0.03		
Hercules	0.37		
---- (I cut out some stuff here)----			
PSU	0.04		
PSU	0.76		
PSU	0.60		
GROUP TOTAL Weight:		1.40	
AVERAGE Weight:		0.47	
Rural Xpres	0.87		
Rural Xpres	0.58		
Rural Xpres	0.08		
GROUP TOTAL Weight:		1.53	
AVERAGE Weight:		0.51	
Zowiefast	0.98		
Zowiefast	0.80		
Zowiefast	0.96		
Zowiefast	0.76		
Zowiefast	0.86		
GROUP TOTAL Weight:		4.36	
AVERAGE Weight:		0.87	
TOTAL Weight:	14.98		
AVERAGE Weight:	0.58		

Figure 7-6:
One of the standard reports that Works can make. (I chopped out the middle so that the report fits on this page.)

To begin your quest for a standard report, awaken the mighty ReportCreator from its slumber by choosing Tools⇨ReportCreator. The first time you create a report, Works displays a First-Time Help dialog box. See Chapter 1 for notes on such help boxes. Click OK to proceed.

A tiny Report Name dialog box requests that you name your report. Use 15 characters or fewer. This name doesn't appear on your report; it just identi-fies your report so that you can use it again.

Then the ReportCreator dialog box swings into action and displays six tabs, as shown in Figure 7-7.

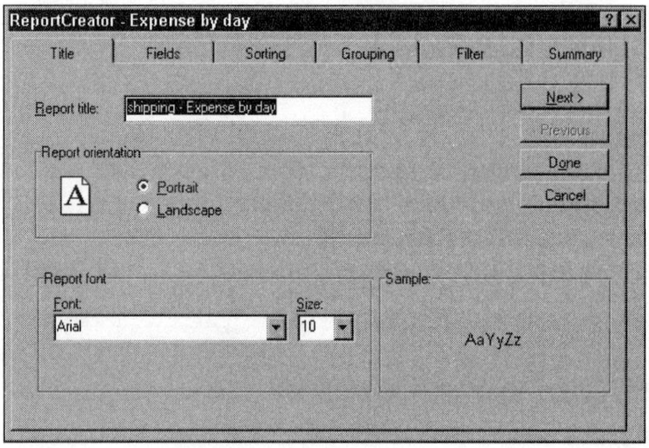

Figure 7-7:
The Title tab
in the
Report-
Creator
dialog box.
Fill out all
six tabs to
win a
report!

You don't need to use the six tabs in strict left-to-right order, but Works presents them to you in that order if you use the Next button in the ReportCreator dialog box. To work on a different tab at any time, just click that tab.

First tab: Title, orientation, and font

The top tab that the ReportCreator shows you is the Title tab. The title is what appears on the top of your report. Works suggests a title for you that it makes up from the database filename and the name that you give the report, but you can probably come up with a better one. Works also suggests that you create the report in *portrait* orientation (taller than it is wide) and the 10-point Arial font, but Works also enables you to change these defaults. To fill out this tab, follow these steps:

1. **Click in the Report Title text box and enter a title (such as *Shipping Costs*) if you don't like the suggestion Works gives you.**

2. **Select Landscape orientation, if you're making a *w–i–d–e* report — that is, a report with a lot of fields in it; select Portrait orientation if your report is tall.**

   The number of fields in your report depends on how wide your fields are.

3. **Select a Font and Size from the drop-down lists in the Report Font area.**

After you finish, click the Next button or the Fields tab.

Second tab: Choose your fields

The second tab that the ReportCreator deals you is the Fields tab, shown in Figure 7-8. Here you choose which of the fields in your database you want to appear in your report and in what order. (In the report, fields appear in columns, going left to right in the order that you specify here.) You can also specify whether you want field names as headings for those field columns.

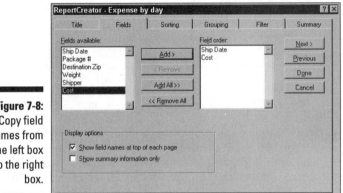

Figure 7-8:
Copy field names from the left box to the right box.

Follow these steps to choose the fields that you want to appear in your report, along with their order:

1. **Click a field name in the Fields Available list box.**

   The list in the Fields Available box is a list of the fields in your database. The basic procedure in this dialog box is to copy field names from the left-hand box to the right-hand box.

2. **Click Add to copy that field to the Field Order list box.**

   The right-hand box is where you accumulate a list of the fields that you want to appear in the report.

   (Every time you add a field, the highlight in the left-hand box moves down, for your pleasure and convenience. So to copy a consecutive series of field names, you can just keep clicking the Add button.)

3. **Repeat Steps 1 and 2 for each field that you want in the report.**

   If you want them all, click the Add All button.

   If you change your mind about a field, click that field's name in the Field Order list box and then click the Remove button that is now available. To remove all the fields from the right-hand box and start again, click the Remove All button.

4. **If you don't want the field names to appear at the top of your page, select the Show Summary Information Only check box.**

Normally, you want them. Figure 7-6, for example, has 'em.

After you finish, click the Next button or the Sorting tab.

Third tab: All sorts of stuff!

This tab may look familiar to you if you've already done sorting in the Works database or spreadsheet program. *Sorting* is the ordering of records alphabetically, numerically, or by date or time.

For sorting instructions, see the section "Sorting," earlier in this chapter. After you finish, click the Next button or the Grouping tab.

Fourth tab: Groupings

Whenever you sort any kind of data, similar items inherently wind up grouped together. All the Zimmers in the telephone book, for example, end up grouped together because the phone book sorts entries by last name. Similarly, sorted databases inherently group records. So why the heck does Works now ask about grouping?

Grouping in Works simply puts *breaks* (space) between the natural groupings that occur during sorting. Works needs breaks if you want headings above each group (*Zimmer* above the Zimmer group, for example), if you want a separate page for each group, or if you want to create a statistical summary of some kind for the group (say, total package weight for each zip code).

The following list gives you the scoop on grouping:

- ✔ You don't need to group at all. If you want one long list of sorted records with a summary at the end, just click the Next button.

- ✔ To create a group, select the When Contents Change check box, as shown in Figure 7-9. The other check boxes for that grouping then come alive.

- ✔ You can group by only those fields that you select to appear on this report (on the Fields tab) and choose for sorting (on the Sorting tab). If I want to group on, say, the Cost field, I must go back to the Sorting tab and add that field. Each field you select for sorting appears on the Grouping tab.

- ✔ You can have groups, subgroups, and sub-subgroups — that's why three identical areas appear on this tab. If, on the Sort tab, for example, I sort shipments by date and *Then By* shipper and *Then By* zip code, the group is all the shipments on that date. Within that date group are the weight totals for each shipper that I used on that date. Within each shipper group are that shipper's shipments, grouped by zip code.

✔ You can create groupings based strictly on the first character of a data entry. If you have a list of last names, for example, you probably don't want to group by each name (because many groups would end up only one name long) but by initial letter: all the *As* together, the *Bs* together, and so on. To accomplish this type of grouping, select the Use First Letter Only check box.

✔ You can use a heading to identify each group. If you're grouping by zip code, for example, you can head each group with its zip code. Heading each group with its zip code is somewhat redundant, however, because the zip code appears in every line of that group anyway, making what group it is rather obvious. Nonetheless, if you like this sort of thing, select the Show Group Heading check box.

Be forewarned that the Works ReportCreator doesn't handle dates as group headings correctly. The ReportCreator doesn't format them correctly, so the dates appear as numbers (the number of days since January 1, 1900)!

✔ For some reports, you may want to print each group on a separate page. In a national sales database, for example, you may need to send a separate page to each region's sales office. To accomplish this task, select the Start Each Group on a New Page check box.

After you finish, click the Next button or the Filter tab.

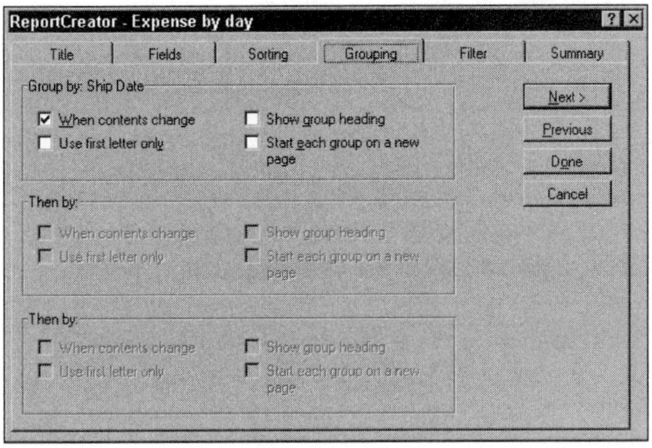

Figure 7-9:
Choosing to group by one field only.

Fifth tab: Filters

Filters enable you to separate the sheep from the goats, so to speak (or the wheat from the chaff, if you're a vegetarian). The filters that you can use here are exactly the same as the ones I discuss in the section "Filtering Your Data," earlier in this chapter.

The executive summary on filters is that filters enable you to selectively hide certain records from your report. Packages that you ship by the U.S. postal service, for example, may not belong in this report, so you can create a filter that says (in filter-ese), "Shipper is not equal to U.S. Postal Service."

To create a filter, click the Create New Filter button and then see the section "Filtering Your Data," earlier in this chapter for further instruction. After you create a filter, the filter appears in the Select a Filter text box. You can modify that filter by using the Modify Filter button, if you need to.

If you haven't created any filters, the ReportCreator gives you two filtering options in the Select a Filter text box anyway. Select one of the following:

> ✓ **Current Records** means that you want to include in your report only the records that are currently *shown* (not *hidden*) in your database. (To include or exclude certain records, see the section "Using Selected Records: Marking, Showing, and Hiding," earlier in this chapter.)

> ✓ **All Records** means just that: Include all the records in the database.

Be brave; you're almost done. Click the Next button or click the Summary tab of the ReportCreator to wrap up your report with a few summaries.

Sixth tab: Statistical summaries

At this point, you're gazing (glassy-eyed) at the Summary tab of the ReportCreator dialog box, as shown in Figure 7-10.

Statistical summaries are useful things. Statistical summaries give you the answers to such questions as, "What are the total sales for January in the Eastern region?" or "What is the batting average for each team?" or "Why are my eyes glazing over?"

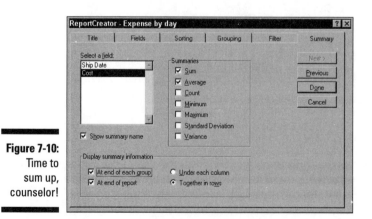

Figure 7-10:
Time to
sum up,
counselor!

Summaries are optional. If you don't specify any summaries and you just click the Done button in the ReportCreator, you get a report that simply lists all the records currently shown (not hidden) in your database, displaying the fields that you chose on the Fields tab — sorted and grouped, if you chose those features.

If you want statistics (including sums) on a certain field or fields, here's what to do:

1. **Click the field name in the Select a Field list box.**

2. **Select the kind of statistical summary (or summaries) that you want for that field by clicking the appropriate check box(es).**

   Click any check box in the Summaries area to select a particular kind of summary. Heck, click a batch of 'em if you want several different kinds of summaries. *Average* computes the average of all the numbers in the field, *Minimum* shows you the smallest (or most negative) value, and so on.

3. **Repeat Steps 1 and 2 for each field that you want to summarize.**

   Each field can have its own set of summaries.

   You must work very carefully in this tab, because you can't easily change summaries after you click the Done button. Be careful that you don't sum if you want to count. Sum adds up the numerical value of all the records in the selected field. Count just counts the records in a field. And don't accidentally sum up the wrong field (such as the date field)!

4. **Select the Show Summary Name check box.**

   This option instructs Works to label the summary as a sum, as an average, or as whatever you choose.

5. **Select where you want your summaries to appear in the report by clicking the appropriate check box(s) in the Display Summary Information area.**

   If you create groups on the Grouping tab, you can have a summary appear under each group by selecting the At End of Each Group check box.

   Select Under Each Column to put your field summaries at the bottom of their respective columns.

   Select Together in Rows to put each of your field summaries in a separate row at the bottom of the report (or at the bottom of each group, if you selected that option).

6. **Click the Done button.**

   Things whiz around on your screen, ultimately delivering . . .

   . . . a big, confusing mess and then one of those little boxes with the exclamation point in it! What the heck?! This result isn't what you had in mind! Where's that nice report??

Hang in there. Read the little dialog box, which is assuring you that `The report definition has been created` and asking whether you want to preview the report or modify it. I suggest that you select Preview. Selecting Modify doesn't gain you much — it just leaves you gazing at the big, confusing mess (called the Report view).

Click the Preview button, and Works shows you your report in Print Preview mode. Remember that the main purpose of a report is to make a nice report to print out — not to view on-screen. The following section helps you to figure out exactly what's going on here.

Viewing your report

If you've filled out the various tabs of the ReportCreator, as I describe in the preceding sections, you're probably now viewing your report in Print Preview. For details on how Print Preview works, see Chapter 1. Click the Cancel button after you finish viewing your report.

After you leave Print Preview, what's on-screen at this point isn't your actual report. Instead, what's on-screen is Report view — a view most people find nearly incomprehensible and that's not necessary for most work. This view displays the rather intimidating report definition that tells Works how to construct your report. Don't be too upset — if not for that nice ReportCreator dialog box, you'd need to enter all that intimidating stuff by hand.

You probably want to get out of Report view and go back to List or Form view. To do so, just choose View➪List or View➪Form.

After you finish defining a report in the ReportCreator, your named report exists as part of your Works database document. As you can with filters, you can access this report at any time, and the report takes into account any new or changed data in your database. Also, as with filters, you can have only eight reports per database; any more, and you must delete one by choosing Tools➪ Delete Report and double-clicking the report name in the dialog box that appears.

You can reuse a report over and over as you add data. Just choose View➪Report. Double-click the report name in the dialog box that appears.

Modifying your report

Works makes modifying your report easy — within limits. You can easily modify the sorting, grouping, and filtering, although certain options that were available at the time you created the report are no longer available. You can't very easily change what fields or summaries your report displays. To access these editing options, you must first be in Report view, so choose View➪ Report. The following list gives you the scoop on how to modify report settings:

> ✔ **Sorting:** Choose Tools⇨Report Sorting.
>
> ✔ **Grouping:** Choose Tools⇨Report Grouping.
>
> ✔ **Filtering:** Choose Tools⇨Report Filter.

All these menu choices open a Report Settings dialog box, where the tabs look exactly like the tabs in the ReportCreator, except that only these three functions (instead of six) are available. Refer back to the discussions of sorting, grouping, and filtering in the preceding sections of this chapter for instructions. Options that are no longer available appear grayed out in the dialog box. If you need an option that's grayed out, sometimes the easiest solution is to construct a completely new report by using the ReportCreator.

Modifying your report by using Report view

To change your report any way other than by using the Tools menu, you need to use Report view. Report view, frankly, is messy to deal with — too messy to cover in this book. The modifications and enhancements that you can make in Report view (including adding fields to the report; performing more sophisticated calculations; and formatting report text, borders, and other features) are invaluable to some users, but most Works users can live without them. If you need a fancier report, consider creating your database by using one of the Tasks instead, such as Home Inventory, found in the Task Launcher, or check the Works Web Site (found in the list of tasks in the Task Launcher).

If you need to enhance your Works report, you can find instructions for basic report enhancements in *Microsoft Works 2000 For Dummies* by yours truly, David Kay, (IDG Books Worldwide, Inc.). The book is available at fine bookstores near you and through www.dummies.com on the Web!

Chapter 8

Works Wizardry for Popular Tasks

· ·

In This Chapter

▶ Creating and using templates

▶ Starting an address book

▶ Sending your own junk mail

▶ Creating envelopes and labels for mass mailings

▶ Working with wizard and template documents

· ·

*T*hrough the magic of Tasks (formerly called TaskWizards) and templates, Works can create some amazing documents for you very quickly. Without the help of a template or Task, you would have to thoroughly study Works in order to create such delightful documents.

Tasks are automated programs that Microsoft provides. When you use one, the Task runs one of Works' programs — such as the word processor or spreadsheet program — to create and format a custom document for you (letterhead stationery, for example). You finish that document by inserting or editing text or values and by adjusting the formatting.

Templates are prototypes that you create for documents you need to create regularly, such as your own letterhead, a design for a monthly newsletter, or a seasonal game schedule for sports teams. From a template, you create a document customized to the occasion. For instance, you might use a newsletter template every month to create a new newsletter document. You can even use a Task to start a document and then save it as a personalized template.

Microsoft Tasks and any templates that you create present themselves on the Works Task Launcher that appears whenever you start Works. (You can view your templates by clicking the Tasks tab in the Works Task Launcher and then clicking Personal Templates.) Chapter 1 shows you how to select Tasks on the Tasks or Programs tab of the Task Launcher. Templates don't have their own tab on the Task Launcher, so they hang out with the Tasks. Works offers too many Tasks to describe here, so instead, this chapter focuses on the most popular ones: those that help you send out form letters and create labels or envelopes for bulk mailing (also called *mail merge*). Here, you'll also find basic instructions for using the Windows Address Book that Works often uses for such Tasks. This chapter also provides some general instructions and hints for using Tasks.

Tempting Templates

For Dummies readers being who they are — intelligent people who would just as soon not do the same thing twice — templates are a fabulous feature. *Templates* are the bare bones of some type of document that you use over and over again. You can create a template in the word processor, spreadsheet, or database program.

For example, if you are a consultant, almost all your invoices look the same except for the details of dates and charges and who the work is for. An invoice template supplies everything but those details, which you fill in each time that you create a new invoice. You can then save that invoice document as a file, and the original template remains untouched. (Some computer users simply modify their last invoice to create a new one, by using Save As to save it with a new name. But a template is better because you don't run the risk of accidentally modifying the original.)

Creating a template

To create a template, begin by creating a document that has all the text and graphics that don't change (such as your address or logo). Format the document and set up the page layout. If you want the text that will be added later to have a particular format, put in *dummy,* or *placeholder,* text and format that. To later replace the dummy text, select it and type the new text; the new text will take on the same format.

To save the document as a template:

1. **Choose File⇨Save As.**

   The Save As dialog box appears. Don't bother opening a folder or typing a name here. Templates are saved in a special folder.

2. **In Works, click the Template button in the lower right of the Save As dialog box. (If you're saving a Word template, select *Document Template* from the Save as Type drop-down list at the bottom of the Save As dialog box.)**

   In Works, a Save As Template dialog box then requests a name.

3. **Enter a name for the template and click OK. (If you're in Word, type a filename for your template into the File Name text box and then click the Save button.)**

    In Works, if this template represents a document that you use nearly all the time (say, it's a blank letterhead), select the Use This Template For New *whatever* Documents check box (with *whatever* being Database or Spreadsheet). This action turns your template into a *default* template. Now whenever you start a new document of that type — a database document, for instance — your document automatically takes the form of that template. (This feature is not available in Word.)

    To turn this feature off, open the template by choosing File⇔Open, return to the Save As dialog box by repeating Steps 1 through 3, and click in the check box again to deselect it.

Works stores your templates in two special folders. Word processor templates are stored as a special type of file that ends in *.dot* in the \Windows\Application Data\Microsoft\Templates folder. Spreadsheet templates are regular *.wks* (spreadsheet) files, and database templates are regular *.wdb* (database) files, stored in the \Program Files\Microsoft Works\ Template folder.

If you need to modify the template in any way, just load it the normal way by selecting it in the Personal Templates in the Task Launcher. (Personal Templates doesn't appear in the Tasks list until you have saved at least one template.) Then make your changes to the template, choose File⇔Save As, and follow the preceding steps.

Using a template

When you use a template, Works creates a new document that exactly mimics the template. To use a template that you have created, do the following:

1. **Open the Task Launcher and click the Tasks tab.**

    At the bottom of the Tasks list, you find the entry Personal Templates. (If the Personal Templates entry doesn't appear after you have created your first template, close the Task Launcher and reopen it.) Your templates also appear in the list of Tasks for each program. You'll see them when you select the appropriate program on the Task Launcher's Program tab.

2. **Click Personal Templates to see a list of templates that you can use.**

    Click your template and then click the Start button that appears. Works creates a document that looks exactly like your template.

3. **Modify this new document as you like and save it as you would any document.**

   (When you save your document, Works saves it as a document and not as a template.)

Creating an Address Book

Microsoft obviously thinks that it's very important for you to have an address book. Because you don't want to disappoint Microsoft, you should probably create an address book. Here are some other good reasons for creating an address book:

- You have lots of people whom you call or e-mail often. The Address Book holds e-mail addresses for Outlook Express, among its many other roles.

- You have lots of friends and want to keep track of their birthdays and anniversaries.

- You want to send out e-mail to groups of people on a regular basis: your relatives, your kids' soccer team, and the like.

- You want to do your own junk mail: "Dear Mr. ___, I know you and others of the ___ family would love to send us your money." (You can use your Address Book to send junk mail, or you can use a separate Works database file that has names, addresses, and possibly other information about each person.)

- You are a salesperson and need to keep a record of all your prospects and clients. When Ms. Steinway calls, you want to be able to say, "Oh, hi, Barbara, I was just thinking of you. How are, um, . . ." (brief pause while you look up her entry in the address book), "George and the kids? Isn't little . . . Sustenuto 12 now?"

Computerized address books make the preceding tasks easier because you can quickly search for people by name, by address (both mail and e-mail), by phone (both home and business), or by other criteria. You can also sort your address book easily — for example, sorting by name, e-mail address, business phone, or home phone.

You may want to create several folders in your address book — one for friends, another for clients, and another for members of the professional organization that you run. You can print out these address book folders as well as use them on the computer.

In previous editions of Works, address books were Works databases. In the new millennium, Microsoft wants everyone — Works users or not — to use the same address book. Microsoft now makes its special Address Book part of Windows and uses it in various Microsoft products. This new Address Book is what Works uses for mail merge and address labels. By way of apology to old users, Works regularly offers to import old Works address books into the new one.

Here's how to create an address book by using one of the Tasks that Works supplies:

1. **Click the Programs tab in the Task Launcher.**

2. **On the left side of the window, click Address Book. Then select Address Book from the list that appears on the right.**

3. **Click the Start button to run the Task.**

   The address book fires up. Depending on whether you've modified the address book previously, Works may ask whether you want to import an address book. (To get rid of this query about importing, select the check box labeled Don't Display This Message In The Future.) If you don't want to import anything, click the Cancel button (odd — but trust me, it works).

   You are now looking at an empty address book, ready to receive information on all your friends and business associates. (However, if you've previously used the Address Book in Outlook Express or other applications, it will be filled with whatever people you've added to it.)

4. **To add a person, click the New button (at the top left) and choose New Contact from the menu that appears.**

   You see the Properties dialog box, which has seven tabs in which you can enter all sorts of useful information about your contact. Do so.

5. **Click OK (in the Properties dialog box) to add this contact to the address book.**

   The Properties dialog box goes away. To review what you have entered for a contact, click the name on the Address Book window and click the Properties button. You then see a dialog box with a Summary tab followed by the seven tabs that were in the original Properties dialog box. Click any of the original tabs to edit the information there.

6. **To arrange your contacts into different folders within your address book, choose View➪Folders and Groups.**

   A window opens on the left side of the address book, showing the book's organization (initially one folder called Main Identity's Contacts within Shared Contacts). Highlight Main Identity's Contacts, click the New button, and select New Folder. You will be prompted to name the new folder (Suzy's friends, tennis partners, whatever); enter a name and click OK.

To add contacts to the new folder, click it first and then add contacts as you did in Steps 4 and 5. To move contacts from Main Identity's Contacts into your new folder, first click Main Identity's Contacts to open it. Then drag contacts from the list of contacts (on the right) to the new folder (on the left). To copy contacts, select a contact in one folder (or press and hold down the Shift key while clicking to select a whole group of contacts) and then choose Edit⇨Copy. Click the folder where you want to copy them to and choose Edit⇨Paste.

7. **To create a single contact for e-mailing to a group, click the folder in which you want the group record to go and then choose New⇨ New Group.**

(By creating a group contact, you can write a single e-mail message, address it to this contact, and have it go to everyone in the group.) The Properties dialog box appears for the new group. Type a name for the group in the Group Name box. You can add group members from your address book by clicking Select Members (or add them directly by typing in the Name filed and E-Mail field and then clicking Add). In the Select Members dialog box that appears, click a person on the left to add to the group, and then click Select to add that person. Click OK to return to the group Properties dialog box.

8. **When you're done filling out and organizing your Address Book choose File⇨Exit.**

Here are a few tips to make your life easier when using the Address Book:

- ✔ To see the information about a contact listed anywhere in the Address Book, click the name for that contact and then click any Properties button that's visible.

- ✔ To find someone by name or other information, the easiest way is to choose Edit⇨Find People. In the Find People dialog box, type whatever information you have (type a full or partial name in the Name box, for instance) and then click Find Now. If your search is successful, the Find People dialog box expands to display a name or list of names.

- ✔ If the person you're looking for is not in your address book, you can look on the Web by using Internet Explorer. In the address book, choose Edit⇨Find People, click in the Look In box, and select any of the Web services listed there. Click the Web Site button that is now active.

- ✔ To open your address book, click the Programs tab in the Works Task Launcher, then click Address Book on the left side, and click Start the Address Book.

Creating Your Own Junk Mail

For that personal touch without actually being personal, there's nothing like junk mail. (Miss Manners, please call your office.) Yes, now you, too — *<your name here>*, of *<your address here>* — can send junk mail just like the pros!

This popular feature, also known as *mail merge* or *form letters,* lets you write a single letter in the word processor, leave blanks in the text, and have Works automatically fill in the blanks *(merge)* from a database (such as an address book). Works prints out one letter for each lucky person in your database.

Of course, in addition to sending falsely personal letters, this feature can be used for more valid personalization, such as:

✔ Sending a letter to members of your organization, telling them how much they have paid, and have left unpaid, of their annual dues or pledge

✔ Welcoming each attendee to some event and telling the attendees what rooms they will be staying in

In these examples, the letter includes a piece of information about each person, which comes from your database. Of course, you must have a database with this information in it in the first place! This database can take one of two possible forms:

✔ **The Microsoft Address Book.** If the only information your form letter needs to use are names, addresses, spouses, children, birthdays, or other information that the Address Book can contain, you can use the Microsoft Address Book as your database. (See the preceding section for details.)

✔ **Some other database file.** If you need to use other information in your form letter (the assigned hotel room, the balance outstanding, or other data), you can use a Works database or any of several types of database files that people commonly use.

You can use only data from a single file; you can't, for instance, take addresses from the Address Book and hotel registration information from another database. You can use any database Task to create the database document. On the Programs tab of the Task Launcher, click Works Database and then create a database from scratch by clicking Start a Blank Database — see Chapter 6 for more information on creating a database.

Creating your form letter

Begin by writing your form letter in Word, leaving out anything that will come from a database. For instance, your letter might begin with your name and address, as usual, and then the salutation, "Dear :" If you were writing to tell event attendees which hotel rooms they've been assigned to (and that information is in your database), you might write, "You have been assigned Room in the hotel."

After you have written your letter, do the following to link it to your database and insert data:

1. **Choose Tools⇨Mail Merge⇨Document Type.**

   You see the Document Type dialog box.

2. **Click OK to select the default Form Letter.**

   The Open Data Source dialog box appears.

3. **Tell Word where to find the data your letter will use.**

   Are you using names, addresses, and other data from Microsoft's official Address Book? Select Merge from the Address Book. If you're using names, addresses, and other data stored in a Works database or other type of file, select Merge Information from Another Type of File. In the dialog box that appears, locate and double-click your chosen database.

4. **For this example, select Merge from the Address Book.**

   The Mail Merge toolbar appears, as shown in Figure 8-1.

Figure 8-1:
Use this toolbar to manage your mail merge and insert fields.

Data is stored in *fields* in your database or Address Book. The fields have names like Title or First_Name. The task at this point is to select fields from the Insert Fields dialog box and insert them into the form letter where you want them.

5. **Click in your document at the point where you omitted something that was to come from the database.**

   For instance, click just before the colon in *Dear :* to insert data there.

6. **Find the field containing the data you want in the Insert Fields dialog box (for instance, *Title*); click that field name and then click the Insert button to copy it to your document.**

   Word inserts the field name in << >> symbols in your document. For instance, your salutation might now read Dear <<First_Name>>:

7. **Repeat Steps 5 and 6 until you have inserted all the fields you need in your document. See the tips following these steps.**

   For instance, the complete salutation might read Dear <<First_Name>> <<Surname>>:

When you're done inserting fields into your letter, your form letter is done! Save it as a file by pressing Ctrl+S. You may then want to clean it up a bit. Here are a few tips for the final cleanup:

- ✔ You can format the text of fields just as you would any other text — make it bold, for instance.

- ✔ If you make a mistake and want to remove a field, highlight the field name in your document and press the Delete key.

- ✔ Add or remove spaces as necessary. For punctuation and spacing purposes, treat the field name as if it were the actual word. Leave no space between <<Surname>> and the colon in the salutation, for instance, but do put a space before and after any field that appears mid-sentence. Press the Spacebar key to leave a space between the fields you inserted and press the Comma key to type a comma — for example, to separate city from state. Figure 8-2 shows you an example of what you see when you're done.

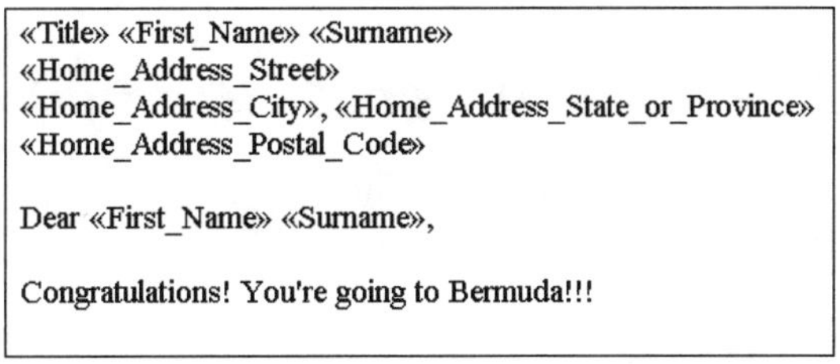

Figure 8-2:
What you
end up with:
a letter with
odd text
in it.

«Title» «First_Name» «Surname»
«Home_Address_Street»
«Home_Address_City», «Home_Address_State_or_Province»
«Home_Address_Postal_Code»

Dear «First_Name» «Surname»,

Congratulations! You're going to Bermuda!!!

Viewing your form letter with real data

When you're done inserting the fields you need, you are basically ready to print. But I suggest reviewing the form letter first, looking at real data from the database, not just field names. Unexpectedly long, short, or missing data in the database can make your form letter look weird.

If the Mail Merge Toolbar Insert Fields dialog box is still on your screen, click its View Merged Data button (the third button from the left on the toolbar). You then see an example of one merged document. To view others, click the buttons with red arrows on them to move through the entire mail merge job.

The arrow buttons advance you from one record to the next (like the ones in Works database program). Click the right arrow to advance from one record (one person, for instance, in your Address Book) to the next. Click the left arrow to move back through the records. The right and left double arrows take you to the first and last records of the database.

When you've finished viewing your letter with a variety of records, click the View Merged Data button again to toggle it off.

Continue editing the form letter if necessary; print for real when the form letter is ready.

Tips for Using Task-Created Documents

Many Works Tasks create documents for you by using the Big Three programs of Works. Works pulls out all the stops for Task-created documents. It uses lots of advanced features in such clever ways that you may not recognize exactly what feature is being used. Following are some tips for working with these clever Task documents. (If you're not sure what kind of document a Task has created, read the title bar on top of the window; it says Microsoft Word, or Spreadsheet, or Database.) See the chapters on the individual programs in this book for more details.

Working with word processing documents

Task and template word processing documents are full of graphical and layout tricks. Here are a few of the most common tricks:

- ✔ In some templates, Word shows multiple columns, WordArt, charts, and graphics. To change any of these features, double-click what you want to change; whatever program is responsible for creating that component then appears.

- ✔ In the Letters and other Tasks, Word uses paragraph formatting and borders extensively. Click some text and choose Format➪Paragraph or Format➪Borders and Shading to see what's going on.

- ✔ To see additional templates, choose File➪New➪More Word Templates.

✔ Some Word Task documents use tabs in creative ways. To see where tab characters appear, choose <u>V</u>iew➪<u>A</u>ll Characters. Tiny arrows represent tab characters. Fill-in blanks are often created by using underlined tab characters.

Working with spreadsheet documents

Task-created spreadsheet documents use lots of tricks with borders, column widths, and gridlines. Here are tips for working around a few of those tricks:

✔ If a spreadsheet appears to have headings with text indented under them, this indentation may have been achieved by using a very narrow column for the heading text and then putting the indented text in the next column over.

✔ If a spreadsheet title is centered over the spreadsheet columns, the actual text of the title is probably in the leftmost cell that the title covers.

✔ If you can't edit the text in a spreadsheet, select the area and choose F<u>o</u>rmat➪<u>P</u>rotection. Click in the Protect Data check box to deselect it.

✔ If a spreadsheet uses colored text that doesn't work well for you, remember that colors are an option on the Font tab of the Format Cells dialog box. (Choose F<u>o</u>rmat➪<u>F</u>ont and Style to get there.) You can also control borders and shading from this same dialog box.

Working with database documents

Task-created database documents come equipped with built-in reports and some tricky formulas, as well as fancy formatting. Here are a few tips for making sense of what you see:

✔ In return-address labels, you have to enter your name and address only once: in the top or upper-left label. You don't have to enter it for every label. (Formulas automatically make copies.) Choose <u>F</u>ile➪Print Pre<u>v</u>iew to see the full set of labels.

✔ Check out what reports are available by choosing <u>V</u>iew➪<u>R</u>eport. Select a report from the list and then click Preview in the dialog box that appears.

✔ To pick up some advanced techniques with formulas, check out the built-in reports in Report view.

✔ To change the formatting, layout, or content of a database document, Form Design view generally works best.

✔ If you need to change a field but Works won't let you, choose F<u>o</u>rmat➪ <u>P</u>rotection and click in the Protect Field check box to deselect it.

Chapter 9

Dating Yourself by Using Microsoft Calendar

- -

In This Chapter

▶ Understanding what's what in the calendar window

▶ Viewing by month, week, or day

▶ Looking ahead or back in time

▶ Creating appointments or events

▶ Entering birthdays and other recurring events

▶ Editing and moving appointments and events

▶ Using categories

▶ Setting up reminders

▶ Printing calendars

- -

Personally, I have trouble remembering the old rhyme, "Thirty days hath whatever, April, March, and whenever, and all the rest have something different."

But all Calendar needs to help you take over the world is for you to put your business, personal, and other appointments (or day-long events) into its calculating little brain. Do so, and not only can you see all your upcoming happenings by day, week, or month, but you also get automatic reminders of appointments, review your notes before meetings, and print out calendars for business associates.

So what are you waiting for? You start Works Calendar from the Works Task Launcher.

Click Programs at the top of the window. Click Works Calendar in the list of programs that now appears along the left side of the window. Click Start the Calendar (which now appears in colorful text) in the right-hand panel, and the Calendar appears.

The Works Calendar page of the Task Launcher also gives you shortcuts so that you can either create a new appointment or find an existing one. Click Calendar, Set Appointment to create a new appointment and then click the Start button that appears. This action takes you to the New Appointment dialog box that you can read about in the section "Setting Up Appointments or Events," later in this chapter. To find an appointment by searching for some of its text, click Appointment Search and then click the Start button. Enter some of the text of the title of the appointment you're looking for in the Find dialog box that appears and then click Find Now.

After you start it up, Works Calendar may ask you whether you want to give it the honor of being your default calendar. If you're not currently using another calendar, click Yes. If you're using another calendar but want to check out Works Calendar before deciding which to use, click No. To get it to stop asking the question, clear the Always Perform This Check When Starting Works Calendar check box.

What's What in the Calendar Window

The Calendar window displays the kind of menu bar and toolbar that you find in any Windows program, plus one of several views of your Calendar among which you can choose (see Figure 9-1). Initially, you see an entire month, but you can choose to view a single day or week instead. (See the following section, "Viewing by Month, Week, or Day," for details.) You can also view your appointments by different categories — displaying, for example, just personal or just business appointments. (See the section "Using categories," later in this chapter, for details.)

As do most Windows programs, Calendar offers you several alternative ways to perform any given task: toolbar buttons, keyboard shortcuts, a pop-up menu that appears after you right-click a date, or the menu bar. The method that you use is up to you. I find that using the toolbar buttons and the pop-up menu are the most convenient methods, but you may prefer to use a different method.

Viewing by Month, Week, or Day

Calendar enables you to choose your view: month, week, or day. (I prefer an ocean view, but they refuse to give me a room with a window.) Click the appropriate button on the toolbar, as shown in Figure 9-1, or choose View⇨Day, Week, or Month from the menu bar.

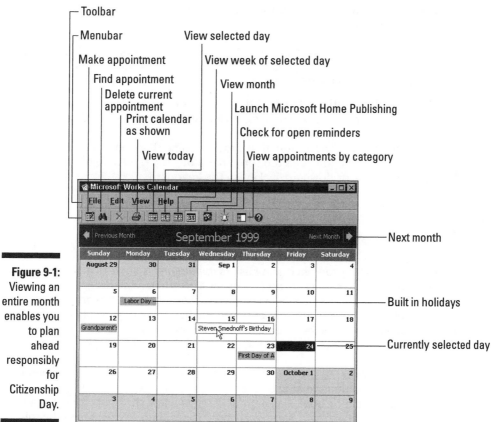

Toolbar
Menubar
Make appointment
Find appointment
Delete current appointment
Print calendar as shown
View today
View selected day
View week of selected day
View month
Launch Microsoft Home Publishing
Check for open reminders
View appointments by category

Next month
Built in holidays
Currently selected day

Figure 9-1: Viewing an entire month enables you to plan ahead responsibly for Citizenship Day.

Following are a few tips for choosing views (I find Day and Month views the more useful ones):

✔ Choose Day view for easiest scheduling of appointments at particular hours. Day view displays all-day events in light gray above the list of time slots.

✔ Choose Month view for easiest scheduling and viewing of all-day events. If an appointment title isn't fully visible in Month view, position your mouse cursor over it and wait a second. The title appears in full (as shown in Figure 9-1 for Steven Smednoff's birthday).

Looking Ahead or Behind

If you're like me (and I don't say that you are), you're always nervously looking ahead and behind to see what's coming or what you forgot to do. In

Calendar, each view provides the following two ways to move your view forward or back in time:

- ✔ Click the Previous *whatever* or Next *whatever* arrows at the left and right sides of the calendar, respectively, just below the toolbar. (By *whatever*, I mean *Day* in Day view, *Week* in Week view, or *Month* in Month view.)

- ✔ Click the month or date text that appears in large type just below the toolbar. Choose a new date from the list of selections that drops down.

If the window isn't large enough to show the time that you want to see, you can scroll the Calendar. Use the scroll bar along the right side of the window, or press the up- or down-arrow key on the keyboard.

Setting Up Appointments or Events

Works' Calendar program distinguishes *appointments* such as meetings or lunch dates from *all-day events* (or *events* for short). (The program is superior to some business people I've known in that regard.) Appointments are happenings that begin and end at particular hours. All-day events are happenings such as holidays, birthdays, or casual days at work. I use the term *happenings* in this chapter if the text applies to both events and appointments.

The key Calendar feature that you use to set up happenings of either kind is the New Appointment dialog box (or its nearly identical twin, the Edit Appointment dialog box). Calendar also offers a few shortcuts for creating and editing happenings. I show you how to use all these features in the following sections.

Making happenings happen

Works Calendar gives you multitudes of ways to enter various happenings. Some ways are obvious because they appear right on-screen and read `Click here to add....` If you click where Calendar indicates, a blank line and cursor appear so that you can type a title for the happening.

Following, however, are my two favorite, universal alternatives for entering a happening of any kind — universal because they work in any view:

- ✔ Click the New Appointment button at the far left on the toolbar (or press Ctrl+N or choose File➪New Appointment). You may want to select the date or time first (by directly clicking the date or the time slot) so that Works enters that date or time for you in the New Appointment dialog box.

✔ Right-click the date (in Month or Week view) or time slot (in Day view) directly and then choose the *top selection* in the list that appears. (The selection reads either New Appointment or New All Day Event. Don't worry about the difference right now; you can choose the type of happening you want in the New Appointment dialog box that appears.)

A shortcut for entering an appointment (not an event) is to switch to Day view and then simply double-click any of the half-hour time slots.

Whichever of those two ways you choose, you end up gazing at the New Appointment dialog box, as shown in Figure 9-2.

If you edit an appointment, you use a nearly identical dialog box known as the Edit Appointment dialog box.

The following steps are the only essential ones for entering an appointment or event in the New Appointment dialog box:

1. **Click the Title text box and type a descriptive title for the appointment or event (see Figure 9-2).**

    This title is what appears in the calendar.

2. **Click the All-Day Event check box to enable or disable the check mark, as necessary.**

    If you're entering an all-day event (such as a birthday or holiday), make sure that the All-Day Event check box contains a check mark. (Click the check box if it doesn't contain one.)

    If you're entering an appointment (which needs starting and ending times), make sure that the All-Day Event check box does *not* contain a check mark. (Click the check box to remove the mark if it does.)

3. **Adjust the dates and/or times for this happening, as necessary.**

    To change the date or specify a *multiday event,* you may edit the dates in the Appointment Starts and Appointment Ends drop-down list boxes. If you prefer to pick dates from a calendar, click the down arrows adjoining those boxes.

    For appointments, type a starting and ending time for the appointment in the second Appointment Starts and Appointment Ends drop-down list boxes, as Figure 9-2 shows. If you prefer to pick half-hour intervals from a list, click the down arrows adjoining those list boxes. You may also enter a new date in the date list boxes above these time list boxes. (If an appointment spans more than one day, it appears in its time slot on each of those days.)

4. **Click OK after you finish.**

Tricky clicking

You must click carefully in Works Calendar or you may find yourself doing something other than you intend. To select a date in Month view, click the day number and *not the appointment or event in the gray bar.* Similarly, to enter an appointment or event by right-clicking, right-click the day number and not the appointment or event. And make sure that you don't left-click before you right-click. Clicking or right-clicking the appointment or event is only for editing it. Press the Esc key if you find yourself accidentally editing a title or viewing a menu with Edit commands.

Set times if *not* all-day event.

Add notes (optional).

Type a location (optional).

Choose a category (optional).

Set reminder (optional).

Figure 9-2:
For a holiday or birthday, click to place a check mark in the All-Day Event check box.

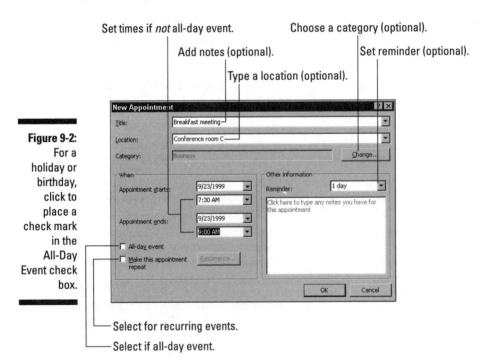

Select for recurring events.

Select if all-day event.

Some of the additional options that you can choose in the New Appointment dialog box are as follows:

- ✔ Click the Make This Appointment Repeat check box to make your happening *repeat* every day, week, month, or year. See the following section, "Entering birthdays and other recurring events," for details.

- ✔ Click the Location text box and type a *location* for the event. Calendar keeps a list of locations you've used in the past. To choose from that list, click the down arrow at the far-right end of the Location text box.

✔ Click the Change button to *categorize* your happening. See the section "Using categories," later in this chapter, for instructions.

✔ Click the Reminder drop-down list box and type a time interval (or click the adjoining down arrow and choose a time interval from the list) to have Works remind you in advance of the happening. See the section "Setting up reminders," later in this chapter, for details.

✔ Click and type notes about the event in the large white text box below the Reminder box.

Entering birthdays and other recurring events

If your event or appointment occurs once a year, a month, or a week, every second Tuesday of each month, or all Mondays through Fridays, you're in luck (unless you're talking about dental-surgery appointments). Calendar enables you to enter the happening just once and make it repeat on any of those intervals. Follow these steps to success:

1. **To enter a new, repeating event or appointment, click the New Appointment button (or press Ctrl+N or choose File⇨New Appointment) or, in Month or Week view, right-click the date that you want and choose New All-Day Event from the menu that appears.**

   To *change an existing event or appointment* to a repeating one, begin by right-clicking it. Then choose Open from the pop-up menu that appears. You open an Edit Appointment dialog box, which is identical to the New Appointment dialog box. (If this existing event is a recurring one, the Open Recurring Event dialog box appears first. Choose Open This Occurrence to make a change for the date you chose. Choose Open The Series to make a change that applies to all dates on which the event recurs.)

2. **Click the Make This Appointment Repeat check box in the New Appointment (or Edit Appointment) dialog box.**

3. **Click the Recurrence button.**

   The Recurrence Options dialog box appears, as shown in Figure 9-3.

You specify how often your happening occurs and for how long it continues to recur by following these steps in the Recurrence Options dialog box:

1. **Click the radio button for your choice of interval: Daily, Weekly, Monthly, or Yearly.**

2. **The options that each different interval offers now appear in the dialog box, and you can choose them by clicking the following check boxes:**

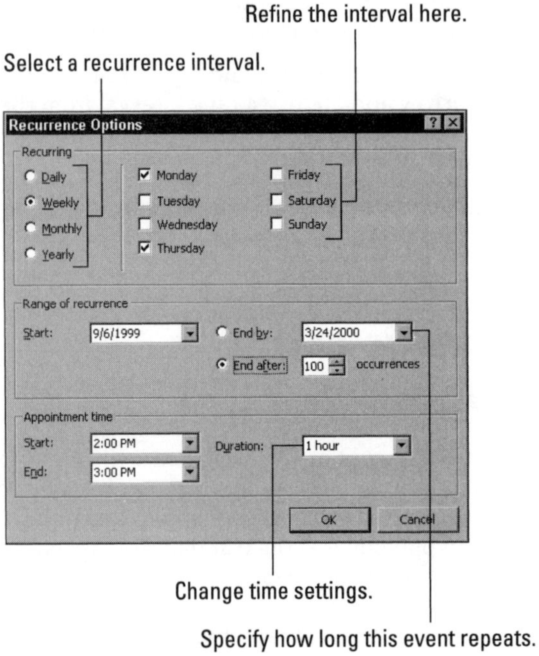

Refine the interval here.

Select a recurrence interval.

Recurrence Options   ? X

┌─ Recurring ───┐
│ ○ Daily   ☑ Monday   ☐ Friday   │
│ ● Weekly   ☐ Tuesday   ☐ Saturday   │
│ ○ Monthly   ☐ Wednesday   ☐ Sunday   │
│ ○ Yearly   ☑ Thursday   │
└──┘

┌─ Range of recurrence ───────────────────────────────┐
│ Start: 9/6/1999 ▼   ○ End by: 3/24/2000 ▼   │
│   ● End after: 100 ⊟ occurrences│
└──┘

┌─ Appointment time ──────────────────────────────────┐
│ Start: 2:00 PM ▼   Duration: 1 hour ▼   │
│ End: 3:00 PM ▼   │
└──┘

                              OK   Cancel

Figure 9-3:
A hypothetical appointment occurs weekly on Mondays and Thursdays.

Change time settings.

Specify how long this event repeats.

- **Options if you choose Daily:** Every Day (seven days a week) or Every Weekday (Monday through Friday).

- **Options if you choose Weekly:** Choose a day of the week.

  For happenings that occur several times a week, you can choose multiple days. If you're a computer book author, for example, this choice is perfect for your electroshock appointments.

- **Options if you choose Monthly:** Choose by *day number* (On the 6th day, for example) or by the *day and week* (such as Every Second Thursday).

- **Options if you choose Yearly:** Choose by *date* (August 13th, for example) or by *day, week,* and *month* (such as Every Second Thursday in August).

3. **Specify how long this happening continues to repeat by giving a beginning date and either an end date or a number of occurrences.**

   Enter a beginning date in the Start drop-down list box. (You may use the "slash" format shown in the figure or type the date as in **August 15, 2000**.)

   Enter an ending date in the End By drop-down list box or click End After and enter a number of occurrences.

By editing the values in the Start, End, or Duration drop-down list boxes in the Appointment Time area (or all of these), you can also adjust the appointment times if necessary.

4. **Click OK in the Recurrence Options dialog box after you finish there to return to the New (or Edit) Appointment dialog box.**

5. **Review — and, if you like, change — the information in the New Appointment (or Edit Appointment) dialog box.**

   If you need to adjust appointment times, click the Recurrence button again and make the necessary corrections in the Recurrence Options dialog box.

6. **Click OK after you finish setting up your appointment.**

To automatically enter birthdays and anniversaries that you store in your Windows address book, choose Edit⇨Birthdays.

Editing and moving appointments and events

If you're like me, your appointments change and move even faster than those giant man-eating chameleons. (You know — the ones crawling up your walls.) Well, maybe you're not like me — you may have fewer mental health appointments — but I bet that your appointments change.

To edit the title of an appointment in any view, simply click the appointment. A blinking cursor appears, and you can type, backspace, select text, and delete text just as you do in the text box of a dialog box.

To edit any aspect of an appointment, including its dates, times, notes, or title, right-click the appointment and choose Open from the pop-up menu that appears. The Edit Appointment dialog box appears, which works identically to the New Appointment dialog box (refer to Figure 9-2) and enables you to change any aspect of the appointment. If the appointment is a repeating one and you need to change its date or time, click the Recurrence button and make the changes in the Recurrence Options dialog box. (See the preceding section for details.)

In Calendar, dragging is the easiest way to move any happening (appointment or event) to another date or time. Click that happening and, holding down the mouse button (don't let go!), drag the happening to another date on the Calendar.

Copying an appointment or event is similar, except that you press and hold the Ctrl key on your keyboard while you drag the appointment.

To move an appointment or event to a date farther in the future than you care to drag it, edit the appointment or event (as I describe in the second paragraph of this section) and change its date.

Using categories

If you get really serious about using Calendar to manage your life, consider using the Calendar *categories*. (Or consider getting a simpler life!) If you have lots of happenings in Calendar — meetings, trips, lunches, therapies, kids' activities, holidays, classes, or the Ludlow, Vermont, Zucchini Festival — your calendar gets pretty cluttered.

By using Calendar's categories, you can assign any happening to one or more categories: business, education, medical, personal, and so on. Then you can restrict (or *filter*) the display to show only certain categories of happenings at a time. Calendar comes with a set of standard categories among which you can choose, and you can create, rename, or delete categories as well.

The place to go to assign categories is the Choose Category dialog box. You can access this dialog box in any of the following several ways — whichever is most convenient for you:

- ✔ To assign a category while you're creating a *new* happening by using the New Appointment dialog box (refer to Figure 9-2), click the Change button.

- ✔ To assign a category to an *existing* happening, right-click that appointment or event in the Calendar and choose Categories from the pop-up menu that appears. (This option is available only if you haven't previously assigned a category to this happening.) If you're editing the happening anyway by using the Edit Appointments dialog box, click the Change button in that dialog box.

The Choose Categories dialog box consists simply of a list of check boxes, one for each category. Check one or more categories for your happening and then click OK.

To add a category of your own design or to delete or rename a category, you need to access the Edit Category dialog box. Choose Edit➪Categories from the menu bar or click the Edit Categories button in the Choose Categories dialog box.

In the Edit Categories dialog box, click a category to delete or rename it and then click the Delete or Rename button. To create a new category, click the blank text box at the bottom of the dialog box, type a new name, and then click the Add button.

To make your calendar display only certain categories of appointments or events (say, medical appointments), you *filter* out the other happenings by using the filter control panel. Click the Category Filter button on the toolbar (the button second from the right, as shown in Figure 9-1) to display or hide that pane.

A list of check boxes appears to the left of your calendar; check marks in these boxes indicate which categories Calendar is displaying. Click the appropriate check boxes to clear the check marks for categories that you don't want to see, and your calendar changes accordingly.

To restore all happenings to your calendar, click the words Category Filter at the top of the filter control panel, and choose Show Appointments in All Categories from the menu that appears. To hide the filter control panel, click the Category Filter button on the toolbar again.

Hiding the filter panel doesn't remove filtering. Only by choosing Show Appointments in All Categories do you remove filtering.

Setting up reminders

Calendar can remind you of upcoming happenings (events or appointments) by popping up a reminder window and, optionally, making a sound. All you need to do is tell Calendar how far in advance to remind you.

To create a new event or appointment that includes a reminder, click the New Appointment button (or press Ctrl+N or choose File⊅New Appointment) or, in Month or Week view, right-click the date of the happening.

To add a reminder to an existing event or appointment, begin by right-clicking it. Then choose Open from the pop-up menu that appears.

In the New Appointment (or Edit Appointment) dialog box that appears (refer to Figure 9-2), enter an interval into the Reminder drop-down list box that reflects how far in advance of the happening you want Works to remind you about it. Either type an interval (in minutes, hours, days, weeks, months, or years) or click the down arrow adjoining the Reminder text box and choose a standard interval from the drop-down list that appears.

Calendar doesn't need to be running for the reminder to work. You can now exit Calendar by choosing File⊅Exit.

At your specified interval before the appointment or event begins, a View Reminders dialog box appears. You may leave the View Reminders dialog box on-screen to help you remember the appointment. The dialog box displays all current (*active*) reminders in its Reminders text box. To view your notes on a given happening, click the happening in the Reminders text box, and then click the Open button.

After you're sure that you're going to remember an upcoming happening (or after it passes), you may clear (*dismiss*) its reminder from the View Reminders dialog box. Click that happening and then click the Dismiss Item button. To dismiss all current reminders, click Dismiss All; they don't appear again. Dismissing a reminder is the same as deleting or canceling it.

Click the Close button to remove the View Reminders dialog box from your screen. You can check your reminders at any time by choosing View➪Reminders from the Calendar menu bar or by clicking the Reminders button on the toolbar, which displays a bell icon.

Printing Calendars

Computers — phooey! Nothing beats a paper calendar or appointment book for keeping you current with events and appointments and for sharing a schedule with others. Works Calendar gives you more ways to print your schedule than you probably can ever use.

Choose File➪Print (or click the Print button on the toolbar or press Ctrl+P). The Print dialog box appears.

Begin by selecting a calendar style. To print out a day's appointments, choose one of the following Day styles from the Style list box.

- **Day by appointments:** Similar to Day view; shows a space covering each appointment's duration.

- **Day by hours:** Similar to Day view but lists every half-hour time slot and shows what appointment begins in that half-hour.

- **Day list:** Lists each appointment in order and its start and end times; shows no time slots.

- **Day list by sections:** Groups appointments into Morning, Afternoon, and Evening, showing start and end times for each appointment.

Calendar also offers Week and Month calendar styles in the Style list box. Choose Month-Portrait for a calendar that prints vertically on a page or Month-Landscape for the horizontal orientation that's more common for calendars.

Enter a Start and End date and time in the Range area of the Print dialog box. (Or use the default dates and times that Calendar suggests.)

Make sure that Calendar applies any filtering the way you actually want it to appear. In the Include area of the Print dialog box, Calendar assumes by default that any filtering you're currently applying (displaying Personal appointments only, for example) also applies to this printed calendar. If you want to print all appointments and events instead, click All Appointments.

Part II

Putting Words in Word

The 5th Wave   By Rich Tennant

"NOPE - I'D BETTER WAIT 'TIL ALL MY FONTS ARE WORKING. A HATE LETTER JUST DOESN'T WORK IN *Filigree Flowerbox Extended*."

In this part . . .

Microsoft Word 2000 is the big bargain of Works Suite. Thanks to the influence of Microsoft, Word is probably the most commonly used word processor in the business world today. Knowing Word is a skill useful in nearly any job. (Academic, legal, and government organizations tend to prefer Corel WordPerfect.) Word, like other top-end word processors, is overflowing with features. Many features are useful to everyone, some are useful to only a select few people, and nearly all are as confusing as heck to new users!

If you've never processed a word electronically in your life, this part gets you past the confusion and into creating and formatting basic documents. This part gives you key fundamentals behind the power of word processing, such as using paragraph formatting and styles. This part then tells you how to add common and essential features, such as tables, headers and footers, columns, charts, and illustrations.

Chapter 10

Creating and Editing a Document

- -

- -

*I*n the beginning, there was Word. Yes, Microsoft Word has been around for many years, and in that time, it has acquired many fancy features. In this book, however, I'm focusing on the basics. (Well, okay, maybe a few fancy features.) If you want to get seriously into Word, I suggest you pick up a copy of Dan Gookin's *Word 2000 For Windows For Dummies* (IDG Books Worldwide, Inc.).

This chapter gives you the really basic basics: getting the words right. I include information on starting a document and typing the words, plus finding, editing, and checking those words. Anything having to do with appearances and other frilly stuff is in the next chapter.

Starting and Exiting Word

Just as you do for any other Windows program, you can start Word from the Windows Start button or with a shortcut icon. Do one of the following:

- ✔ On the Windows taskbar, choose Start➪Programs➪Microsoft Word.

- ✔ If you prefer to start Word from the Works Task Launcher, choose Start➪Programs➪Microsoft Works. Then in the Task Launcher, click Programs (just under the menu bar), click Word in the list box on the left, and then click the W icon labeled Start a blank Word document. See Chapter 1 for an in-depth look at the Task Launcher.

- ✔ If you have a Microsoft Word icon on your screen, double-click that icon.

Unfortunately, you cannot assign a Ctrl+Alt+[Shortcut key] to Word (when it's installed as part of Works), although you can with the other Works programs such as Encarta or Money. See Chapter 1 for a tip on this subject.

To exit the Word program, choose File➪Exit (or you can more quickly exit *any* Windows program by pressing Alt+F4). If you haven't already saved your work (your *changes* in Word-speak), a dialog box asks you if you want to do so. Click Yes to save your work, click No to discard your work, or click Cancel to return to Word.

To read more about starting Windows programs, see the appendix. Likewise, turn to the appendix if you're a little shaky on using the mouse or keyboard, windows, menus, or dialog boxes.

Starting Documents

When you start Word (unless you start Word by double-clicking a Word document's name in Windows Explorer), it gives you a brand-new, daisy-fresh document right from the start: that big area of sparkling white you're looking at in the Word window. Just start typing! See "Typing and Deleting," later in this chapter, if you're new to word processing.

To start a new document while Word is already running, do as you would in most other Windows programs. Do any of the following:

- ✔ Choose File➪New.
- ✔ Press Ctrl+N.
- ✔ Click the icon on the far left of the standard toolbar (it looks like a blank sheet of paper), as shown in Figure 10-1.

The paper clip guy

Word may occasionally display a very cute animated paper clip, called *Office Assistant,* who tries to help out. He gives you pretty explicit directions, so you don't need me to repeat them. You type a question, and he lists subjects that he thinks are related.

Unfortunately, he's not very smart. But then, he's a paper clip. Click one of the listed subjects to read about it. To make him go away, right-click on him and choose Hide from the context menu. To wake him up, click his "?" button on the toolbar or just press F1. (See Figure 10-1.)

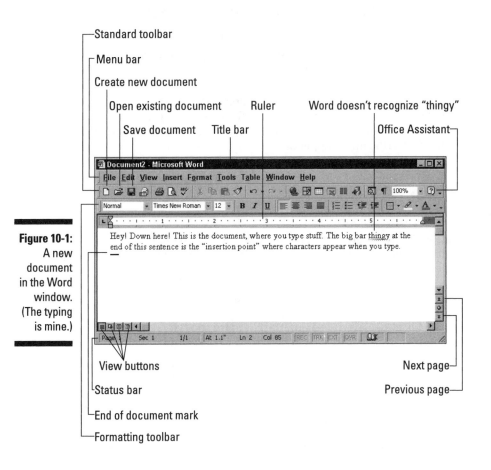

Figure 10-1: A new document in the Word window. (The typing is mine.)

Standard toolbar

Menu bar

Create new document

Open existing document

Save document

Ruler

Title bar

Word doesn't recognize "thingy"

Office Assistant

View buttons

Status bar

End of document mark

Formatting toolbar

Next page

Previous page

If you choose File➪New, you get a choice of what kind of new document you want. A submenu appears, which includes the Blank Document option. Click this option to start a normal, blank document. But if you would rather create a fancier document, click the More Word Templates option. You then see the New dialog box, with its variety of templates and wizards displayed on what appears to be several tabbed cards. If you click the New button on the Word toolbar, or press Ctrl+N, a blank document opens immediately.

To open an existing document, do as you would for most other Windows program documents: Chew open the wrapper. No, just kidding. Do one of the following:

✔ Choose File➪Open or press Ctrl+O (the letter, not the numeral zero).

✔ Click the Open button on the standard toolbar.

✔ Choose File, and then at the very bottom of the File menu, choose a recently-worked-on document by its name.

In the first two instances, you then choose the file from the Open dialog box that appears. Double-click the file in the Open dialog box to open it. If the file you want is not displayed, use the standard Windows file-finding techniques that I describe in the appendix.

Saving Documents

As with any program, you must save your document as a file on your hard drive or on a diskette before exiting Word (assuming you want to keep the document). Saving Word documents is very much like saving a document in any Windows program, so please see the appendix for basic instructions on saving and managing files. Following are some tips for saving in Word:

✔ Click the Save button on the standard toolbar (refer to Figure 10-1), or choose File➪Save, or press Ctrl+S to save your document.

✔ The first time you save a new document, a Save As dialog box asks you for a name and a location for where you want to save your document. Word suggests a default filename based on words taken from the start of your document. Type a new name if you like and then press the Enter key (or click the Save button).

✔ You don't have to type the *.doc* part of the filename, Word does that for you.

✔ Unless you give a different location in the Save As dialog box, Word saves your documents in a default folder, typically *My Documents* on your C drive.

The Word Window and Toolbar

Figure 10-1 shows the names of parts of the Word window. In the window is a document with one of the dweeby sort of startup titles that Word gives new documents — *Document 2,* for instance — appearing in the title bar.

Figure 10-1 shows only one of several possible *views* of your document. This view, which Word uses unless you choose otherwise, is called *Normal view.* Another common view is *Print Layout* view. See "Document Views," later in this chapter, for more information.

To find out the name of a button in Word, position your mouse cursor over the button and pause for a second. Word displays the button's name. You can then move your cursor over the other buttons, and pause it there, to see their names. Word offers so many buttons, and so many of them are rarely used that I don't waste space discussing them all here. In the appendix, I identify basic buttons shared by nearly all Windows programs.

Typing and Deleting

Typing and deleting are the big existential issues of word processing: existence and nonexistence — calling into creation and returning to the void. All else is illusion (or maybe illustration).

Typing

If you're looking at a Word window, away you go. Just start typing. All the regular keys on the keyboard — the letters, numbers, and punctuation — put characters on the screen when you press them. The spacebar, the Tab key, and the Enter key put invisible (white space) *characters* in your document.

If you're new to word processing, remember: Do *not* press the Enter (or Return) key when you get to the end of a line. Just keep typing. The text you type automatically starts on the next line, a phenomenon called *line wrap.* When you get to the bottom of the document window, the document scrolls up, like paper in your typewriter. Press the Enter key only when you get to the end of a paragraph — *not before!!!*

To add space between your paragraphs, you can press the Enter key twice at the end of the paragraph; however, a better way is to use *paragraph formatting,* which I get into in the next chapter. For now, try this technique: To put a line's worth of space above the paragraph that you're currently typing (and a line's worth of space above subsequent paragraphs), press Ctrl+0 (that's zero, not the letter O). If you want that space to go away, press Ctrl+0 again.

The insertion point

As you type, you start pushing around that big, blinking vertical bar called the *insertion point.* The insertion point's main function in life is to show you where the next character appears when you type or which character disappears when you delete.

Click anywhere in existing text to move the insertion point. As you type new text, any existing text (to the right of the insertion point in the same paragraph) moves to the right. When you place your insertion point in existing text, the characters you type take on the appearance *(character formatting)* of the character immediately *before* the insertion point — even if that character is a space or other invisible character!

You can nudge the insertion point up, down, or sideways by pressing the arrows and other navigation keys on your keyboard. Or you can just click the mouse pointer at the place in your document where you want to start typing.

Notice what happens to your mouse pointer when you move it off a toolbar and into the white area where you type. The bulky, arrow-shaped mouse pointer changes into an *I-beam* cursor, which is a little easier to fit in between characters than the arrow is.

Beware the insidious Insert key

Word provides two ways for you to type with your keyboard: *insert mode* and *overtype mode.* (A third mode, *à la mode,* is when your ice cream cone drops onto the keyboard.) By default, you're in insert mode, which means that if you move the insertion point into the middle of the text and start typing, the existing text scoots to the right to make room. If, however, you accidentally press the Insert key (which lives over by your navigation keys, just waiting to be pressed accidentally), you find yourself transported to the parallel dimension of *overtype* mode. (A little OVR shows up near the bottom-right corner of your Word window.) Now, if you move the insertion point into the middle of text and type, the existing text vanishes as you type over it. If you find yourself typing over existing text, you probably pressed the Insert key. Press the Insert key again to return to your home dimension.

Undoing your doings

Word (and many other programs) lets you *undo* whatever you just did. For instance, to undelete (that's *undelete*, not *undulate* — don't get excited) something that you deleted by accident, press Ctrl+Z or choose Edit➪Undo. To untype something that you just typed, you can also press Ctrl+Z. Word lets you undo many actions into the past; just keep pressing Ctrl+Z.

Deleting

You can delete stuff with either the Backspace key or the Delete key. To delete a character you just typed, press the Backspace key (usually on the upper-right corner of the typewriter keys). Technically speaking (geek-speak), the keys work as follows:

- ✔ The Backspace key deletes the character *before* the insertion point.
- ✔ The Delete key deletes the character *following* the insertion point.
- ✔ Either key deletes a block of text that is selected. (You can select text by holding down the left mouse button and dragging your mouse cursor across it, or by holding down the Shift key while using the arrow keys.) The selected area can span as many words, lines, paragraphs, and pages as you want, or even the entire document. For more on selecting text, see the appendix.

Typing spaces, tabs, and other invisible characters

You probably already suspect that your document is haunted by powerful invisible beings. What you probably didn't know is that you pressed the keys that brought them into existence.

Some of these characters are commonsensical and fairly innocuous. Other characters, such as the following, are somewhat more mysterious:

- ✔ The spacebar puts a space mark (character) in your text that is (unlike the space on a typewriter) thinner than most other characters that you type.
- ✔ When you press the Tab key, you insert a tab mark. The tab mark creates space in your text between the preceding character and the next *tab stop* location. See Chapter 11 for more on tabs.

✔ The elite of these invisible beings, the paragraph mark that you get when you press the Enter key, is so powerful that it gets its own section in this chapter, "Understanding paragraphs and paragraph marks," coming up soon.

"What tab mark? What paragraph mark?" you ask. Well, these marks are *invisible,* of course, which is why they don't stand out in a crowd. They're easy to overlook when you format or delete. But they do affect the way your document looks, and they can cause weird, spooky, inexplicable things to happen, such as a big gap appearing in your text (due to a tab mark or a line of spaces you didn't know was there), or one paragraph merging with another (when a paragraph mark gets deleted), or finding a font you didn't expect (when the insertion point gets plunked down next to an invisible character that has a different font attached to it).

For all these reasons, you need to be able to see these invisible characters, at least occasionally. Read on to find out how.

Seeing invisible characters

To see the creepy invisible characters inhabiting your document, click the Show/Hide paragraph button (the backward-P thingy next to the zoom percentage) on the standard toolbar.

AAAaaggghh! Your document is filled with nasty dots and funny marks! In fact, it looks almost as bad as the document shown in Figure 10-2! Those dots between your words are spaces. The little backward-P-looking thing is a paragraph mark, and it hangs out with the text that precedes it. If you have any tab marks, they look like arrows with deodorant-failure problems (lots of space around them). Manually inserted page breaks are dotted lines.

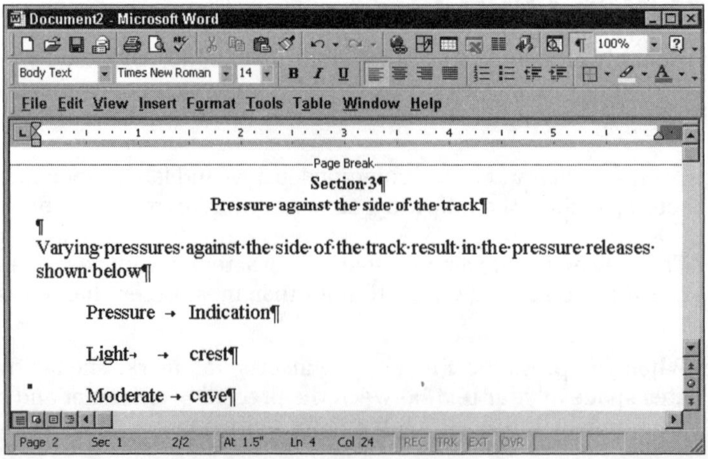

Figure 10-2:
Invisible
characters
are lurking
in your
document.

Now, if any of these invisible dudes are giving you trouble, just revoke their existence (delete them). The visible text moves around to fill the gap.

To make these characters invisible again, click the Show/Hide paragraph button again. However, until you get used to having these characters lurking around, your life may be easier if you leave the characters visible.

Understanding paragraphs and paragraph marks

You remember what your English teacher told you a paragraph is, right? Topic sentence? Two or more related sentences? Well, Word has its own ideas about paragraphs. A Word paragraph is created when you press the Enter key and therefore insert one of those secret, invisible paragraph marks that I talk about in "Typing spaces, tabs, and other invisible characters" earlier in this chapter.

That paragraph mark is very powerful, as invisible beings tend to be. Here are three extremely important and utterly critical things to know about the paragraph mark:

- ✔ **A paragraph mark tells Word, "Do not line wrap beyond this point; start a new line."** A paragraph mark is what keeps paragraphs apart.

- ✔ **The paragraph mark controls paragraph formatting for its paragraph.** In other words, the mark affects all the text preceding it (up to the preceding paragraph mark).

  Paragraph formatting is indentation, spacing between paragraphs, tab stops, alignment, justification, and other stuff that I talk about in the next chapter. When you format a paragraph, all this formatting information is *owned* by the paragraph mark and applies to the text preceding it. So if you copy a paragraph mark and paste it somewhere else, *it brings its paragraph formatting with it!* (The paragraph mark does *not*, however, specify type — meaning the typeface [font] or any aspect of type, such as style or size.)

- ✔ **Every time you press the Enter key (creating a new paragraph mark), the new paragraph inherits all the formatting of the paragraph you were just in.** The indentation, the spacing, the tab stops, and all the other paragraph stuff is just the same. In other words, just type, and new paragraphs look just like the first one. To change appearances of new paragraphs, adjust the final paragraph's formatting. Any new paragraphs you create from it inherit its appearance.

What these points mean for you is

- Don't press the Enter key at the end of every line; press it only at the end of your paragraphs. Otherwise, Word thinks your paragraph is actually a bunch of paragraphs. And then, if you want to do something stylish with your paragraphs — like indenting every line except the first one — the format won't work properly because (as far as Word is concerned) every line *is* the first line!

- Do press the Enter key at the end of short lines in a list, like this one.

- To split one paragraph into two, put the insertion point where you want the split and press the Enter key. The two new paragraphs share identical paragraph formatting.

- To create a new paragraph in front of the one that you're currently in, move your insertion point to the beginning of the current paragraph and press Enter.

- To create a new paragraph to follow the one that you're currently in, move your insertion point to the end of the current paragraph (click the last line and press the End key to be sure) and press Enter.

- If you delete text that includes a paragraph mark (for example, if you select and delete text crossing two paragraphs), the two paragraphs merge. The remaining single paragraph takes on the paragraph formatting of the bottom of the original pair. Try pressing Ctrl+Z to undo whatever you did, if you need to.

Unfriendly mergers and takeovers of paragraphs

The Backspace and Delete keys delete invisible characters the same way they delete visible characters. If your insertion point is at the beginning of a paragraph and you press the Backspace key, you delete the preceding character: the invisible paragraph mark at the end of the preceding paragraph! Likewise, if you press the Delete key at the end of a paragraph, you delete the paragraph mark. Without a paragraph mark to hold it back, the first paragraph spills into the following one and forms one humongous paragraph. What's worse, if the two paragraphs were formatted differently — say that the first paragraph was centered and the second paragraph wasn't — both of them are now formatted like the second paragraph.

You can get out of this mess by pressing Ctrl+Z (or choosing Edit➪Undo) immediately. Another option is to reinsert the paragraph mark by clicking where you want the paragraph break and pressing the Enter key; however, you still may need to reformat the first paragraph. But don't worry, most people use the same paragraph format all the way through.

Moving around

To work on another area in your document, move the insertion point. To move your insertion point by using the mouse, just click somewhere in your document. To move to another page, click the blue double-arrow buttons (shown in black, back in Figure 10-1) in the vertical scroll bar.

To move your insertion point by using the keyboard, press the arrow or other navigation keys, like Page Up and Page Down. Table 10-1 shows you how.

Table 10-1	Navigating with Keys
Navigation Key	*Where It Moves the Insertion Point*
←/→	One character's worth left or right
↑/↓	One line's worth up or down
PgUp/PgDn	One window's worth up or down
Home	Beginning of the line
End	End of the line
Ctrl+Home	Beginning of the document
Ctrl+End	End of the document

Document Views

One of the weird things about word processors is that they're all a little reluctant to show you *exactly* what your document looks like. Word offers you several ways of looking at your document (apart from printing it), with varying amounts of fidelity to how the document looks on the printed page.

Choose View⇨Normal or choose View⇨Print Layout to select one of the two main views:

- ✔ **Normal view** is best for actually writing text. It doesn't show page margins. It treats your document like a long, continuous scroll.

- ✔ **Print Layout view** is a bit more exact. You can see your page breaks and margins realistically. If you use page numbers, headers, or footers, Print Layout view shows them. Normal view doesn't.

Print Preview is not exactly a view, but it lets you see something that's as close to the paper printout as your word processing program can manage. For more on this feature, see Chapter 11.

As you add and delete text in your document, the page breaks move fairly often. In the Normal view, the top of each page is marked by an unobtrusive, dotted line. In the Print Layout view, your pages appear against a gray background, and a gap appears between one page and the next. This gap makes working in the vicinity of the page break — doing things like selecting text across the break — rather awkward. You probably want to use Normal view for most of your writing and then switch to Print Layout for any necessary final formatting.

Selecting Text for Editing or Formatting

To format or otherwise change a whole chunk of text at one time, you *select* or *highlight* that text. Because selecting works pretty much the same in all Windows programs, I put the details in the appendix.

In a nutshell, however, to select text, you can either hold down your left mouse button and drag the cursor across text, or hold down the Shift key and press the navigation keys on the keyboard. (The navigation key method is sometimes easier to control.)

Your word processing program has some funky selection quirks not found in other tools:

- When selecting with your mouse, the highlight envelops one character at a time within the first word, but in subsequent text, it switches to enveloping one word at a time. Sometimes that behavior selects more text than you want. However, if you back up the cursor (while still holding down the left mouse button), you then release individual characters from the selection.

- To select a line, click in the white area to the left of that line; to select several lines, hold down the left mouse button and drag the mouse.

- To select a paragraph, double-click anywhere in the white area to the left of the paragraph. To select several paragraphs, hold down the left mouse button when you make the second click, and then drag the text up or down.

- To select the whole document, choose Edit➪Select All (or press Ctrl+A or click in the white area to the left while holding down the Ctrl key).

Moving and Copying

If you want to rearrange the order of your sentences or paragraphs, Word provides a variety of features that let you reorganize your document by moving and copying blocks of text.

Basic cutting and pasting are pretty much the same in every Windows program, so I give details of those activities in the appendix. Following are two special tricks for word processing:

- **To move text:** Select the text, and then drag that selection with the mouse. The vertical bar that follows you as you drag shows you where the selection will go when you release the mouse button.

- **To copy text:** Do the same thing as for moving text, but hold the Ctrl key down while you drag.

Finding Elusive Fauna (Or, Where's That Word?)

In the jungle of words that is the typical document, losing track of important words and phrases is easy. Finding a word or phrase is no problem for your efficient and jungle-wise guide, the Find and Replace dialog box.

Before you give the Find and Replace dialog box its marching orders, click to put the insertion point wherever you want Find to start looking. (Press Ctrl+Home to put it at the beginning of the document.) Or, if you know that what you seek is in a certain area, highlight (select) that area. The Find feature then restricts its search to the selected area.

1. **Choose Edit⇨Find or press Ctrl+F.**

   The Find and Replace dialog box springs into action and presents itself for duty.

2. **Type the word or phrase that you want to look for in the Find What box.**

3. **Click the Find Next button or press the Enter key.**

   Word scurries forward into the underbrush and highlights (selects) the first *wildebeest* (or whatever word or phrase you're searching for) it finds. Highlighting makes doing stuff to the word (deleting, formatting, copying, or just observing) easy. Click in the document window to make any changes.

4. **Repeat Step 3 until you finish searching and then click OK.**

Word displays a dialog box to tell you when it has searched your entire document. Repeat Step 2 to change your search word.

5. **Press the Esc key or click the Cancel button in the Find box when you're done.**

Finding words by using fragments

Is it *wildebeest* or *wildebeast?* Your Find feature lets you type just the portion of the word or phrase that you are sure of (*wilde,* in this instance) or that identifies the stuff you're looking for (all *Microsoft* products, for instance). This method also works if you want both singular and plural *wildebeest(s).* Just leave off the *s.* (The Find Whole Words Only check box, described in the next section, must *not* have a check mark in it if this technique is to work.)

A useful alternative is to use a *wild card* in place of text you're not sure of — especially if that text is in the middle of a word or phrase. A wild card is a symbol that takes the place of one or more characters.

In the Word Find dialog box, you must first click the More button to reveal advanced features, and then click in the Use Wildcards check box to select it. Now you can type wild card symbols to represent parts of a word. The two most popular wild cards are the following: * for any set of characters (as in `wildeb*t`), and ? to represent any single character (as in `wildebe?st`). Word's Find dialog box offers additional symbols when you click its Special button, but they are too tricky to describe here. You can safely explore the special world of the Special button on your own, however!

Searching for Oscar Wilde and finding wildebeests

If you send the Find feature off to locate the word *Wilde* (a *Wilde* goose chase), the Find feature may return from the hunt with a *wildebeest* instead of Oscar Wilde. Very embarrassing for everyone. A more annoying example is when you're searching for text like *man,* which also appears in *man*y other words like *man*ufacture and hu*man.*

To tell the Find dialog box to search for whole words only (a bunch of characters set off by spaces or punctuation), first click the More button in the Find dialog box. Then click in the Find Whole Words Only check box to select it.

To find only capitalized words like Wilde, another alternative in the Find dialog box is to click in the Match Case check box (revealed in Word by clicking the More button in the Find dialog box). Then use a capital *W* in Wilde.

Replacing Wildebeests with Whelks

If you're typing along about wildebeests and suddenly realize that you meant *whelks,* not wildebeests, you have some personal problems that go beyond software, and I cannot attempt to deal with them here. I can, however, tell you how to replace *wildebeest* with *whelk.* Here's how:

1. **Narrow the area for your search and replace, if you can, by highlighting (selecting) that area.**

2. **Choose Edit⇨Replace or press Ctrl+H.**

   The Find and Replace dialog box springs into action.

3. **Type the word or phrase (say,** *wildebeest***) that you want to find in the Find What box.**

4. **Type the replacement word or phrase (say,** *whelk***) in the Replace With text box.**

5. **Click the Find Next button or press Enter.**

   The Replace feature scurries forward into the underbrush, and when it discovers your search word *(wildebeest)*, it highlights (selects) the word so that you can see whether this particular *wildebeest* is one that you want to replace.

6. **To replace the highlighted text, click the Replace button. To leave it alone, click the Find Next button.**

   Click the Replace button and — poof! Your wildebeest is a whelk and happy as a clam. If the wildebeest was capitalized, Word likewise capitalizes your whelk (which is pretty businesslike for an ungulate).

   To replace *all* instances of the search text without pausing for your permission in each case, click the Replace All button.

   Replace pops up a message box when it finishes searching the whole document (or whatever text you selected). Click OK.

When you're done with your replacing, press the Esc key or click Cancel to clear the dialog box.

Here are two tips for replacing:

✓ To replace a noun throughout your document, use the singular form (say, *wildebeest* or *whelk*) so that where you once had either wildebeast or wildebeests, you now have *whelk* or *whelks*.

✓ The Replace All button can be dangerous. If you want to change *days* to *weeks,* for instance, make sure that you're not changing Sun*days* to Sun*weeks*. Selecting the Find Whole Words Only check box (described in the preceding section) can help in these special instances.

Meeting the Mighty Thesaurus

Among the various critters roaming around in your word processing program is a thesaurus. Its basic job is to help you find alternative words. This thesaurus is convenient, although it's kind of a baby thesaurus that can't really hold a candle to a printed thesaurus (which is good, because they're generally flammable).

The following steps give you a click-by-click description of how to use the thesaurus:

1. Move your insertion point to or select (highlight) the word or phrase that you want to look up.

2. Choose Tools⇨Language⇨Thesaurus (or press Shift+F7).

The Thesaurus dialog box, shown in Figure 10-3, lumbers out of the wilderness.

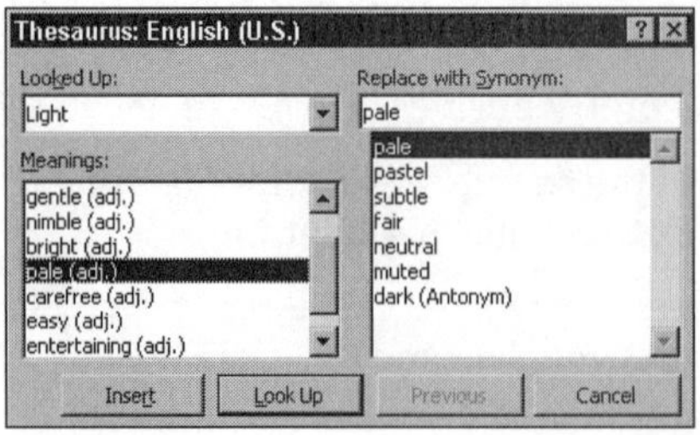

Figure 10-3:
The baby thesaurus in Word is not purple, but it still wants to be your friend.

Thesaurus: English (U.S.)	? X
Looked Up:	Replace with Synonym:
Light	pale
Meanings:	pale
gentle (adj.)	pastel
nimble (adj.)	subtle
bright (adj.)	fair
pale (adj.)	neutral
carefree (adj.)	muted
easy (adj.)	dark (Antonym)
entertaining (adj.)	
Insert	Look Up	Previous	Cancel

3. Click any replacement word or phrase you like, either in the Meanings box or in the list of synonyms that appear below the Replace With Synonym box.

Your substitute word can come from either list. If you click a *meaning*, you get a new list of synonyms to play with.

4. **To look for synonyms for your chosen synonym, click the Look Up button.**

   You can go from synonym to synonym all day. If at any point you want to return to an earlier synonym, click the down arrow adjoining the Looked Up box, and the whole list of what you've looked up so far drops down.

5. **When, in either list, you find a good substitute word or phrase, click it and then click the Replace button.**

   Your original word or phrase in the document is replaced.

Your new word or phrase may not be any better than your old one, but what a good time you had getting it there. Beats working!

Checking Your Spelling and Grammar

One of the classic advantages of using a word processor is that it supposedly can check your spelling. Actually, what the spell checker does is make sure that your document contains 100-percent genuine words — or words it thinks are genuine, anyway, because the words appear in a list of words called a *dictionary*. Word can also check your grammar at the same time that it checks your spelling, so I just call this feature a checker.

The checker does not make sure that you use words write. For example, the word *write* in the preceding sentence is indisputably a word; it just happens to be in the wrong place at the wrong time. The checker doesn't turn up anything wrong with that that sentence. The checker does, however, catch the repeated word *that* in the previous sentence. The spell checker also catches hyphenation and some capitalization errors.

Word can also check your text as you type, and anything that it doesn't like is underlined with a wavy line: red for spelling problems, and green for grammar. (If this feature annoys you, choose Tools⇨Options and then click the Spelling and Grammar tab and deselect the check box labeled Check spelling as you type.)

When you see a wavy line and the problem isn't obvious to you, do the following:

1. **Press F7, or on the toolbar, click the checker's button (the check mark with ABC on it).**

   The Spelling and Grammar dialog box appears (see Figure 10-4), which gives you some interesting suggestions for replacing the word or phrase it doesn't recognize.

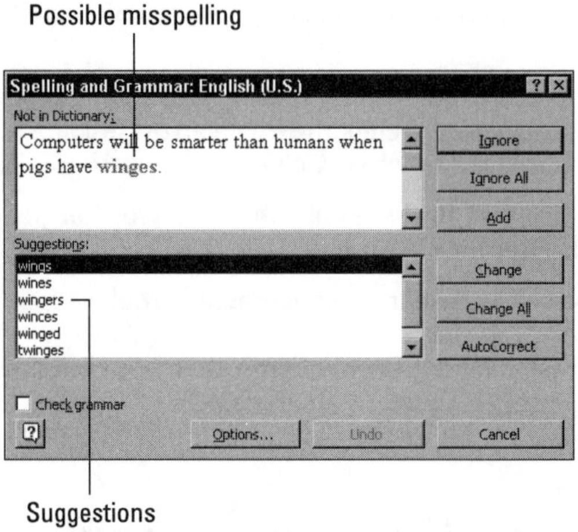

Possible misspelling

Figure 10-4:
Spelling and
Grammar
checking: as
much fun as
fifth grade.

Suggestions

Fortunately, the Spelling and Grammar dialog box often includes a good suggestion among the amusing ones (such as pigs having *wines,* the second suggestion in Figure 10-4), and all you have to do is choose that good one.

2. **To replace your original word with a word in the Suggestions list, click the word and then click the Change button.**

3. **If the word is actually okay, either click the Ignore button or click the Add button to add the word to the dictionary.**

   Click the Ignore button if the word is okay here but may be incorrect later in this document or in another document.

   Click the Ignore All button if the word is okay in this document (as *athwartships* may be in a document about sailboats) but may be a typo or misspelling in some other document.

   Click the Add button if the word is a real word (such as *atlatl*) that you may use again and again. The word is then added to the spell checker's Custom Dictionary and is thereafter and forever ignored in *any* document that you check. Be certain that the word is spelled correctly before you do this!

   After you choose one of the preceding actions, the checker moves on to scan the remainder of the document.

4. **You may also edit the original text directly in the checker's dialog box.**

   If you know that a correction is necessary, click the text in the upper Not In Dictionary text box and then edit it. Click the Change button to transfer the edit to your document and move along to the next apparent blunder in your text.

   Eventually, the spell checker reaches the end of your document and opens up a little box letting you know that the checking process is done.

5. **When you're finished, click OK.**

Chapter 11

Controlling Appearances and Printing

. . . .

. . . .

*Y*ou must keep up appearances. There is no excuse for frumpy fonts, untidy indentation, improper alignment, unkempt tab stops, and mis managed margins. Indeed, those who format fastidiously can even print sideways and control where their pages start and end.

In this chapter, I show you how to attain all those niceties of civilization — first-line indentation, line spacing, paragraph spacing, and more — automatically, without typing a bunch of tabs and blank lines. I work from the small to the large — from characters to paragraphs to documents — and explore how Word can help give your document a civilized and smart look.

Charming Characters

When your characters are losing their charm, it's time to look for a prettier face — typeface, that is (or *font,* as it is misnamed in the geeky world of computers). Word can put your type in any font or any size. But wait! There's more! You can also easily change your font's *style,* making it **boldface,** *italic,* underlined, ^{superscript} _{subscript,} or ~~strikethrough~~.

All told, you have three different kinds of formatting to play with: font, size, and style. These different aspects of type are called *character formatting.*

Word offers you three methods for formatting your characters:

✔ Use the formatting toolbar to change the type of font, font style, or font size. Clicking the B, *I,* or U buttons — just to the right of the center of the toolbar — puts bold, italic, or (single) underline style at your service. The toolbar's Font drop-down list box and Font Size drop-down list box (shown here) lets you choose from a range of font types or font sizes.

Times New Roman ▼	12 ▼

To use either box, click the down arrow attached to the box and choose from the list that drops down.

✔ Use the Font dialog box (shown in Figure 11-1) to choose from the complete range of fonts, sizes, and styles. Choose Format⇨Font to open this dialog box.

✔ Press Ctrl+B for bold, Ctrl+I for italic, and Ctrl+U for underline, to change the style.

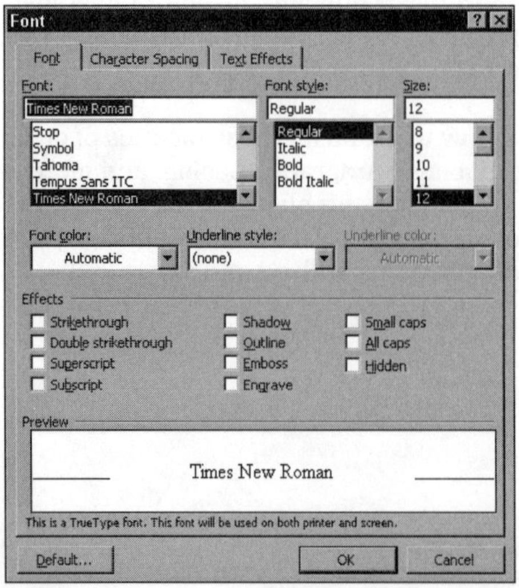

Figure 11-1: The Font dialog box offers more formatting options than the toolbar.

To change the format of the text that you're currently typing, use one of the preceding alternatives with no text selected. The formatting toolbar's boxes and buttons reflect the character formatting in effect at the point you are typing. To change the format of text after you type it, first select (highlight) that text and then choose one of the alternatives.

Pretty Paragraphs

There's no accounting for taste. (In fact, there's no Personnel, Purchasing, or any other department for taste.) Some folks like the first line of their paragraphs indented. Others, perhaps plumbing professionals, like them flush right. Some folks like their text double-spaced, and maybe they like bigger-than-average spaces between paragraphs, too. All this stuff is called *paragraph formatting*, which boils down to a few things that you can fool around with:

- ✔ **Indentation:** How far the paragraph's margins are indented from the page's margins.

- ✔ **Alignment:** How all the lines of the paragraph line up: against the left and/or right page margins, centered between them, or evenly spaced between them.

- ✔ **Breaks:** Whether to split up a paragraph when it crosses over onto the next page or to keep the paragraph as one solid lump; also, whether two paragraphs stay with each other on the same page.

One big deal about using paragraph formatting is that often you need to format only the first paragraph you type. As you type, you spawn new paragraphs from the original whenever you press the Enter key, and the same paragraph formatting applies to those descendants. (This inheritance will *not* happen in the relatively advanced situation where you apply a certain Word "style," such as Heading 1, to your initial paragraph, and that style happens to specify that the next paragraph should be in a particular style! If you don't use styles, delete that last sentence from your brain.)

Alignments: Making your lines line up

Alignments are the simplest kind of paragraph formatting, so I get them out of the way first. You can choose from four kinds of alignment.

Left, left.

Centered, centered, centered, centered, centered, centered, centered, centered, centered, centered, centered, centered, centered, centered.

Spooky formatting changes

If you find yourself typing in a format you didn't intend, you probably placed your insertion point just before a formatted character. The character may even be invisible (like a space, a tab, or a paragraph mark). Text entered at the insertion point always takes on the format of the character that precedes it. Press the Backspace key to remove the invisible character. (Check out Chapter 10 for details on seeing, typing, and deleting these invisible characters.)

Right, right.

Justified, justified.

Check out these two really easy ways to change alignment. First, select the paragraphs you want to realign (or, for a single paragraph, simply click to place your insertion point anywhere within it) and then do one of the following:

✓ **Click one of the following four formatting toolbar buttons.** The buttons are, in order, Align Left, Align Center, Align Right, and Justify.

✓ **In the Paragraph dialog box, select one of the four alignment options in the Alignment drop-down list box.** I explain the Paragraph dialog box later in this chapter.

Spaced-out paragraphs

Space is the final frontier of paragraph formatting. If you need a little air in your text, you can always ventilate your paragraph by double-spacing or by adding space between paragraphs. But you don't add spaces the way your grandparents did on their old Dumbrowski-Stanowitz steam-powered typing machine:

✓ Don't press the Enter key twice at the end of every line to double-space. (Don't even press it once at the end of every line.)

✓ Except for short, informal documents, don't press the Enter key twice at the end of every paragraph to put space between your paragraphs. Having two paragraph breaks makes going back to change your paragraph spacing both confusing and tedious. In addition, having to remember to press the Enter key twice means you're likely to make a mistake and enter it once, somewhere, or three times somewhere else. If you want consistent spacing that is easy to fiddle with, better to use Word's paragraph formatting properly from the start.

The quick way to add space between paragraphs is to press Ctrl+0. (That's zero, not the letter *O*.) This command puts one line of space before the current paragraph if that space isn't there already. If a line of space is already there, this action takes it away. You can also use keyboard commands to set the line spacing within a paragraph:

✔ Ctrl+1 single-spaces the current paragraph (where your insertion point is).

✔ Ctrl+2 double-spaces the current paragraph.

✔ Ctrl+5 imposes one-and-a-half-line spacing on the paragraph.

To change the spacing on a group of paragraphs, select them first. To change the spacing of all the paragraphs, press Ctrl+A to select them all.

You can also do this stuff (and lots more) with the Paragraph dialog box. See "Having it your way: The Paragraph dialog box," later in this chapter.

Quick indenting and outdenting

Indentation is one kind of paragraph format. A quick way to add left-side indentation to your paragraph is to select the paragraphs you want to indent (or, to indent a single paragraph, click anywhere in it), and then use Ctrl key combinations as follows:

✔ **To indent the left side:** Press Ctrl+M; the paragraph indents to the next tab stop (which, unless you add a tab stop, is the first so-called *default* tab stop, normally at ½ inch). Press Ctrl+M again, and your paragraph indents to the next tab stop, and so on. (The *default* is the setting that Word uses until you tell it otherwise.)

✔ **To left-indent every line but the first line of the paragraph (called a *hanging indent*):** Press Ctrl+Shift+H.

✔ **To undo any left-side indentation:** Press Ctrl+Shift+M; this action *outdents* (reverses indentation) by one tab (moves the left edge of the paragraph left one tab stop).

You also have toolbar buttons that do indenting and outdenting. The *outdent*ing button is on the left, as the following shows; the *in*denting button is on the right:

What's wrong with simply using the Tab key to indent everything, as you would on a typewriter? In Word, the Tab key does peculiar things. (See "The tab stops here," later in this chapter.) If you want to use the Tab key for indentation, I suggest that you use it only for left-side indentation of the first line or of the whole paragraph, and use it only after typing the paragraph. That is, click at the beginning of an existing line and then press the Tab key.

Pressing the Tab key normally inserts a tab character in Word. (For more about tab characters, see the next section, "The tab stops here.") However, in Word, when you click at the beginning of an existing line and press the Tab key, Word actually decides, "Whoa! This dude wants to add indentation to the paragraph formatting." It does not insert tab characters at the beginning of the line.

The indentation described here is limited to the default intervals (initially ½ inch). For more control over the indentation of a paragraph, you can either use the Paragraph dialog box or the ruler bar. Check out "Indenting with the ruler" and "Having it your way: The Paragraph dialog box" later in this chapter.

The tab stops here

You know all about tab stops, right? Those things that you used to set on your Smith-Corona where, when you pressed the Tab key, you moved to the next stop? Nice and simple. Well, tabs are a tad (or a tab) more complex than they were on the old Smith-Corona, but they also do a few new tricks.

Using the Tab key

The Tab key worked fine on typewriters, but it's kind of a problem for word processors, for complex reasons. (The reasons have to do with the fact that text flows freely from line to line as you edit on a PC, whereas on a typewriter, text stays put.)

As a result of this problem, the Tab key is actually obsolete for most uses. Indenting lines and creating tables are the most common reasons people use the Tab key. But paragraph formatting is a better way to indent; see the earlier section "Quick indenting and outdenting" for indentation instructions. And you're usually better off using an official Word table for tables (Word offers a whole menu for tables).

For more information on indentation, see "Having it your way: The Paragraph dialog box," later in this chapter.

Most of the time, the Tab key works much like it does on a typewriter: When you press the Tab key, the insertion point jumps to the next tab stop. (Unless you change the tab stops yourself, stops are at every ½ inch from the left margin.)

The big difference between tabs in your word processor and tabs on a typewriter is that in Word, when you press the Tab key in the middle of a line, you insert a special tab character (normally invisible), whose job could be described as "creating a space between the preceding character and the next tab stop." (If you want to see the tab character, click the Show/Hide Paragraph button on the toolbar.) "Fine," you say, "Who cares?" You care — if you edit the line after the tab! If, for instance, you delete enough text preceding a tab character that currently skips to the 1-inch tab setting, the tab skips to the ½-inch tab setting instead! Because all subsequent text in the paragraph moves left to fill the space, subsequent tabs in the same line or paragraph may also be seriously wrong!

Newfangled tab stops

Your old Smith-Corona typewriter had only one kind of tab stop. Word (like most word processors) has four kinds of tab stops:

- **Left tab stop:** The conventional tabs that you're accustomed to are called *left tabs* in a word processor, because after you press the Tab key, what you type begins after the stop; therefore, the text has its left edge at the tab. Your word processor uses left tab stops — unless you tell it otherwise (the default tab setting) — which are preset to appear every ½ inch.

- **Decimal tab stop:** To better align numbers that appear in a column, you may want to use the decimal tab stop, which aligns every number at the decimal point. You set the tab stop in the position where you want the decimal point to be (or at the end of a number without a decimal point). After setting up the tab stop, press the Tab key to advance to this stop and then type a number. Your word processor types — oddly enough — to the left of this stop. It continues to type to the left of the stop until you type a decimal point; then it types to the right of the stop.

- **Right tab stop:** Unsurprisingly, the right tab stop is the opposite of the traditional or left tab stop. Instead of the left edge of text aligning with this stop, the right edge does. When you type (having first set up the tab and then pressed the Tab key to move to this stop), your word processor shifts text over to the left, keeping the right edge of the text aligned with the tab stop.

✔ **Center tab stop:** After you set up one of these guys, press the Tab key to move to it and then start to type. Your word processor shuffles your characters left and right as you go, in order to keep your text centered on the tab position. Whatever you type ends up centered at the tab stop.

To see the four kinds of tab stops in action, skip ahead in this chapter and check out Figure 11-3.

How do you set tab stops? You can set all four types of stops with the help of the Tabs dialog box, which I introduce in the next section. Unless you need to set tabs very precisely, however, your word processor's *ruler* is often an easier tool to use for setting tabs. See the section "The ruler: A benevolent monarch," later in this chapter.

Setting, clearing, and changing tab stops in a dialog box

If you want something other than the conventional, every-½-inch tab stop, try using Word's Tabs dialog box, shown in Figure 11-2. You, too, can get one of these lovely dialog boxes by choosing Format➪Tabs.

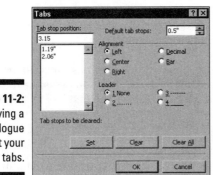

Figure 11-2: Having a dialogue about your tabs.

The Tabs dialog box works like this: You create one tab stop at a time — specifying its position, its alignment, and its (optional) leader (characters, such as a line of dots, that fill the space that the tab creates) — and then you click the Set button. As you create each new stop, your word processor adds it to the list of stops.

The blow-by-blow instructions for using the Tabs dialog box to add, remove, or modify a tab stop are as follows:

1. **Select the paragraphs whose tab stops you want to set or change.**

   If you don't select anything, your word processor assumes that you want to set tabs in the paragraph where the insertion point is. Select multiple paragraphs to give them all the same tab stops.

2. **Choose Format⇨Tabs. (If you don't see Tabs on the Format menu, click the double-arrow symbol on the bottom of the menu to display the complete Format menu.)**

   Any tab positions already set in the selected paragraph are listed in the largest white box at the left side of the dialog box. The interval at which default tab stops appear (0.5 inch initially) is listed in the Default Tab Stops box.

3. **To add a new tab stop, enter its position in the Tab Stop Position box.**

   Click the box immediately under the Tab Stop Position label and type in the position you want the tab stop to take (as measured from the left column margin). Whatever you do in the dialog box — changing alignment and so on — now applies only to that tab stop.

   To modify or delete (or clear) an existing tab stop, click it in the list box (the largest white area) at the left of the Tabs dialog box.

4. **Select an alignment for this tab stop in the Alignment area.**

   See the preceding section for a discussion of the different types of alignment.

5. **Click the Set button to add this tab stop to your paragraph.**

   When you add your own tab stops, your word processor removes any default tab stops between the left margin and your new tab stop. To review the tab alignments, just click them in the list box.

6. **To remove this tab stop, click the Clear button.**

7. **To clear out all the tab stops in this paragraph (except the default tabs), click the Clear All button.**

8. **Repeat Steps 3 through 5 to create additional tab stops until you have just the tab stops that you want in the Tab Stop Position list box.**

   To review the tabs' alignments, just click the tabs in the list box.

9. **Click OK.**

The Tabs dialog box also says something about a leader. No, the tabs haven't formed a political system. A *leader* is what your word processor puts in the area occupied by the tab character. For example, in a *table of contents,* you use a right tab between the topic and the page numbers, and you may want a line of dots or something in that space (as in the table of contents of this book). To associate a leader with a tab stop, select one of the styles shown in the Leader area; otherwise, select None.

Finally, if you really don't want to set a bunch of individual tab stops but want to change the intervals between the tab stops that your word processor provides (the default tab stops), just type a new interval in the Default Tab Stops box. These tab stops are important because your word processor uses them for indenting paragraphs.

The ruler: A benevolent monarch

Nothing keeps order like a good ruler, so your word processor comes equipped with a royal one. Sometimes your word processor is a *royal* something else, but this ruler is a benevolent monarch.

If your ruler is missing, choose View➪Ruler. (If you don't see it on the View menu, click the double-arrow symbol on the bottom of the menu to display the complete View menu.) Don't be shy; if a cat can look at a king, you can view your ruler. (The same command also lets you hide the ruler if it takes up too much real estate.)

The ruler reigns over indentations, alignments, and tab stops. A modest kingdom, perhaps, but an important one. See how it rules the indentations, alignments, and tab stops in the nonsensical paragraph shown in Figure 11-3.

Choose what kind of tab stop to set

Zero=Left page margin

Paragraph indent

Hanging indent, if any

First line indent

Left tab stop   Decimal tab stop

Right tab stop

Right paragraph indent

Right page margin

Figure 11-3:
The ruler: a kindly and powerful monarch in the word processing realm.

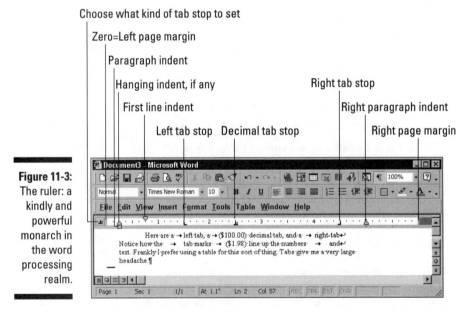

Notice how the left side of the paragraph in Figure 11-3 aligns with the paragraph indent mark. Also, the first line aligns with the first-line indent mark. (Pretty reasonable, huh?) Notice how text aligns in the paragraph with the left, decimal, and right tab stops, and with the right indent mark.

The ruler shows you what's going on in the paragraph that your insertion point is in. Or, if you select a paragraph, the ruler tells you about the paragraph you selected. The ruler can apply itself to only one paragraph at a time. If you select a bunch of paragraphs, it shows you what applies to the first one.

The totally, utterly cool thing about the ruler is that it not only *shows* you the paragraph stuff but also lets you *control* the paragraph stuff. Exciting, right? (If you find it exciting, I fear for your well-being, but read on, regardless.)

Indenting with the ruler

The exciting thing about using the ruler for indents is that the ruler lets you adjust them graphically. Just click the left or right indentation mark (check out Figure 11-3 to see where they are) and drag it. As you drag, you move the edges of the paragraph that your insertion point is currently on! To set the edges of a bunch of paragraphs, select the paragraphs before you drag the marks. (To set the edges of all the paragraphs in your document, press Ctrl+A to select everything!) These edges are technically called the left and right *paragraph indentations,* not paragraph margins. (Not to think of them as margins is hard, but that would be marginal thinking.)

The tricky thing about the pair of indentation icons (the small triangles on the left side of the ruler) is that they are related, like twins. The top half of this split pair controls only the first line of the paragraph. The bottom half of the pair controls the entire paragraph. These two triangles can be dragged independently, but if you want to move them both at the same time, drag the small rectangle icon beneath them.

So having said all that, I give you the blow-by-blow on changing paragraph indentations with the ruler:

1. **Select the paragraphs you want to indent.**

   If you don't select anything, Word assumes that you want to format the paragraph where the insertion point is.

2. **To indent the first line, drag the top of the pair of indentation marks on the left of the ruler bar.**

3. **To indent everything in the paragraph *except* the first line, drag the bottom of the pair of indentation marks on the left of the ruler bar.**

4. **To indent the whole paragraph, drag the rectangle icon just below the two indentation marks.**

5. **To indent the right side of the paragraph, drag the triangle on the right side of the ruler bar.**

You can also change indentations by using a dialog box. The dialog box is not as cool and graphical as the ruler, but the dialog box is more precise and is easier to use for those of us with poor hand-eye coordination. See "Having it your way: The Paragraph dialog box," later in this chapter.

Tab stops on the ruler

Your word processor already provides a nice set of built-in (default) tab stops, spaced every ½ inch. If you want other tab stops, follow this complicated instruction:

> Click in the ruler where you want your tab.

In Word's ruler, you can choose what kind of tab stop to set: left, right, center, or decimal. As you click the button that shows a tab symbol at the far left, the symbol cycles through the different varieties of tab stops you can set. When the symbol for the variety of tab you want appears, click in the ruler where you want that variety of tab. (Figure 11-3 shows the varieties.)

What if you don't like your tabs after you have them? Try the following:

- ✔ To move your tab marks around, drag 'em. The built-in default tabs that fall before or between your marks are removed.

- ✔ To remove one of your tab marks, drag it off the ruler and into the document, where it evaporates in the rarefied atmosphere of your prose.

Having it your way: The Paragraph dialog box

For one-stop shopping in the world of paragraph formatting, use the Paragraph dialog box, shown in Figures 11-4 and 11-5. This two-tab dialog box supplies nearly all your paragraph formatting needs. Indentations, alignments, breaks, mufflers — you name it; everything for the well-formatted paragraph except tab stops.

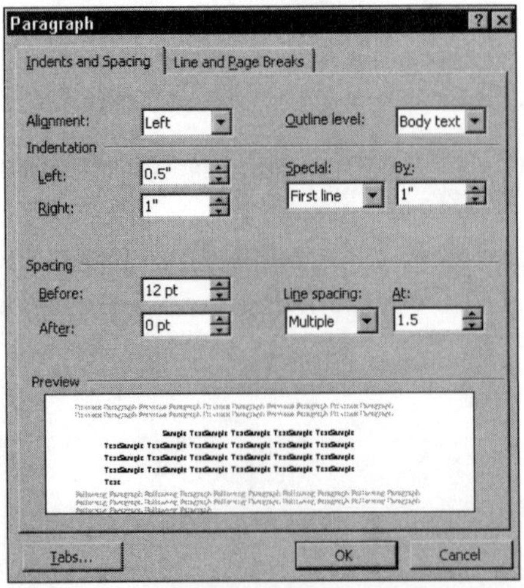

Figure 11-4:
The Indents
and Spacing
tab in the
Paragraph
dialog box.

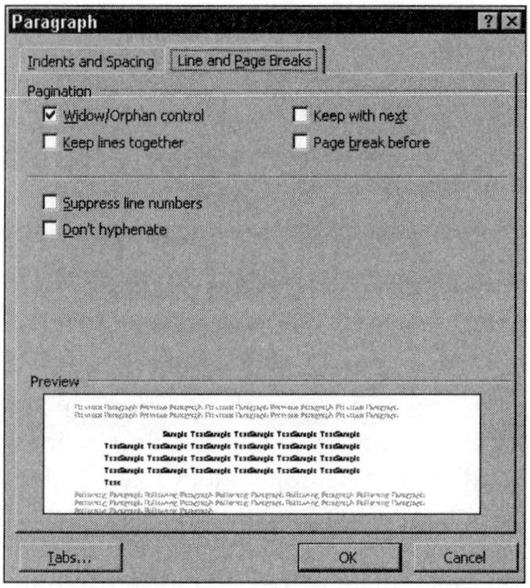

Figure 11-5:
The Line
and Page
Breaks tab
in the
Paragraph
dialog box.

Begin formatting a paragraph by placing your insertion point in a paragraph to be formatted or by selecting several paragraphs. Then you can open the Paragraph dialog box in either of two ways:

✔ Choose Format➪Paragraph.

✔ Double-click the left or right indent marks on the ruler bar.

The dialog box looks like two index cards — Indents and Spacing, and Line and Page Breaks. You can switch between the two tabs by clicking the top of the hidden tab. Both tabs have preview boxes that show you what the reformatted paragraph looks like on a page.

You use the Paragraph dialog box by making whatever changes you want on the two tabs and then clicking the OK button. Nothing changes in your document until you click OK. If you click the Cancel button at any time, you return to your paragraph without making any changes.

Indents and spacing

The Indents and Spacing tab (refer to Figure 11-4) controls not only indentations, but also the text alignment, the spacing between lines of the paragraph, and the spacing between paragraphs. The options are as follows:

✔ **Alignment:** Click to select Left, Right, Center, or Justified.

✔ **Outline Level:** A Word format that applies only in the Outline view, which I don't discuss in this book.

✔ **Left Indentation:** Sets the distance between the left paragraph margin and the left column margin.

- ✔ **Right Indentation:** Sets the distance between the right paragraph margin and the right column margin.

- ✔ **Special:** Specifies a first-line indentation or a hanging indent. Click the Special drop-down list box and select an indentation style, and then click the By box and enter the indentation distance.

- ✔ **Before Spacing:** The spacing you want preceding the selected paragraph(s).

- ✔ **After Spacing:** The spacing you want following the selected paragraph(s).

- ✔ **Line Spacing:** Specifies the spacing within the paragraph: Single, Double, or 1.5 Lines. Or, select Multiple and enter the spacing in lines (enter **3** if you want triple-spaced text) in the At box. Select Exactly if you prefer to specify spacing in points (typesetting measurements ½ inch per point) in the At box; in-line characters or graphics that are too tall to fit in that space will be chopped off. Select the At Least option not only to specify points, but also to allow your word processor to adjust for tall characters or graphics on a line.

Line and page breaks

The Line and Page Breaks tab of the Paragraph dialog box (refer to Figure 11-5) tells Word how each paragraph relates to its neighboring paragraphs and where to place page breaks with respect to paragraphs. Following are the various options on this tab and what they do:

- ✔ **Widow/Orphan Control:** Prevents Word from leaving a single line of a paragraph on one page, if the page happens to break mid-paragraph.

- ✔ **Keep Lines Together:** Keeps the entire paragraph on one page.

- ✔ **Keep with Next:** Keeps the paragraph on the same page as the start of the following paragraph. (Of course, if the combined paragraphs are more than a page long, the second will break and continue on the next page.)

- ✔ **Page Break Before:** Forces a page break before the paragraph. (This choice can be useful for the first paragraph of a chapter or section.)

- ✔ **Suppress Line Numbers:** If you're using line numbers (which this book does not discuss), this choice hides the number of the paragraph.

- ✔ **Don't Hyphenate:** Turns off Word's automatic hyphenation feature for the paragraph.

(Clicking the Tabs button, naturally enough, takes you to the Tabs dialog box.)

Having it their way: Styles

Often, you want to use a particular kind of formatting over and over again for consistency. All headings of a particular level in a document, for instance, should be similarly formatted, and most body text should appear the same. Word lets you format text with named *styles,* which can include character formatting, paragraph formatting, or a combination of both. If you change the definition of the style (say, increase the font size), everything in that style that has not been individually formatted changes accordingly.

In fact, Word has several built-in styles, including the default style, Normal, which is what it uses unless you select a different style. Word also offers three levels of heading styles and several body text styles. You can use Word's styles as they are, change them to your own preferences, or create your own from scratch.

The quickest way to apply one of Word's standard styles is to click in or select the paragraph(s) that you want to format and then select a style from the Formatting toolbar. Click the down arrow on the Style box, which is at the far-left end of Word's Formatting toolbar. (Unless you've fooled around with styles, the Style box probably has the word *Normal* in it.) Each style has a name and shows a format; click one to apply it.

The list that you get from the toolbar doesn't display the details of the formatting very clearly, however. If you need to review the details before applying a style, choose Format➪Style to open the Style dialog box. Click any style listed in the Style dialog box and read the description provided. Click the Apply button to apply that style to the paragraph where your insertion point currently resides (or to currently selected paragraphs).

Although I don't have the room in this book to get into templates in detail, you should know that styles (plus various customizations to Word) can be lumped together into something called templates, typically used in the creation of new documents. Chapter 8 talks a bit more about templates.

Having it your way: Creating your own styles

If you find yourself using the same combination of character and paragraph formatting again and again, you can add it to Word's list of styles. All you have to do is follow these steps:

1. **Click or select a paragraph that is already formatted the way that you want.**

2. **Choose Format➪Style and click the New button in the Style dialog box that appears.**

3. **In the New Style dialog box that appears, type a name for your style in the Name text box.**

4. **If you want this style to be available to you in future documents (those created by using the current *template* — usually the Normal template), select the Add to Template check box.**

5. **Click OK in the New Style dialog box and then click the Close button in the Styles dialog box.**

Now your newly named style appears on the list of styles on the toolbar, where you can easily select it to format any future paragraph.

Perfecting Your Page Layout

Most of this chapter talks about the small stuff: character and paragraph formatting. But what about the big picture? How big is a page, which way does it print, and what are the margins? Good questions. I'm glad you asked.

Word begins by assuming a bunch of stuff about the page — the *page defaults:*

✔ You're using 8½-x-11-inch paper, oriented the normal way for a letter.

✔ The top and bottom margins are 1 inch. Left and right margins are 1¼ inches. If you're using headers and footers, they are ½ inch from the top and bottom of the paper.

Word automatically inserts page breaks based on these settings and based on how you format your characters and paragraphs. You can also add page breaks manually (press Ctrl+Enter).

Most of the formatting-of-the-overall-document stuff is tucked away inside the Page Setup dialog box, which I discuss in the next section.

Page setup

To set up your document's overall appearance (which is not to imply that it looks like a pair of old overalls), do the following:

Choose File➪Page Setup.

This action wins you a Page Setup dialog box. When you first use this Page Setup command, the top tab is the Margins tab, shown in Figure 11-6. The tabs in this dialog box all deal with different aspects of page setup and printing. Click a tab, sticking out at the top, to choose it.

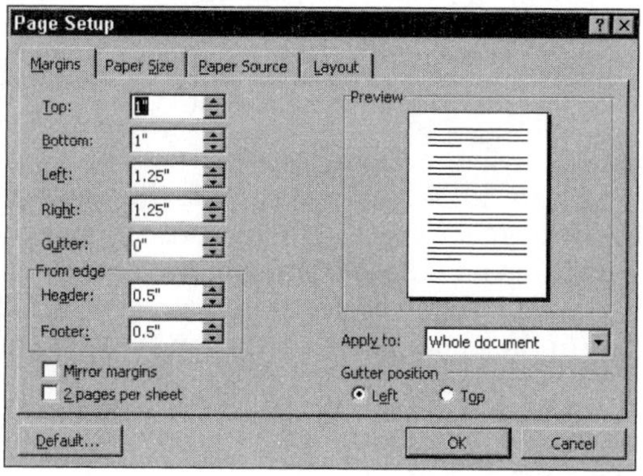

Figure 11-6:
Page Setup
has tabs like
Mom's
recipe card
file, but
without the
blueberry
pie stains.
One of these
is the
Margins tab.

Each tab in the dialog box also shows you a preview to give you a rough idea of what your document will look like with the changes you make. One quirk to be aware of is that if you type something into one of the boxes on these tabs (say, Top Margin), the preview doesn't show your changes until you click a different box on that tab (say, Bottom Margin) or press the Tab key.

Margins

In the Page Setup dialog box (choose File⇨Page Setup if the Page Setup dialog box is not already up), click the Margins tab. Then enter new values in the various margin boxes. Following are a few tips for setting margins:

✔ Headers and footers are supposed to fit within the top and bottom page margins, respectively. If you make the header or footer margin larger than the page margin, Word increases the page margin.

✔ The default unit is inches, so if you want inches, just type the number of inches you want. If you want to use another unit, type the number and then one of the following abbreviations for the unit: **cm** for centimeters, **mm** for millimeters, **pi** for picas, and **pt** for points. (Whatever you type, it will be converted to inches when you return to this dialog box later!)

✔ Remember that the preview doesn't show your changes until you click in a different margin box from the one you just edited or press the Tab key.

✔ To change margins, place your insertion point where you want the margins to change before choosing File➪Page Setup. And then click the arrow icon attached to the Apply To drop-down list box and select This Point Forward from the list that appears.

✔ If you're printing an *edge-bound document* that will be printed on both sides of the paper (a book, for example), increase the left margin to allow for binding space and then select the Mirror Margins check box. The left margin becomes the inside margin (for the bound edge), and the right margin becomes the outside margin. (That is, the margins are the "mirror image" of each other.)

✔ Another setting necessary for bound materials is the Gutter Position. The "gutter" is the white space created by the two adjoining inner margins of two facing pages in a bound document, like a magazine. Select the Gutter Position option based on where you are going to bind your pages (the long side of the paper like an ordinary book, or the shorter side like some books of cartoons, graphics, and so on).

✔ The 2 Pages Per Sheet option is useful if you're creating a folded flyer, where the printed matter appears inside the flyer. In other words, page 1 and page 2 are *both* printed on one side of the sheet of paper, and then it's folded.

Click OK when you're done setting up the page.

Sideways documents

Most printers these days let you print sideways (known to printers as *landscape orientation*). You can let Word know that sideways printing is what you have in mind by using the Page Setup dialog box (choose File➪Page Setup if the box is not already open).

In the Page Setup dialog box, click the Paper Size tab. Then select the Landscape radio button in the lower-left corner to print sideways. (Portrait is the other, more customary printing orientation, like the portrait of *Mona Lisa*.) The page icon, with the letter *A*, illustrates how type is to be printed on the page. The preview also changes to show you how the lines of text run.

To change printing orientation within a document (perhaps where large tables begin), first place your insertion point where you want the change to begin. Choose File➪Page Setup to open the Page Setup dialog box; then click the Paper Size tab, select your orientation, click the Apply To drop-down list box and select This Point Forward. To resume your earlier printing orientation on a later page, move your insertion point to that page and repeat the process.

Click OK unless you need to set up something else, such as the paper size.

Different-sized documents

If you're using anything other than 8½-x-11-inch paper (or if you're using an envelope), you need to tell Word about it. (Word has special features for envelopes; see Chapter 12 for details.) You can do so by following these steps in the Page Setup dialog box (choose File⇨Page Setup if the box is not already up):

1. **In the Page Setup dialog box, click the Paper Size tab.**

2. **On the Paper Size tab, click the Paper Size drop-down list box.**

3. **Select one of the standard paper or envelope sizes from the drop-down list.**

   If your paper size is not shown, click the Width box and enter a new value; then do the same for Height. (Width always refers to the direction that a line of text runs.) After your last change, click in a different box from the one that you're in and check the preview to see if things look roughly correct.

4. **Click OK when you're done setting up the page.**

Page breaks

After you fill one page, Word begins another page automatically as you're typing. If you want the page to break at an earlier location, you can put in a page break yourself. If you want the page to break later, forget it. Word can't squeeze any more on a page unless you change some formatting, such as reducing the font size.

Most of the time, the automatic page breaks are just fine because Word counts lines and measures spaces much better than humans can (it being a computer program and all). But occasionally, you know something that Word doesn't, such as the fact that this particular line is the start of a new chapter and really needs to come at the top of a page. Then you want to be able to insert a page break yourself.

You can tell Word not to put a page break within a paragraph or between two consecutive paragraphs. Take a look at "Line and page breaks," earlier in this chapter.

You can also put in a pair of page breaks to create a blank page or insert a page break to force a page to appear on the right side in a bound document (such as this book). Don't try this last trick until you finish all the editing. (Otherwise, you may have to repaginate the entire book.)

You can put in your own page break by following these two easy steps:

1. **Click exactly where you want the page break to occur.**

   Click the first line of a paragraph and then press the Home key to ensure you are at the very start of a paragraph, to avoid any problems with tabs or other invisible characters.

2. **Press Ctrl+Enter, or choose Insert⇨Break and then select the Page Break radio button.**

   A dotted line appears; this is your page break symbol. You can delete, cut, paste, or drag the page break symbol just like any other symbol on the page. To select the page break by itself, click the left margin next to the symbol.

After your page break, Word continues to do its own normal, automatic page-breaking thing. Let it. Don't do any more manual page-breaking than you absolutely must.

Printing

You may think that with all this computer wizardry, humans would advance beyond flattening a bunch of trees into thin sheets, smearing ink on them, and then tossing them away when they finish reading them. But no, computer use has actually increased paper consumption. In this section, I tell you how to get good printing results without wasting any more paper than absolutely necessary.

Previewing: Printing without paper

If you really want to save a tree, use Print Preview, shown in Figure 11-7. Print Preview shows you how your document will look in print, without wasting paper.

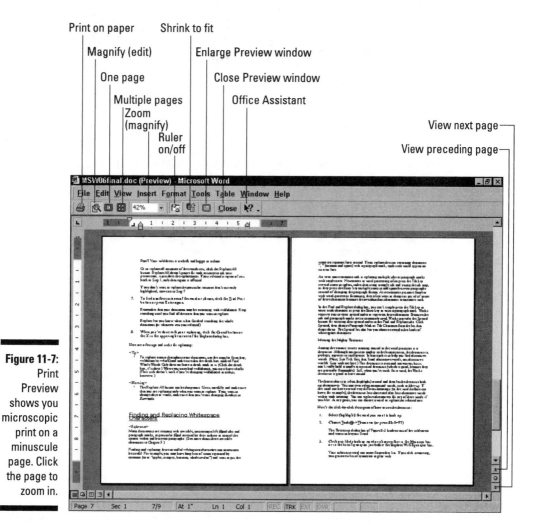

Print on paper
Shrink to fit
Magnify (edit)
Enlarge Preview window
One page
Close Preview window
Multiple pages
Office Assistant
Zoom (magnify)
Ruler on/off
View next page
View preceding page

Figure 11-7:
Print Preview shows you microscopic print on a minuscule page. Click the page to zoom in.

Most Windows applications provide a Print Preview feature similar to the one in Word.

You can get into Print Preview in one of two ways:

⍦ Choose File➪Print Preview.

⍦ Click the Print Preview button on the standard toolbar, as shown here:

Figure 11-7 identifies the various options in Print Preview.

To switch between maximum and minimum magnifications of the document, click the document itself. To magnify at intermediate levels, click the Zoom button and choose a magnification percent level.

When magnifying, use the vertical and horizontal scroll bars to view parts of the document that extend beyond the window. (See the appendix if scroll bars are new to you.)

Following are some additional tips for using Print Preview:

- ✔ The Print button starts the printing process immediately, without displaying a Print dialog box.

- ✔ The Magnify button is normally enabled (depressed), which means that clicking the document zooms you in or out. Click the Magnify button to disable it and then click the document to edit it.

- ✔ Click the Multiple Pages button and move your cursor diagonally across the array that appears to display a similar multipage array.

- ✔ The Shrink to Fit button adjusts font size to avoid having a fractional last page. Press Ctrl+2 to undo.

- ✔ The Full Screen button fills your monitor with a preview.

- ✔ Click Close, or press Esc, to return to your regular editing view.

Printing on actual paper!

The time has come to smear ink on dead trees. Printing is pretty simple when things go right. Do the following:

1. **Turn on your printer and wait until it comes on-line.**

   Most printers have an indicator light somewhere to tell you when the printer is paying attention to your PC. Consult your printer manual if you have questions. The latest printers do not need to be turned on at all when you request printing; they power up automatically. Much more sensible.

2. **To print the whole document right now (that is, you "don't need no stinking Print dialog box"), click the Print button on the standard toolbar (the button with picture of a printer on it).**

At this point, the rest is up to Windows and your printer. Read "Terminating printing," later in this chapter, if you change your mind about printing the document.

3. **To print the document in any other way, choose File⇨Print or press Ctrl+P.**

   The Print dialog box, shown in Figure 11-8, comes to your aid. Click OK when you're ready to print.

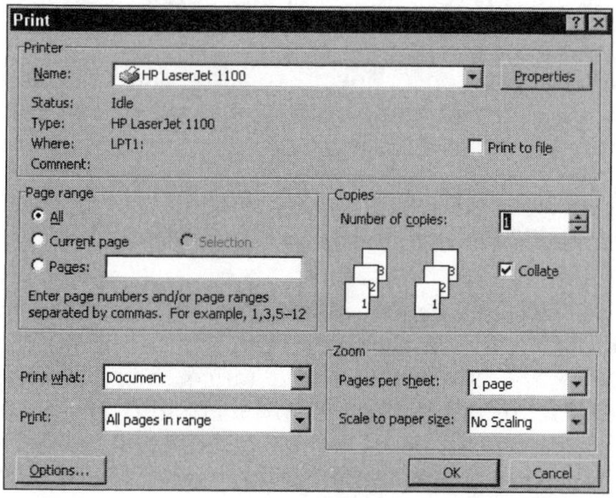

Figure 11-8:
Print what
you want,
how you
want it.

Use these features to make good use of the main printing options that Word provides in the Print dialog box:

✔ For *multiple copies,* click the Number of Copies box and enter the number of copies you want (but don't press the Enter key). If you want to print all the page 1 sheets in a batch, followed by a stack of all the page 2 sheets, and so on, deselect the Collate check box. Otherwise, the document will be printed with the pages in order, followed by a second copy of the entire document, and so on until the number of copies you requested have been finished.

✔ To print just the *current page* (where your insertion point is), select the Current Page radio button.

✔ To print *selected (highlighted) text in the document,* select the Selection radio button. The selected button is gray in Figure 11-8 (meaning it cannot be clicked). It's gray if you have not selected any of the text, so "print selected text" is therefore meaningless.

✔ To print a specific *group of pages,* select the Pages radio button and enter the page numbers as the instructions under the Pages box describe.

✔ To *print on both sides of the paper* (as for a bound document) — unless you have a two-sided printer — first check your printer manual to make sure that you can manually reinsert paper. If all systems are go, print the odd-numbered pages first by selecting Odd Pages in the Print drop-down list box. When the odd pages finish printing, reinsert the pages blank-side-up in the printer (with the top edge pointing the same direction as before), and then go back to the Print drop-down list box and select Even Pages. Before printing the even pages, check the stack of pages to be sure that page 1 will be taken first (so that page 2 goes on the flip side of page 1). If the order is reversed, click the Options button and then select the Reverse Print Order check box.

✔ To *change to another printer* (or "print" to a fax modem — another way to say *send a fax*), click the Name drop-down list box and select a printer (or fax modem).

✔ To use any of the *special options of your printer,* click the Properties button. A printer-specific dialog box appears. Check your printer manual for instructions.

✔ To print several pages on a single sheet of paper, click the Properties button and adjust the Pages per Sheet option in the dialog box that appears. If you set the option to 4, for instance, then a single sheet of paper will contain four of your pages shrunk to fit (the size of the type will be very small). This is useful if you want to create a set of thumbnails, showing the overall formatting of the pages side by side.

✔ The Scale to Paper Size option allows you to specify a different paper size than the one you're actually using. In effect, you can use this feature to enlarge or shrink your pages just as you can on most copiers. For example, if you're using 8½-x-11 paper, but specify 4⅛-x-9½ Scale, considerable white space will appear around the text (about 2 inches on the sides and top, and 4 inches on the bottom), and the text will shrink (the entire printed page will measure about 3 x 4 inches).

Although both the Pages per Sheet and Scale to Paper Size options are located in the Zoom area, I suggest that you avoid trying to *combine* them. These features do different things and aren't intended to be used at the same time.

Terminating printing

If you just sent your resumé to the printer and you discover that your boss is standing next to the printer, you need to take action, fast! Here's what to do.

Don't just turn off the printer. Your paper may get stuck halfway, and your PC may get confused and send you error messages. Don't just turn off the PC, either, or it may be confused when you restart it.

Depending upon what printer you use, a dialog box for your printer may appear on your screen as soon as you click OK in the Print dialog box (Step 3 of the preceding section). If such a dialog box appears, click the stop button (sometimes marked with a black square). I can't tell you exactly what to click because the dialog box comes from your printer's manufacturer. Check your manual for details.

If no dialog box for your printer appears on your screen, Windows provides a quick emergency stop procedure, which is outlined in these steps:

1. **Double-click the printer icon on the system tray (the space on the right side of the taskbar where the current time is displayed).**

   A dialog box appears with the same name as your printer, and displays your file's name.

2. **Right-click on your file's name and choose Cancel Printing from the context menu that pops out.**

   Printing may continue for a page or so, depending on how many pages are already downloaded to your printer's memory.

Chapter 12

Dressing Up Your Document and Sending It Out

. . . .

In This Chapter

▶ Making bullets

▶ Repeating yourself with headers and footers

▶ Paging all numbers (or numbering all pages)

▶ Comparing footnotes

▶ Setting up tables

▶ Surrounding your text with lines and borders

▶ Building columns

▶ Printing addresses on envelopes and labels

. . . .

*Y*ou've seen your document through the basics: writing, editing, formatting, and printing. Now your document is grown up enough for you to dress it up, introduce it to society, and generally have a little fun. (*Fun* in the highly abstract, metaphoric sense of the word, that is. If you really find yourself eagerly looking forward to word processing, you may want to consider enlisting the aid of a competent lifestyle advisor.)

Dress your document in a top hat and tails: Add some headers and footers! Teach its pages to do a few numbers; show it how to dance some footnotes, sit down correctly at a table, go to a few shady places across the border, and still get written up nicely in columns. Then send it out "enveloped" with pride!

One way to make a fancier document is to add graphics of various kinds, such as charts, photographs, or other pictures. This chapter discusses charts; see Chapter 13 for tips on dealing with every photo issue *except* the paparazzi.

Bulleted Lists: Shooting from the Toolbar

It's a jungle out there, and a few bullets may come in handy — bulleted lists, that is. Bulleted lists are made up of indented paragraphs like these:

- Each paragraph has
- a little dot next to
- its first line.

If you want simple, big-black-dot-style bullets, you can get them easily by clicking the Bullets button on the toolbar. (The icon on the Bullets button looks like a bulleted list.) All you have to do is type your paragraphs in the usual way, select (highlight) the ones you want bulleted, and click the Bullets button.

In Word, a bullet is a special character, separated from the text by a tab character. Word uses a hanging indent of ¼ inch and places a left tab stop at the ¼-inch point to make the text line up. (You can adjust this indentation in the Bullets and Numbering dialog box, discussed in the next section.) For some bulleted lists, you may also want to indent the whole bulleted paragraph: Press Ctrl+M to increase the indentation by one tab stop. Press Ctrl+Shift+M to reduce the indentation by one tab stop.

You can remove bullets without an anesthetic. Just select the proper paragraphs and click the Bullets button again.

Bullets behave like paragraph formats do: When you press Enter within any bullet-formatted paragraph, you get a new, pre-bulleted paragraph. This feature lets you type with bulleting *on* and spawn new bulleted paragraphs as you go. To stop using bullets, click the Bullet button. (You can also stop bullets by positioning your cursor at the start of a bulleted paragraph, and then pressing the Backspace key.)

Heavy Ammo: The Format Bullets Dialog Box

Bullets of any make and caliber are available from the Bullets and Numbering dialog box. To use this dialog box for your ammo, just right-click anywhere in your text and then choose Bullets and Numbering from the menu (called a *context menu*) that pops up.

In the Bullets and Numbering dialog box, simply click a bulleting style — or disarm your selected paragraphs (remove their bullets) by clicking the None option. Then click OK.

Word comes with dozens of really cool bullets boasting color, shading, 3-D effects, and more — even a couple of animated ones! To see the catalog, click the Picture button in the Bullets and Numbering dialog box. You can then scroll through the huge Picture Bullet catalog. Right-click on the one you want and choose Insert from the menu that appears. And if you're super picky and cannot find *exactly* the bullet that you want, click the Clips Online button to import more of them via the Internet.

Convinced that no one out there can make a better bullet than little old you? Need more space between your text and its bullet? Visit the custom bullet shop by clicking the Customize button in the Bullets and Numbering dialog box. The Customize Bulleted List dialog box opens its doors to you.

Any character in any font on your PC can become a bullet; just click the Bullet button to select your symbol. Click the Font button to adjust the bullet size or select a different font by using the familiar old Font dialog box that I introduce in Chapter 11.

Page Numbers, Headers, and Footers

Headers and *footers* are chunks of text that appear in a special location, either at the top (header) or at the bottom (footer) on every page of a document. You typically use headers and footers for chapter or section titles or to remind everyone who the author is.

A *page number* is an automatically computed number that appears in a footer or a header. It appears either by itself or with other text, such as after the word *Page*. You can insert page numbers while creating headers or footers, or use the separate Page Number dialog box, described in the following section.

Inserting automatic page numbers

If all you want is plain old page numbers without having to think about this footer and header stuff, choose Insert➪Page Numbers. The Page Number dialog box that appears gives you several options:

- ✔ **Position:** Select Top of Page (Header) or Bottom of Page (Footer).
- ✔ **Alignment:** Select Left, Right, or Center; or for documents such as bound books, select Inside (the edge the binding is on) or Outside (used in the very book you're holding).
- ✔ **Show Number on First Page:** Most documents don't bother numbering the first page. Select this check box if you prefer to number page 1.

✔ **Format:** This button leads you to a dialog box where you can select fancy options for numbering pages. Several options involve complicated schemes for automatically numbering sections or chapters — topics that I don't explore in this book. The others are

- **Number Format:** Click to select Roman numerals or letters.

- **Page Numbering:** In the Start At box, click the up and down arrows to start at some number other than 1 (or *i* if you are an ancient Roman) or enter that number here.

Word automatically keeps page numbers up-to-date as you add or delete pages.

Creating headers and footers

A header or footer is text that is reproduced on every page of a document. Usually the text of a header or footer is exactly the same on every page, but a few special cases exist, all of which the headings of this very book illustrate. One special case is page numbers, which change automatically for every page. (For every page to have the same number would be kind of useless.) Another special case is the first page of a document (like the first page of each chapter in this book). The third special case is header or footer text that differs between odd-numbered and even-numbered pages.

To put a header or footer into your document, just follow these instructions:

1. **Choose View➪Header and Footer. (Or if you're in Print Layout view, where the headers and footers appear in light gray, double-click the header or footer.)**

   This step does several things. First, it plops a floating Header and Footer toolbar (a toolbar that you can drag around) on your screen, as shown in Figure 12-1. Second, it puts your document into Print Layout view. Third, it moves the insertion point to the header area on the current page. Header and footer areas are enclosed by a dashed line marked with a Header or Footer label.

2. **Choose whether to work on a header or footer.**

   If you start out working in a header, you can switch to a footer by either scrolling down in your document window to the footer and clicking there, or by clicking the Switch Between Header and Footer button shown in Figure 12-1.

3. **Click the Insert AutoText button (see Figure 12-1) to choose from pre-designed header or footer text, which includes various page numbering styles and options for inserting the date, the time, your name, or the document name — or any combination of these.**

   The AutoText selections may well be everything you need. If they're not quite perfect, you can edit them or type in your own stuff.

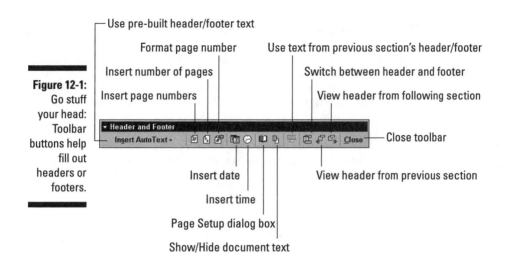

Use pre-built header/footer text

Format page number   Use text from previous section's header/footer

Insert number of pages   Switch between header and footer

Insert page numbers   View header from following section

Figure 12-1:
Go stuff
your head:
Toolbar
buttons help
fill out
headers or
footers.

Close toolbar

Insert date   View header from previous section

Insert time

Page Setup dialog box

Show/Hide document text

4. **Edit or type your own header or footer text.**

   Anything that you can do in ordinary text, you can do in a header or footer. You can use italics, giant fonts, different alignments, Word styles — anything goes.

   In addition to typing, you can insert special text from the toolbar: the page number, the total number of pages in the document (for text like Page 3 of 15), or a date or time that is updated every time you open or print the file. Figure 12-1 shows you which buttons to click.

   Word automatically numbers pages as the header or footer is reproduced on each page. Although you see only the current page's number at the moment, each page always displays its proper page number. Don't think you need to make a new header or footer for each page!

5. **For a special header on the first page, or for different headers on odd and even pages, click the Page Setup button (refer to Figure 12-1).**

   The Page Setup dialog box appears, laying out its Layout tab. Select one or both check boxes: Different Odd and Even, and Different First Page. Click OK in that dialog box to return to your document. Scroll through your document to the appropriate page (the first page, or an odd- or even-numbered page), and click in its header or footer area to create your header.

6. **For special page numbering, like Roman numerals, click the Format Page Number button.**

   See the discussion of the Format button in the preceding section, "Inserting automatic page numbers."

   When you're done with the Page Setup dialog box, click OK.

Adjusting header and footer margins

Anyone who has ever slept in a short bed is sensitive to having suitable margins for their headers and footers. To change your header or footer margin, choose File⇨Page Setup to open the Page Setup dialog box. Click the Margins tab and type in a new margin value for your header or footer in the text boxes under the label `From Edge`.

Headers and footers are supposed to appear within (be less than) the top and bottom page margins, respectively. If you make header or footer margins larger than the page margins, Word adjusts the page margins.

Footnote Fundamentals

When I get old (which should be by next Friday, at the very latest), I won't bore younger people with tales of how I trudged miles to school in the deep snow. Oh, no — I plan to bore younger people by telling them how I used to do footnotes before word processors existed. But if you want to be bored, you don't need me; you can just read the Word manual. (Besides, how can I tell whether you're younger than I am?)

Here's how to create automatically numbered footnotes:

1. **Put the insertion point just after the text that you want to footnote.**

2. **Choose Insert⇨Footnote. (If you don't see *Footnote* on the Insert menu, click the double-arrow symbol at the bottom of the menu to display all the options.)**

   The footnote footman (in the form of a Footnote and Endnote dialog box) comes to your aid.

3. **Choose either Footnote (to put your note at the bottom of the page) or Endnote (to put your note at the end of the document), and click OK if you want a normal, numbered footnote.**

   If you prefer asterisks or some other symbol, select the Custom Mark radio button. Then type the mark that you want (usually * or **) in the Custom Mark text box and click OK.

4. **The insertion point moves to the footnote area at the bottom of your current page, right after an automatic footnote number. Type in your footnote text, beginning with a space (for appearance's sake).**

5. **To return to your place in the text, double-click the footnote number (or other symbol) in the Footnotes window.**

To delete a footnote, just delete its reference mark in the text (you have to press the Delete or Backspace key *twice*). The mark *and* the footnote go away, and the remaining footnotes are renumbered.

Serious scholars may need to adjust the location of footnotes, choose a different number format, or adjust the starting numbers. Word provides controls for such changes, which you can find by clicking the Options button. Their use is straightforward, and so is "left as an exercise for the student."

Tables

Word lets you create nearly any kind of table you can imagine, but its table-handling features can be a bit overwhelming. The following sections should help reduce the confusion.

Creating a table

Tables work best if you first start a new paragraph and then create your table — although you can certainly insert a table in the middle of an existing paragraph if you like.

Each cell (square) of your table has the same formatting as the paragraph in which you insert the table. For a nice, cleanly formatted table, select Normal from the Style box on Word's Formatting toolbar and check the toolbar to make sure bullets and numbering are turned off.

Word gives you several ways to make tables. Here's the most straightforward way:

1. **Choose Table⇨Insert Table.**

   The Insert Table dialog box appears on the scene.

2. **Size your table.**

   Enter the number of rows and columns that you need into the Number of Columns and Number of Rows boxes. Don't forget to add a row for your column heads and a column for your row heads.

3. **Click the AutoFormat button to format your table.**

   The Table AutoFormat dialog box, shown in Figure 12-2, makes an appearance. On the left side of the dialog box is a list of possible formats. Each time you click a name, the Preview box on the right changes to show you how that format looks.

   To further customize a format, you can disable its borders, colors, chosen font styles, or heading row or column. Select or deselect various check boxes in the bottom of the Table AutoFormat dialog box, as shown in Figure 12-2, and watch the result in the Preview box. If your table has a row or column of totals, select the Last Row or Last Column check box. To automatically size the table to fit its contents, select the AutoFit check box.

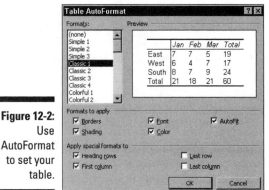

Figure 12-2:
Use
AutoFormat
to set your
table.

4. **OK! OK! Click OK in the Table AutoFormat dialog box and then click OK in the Insert Table dialog box.**

   Pouf! Your table is ready, *monsieur* or *madame*. Simply click any cell and then type to fill it in. You can put or format nearly anything in a table — including tab stops (decimal tabs are useful for columns of numbers), illustrations, and bulleted paragraphs — but you can't insert a table in a table!

Modifying your table

Tables in Word are immensely flexible. Following are some tips for modifying your tables. Most tips involve commands on the Table menu on the menu bar; you can often give the same commands by right-clicking on the table and choosing the command in the context menu that appears.

   ✔ To select multiple cells, drag across them.

   ✔ To select (highlight) an entire row, column, or the entire table so that you can format its contents, delete it or its contents, or do something else to it, click the row, column, or table and choose Table➪Select Row, Table➪Select Column, or Table➪Select Table. Or you can just drag your mouse across it.

   ✔ To insert a new row above the row where your insertion point lies, choose Table➪Insert Rows.

   ✔ To insert a new column, choose Table➪Select Column and then choose Table➪Insert Columns. To insert multiple new columns, drag across the many existing columns before issuing the commands.

   ✔ To insert new cells, select one or more existing cells and then choose Table➪Insert Cells. The Insert Cells dialog box that appears lets you choose which direction to shift existing rows or columns.

✔ To adjust column width, slowly move your cursor over the dividing line between columns until the cursor changes to a double line with arrows. Then click and drag the line.

✔ To adjust row height (or nearly anything else about the table), select the rows you want to change and then right-click on them. Choose Table Properties from the menu that appears, and the Table Properties dialog box makes a scene, displaying tabs with controls for all kinds of stuff. To adjust rows, click the Row tab in that dialog box. Click in the Specify Height check box to select it, and enter a new height value to the right. The At Least option in the Row Height Is box means that the row height will also adjust upward to fit the contents; to fix the row height, click At Least and choose Exactly to take its place.

Borders and Shade

Nothing like a few good lines and a little shade to liven up a party! Word's got 'em, in the form of *borders* and *shade* around paragraphs or pages. Borders are boxes around text; shade (well, *shading,* actually) is a colored background behind the text. You find these options by choosing Format⇨Borders and Shading.

I'll give you the details in a minute. First, here are a few shady, borderline tips on how to use borders:

✔ To create a horizontal line, apply a bottom or top border to a paragraph (see "Marking your borders," later in this chapter, for details).

✔ To create a vertical line, apply a left or right border to your paragraph(s).

✔ You can apply borders or shade to nearly anything — one paragraph, a group of paragraphs, or every page in your document — by using different styles, line types, and colors.

✔ Because borders and shade are actually a sort of paragraph formatting, if you spawn a new paragraph by pressing the Enter key in a bordered or shaded paragraph, the new paragraph is bordered or shaded, too.

✔ Consecutive, identical paragraphs, identically bordered or shaded, merge into one bordered or shaded block.

Selecting what to border or shade

You can apply borders or shade to darn near anything. Just select the "anything" first:

✔ To border or shade a single paragraph, click anywhere within the paragraph.

✔ To border or shade a group of paragraphs, select the group (double-click in the left margin and drag).

For this effect to work well, the selected paragraphs should all have the same left and right indents. With the group selected, drag the left and right indent marks on the ruler to set common indentations.

✔ To border or shade any old chunk of text, select the text.

✔ To border an illustration, click it. (Shading is not available for illustrations.)

Marking your borders

Here's how you, too, can create borderline documents, just like the pros. With your target selected, do the following:

1. **Choose Format⇨Borders and Shading.**

   The border patrol arrives on the scene in its three-card, four-wheel-drive dialog box. Have your passport ready.

2. **Click the Borders tab to put borders on paragraphs. Click the Page Border tab to border entire pages.**

   Figure 12-3 shows the Borders tab. The Page Border tab is nearly identical.

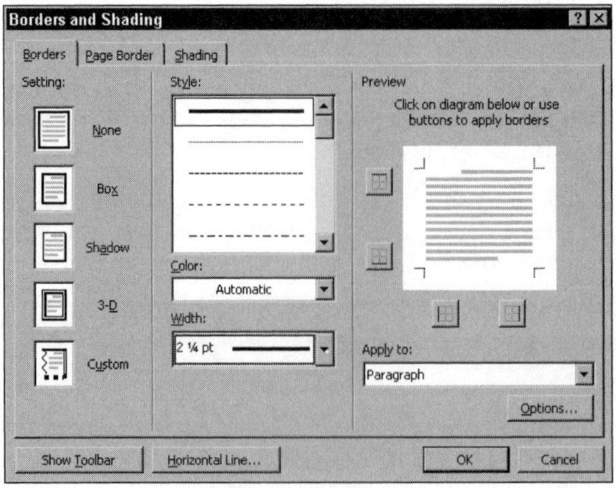

Figure 12-3: Selecting fine bordeaux.

3. **Choose a border Setting (appearance), line Style, Color, and line Width.**

   Click stuff and see what happens in the Preview box. You need not make your selections in any particular order.

4. **If you don't want a complete outline border, click individual borders (left, right, top, bottom) in the Preview box to turn them off. (Click again to restore a border.)**

5. **To use different line styles, colors, and widths for different borders, adjust those attributes in the Style, Color, and/or line Width boxes, and then click a border in the Preview box.**

   (Click the Horizontal Line button in the Borders and Shading dialog box to see zillions of graphic lines that you can drop into your pages to liven them up. Right-click on the one you want and choose Insert from the menu that appears.)

6. **Examine the Apply Style To box and make sure that your border is being applied as you intended (to one or more paragraphs, some selected text, or one or more pages).**

   If you're using the Page Border tab, your main choices are Whole Document, This Section – First Page Only (translation: page 1 of your document), and This Section – All Except First Page (translation: all pages *but* page 1). (In most of this book, because I don't discuss sections much, I assume your entire document is a section.)

7. **Click OK in the dialog box.**

To delete a line, choose Format⇨Borders and Shading, and then click the line again — to toggle it off — in the Preview section of the Borders and Shading dialog box. You cannot delete these lines by simply using the Delete or Backspace keys, nor can you select these lines.

Making shady paragraphs

If you have a really red-hot paragraph, you can draw the reader's attention to it by putting it in the shade. By selecting multiple paragraphs, you can create one continuous block of shade for all of them to lounge in. Here's how:

1. **Select your target and then choose Format⇨Borders and Shading.**

   You should now be looking at the Borders and Shading dialog box.

2. **Click the Shading tab if it's not already displayed.**

3. **For a solid background, click one of the shades of gray or a color in the Fill area on the Shading tab.**

4. **For a patterned background blended from two colors (including black and white), select the first color in the Fill area, select a percentage in the Style box, and then select the second color in the Color box. Observe the effect in the Preview area.**

5. **Click OK in the dialog box.**

Keep your eye on the Preview box as you go to make sure that you aren't creating something hideous. Hideosity happens — there's a little Dr. Frankenstein in all of us.

Columns

You can't have a newsletter, newspaper, or magazine without columns. So if you're pursuing a career in self-published journalism, you need to know how to put your text into columns.

You can either put the entire document into columns or start columnizing (columnifying?) — well, change the number of columns, then — from your insertion point forward. Just follow these steps:

1. **Choose Format⇨Columns. (If you don't see *Columns* on the Format menu, click the double-arrow symbol at the bottom of the menu to display all the options.)**

   The Format Columns dialog box appears, as shown in Figure 12-4. (If you are not already working in Layout view, Word — or its paper clip guy, who squawks and clinks first — asks if you want to switch to that view; click Yes.)

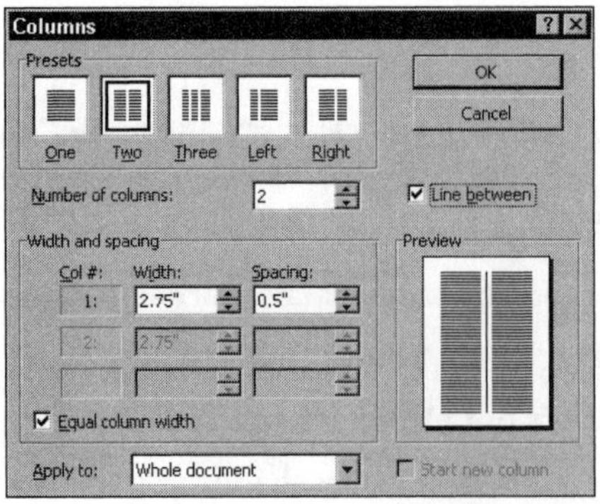

Figure 12-4:
Getting
columnar.

2. **Click the number of columns that you want in the Presets area or enter a number in the Number of Columns box.**

3. **If you don't want columns of equal width, deselect the Equal Column Width check box.**

4. **Enter how wide you want your columns in the Width box(es).**

   If your columns are of equal width, the width that you enter in the Col # 1 row applies to all columns.

5. **Enter the amount of space you want between the columns in the Spacing box.**

6. **Select the Line Between check box if you want a vertical line between your columns.**

7. **Click the Apply To drop-down list box and select This Point Forward if you intend to affect the column only from the insertion point forward.**

   You probably want the following text to begin a column. If so, select the Start New Column check box.

8. **Click OK.**

Here are a few tips for dealing with Word quirks when using columns:

- ✔ If you're using columns to create a newsletter, you probably want a banner at the top of the newsletter, spanning all columns. Create the banner by using a single column, and then in the subsequent paragraph, switch to multiple columns.

- ✔ Text flows automatically through the columns. To force a particular piece of text to wrap to the top of a column, insert a column break: Choose Insert⇨Break, and then in the Break box that appears, select Column Break.

- ✔ To create *balanced columns* (in which every column has equal length), click at the end of the text, choose Insert⇨Break, and then in the Break box that appears, select Continuous.

The Envelope, Please!

May we have the envelope, please? And the winner is . . . you! You win because printing envelopes and labels is one of the dirty little jobs that Word makes easier than it used to be. In the dark ages of word processing (seven or eight years ago), printing envelopes or labels was a job that took a squadron of software engineers five phone calls to the printer and software vendors, four Tylenol tablets, and ultimately, a ballpoint pen. (Another tale I can bore young people with when I get old.)

Don't toss out the ballpoint pen yet. Some days, turning on the PC and printer to address an envelope is just not worth the effort!

Creating and printing an envelope

Printing a single envelope is usually a pretty fast job in Word. Word knows all about your printer and makes all the right choices about sending the address to it. Usually. So, usually, the following steps go quickly, despite the length of this section. The reason these instructions are as long as they are is so that you can check out all of Word's choices. When envelope printing doesn't go well, the result is a lot of frustration and expense as you chew up envelope after envelope. Here's what to do to minimize hair pulling:

1. **If your document is a letter and already has the recipient's name and mailing address in it, select (highlight) the name and address portion.**

   Otherwise, move on to Step 2.

2. **Choose Tools⇨Envelopes and Labels.**

   The Envelopes and Labels dialog box makes an appearance.

3. **Click the Envelopes tab and examine the Delivery Address text box.**

   If, in Step 1, you initially highlighted the recipient's name and address in your letter, it appears in the Delivery Address text box. You can edit the recipient's address now if you like. If you didn't select an address, this text box is blank, and you can fill it in by clicking the text box and typing.

4. **Click the Return Address text box.**

   If you have never printed an envelope before, the Return Address text box is empty. Type in your name and address. If you have printed an envelope before and saved the return address as the default return address, the default address is displayed here; edit the return address if you need to.

5. **Click the Options button to check or change settings.**

   You probably don't need to change anything, but checking the settings is a good idea. The Envelope Options dialog box appears with two tabs: Envelope Options, and Printing Options. These tabs give you the chance to make sure that you're printing on the correct size envelope or make adjustments to the way the envelope is printed. Click OK when you're done.

   On the Envelope Options tab, click the Envelope Size drop-down list box and select a size from the list. If your envelope doesn't match any of the standard sizes listed, select Custom Size from the list and enter your envelope's dimensions in the Envelope Size dialog box that appears.

   Other frequently useful options on this tab are

   - **Add a bar code for the zip code.** Select the Delivery Point Barcode check box.

- **Change the font for the delivery or return address.** Click the Font button for Delivery Address or Return Address to use the usual Font dialog box.

- **Reposition the addresses.** The From Left and From Top boxes adjust the position of the delivery and return addresses from the upper-left corner of the envelope. Auto uses standard settings for standard envelopes.

Click the Printing Options tab to see the tab shown in Figure 12-5. This tab tells Word how you're feeding envelopes into your printer. (Check your printer manual to make sure that *you* know how you're feeding envelopes into your printer!) If Word thinks you're using a different printer than you actually are (or a fax modem!), you need to click the Cancel button to exit the Envelope dialog boxes and then choose File⇨Print to select the correct printer.

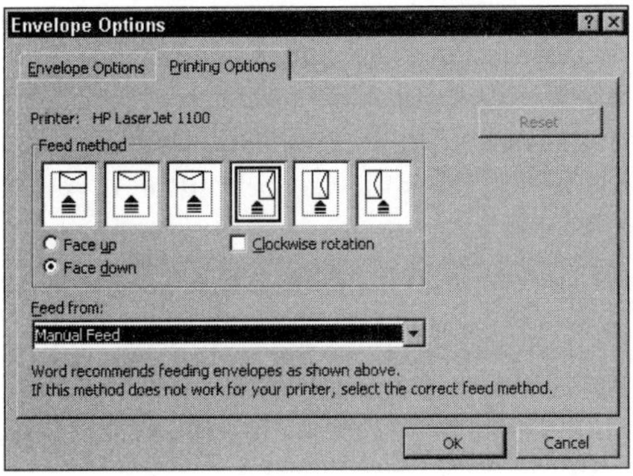

Figure 12-5:
Make sure that Word knows how you're inserting your envelope.

Check three settings on the Printing Options tab:

- **Feed method:** In the pictures in the Feed Method area, Word chooses (by framing it) the most likely way for you to orient and position the envelope in your printer's feed tray. Look very closely at the selection and click a different way, if necessary. Certainly make sure that your envelope's left or right edge is aligned with the tray's edge as the picture shows. An arrow shows how the envelope moves when it's fed into the printer. Make sure that you're not thinking that the envelope will feed the other way! If you feed your envelope sideways, but not the way shown, select the Clockwise Rotation check box.

- **Face Up/Face Down:** Most printers print envelopes face up, but check your manual and choose the proper option.

- **Feed From:** Most small home or office printers feed envelopes from the standard paper tray, but some have a special manual feed option (probably already chosen by Word). Click the Feed From drop-down list box and select the correct feed tray.

  Click OK in the Envelope Options dialog box to return to the Envelopes and Labels dialog box.

6. **Click the Print button to physically commit ink to paper.**

   Word may pop up a dialog box, asking whether you want to save the return address that you entered as the default return address. If you intend to use this same address for the next envelope you create, click Yes. Otherwise, click No.

   After a few seconds, your printer is ready to print. Your printer may wait for you to put an envelope in it manually, unless it has a stack of envelopes already in an envelope feed. Every printer handles envelopes differently; insert a blank envelope the way the printer manual tells you to. Your printer's software may also pop up a dialog box or two, either to keep you informed on the printer's progress or to remind you to do something.

7. **Click the Add To Document button to save the envelope as part of the currently open document. (Click the Cancel button if you don't want to save the envelope.)**

   The envelope tool creates something called an envelope page and puts it at the top of your document. A special envelope/page break (the dotted line) separates the envelope page from the rest of your document.

Choose View➪Print Layout or File➪Print Preview to see your envelope more realistically before you print.

You can edit the envelope page or format it just like any other page of your document. If the envelope is all that the page contains, you can save the file to reuse later. You can also call on the envelope tool again to edit the text, if you prefer. (If so, the Add To Document button becomes the Change Document button.) If at any time you decide that you won't need the envelope again, you can delete it. Click and drag across the entire envelope page, including the page break and press the Delete key on your keyboard.

After you attach an envelope to a document, whenever you print your document, you get an envelope, too — unless you tell the Print dialog box otherwise. Chapter 11 tells you how to print selected pages of a document. Use those instructions to determine what you print. To print only the envelope, for instance, click in the envelope page before choosing File➪Print; then in the Print dialog box, select the Current Page check box.

If all works well, you soon have a nicely printed envelope. If not, well, there's always the ballpoint pen.

A few things can go wrong; here's information on how to fix 'em:

- ✔ **Nothing happens when you print.** Your printer may be waiting for you to manually feed an envelope into it. If no way is available to manually feed the printer an envelope, follow these steps: Click the envelope page. Choose File➪Page Setup. Click the Paper Source tab, and in the First Page box, select Default Tray. Try printing again.

- ✔ **The envelope jams.** After you carefully extract the smushed envelope, try printing again with a new envelope, but this time, sharpen the crease of the edges of the envelope by running a hard object across them (or by running the edge between your thumbnail and middle finger tip). If this fails, try adjusting the paper thickness control of the printer or using a thinner envelope.

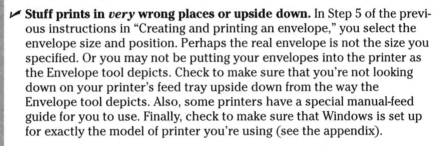

- ✔ **Stuff prints in *very* wrong places or upside down.** In Step 5 of the previous instructions in "Creating and printing an envelope," you select the envelope size and position. Perhaps the real envelope is not the size you specified. Or you may not be putting your envelopes into the printer as the Envelope tool depicts. Check to make sure that you're not looking down on your printer's feed tray upside down from the way the Envelope tool depicts. Also, some printers have a special manual-feed guide for you to use. Finally, check to make sure that Windows is set up for exactly the model of printer you're using (see the appendix).

- ✔ **Stuff prints in *somewhat* wrong places.** See the possible reasons given in the preceding paragraph. Another possible remedy is to click the envelope page and adjust the margins by choosing File➪Page Setup.

Printing labels

People who want to print labels typically have one of two different jobs in mind: printing pages of labels with a single address (or other text), or performing a rather complex operation called *mail merge* to print labels from an address database.

To print labels, you need to buy special labels for the kind of printer you have. Unless you have a special label printer, your labels come on sheets that you use like paper in your printer. After printing, you peel the labels off the sheets. Two common label vendors are Avery and Maco, and the two most common types of labels are those for laser printers and those for inkjet printers. Check your printer manual for its suggestions on label printing.

Don't try to use laser printer labels in an inkjet printer, or vice versa. Problems can include smearing, misalignment between the print and labels, and sticky paper jams!

In Word, printing labels that all have the same text (or just a single label) is usually a piece of cake. Here's how to cut that cake:

1. **If your document already has the label text in it, select (highlight) that text.**

   Apply any special character formatting that you want, such as color or special fonts. Otherwise, move on to Step 2.

2. **Choose Tools⇨Envelopes and Labels.**

   The Envelopes and Labels dialog box skitters into existence.

3. **Click the Labels tab and examine the Address text box.**

   If, in Step 1, you initially highlighted text, it appears in the Address text box. You can edit this text now if you like. If you didn't select any text, this text box is blank, and you can fill it in by clicking the text box and typing.

   If your intention is to print return address labels for yourself, try selecting the Use Return Address check box. If the address is correct, proceed to Step 4; otherwise, edit the address.

4. **Check the Label area of the dialog box to see if the label part number matches your labels; if not, click the label displayed (or click the Options button) to access Label Options.**

   In the Label Options dialog box, shown in Figure 12-6, select the label vendor and series in the Label Products drop-down list box and then select the label's product number in the Product Number list box. The Label Information area provides details on label and page size.

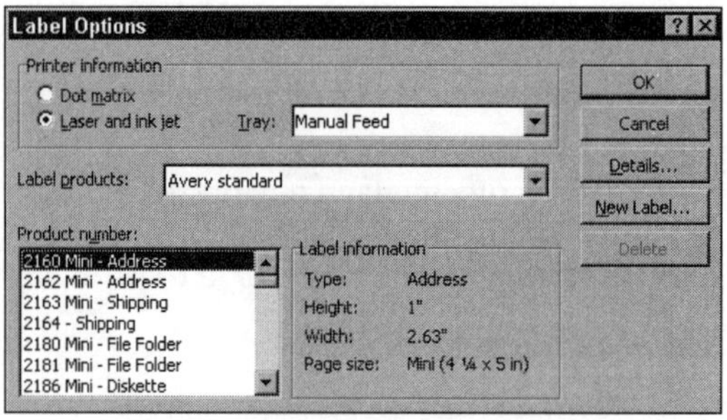

Figure 12-6:
Select a type of label and make sure that you feed it properly to the printer.

Inspect the type of printer feed listed in the Tray drop-down list box. Click to select a different option: Default Tray, for instance, if you are printing a stack of label sheets, or Manual Feed to print a single sheet.

Click OK in the Label Options dialog box when you're done, to return to the Envelopes and Labels dialog box.

5. **If you want only a single label, select the Single Label check box in the Envelopes and Labels dialog box.**

   Specify which label on the page of labels you want to print, by entering the label's row and column number in Row and Column.

6. **Keep your label setup as a document by clicking the New Document button.**

   A page of labels is created as a document and displayed in your Word window.

7. **Ready to print? Click the Print button, but first . . .**

   . . . insert a regular piece of paper in your printer's feed tray or slot. In case anything goes wrong, you haven't wasted a sheet of labels. After printing, hold the paper over a sheet of labels and see how the text lines up with the label.

   If all is well on plain paper, place a single sheet of labels in your printer's feed tray.

   The Envelopes and Labels dialog box goes away after you click the Print button.

8. **You created a new document in Step 6; save it by choosing File⇨ Save now.**

9. **To print on a sheet of labels, choose File⇨Print.**

Many of the same problems that afflict envelope printing also afflict label printing. See the tips at the end of the section, "Creating and printing an envelope," earlier in this chapter. In addition, two other problems are

✔ High humidity can cause your labels to warp, print badly, stick together, or stick to your printer's innards. Wait for a dry day or buy a dehumidifier.

✔ Label sheets can slip or bind in the printer's rollers. You may need to adjust the printer for the label sheet thickness.

Chapter 13

Adding Graphics, Charts, and Sidebars

· ·

In This Chapter

▶ Reproducing some art for your document

▶ Hanging some pictures

▶ Making your own art

▶ Getting glitzy by adding sidebars

▶ Using art in the public domain

▶ Exploring WordArt

▶ Keeping up-to-date with charts

▶ Tweaking your art

· ·

A picture is worth a thousand words, so I figure a chapter about pictures warrants several thousand words. But I'm not just talking pictures, here. Word lets you add all kinds of useful visual stuff to a document, including drawings, spreadsheets, charts, and sidebars. But I'm wasting my thousand words; read on!

Copying and Pasting Images

If you can see an image on your PC, you have a reasonable chance of being able to *copy and paste it* into a document by using the Windows *Clipboard*. (See the appendix for a discussion of the Windows Clipboard.) Whether or not you *can* copy an image depends on the application (program) that you're using to view the image. Try the following:

> ✔ If, when you click on the image, a frame (a box) appears around the image and remains after you release the mouse button, you can probably copy it. Click the image to select it for copying, and then choose Edit⇨Copy from the viewing program's menu bar (or from the right-mouse menu).

> ✔ See if the image fills the program's window, and when you peek in the program's Edit menu, see if a Copy or Cut command is present and not grayed out. If so, choose Edit➪Copy from the viewing program's menu bar (or right-mouse menu).

In a document in Word, click where you want the image to go and press Ctrl+V or choose Edit➪Paste.

To adjust the position, the size, or anything else about the picture, see the last section of this chapter, "Messing Around with Art in the Document."

Inserting Pictures from Files

To insert a picture from a file, just click where you want the picture to go, and use Word's rather obvious command: Choose Insert➪Picture➪From File. The Insert Picture dialog box that appears (as shown in Figure 13-1) includes a Preview feature: Click a file (like rustfris.jpg in Figure 13-1), and the image is displayed on the right side of the box.

Figure 13-1:
Insert
Picture
offers
convenient,
but slow,
previewing.
Pictures of
cute dogs
are worth it.

Here are some instructions and tips for using the Insert Picture dialog box shown in Figure 13-1:

> ✔ Browse through folders on your PC just as you do in the File Open dialog box. (See the appendix if browsing through folders is a new concept for you.)

> ✔ To select a picture, click its file in the left-hand window.

> ✔ To insert your selected picture into your document, click the Insert button.

After you insert the picture, you can size, position, or otherwise mess around with it. See "Messing Around with Art in the Document" later in this chapter for instructions.

Drawing "Blob Art"

Few things strike more dread into the heart of the average adult than being asked to draw something. Otherwise, brave souls who daily undertake such daunting ventures as business trips, advanced courses in physics, or even (shudder) field trips with their child's class shiver in their berets at the thought of drawing something.

Fortunately, the most artistic endeavor that most of us are ever called upon to do in Word is what I call blob art. *Blob art* is the art of putting together a bunch of simple shapes with lines and text. Word gives you a convenient drawing feature for making your blob art attractive. Here are some useful factoids about using Word's drawing feature:

- Word lets you draw anywhere in your document — even on top of your text!

- To draw on your document, just display the Drawing toolbar shown in Figure 13-2: Choose View⇨Toolbars and then select Drawing in the list of toolbars that appears. The Drawing toolbar normally appears at the bottom of your Word window. Repeat these steps to remove the toolbar.

- The Drawing toolbar includes a blob art feature called AutoShapes, which contains predesigned blobs of all kinds.

Making shapes and text

Any shapes and text that you create with the drawing tools are separate, movable objects, like cutouts lying on a piece of paper. You can even stack them in any order, like paper shapes, in which case they often partially obscure each other. You can also group them for purposes of moving them or changing various attributes like color.

To use a tool, click the tool and then move your cursor into the document area. After you do that, using the tool is generally a matter of clicking at various points, or clicking and dragging. Pressing the Shift key while you click (which this book refers to as *Shift+click*) allows you to get certain specialized objects, such as circles and squares, from the more general ellipse and rectangle tools.

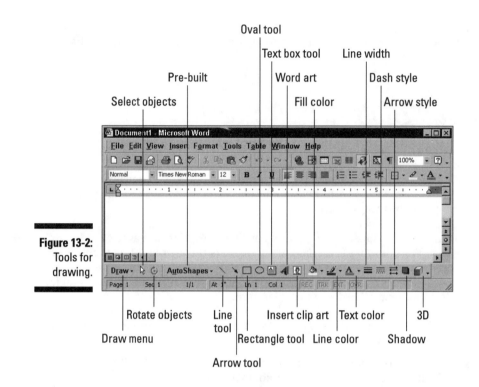

Figure 13-2:
Tools for drawing.

Refer to Figure 13-2 to identify these basic shape and text tools on the Drawing toolbar:

- ✓ **Line:** Click where you want one endpoint and drag to where you want the other endpoint. Pressing Shift+click forces a line to be drawn at even multiples of 15 degrees (15, 30, 45, 60, 75, 90, and so on).

- ✓ **Oval:** Click and then drag in any direction to create an ellipse. Dragging diagonally makes the shape more circular. To force it to be a true circle, press Shift+click.

- ✓ **Rectangle:** Click where you want one corner and drag to the opposite corner. For a square, press Shift+click.

- ✓ **Text box:** Click where you want one corner and drag to the opposite corner. For a square, press Shift+click. Click inside the box to type text. Use the same font controls that you use for document text, plus the text color button in the attributes group shown in Figure 13-2.

- ✓ **WordArt:** See "Creating WordArt," later in this chapter.

- ✓ **Insert Clip Art:** See "Clipping Clip Art" later in this chapter.

- ✓ **AutoShapes:** AutoShapes are, for the most part, pre-designed shapes like stars and arrows that you simply choose from the AutoShape menu, and then click and drag in your document.

TIP

Make this sidebar!

Text boxes are ideal for sidebars, like this one! See "Messing Around with Art in the Document" for tips on making text flow around a text box.

Modifying objects

Drawing objects have a variety of qualities, or *attributes,* controlled by the attribute buttons shown in Figure 13-2. To change any attribute, select the object by clicking it (if it isn't selected already) and click the attribute button.

Selected objects are marked by tiny squares at various points on the shape. To select a *group* of objects, choose the selection tool (labeled "Select objects" in Figure 13-2) and drag a rectangle to completely enclose the objects. To select a bunch of objects scattered all over the drawing, hold down the Shift key and click each object individually.

Check out some of the attributes that you can set by using the buttons on the Drawing toolbar (refer to Figure 13-2):

- **Fill Color** applies the fill color displayed on that button. (A *fill color* is a solid-colored center for closed shapes, like ovals.) Click the triangular down arrow on the Fill Color button to select a color from a palette (or choose None).

- **Line Color** applies the color displayed on that button. (For closed shapes, line refers to the shape's outline.) Click the triangular down arrow on the Line Color button to select a color from a palette.

- **Line Width** lets you choose a line width (which, for a closed shape, refers to its outline).

- **Dash Style** lets you choose a solid or broken line (which for a closed shape, refers to its outline).

- **Arrow Style** lets you turn a line into an arrow and choose the direction for the arrow points. (Not for closed shapes.)

- **Shadow** lets you apply a shadow to an object. Choose both a direction for the shadow and a style from the graphical menu that appears.

- **3D** switches an object to a three-dimensional appearance. Choose a 3D style from the graphical menu that appears or click No 3-D to restore a two-dimensional appearance.

Here are ways that you can adjust an object (or a bunch of objects). Click the selection tool and select the object(s) before you attempt any of these actions:

- **Move:** Click anywhere on the object and drag. To move straight horizontally or vertically, hold down the Shift key and drag. (Don't forget: You can select a bunch of objects and move them all together.)

- **Copy:** Press Ctrl+C and then Ctrl+V. A copy appears somewhere nearby; click and drag it to the place where you want it.

- **Stretch or shrink:** (For shapes, not text.) Click any of the squares around the shape and drag. Shift+drag constrains dragging to certain directions: Shift+drag a side square to move it straight horizontally or vertically; Shift+drag a corner square to move it at a 45-degree angle. To stretch or shrink while keeping the shape's center in place, hold down the Ctrl key.

- **On-top/underneath:** Objects overlap each other in Draw; to change a selected object's position in the pile, choose Draw⇨Order on the Drawing toolbar and choose an order from the menu that appears.

- **Rotate or flip:** Choose Draw⇨Rotate or Flip on the Drawing toolbar and choose a rotation or flip in the menu that appears. Rotate Left and Rotate Right turn the object 90 degrees. Click Flip Horizontal for a mirror image or Flip Vertical for upside down. Choosing Free Rotate (which is also a button on the Drawing toolbar) puts exciting green dots around the shape. (I get excited easily.) Drag a dot to rotate the shape around its center. Hold the Ctrl key down to drag the shape around the dot on the opposite corner. If you choose Free Rotate, it stays on; choose Free Rotate again to turn the tool off.

If you realize that you made a mistake (maybe you accidentally nudged something that took you a long time to get in exactly the right place), you can undo it. Choosing Edit⇨Undo or pressing Ctrl+Z works here just like it does everywhere else in Word.

If you get a few objects perfectly positioned relative to each other, you can freeze them in their relative positions by selecting them all and choosing Draw⇨Group.

To apply a border, adjust position, size, or do anything else for a particular blob, see the last section of this chapter, "Messing Around with Art in the Document."

Creating Sidebars (Text Boxes)

All the highest-quality magazines and books (like this one) use sidebars, right? (See the "Make this sidebar" sidebar, earlier in this chapter, for an example of a sidebar.) So why shouldn't your document?

A sidebar in Word is nothing more than a special piece of blob art called a *text box.* Because a text box *is,* simply, a piece of blob art, you can create a text box by using the Text Box tool of Word's Drawing toolbar, as described briefly in the "Drawing 'Blob Art'" section. Or, to avoid dealing with the drawing tools, you can do the following:

1. **Choose <u>I</u>nsert⇨Te<u>x</u>t Box.**

   Your cursor changes to a set of cross-hairs. Ready, aim,. . . .

2. **In your document, click where you want one corner of the box and drag diagonally across your text to where you want the opposite corner.**

   A text box with a shaded frame and eight *handles* (tiny squares) appears, overlaying your document text, with a blinking cursor in the box.

3. **Type your sidebar text.**

   Format characters and paragraphs just as you would any other text in a Word document. In Figure 13-3, I used bold text and center alignment for the sidebar heading, and bullets for the sidebar text.

4. **Click anywhere outside the text box when you finish typing and formatting your text.**

   To edit your sidebar text at any later time, just click in the text box.

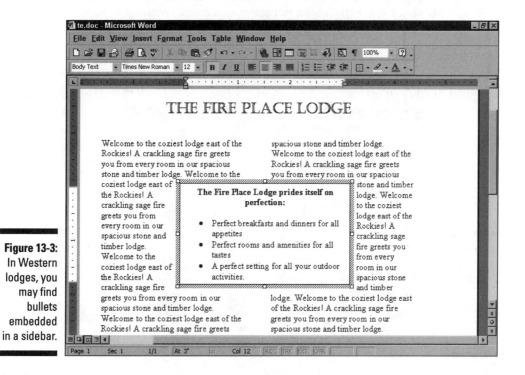

Figure 13-3: In Western lodges, you may find bullets embedded in a sidebar.

You're not done yet, though; your text box needs some fine-tuning to become a real sidebar. Most noticeably, your sidebar, unlike the one in Figure 13-3, is probably sitting right smack on top of your document text!

What you need to do now is to adjust how text *wraps* around the sidebar. You may also want to fine-tune the size and position of your text box in the document, the margins between the box and the text, the border *(line)* around the box, or the box's background color or pattern *(fill)*. The dialog box that controls all these features is the same for text boxes as for graphical objects, like pictures, WordArt, and blob art. See the final section of this chapter, "Messing Around with Art in the Document," for details.

Clipping Clip Art

When your document needs a little pizzazz — not functional, industrial art like blob art or charts — use some clip art. Clip art is nothing more than a bunch of illustrations that you can use in your documents. Works Suite comes with a batch of drawings; you can add more by connecting to the Internet with Microsoft Internet Explorer, which is discussed in Chapter 19.

The clip art feature that comes with Works Suite is called the Clip Gallery. It's designed to let you find, choose, and organize not only the artwork that's prepackaged with Works, but also any images, sounds, or video files that you add from the Microsoft Web site or other sources.

Summon the Clip Gallery by choosing Insert⇨Picture⇨Clip Art, and it appears as shown in Figure 13-4.

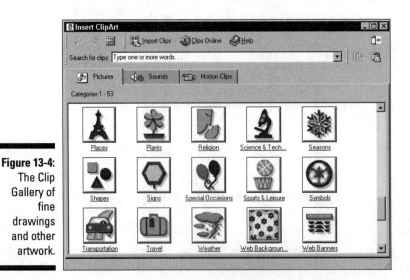

Figure 13-4: The Clip Gallery of fine drawings and other artwork.

Clip art often looks much better in your document than it does in the Clip Gallery, where certain types of art appear rather grainy and blotchy. To see how it will actually appear full-size in a document, click the clip and a pop-out menu appears. Select the second icon — it looks like a magnifying glass. The image will be displayed full-size.

To insert a clip in your document follow these steps:

1. **In your document, click where you want the art to appear.**

2. **In Word, choose Insert➪Picture➪Clip Art.**

    You may have to wait, staring at a cursor-turned-hourglass, while Word quietly builds its museum of masterpieces or reads the clips from the CD. Eventually, the Insert ClipArt dialog box appears.

3. **Click a subject category, illustrated by the icons in the window.**

    The clip art illustrations are divided by subject category for your artistic critique and selection. Scroll through the gallery window to see more of the categories.

4. **Click the image that you want to insert into your document.**

5. **Click the top icon (Insert Clip) on the pop out menu that appears.**

6. **Close the Insert Clip Art dialog box by clicking the X in the upper-right corner of the gallery, or you can leave it open to insert more clip art.**

After you insert the art into your document, you can size it and otherwise fine-tune it the same way you do your own drawings. See the final section of this chapter, "Messing Around with Art in the Document" for more information.

Creating WordArt

Oh, those madcap Microsoft engineers! First blob art, then clip art, and now WordArt. What's next, punctuation art? Well, WordArt is definitely fun, and it's also great for getting readers' attention (see Figure 13-5). The WordArt feature lets you create special effects for text — like you see in advertisements and brochures.

The basic procedure for getting swoopy, loopy text in your document goes like this:

1. **Click at the place you want your text art.**

2. **Choose Insert➪Picture➪WordArt.**

In Word, a way-cool WordArt style gallery appears. Click any style that appeals to you and then click the OK button. You can vary or customize the style later to suit your needs.

An Edit WordArt Text dialog box appears. `Your Text Here` appears in the dialog box. The phrase "Your Text Here" probably doesn't quite get *your* point across, so move on to Step 3!

Figure 13-5:
Playing with
WordArt:
Curved text
can turn
heads.

3. **Type your text in the dialog box and then click OK.**

   The document displays your cool WordArt (refer to Figure 13-5). You also see the WordArt toolbar shown in Figure 13-5.

4. **To change the shape of your WordArt, click the WordArt Shape button (marked ABC) on the WordArt toolbar.**

5. **A gallery of weird shapes appears. Click any shape in the gallery. (Shapes with multiple lines are intended for multiple lines of text.)**

When you're happy with your WordArt, click the X in the upper-right corner of the WordArt toolbar to dismiss the toolbar.

Inserting Charts and Other Foreign Objects

As a kid, I was always amused at the medical world's use of the phrase "foreign object" to describe the various kinds of specks I got in my eyes. (What can I say? I was easily amused as a child, and dirt was one of my favorite toys.)

Today, thanks to the wonders of software, you can not only get foreign objects in your eyes but also deliberately put foreign objects in your documents. By *foreign objects,* however, I now mean stuff that you make with another program — like charts, graphs, spreadsheets (entire spreadsheets or named ranges), or even other documents — that you want to use as an illustration. You put such foreign objects into your Word document several ways:

- ✔ **Copy and paste the object as a graphical image.** See the first section of this chapter, "Copying and Pasting Images," for instructions. You cannot easily edit this object, so if you want to alter it in the future, you need to edit it in the other program, and then copy and paste it again.

- ✔ **Paste a link to the object.** This special form of pasting allows you to keep your illustration (a chart, for example) up-to-date by incorporating the latest changes in the data. Whenever you change the chart in the other program, that change automatically shows up in the Word document.

  If you paste a link to an object, you can't move that object's file to another folder, change that file's name, or copy the document to another person's computer. If you do any of these things, you must get into editing links, which I don't have room to discuss here!

- ✔ **Embed the object.** This special form of pasting actually stores a copy of the object — a chunk of spreadsheet data, for instance — in your Word document. You can edit the object by double-clicking it.

Following are the steps for pasting a link or embedding an object. These steps work for objects created under many Windows programs, but not all of them. If these steps don't work for you, you must resort to copying and pasting the object as a graphical image.

1. **Create your object (a spreadsheet, chart, or drawing, for instance) by using a Windows program.**

2. **Save your work in that program as a file.**

3. **Select your chart window or other object in that program, and then copy the object by choosing Edit⇨Copy. Don't exit the program.**

4. **Open (launch) Word if it isn't already running, click your document where you want the object to appear, and choose Edit⇨Paste Special.**

The Paste Special dialog box appears. Within it, the As selection box offers several ways of pasting your object, with one of those ways highlighted for you.

5. To link or embed an object, look for an *object* in the As list box and click that selection if it is not already highlighted. For instance, if you are copying a Works chart, look for a Microsoft Works Sheet or Chart *Object*.

If none of the selections offers an *object,* you cannot link or embed. Press the Esc key and resort to ordinary copying and pasting.

6. Choose Paste Link to paste a link, or choose Paste to embed the object.

If Paste Link is grayed out, you cannot paste a link to this object. You can only embed it.

7. Click OK in the Paste Link dialog box.

You may now exit the Windows program in which you created the object.

You can now format and edit this object like most other graphics objects. See the last section in this chapter, "Messing Around with Art in the Document" for instructions. As with other graphics objects, you can edit the object by double-clicking it. If you pasted a link to the object, you then return to the original program in which you created the object; save your work as a file in that program.

If you pasted a link, you can use the Windows program that created the file to change that file, even when Word is not running. (After changing the file, however, don't move the file to another folder or change the file's name, or the link will no longer work.) When you next open your Word document, the object in that document will be up-to-date.

Messing Around with Art in the Document

To do anything to a figure of any sort (blob art, WordArt, picture, or other object), first click the figure to select it. The figure then appears framed — as is usual when any object is selected — with eight tiny squares *(handles)* around the outside. To select a group of figures so that you can move or otherwise operate on them all together, hold down the Ctrl key while clicking each one.

Here are some of the ways you might want to mess with art:

✔ **To move a figure:** Position your cursor over it until the cursor changes to a four-way arrow, and then click and drag the figure. (If a figure's center is transparent, click its border.)

✔ **To delete a figure:** Press the Delete key.

✔ **To resize a figure:** Click and drag any of the handles around the figure.

✔ **To modify a figure:** Double-click the figure, and you return to the original program that created it, or in some cases (such as clip art), you see a special dialog box where you can choose various options to modify the figure.

To more precisely control size and position, to choose a border or fill, to control text wrapping around a figure, or to set interior margins in a text box, choose Format from the menu bar, and then click the last selection on the Format menu that drops down. That selection reads Format Object, Format Picture, Format WordArt, or Format something-or-other, depending upon what sort of something you selected. A Format something-or-other dialog box appears. Do the following:

✔ **To adjust the frame around your figure:** Click the Colors and Lines tab. Choose a color, line width (weight), and dashed style, if you like. If your object is a line or arrow, you can choose arrowhead size and style. (You can also access the Colors and Lines tab by choosing Format➪ Borders and Shading.)

✔ **To change the figure's dimensions or rotation:** Click the Size tab. To adjust the figure's height and width (proportions) separately, click to deselect the Lock Aspect Ratio check box. You may either enter *absolute values* (inches) in the Height and Width boxes of the Size and Rotate area, or adjust *scale* by entering percentages in the Height and Width boxes of the Scale area. Enter rotation in degrees (360 being a complete turn) in the Rotation box.

✔ **To make text wrap around the figure in the word processing program:** Choose Format➪Picture and click the Layout tab. Then click the Wrapping Style button of your preference. Also click the Advanced button to see additional options. Never be frightened of a button labeled Advanced in Word. Quite often the features revealed are not any more sophisticated than those displayed on the default tab. I often think they should change the caption *Advanced* to *Other Options*.

✔ **Additional Options:** Click the Layout tab, then click the Advanced button, and then click the Picture Position tab. Enter Horizontal and Vertical values (which set the distance to the figure's upper-left corner). A bunch of options here control how the graphic moves as text is added or deleted from your document:

- Click to select the Move Object with Text check box if you want the figure to move vertically with the paragraph it appears in.

- Click to select the Lock Anchor check box to ensure that the figure stays on the same page as the paragraph it is inserted in.

✔ **To crop or adjust several qualities of a picture:** Click the Picture tab. Enter crop distances for the left, right, top, or bottom of the picture. To adjust picture appearance, use the Image Control settings. Choose from the Color selection box: Automatic to use original colors, Grayscale to convert the image to shades of gray, Black & White to reduce the image to lines and dot patterns, or Watermark to fade the image by applying predetermined Brightness and Contrast settings. You may also adjust Brightness and Contrast yourself by using the horizontal scroll gizmos or by typing in percentages.

✔ **To adjust the space between a text box border and the text it contains:** Click the Text Box tab. Set values for the top, bottom, left, and right interior margins.

Part III
Learning to Love Money

The 5th Wave   By Rich Tennant

"The first thing you should know about investing online is that when you see the exploding bomb icon appear, it's just your browser crashing — not your portfolio."

In this part . . .

The love of money may be the root of all evil, but the love of Microsoft Money is more benign. Understandable, too, considering how nicely Microsoft Money helps you keep tabs on your expenses and income, generates reports and charts to help you understand why you aren't richer, and prepares you for tax time (to help the IRS understand why you aren't richer).

In this part, you see how to set up your various bank and other accounts in Money, enter transactions, track investment performance, analyze the results, and download performance data on potential new investments. And if, along the way, you develop a certain fondness for Money, that's quite understandable.

Chapter 14

Setting Up Banking and Checking Accounts

So you have *Money,* have you? How *Suite* it is to have *Money!* And how *Suite* it *Works* . . . after you get the basic instructions. But before you commit yourself to this electronic bookkeeping marvel, ponder the following question: "Is Money good for me?"

If your answer is "*You bet* Money is good for me," your next step is to set up some accounts, and this chapter helps you do that. (After all, who wants no-account software?) This chapter also shows you how to set up categories of expenses and income so that you can analyze your finances by using the planners, charts, and reports that Chapter 16 describes.

Money is a big topic. And *Microsoft* Money is a fairly chunky topic in its own right. So chunky, in fact, that IDG Books Worldwide, Inc., offers an entire book, Peter Weverka's *Microsoft Money 2000 For Dummies.* If you want the big picture — the entire chunky enchilada — check out that book. I'm just going to hit the basics here. In particular, I'm going to avoid much discussion of online banking or electronic transactions, except for getting security prices online (see Chapter 17).

Deciding Whether Money's Good for You

If the love of money is the root of all evil, can Microsoft Money 2000 *really* be good for you? You decide. Some of the most useful jobs (in my opinion) that Money can do are as follows:

- ✔ Money provides a single place (your PC) for you to record all payments, deposits, and transfers; to review these transactions; and to see your balances. If your bank provides online services, Money can automatically get this information from your bank over the Internet; you don't need to type it in.

- ✔ Money prints checks (or pays bills online — in theory), recording the transactions and adjusting your account balances.

- ✔ Money reminds you when regular payments are due and the amount due.

- ✔ Money tells you how much you owe on mortgages and/or car loans.

- ✔ Money tells you how much money you spend on various things (categories of expenses, such as dining out).

- ✔ Money helps you plan and stick to a budget.

- ✔ Money totals your tax-exempt expenses, separated by categories, so that you can simply enter the expenses on your tax forms.

- ✔ Money records in one place all your investment holdings, your purchases, and your sales and displays the value of your investments.

- ✔ Money updates the value of your investments automatically by obtaining stock, bond, and mutual-fund prices off the Internet.

"What's the downside?" you ask (using your best financial jargon). The downside (or disadvantage, if you prefer) is that you must perform the following tasks yourself:

- ✔ **Take the time to tell Money all about your accounts.** This job can take anywhere from hours to days, depending on how many different accounts you have! The more complicated the account (say, a mortgage), the more information you must enter.

- ✔ **Take the time to enter every transaction into the computer.** If you're the kind of person who balances your checkbook every month, you don't find this task too onerous. Otherwise, you may want to consider using Money's online features and your banks' online services (if available) to automatically download your transactions, because manually entering all those transactions can be a pain in the wrist.

- ✔ **Take the time to learn how to use Money.** Compared to the previous two points, this job is a snap.

Preparing to Use Money

The main job facing you before using Money is to assemble your financial information; at the very least, you need to gather your most recent statements from financial institutions. If you want to analyze your past expenses (say, for example, that today's date is April 14, and you're doing your taxes), you also need past statements. (And if today *is* April 14, you also need a *very* large pot of coffee.) If you're entering a mortgage, you need initial amounts from the mortgage papers.

You need these records so that you can copy information from them into Money. You don't *need* to record *all* your account information in Money. You can start with, say, household checking and savings accounts. If your main reason for using Money is to summarize tax-related income and expenses, don't bother recording any accounts for which the financial institution already sends you tax summaries!

If, from the descriptions I gave in the preceding section, "Deciding Whether Money Is Good for You," you think that you want to use online banking, I suggest that you get your PC online before starting to use Money. Turn to Chapter 18 in this book for instructions on getting your PC online.

If you've been using Quicken, Money can translate your Quicken account files into Money 2000 files. In the Money window, choose File⇨Convert Quicken File from the menu bar and, in the Convert Quicken File dialog box that appears, browse to your Quicken file. (Quicken files end in the extension QDB.) See the appendix for details if browsing for files is new to you.

Starting Money, Exiting, and Saving Your Work

Just as you do any other Windows program, you can start Money from the Windows Start button or a program icon. Perform one of the following actions:

- ✔ If you have a Microsoft Money icon on-screen, double-click that icon.
- ✔ On the Windows taskbar, choose Start⇨Programs⇨Microsoft Money.

To read more about starting Windows programs, see the appendix. Likewise, turn there if you're a little shaky on using the mouse or keyboard, windows, menus, or dialog boxes.

To exit the program, choose File⇨Exit from the menu bar. Money automatically saves your work as a file if you exit.

If you exit, Money may also ask whether you want to back up your files to a floppy disk. This suggestion is an excellent one because, if your PC or hard disk fails and you have no backup file, you lose all your work — and you're one very sorry person. Pop a floppy into your disk drive and click BACK UP NOW. The process may take a few minutes. You may also choose File⇨Back Up at any time to back up your file to a floppy disk.

What's What in the Money Window

Figure 14-1 shows you approximately what the Money window looks like after you start the program. Your window may look different, depending on what accounts you set up and how you customize this window. This window is known as your *Money Home Page*, the *Financial Home Page*, or just *Money Home*. Money offers several different windows besides the Home Page, one window for each different kind of activity.

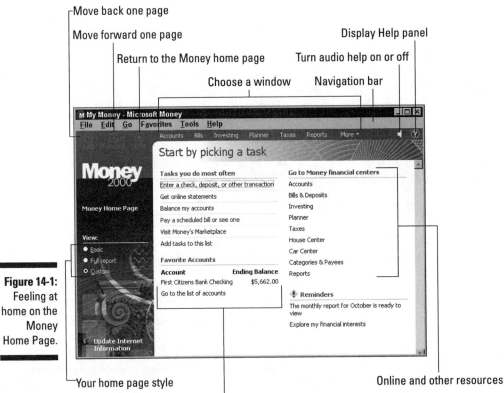

Move back one page

Move forward one page

Return to the Money home page

Display Help panel

Turn audio help on or off

Choose a window

Navigation bar

Figure 14-1:
Feeling at home on the Money Home Page.

Your home page style

Accounts you said were your favorites

Online and other resources

Unusual behavior

Money's operation and controls are a bit different from those of the other Works Suite programs. The user interface (how the program looks and responds to your actions) looks more like the user interfaces that you see on Web pages. If you're not a Web user yet, following are Money's main distinctions from other Windows programs:

✔ Money uses *links* or *hot text* extensively — text that does something if you click it. You can sometimes identify links or hot text because they change in some way as you pass your cursor over them and your cursor changes to a pointing finger icon. Links are generally entirely underlined; hot text may have one letter underlined.

✔ You may find that the *boundaries between windows* or areas of windows seem vague; these boundaries should become clearer to you, however, as you become more familiar with the program. You can know whether a boundary is movable by seeing whether, after you pass your cursor over the boundary, the pointer changes to a double-arrow. That change means that you can click and drag the boundary.

✔ You can customize the Money opening screen (its *Home Page*) like crazy and significantly change its appearance. I don't discuss customization here, but you can fool with it yourself by choosing Tools⇨Options from the menu bar and clicking the Money Home tab in the Options dialog box that appears.

The Home page is your starting place for many different activities. Here's how to use the various controls on Money's home page:

✔ Click any of the navigation bar choices *Accounts* through *Reports* to move to that page. (Click More to see more reports.) If you start hearing a voice, fear not. It's only your recorded tour guides, Eric or Carrie, speaking to you from your Money CD-ROM! To control them, see the following bullet about the speaker icon.

✔ Click the speaker icon (near the question mark at the right end of the navigation bar) to control Eric and Carrie, the narrators of the audio Help that your PC may play (if it's equipped for audio). In the menu that appears, you can choose either Turn All Audio Help Off or Replay Previous Clip. (Play it again, Sam.)

✔ Click the Back button to return to whatever page you were looking at previously.

✔ Click the red question-mark icon to display or hide the Money Help panel. The Help panel occupies the right side of the Money window.

If you turn on the Money Help panel, you can view documentation on all kinds of subjects. I don't need to detail the controls here because the panel offers one nice, simple way to get Help. To search for a subject, first click Help's magnifying-glass icon. Next, click the Ask Money area at the bottom of the Help panel and then type a subject on which you need Help. Press the Enter key on your keyboard, and the Help panel displays several topics; click any of those topics to read documentation.

Setting Up Accounts

What are accounts? An *account* in Money is any pool of money — or any asset or liability — with which you're involved. That includes bank accounts, checking accounts, credit cards, CDs (Certificates of Deposit), stocks, bonds, mutual funds, the cash lying around the house and in your wallet, the equity in your house, loans (which are simply pools of money that someone else owns), liabilities (money you owe but haven't paid yet), and lines of credit. Microsoft Money can deal with them all.

The first time you use Money, it leads you through setting up an account. You can use the following steps to set up additional accounts. (I suggest that you start with your checking account, if you haven't already done so.) To set up any account, follow these steps:

1. **Click Accounts on the navigation bar.**

   Your screen displays either the Accounts page (which lists all your accounts) or the account you viewed most recently. In the latter case, click the Accounts bar again so that you can view all your accounts. Figure 14-2 shows one view of the Accounts page.

2. **Click the New Account button at the bottom of the Accounts page.**

   A New Account dialog box (a *wizard*, or automated program) appears and steps you through the process of setting up an account.

Money offers a different wizard for every kind of account, and this book doesn't have room for me to take you through them all. Fortunately, Microsoft does a good job of making its wizards self-explanatory, so you shouldn't need much help from me.

Fill out the wizard's various forms as they appear, reading the explanations. (If you have audio capability on your PC and the Money CD in the CD drive, a narrator speaks to you soothingly.) To move from step to step, click the Next button. To return to an earlier step, click the Back button. Check out the following suggestions to help you along:

✔ You can change anything that you set up in the wizard later or add information that you don't currently have on hand. See the following section for details.

✔ As you set up your first accounts, avoid any options that deal with online banking. It's a complicated process, and you can add the online stuff later.

✔ If a wizard offers to "associate" your account with another account (for example, to associate an asset with a mortgage or loan account), choose association only if you expect to make regular transfers between those accounts (which you do with, say, a mortgage and the account from which you pay it).

✔ As you set up credit card accounts, you get the option of adding the card payment to your Bill Calendar. Choosing this option means that Money reminds you as the payment date approaches and automatically fills out a payment entry form for you. You then can opt to pay the card from a particular account (typically, your checking account).

After the wizard finishes, a new icon with the account name appears on your Accounts page. Double-click that icon to view or modify the account.

Money gives you several ways to view the Accounts page. Click Sort Account List By (see Figure 14-2) and choose any of the views that the drop-down menu that appears lists.

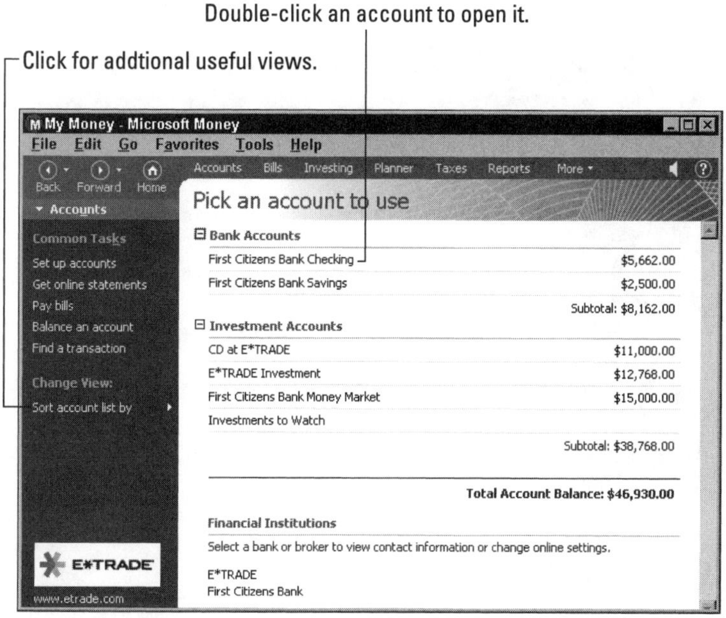

Double-click an account to open it.

Click for addtional useful views.

Figure 14-2:
Taking account of your accounts on the Account page.

M My Money - Microsoft Money

File   Edit   Go   Favorites   Tools   Help

Back   Forward   Home | Accounts   Bills   Investing   Planner   Taxes   Reports   More ▾

▾ Accounts

Pick an account to use

Common Tasks

Set up accounts
Get online statements
Pay bills
Balance an account
Find a transaction

Change View:
Sort account list by ▸

⊟ **Bank Accounts**

First Citizens Bank Checking	$5,662.00
First Citizens Bank Savings	$2,500.00
	Subtotal: $8,162.00

⊟ **Investment Accounts**

CD at E*TRADE	$11,000.00
E*TRADE Investment	$12,768.00
First Citizens Bank Money Market	$15,000.00
Investments to Watch	
	Subtotal: $38,768.00

| **Total Account Balance: $46,930.00** |

Financial Institutions

Select a bank or broker to view contact information or change online settings.

E*TRADE
First Citizens Bank

E*TRADE
www.etrade.com

Viewing and Modifying Individual Accounts

Money gives you several convenient ways to view an individual account so that you can enter data, modify the account's setup, or review recent transactions. Two ways to view an individual account are as follows:

- ✔ **From the Money Home Page:** Click any account shown. (They appear in the Favorite Accounts listing.)
- ✔ **From the Accounts page:** Double-click the account's name in the list that appears.

The first view that Money presents of your account is the Register view, where you enter transactions. See Chapter 15 for more details on using this view.

To modify the setup of an individual account (if, for example, you didn't know your closing balance at the time that you first set up the account), click Details on the left side of the Account page; Money then displays the Details view, as shown in Figure 14-3.

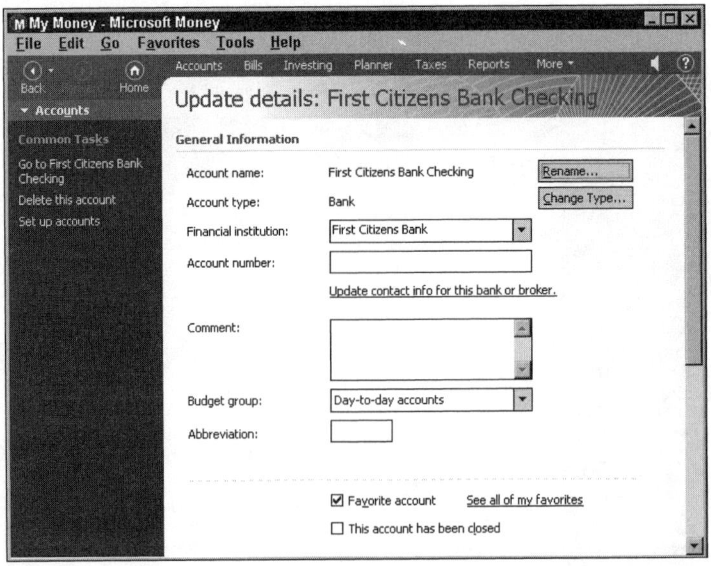

Figure 14-3: Fine-tuning an account's details.

Click any of the text or list boxes to edit its contents, or choose a different value from a drop-down selection list. Following are a few tips for working on this page:

- ✔ Click to place a check mark in the Favorite Account check box; thereafter, you can go immediately to this account by choosing Favorites⇨*Account name* from the Money menu bar. The account also appears among the Favorites on the Money Home Page.

- ✔ To change the name of the account, click the Rename button. Enter the new account name in the Modify Account dialog box that appears. To change the *type* of account — say, from savings to checking, which is rarely necessary — click the Change Type button.

Setting Up Categories and Subcategories

Categories are how Money lumps stuff together in reports and charts. Setting up categories is important if you want Money to tell you how much you spend on certain things (or earn from certain sources).

You probably have, for example, household expenses of various types: electricity, fuel, postage, home maintenance, home improvement, and so on. As you enter these expenses into Money, you can assign them all to a category of *Household* and then generate a report to show you the total (by year or month, for example) of all household expenses. (You can do similarly for entertainment expenses, education expenses, and so on.) If you want to total each kind of household expense separately, add electricity, fuel, postage, and the like as subcategories to the Household category.

While you're categorizing things, you probably also want to designate certain categories as tax-related, such as wages or tax-deductible contributions. Money can then generate a report that shows only the income and expenses that affect your taxes. See Chapter 16 for instructions on creating reports and charts.

Just to make life confusing, Money can also create "classifications." You typically use these to group together income and expenses for a particular project or investment. I don't go into classifications in this book, but Peter Weverka's *Microsoft Money 2000 For Dummies* (IDG Books Worldwide, Inc.), does.

Viewing Money's categories

The good news about setting up categories is that you may not need to do it! Money already includes a bunch of categories that you can use. To see Money's list of categories, follow these steps from Money's home page (click the Home button on Money's toolbar if you're not already on the Home page):

1. **Click Categories & Payees in the Go to Money Financial Centers list, on the right side of the Money Home Page.**

   The Categories & Payees page appears, displaying one of several possible views: Payees, Categories, Classification 1, or Classification 2. (See Figure 14-4.)

2. **If the page doesn't already show the heading "Set Up Your Categories," as shown in Figure 14-4, click Categories at the left side of the page.**

   The page should now be headed, "Set Up Your Categories."

3. **Review the list of categories by using the vertical scroll bar on the right.**

   (See the appendix if scroll bars are unfamiliar to you.)

The Categories & Payees page can display categories in different views. They are listed on the left of the page. Choose one of these alternative views if you wish.

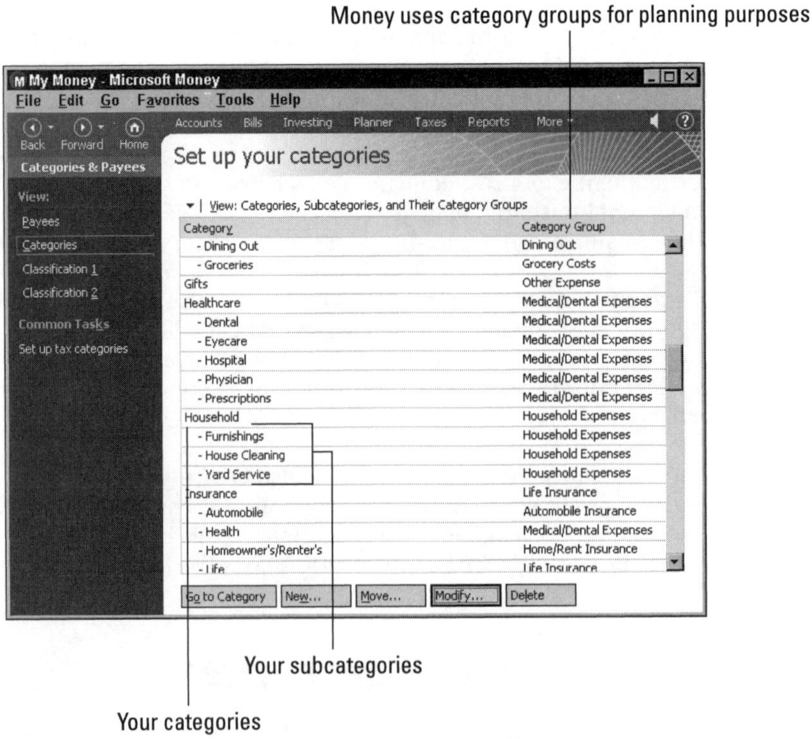

Money uses category groups for planning purposes

Figure 14-4:
Being
categorically
correct.

Your subcategories

Your categories

What the heck are category groups?

Money uses categories, subcategories, and something called "category groups." *Category groups* mystified me until I realized that they're just Money's way of relating *my own, custom* categories (which Money doesn't really understand) to the various kinds of income and expenses that it *does* understand.

If I add the expense category Photographic Supplies, for example, Money has no idea how expenses in that category fit into my life. Are they essential? Money needs to know so that it can help me plan my life with its planners, reports, and other tools. If the category group for Photographic Supplies is Entertainment, money may advise me to trim that expense. The Money category groups are fixed and immutable.

Adding your own category or subcategory

Money offers a fine selection of starting categories, but you may want to add your own. To add a category or subcategory, follow these steps:

1. **If you're adding a category, skip to Step 2; if you're adding a subcategory, first click its parent category.**

   To add Pet Supplies as a subcategory to Household expense, for example, click Household.

2. **Click the New button on the bottom of the page.**

   The New Category dialog box appears.

3. **Click New Category or Subcategory and then click Next.**

   You see a page where you're asked to define your category.

4. **Type a name for your category or subcategory in the Name text box and then click Next.**

   You're shown a page where you're asked to add the category to a Group.

5. **Click the category group that most closely describes the nature of your new category and then click Finish.**

   You may choose Grocery Costs for your Pet Supplies subcategory, for example. A subcategory doesn't need to be in the same category group as the parent category.

To delete a category, simply click it and click the Delete button at the bottom of the page.

Chapter 15

Doing Banking and Checking Transactions

. . . .

In This Chapter

▶ Using an account register

▶ Recording your transactions

▶ Scheduling recurring bills and transactions

▶ Printing checks

▶ Balancing your checkbook

. . . .

*Y*ou know what a transaction is in real life, but what do I mean if I tell you to "do" transactions in Money? Well, you can "do" transactions in Money in one of the following two ways:

✔ You can *record* your real-life transactions (checks that you write or funds that you transfer, for example) after the fact by using your checkbook and other records as references.

✔ You can actually *perform* transactions in Money (check printing, electronic payment, and the like) as well as *record* those transactions. In that case, you enter the data before printing the check (or making the payment electronically, which this book doesn't cover.)

If you record transactions after the fact, you get your transaction information from one of the following two possible sources:

✔ **From your own checkbook(s), records, and receipts:** Sit down at your PC periodically with, for example, your checkbook, automatic teller receipts, credit-card receipts, and other tiny illegible scraps of paper and copy the information on them into Money. The benefit of doing all this copying is that Money turns your creased and scribbled-on papers into a legible, organized record against which you can reconcile your bank's records.

✔ **From the bank's records:** Sit down at your PC (or stand up, if you like) and copy information from your monthly statements. If you trust the bank to record your transactions correctly most of the time, you may want to work this way. You can always check Money against your checkbook and credit card receipts later to discover any errors.

Recording Transactions in an Account Register

The task on which you may spend most of your time in Money is entering your deposits, withdrawals, and payments of various kinds into a Money account register. The following steps show you in detail how to record those transactions for bank and checking accounts. You handle investment accounts similarly but with a few differences; see Chapter 17 for details.

If you're unfamiliar with basic Windows tasks, such as filling out dialog boxes, please see the appendix before proceeding.

The following process may look long and complex, but it's really not so bad. Before entering into your account register any transactions that occur regularly (say, mortgage or insurance payments), however, check out the following section, "Setting Up Recurring Bills and Scheduled Transactions." Otherwise, just follow these steps:

1. **Open your account register by performing one of the following actions:**

   Clicking Accounts on the Money navigation bar is one way to access your account register. You see the main Accounts page appear (listing all your accounts), where you can now click your chosen account.

   If an account is in your list of Favorites, another way to open the account register is to click the account name in the list of Favorites on the Money Home Page. Or click Favorites in the menu bar and then choose your account from the menu that opens. (Choose Favorites⇨ *Your account*.)

   Either way, an account register page appears resembling the one shown in Figure 15-1. Click View to see other views of the register page. Other views include: transactions sorted by check number or by date entered; unreconciled transactions only; or a register page without the data entry form at the bottom (so that you can enter transactions directly into the register).

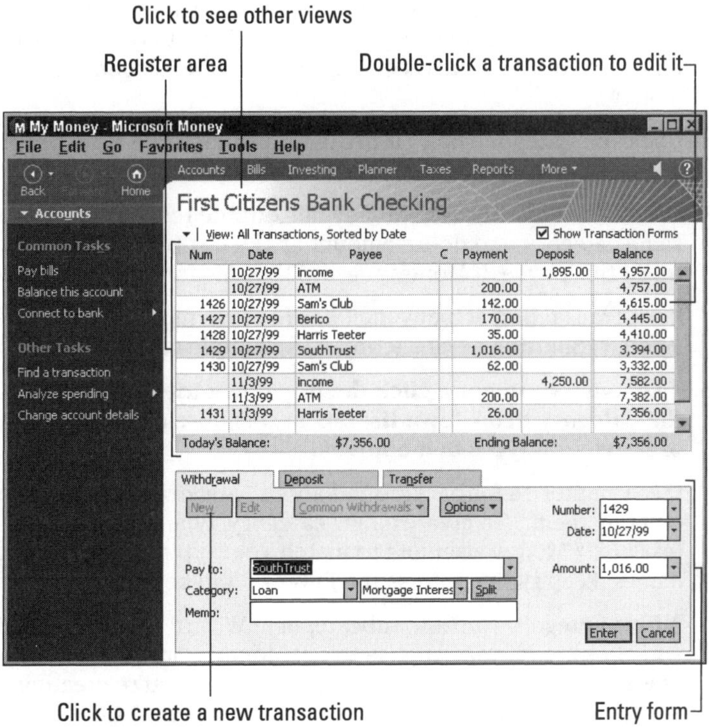

Click to see other views

Register area   Double-click a transaction to edit it

Figure 15-1:
The usual
register
view,
showing
transactions
by date.

Click to create a new transaction   Entry form

2. **Click the New button to create a new transaction (or double-click any transaction appearing on the register to edit it).**

   The form area shown in Figure 15-1 wakes up and displays text boxes and various gizmos for data entry.

3. **At the top of the form area, click the tab for the kind of transaction you want to enter: Withdrawal, Deposit, or Transfer (refer to Figure 15-1).**

   The types of transactions shown on the tabs depends on the type of account you're using: checking, credit card, loan, or other.

4. **Click the Pay To text box and type the payee's name.**

   If you're making a Deposit or Transfer, click the From text box that Money displays instead of the Pay To box and enter the payer's name.

   Money keeps a list of the names of every payee (and payer) that you ever enter. So, as you type, Money tries to match your typing to previous names, filling out the rest of the line; keep typing until Money guesses correctly. (If you're just starting to use Money, you must type the entire name.) To choose a name from Money's list of names, click the tiny down-triangle at the right end of the Pay To (or From) text box.

If you're making a transfer, type your own name (or the name of whoever owns the receiving account) in the Pay To text box. Open the To drop-down list to select the receiving account (the account that gets the money).

5. **Click the Category box (if present) and then see whether Money guesses the correct category.**

Unless the payee is new, Money fills out the rest of the form, using the same category and dollar amount as the last payment to (or receipt from) this payee. If Money guesses the category correctly, skip to Step 7.

If the transaction actually includes funds in multiple categories, see the sidebar "Splitting a transaction into multiple categories."

6. **To choose a category, click the tiny down-triangle at the right end of the Category drop-down list box and choose a category from the list of previous payees that appears.**

(See Chapter 14 for background about categories and instructions for creating them.) To create a new category, type its name in the Category text box. (Money attempts to match your typing with existing category names; keep typing.) Press the Enter or Tab key after you're done.

A New Category (or New Subcategory) Wizard then appears, in which you click Income or Expense to tell Money what kind of category your new category is. (You don't click anything if you're creating a new sub-category — it inherits its type from the category.) Click Next and, on the next wizard page, click one of Money's standard groups with which to associate your category. Click Finish after you're done.

7. **See whether the figure appearing in the Amount drop-down list box is correct and, if not, click the text box and type a new value.**

(As is the case with any Windows text box, you can double-click to high-light the entire value; then the new value that you type replaces the old one entirely.) If the value is already correct, just go on to Step 8.

You can choose one of the five most recent dollar-amounts that you paid to this same payee by right-clicking the Amount or Pay To text boxes.

8. **Click the Memo text box and, if you want, type a memo to yourself about the transaction.**

9. **Record how you're making this payment: by check, electronic pay-ment, funds transfer, blood, Green Stamps, or other medium.**

If you're copying a check transaction from your checkbook, examine the check number Money guessed at and places in the Number drop-down list box. If the number's wrong, click it, edit it, and then press Enter or Tab.

If you're recording an ATM (Automatic Teller Machine) transaction, type **ATM** or any code (text) that you choose in the Number text box. Similarly, you may create your own code if the transaction is an automat-ically deducted fee or other special transaction for which Money doesn't already provide a code in the Number text box.

Splitting a transaction into multiple categories

You need to divide some transactions into two or more categories. The charges of a credit card payment, for example, you often need to split into individual categories. To split a transaction, click the Split button adjoining the register's Category text box. The Split Transaction box that appears contains several rows, one row for each category.

To add or modify a category, click the Category column of a row and choose from the list of categories that appears. (The bottom half of each category row is for classifications, which I don't deal with here.) Enter a dollar amount for each row until the amounts equal the total. To divide any remaining amount (such as sales tax) equally among all parts of your split, press the F6 key. Click the Done button after you finish.

10. **Look at the Date text box and, if you need to change the date, click the date that appears here and then edit it.**

    The date that you want to use is the date of the transaction (although Money always first puts today's date in this text box). Click the tiny down arrow at the right of the date text box to choose a date from a drop-down calendar, or press + or – on the keyboard to advance or regress the date by one day. (For electronic payments, you need to use a date in the future to give your bank time to process the transaction.)

11. **Click the Enter button or press Enter on your keyboard.**

    If you entered everything to Money's satisfaction, Money enters your transaction in the account's register. If not, Money displays a dialog box to help you straighten things out.

Setting Up Recurring Bills and Scheduled Transactions

Everyone has recurring bills, and Microsoft is doing something about it! (No, Bill Gates isn't going to pay your debts for you. In fact, he's kind of a recurring Bill himself, with his products all over your PC.) But Microsoft Money can do the following two things for your recurring bills:

✔ Remind you when to pay a bill. (Again, not Bill Gates. You already paid him by buying Works Suite 2000.)

✔ Reproduce the same transaction in Money each time, on time, so that all you need to do is verify or correct the amount and pay the bill.

I'm talking about recurring bills, but heck — the bills don't need to *recur*; they only need to 'cur once, at some time in the future. Got a one-time payment to a bookie due by New Year's Day? Put Mr. Armbracher on your Money calendar. And you can also set up Money to handle paychecks and other regular deposits, withdrawals, transfers, and even regularly purchased investments (which investment advisors generally recommend).

You can't always set up all the details about a transaction in advance. Paying your phone bill, for example: Who knows how often your kids may call collect? But Money enables you to review and change the details before the transaction actually happens. Fill in your best guess now to save time later if you happen to be right.

Set things up by following these steps:

1. **Click Bills on the Money navigation bar.**

   Money displays the Bills & Deposits window.

2. **On the left side of the Money window, click Set Up Bills & Deposits.**

   The Recurring Bills & Deposits page appears, as shown in Figure 15-2.

3. **Click New to set up a scheduled transaction.**

   A Create New Scheduled Transaction Wizard leaps nimbly into action (despite having a rather ponderous name). Its first page asks what kind of transaction you have in mind.

4. **Choose one: Deposit, Bill, Transfer, or Investment Purchase, and then click Next.**

5. **Tell Money how often the transaction happens: Click Only Once or More Than Once, at Regular Intervals; if more than once, click Frequency and choose one of the intervals listed; finally, click Next.**

   If you're entering a scheduled investment, skip to Step 8.

6. **Tell Money how you plan to pay by clicking the Payment Method drop-down list box and selecting a method from its list; then click Next.**

   You can still choose a different payment method before Money records or makes the transaction. If you're setting up a bill or a transfer, the drop-down list displays many ways of making the transaction happen. If you're setting up a deposit, your selections are Write Check, Direct Debit, Print This Transaction, or the mysterious Other. (Money? What money? Did someone give me some money?)

7. **Tell Money whether the amount is to be the same each time by clicking either Yes, It's The Same Amount Each Time or No, The Amount Usually Varies; then click Next.**

   Whichever selection you choose, you still can change any individual payment before Money records it. After you click Next, a transaction form appears.

Figure 15-2:
Money
makes your
PC a star at
knowing
when a bill
is coming.

M My Money - Microsoft Money

File Edit Go Favorites Tools Help

Accounts Bills Investing Planner Taxes Reports More ▾

Back Home

Bills & Deposits

Common Tasks

See payee details ▸
Turn on online bills
Tell Money how you'd like
to be reminded about bills

Schedule your upcoming bills and deposits

If you have recurring bills and deposits, entering them here makes it easy to record them each
time they occur. Money also reminds you before they are due and helps you anticipate account
balances.

Payee	Account	Frequency	Amount
Scheduled Paychecks & Deposits			
Click New to schedule a recurring deposit			
Scheduled Bills & Withdrawals			
DSS & Cable	First Citizens Bank ...	Monthly	($100.00)~
Duke	First Citizens Bank ...	Monthly	($150.00)~
Garbage people	First Citizens Bank ...	Every three months	($45.00)~
News & Record	First Citizens Bank ...	Every three months	($60.00)~
Peerless	First Citizens Bank ...	Monthly	($100.00)~
Peerless	First Citizens Bank ...	Monthly	($140.00)~
Phone	First Citizens Bank ...	Monthly	($55.00)~
SouthTrust	First Citizens Bank ...	Monthly	($1,019.00)~
Visa	First Citizens Bank ...	Monthly	($19.00)~
Scheduled Transfers			

New...   Edit Details...   Delete   ~ Estimated

Done

8. **Fill out the payment, deposit, or transfer form, just as in your account register, making sure that you enter the date the transaction is next to occur in the Next Due text box, and then click Finish.**

If you're scheduling an investment, see the sidebar "Scheduling an investment."

Being aware of upcoming transactions

You need never again miss another mortgage or credit card payment thanks to Money. Money provides a monitor for staying on top of your recurring bills (or other financial transaction). This monitor is known as Microsoft Money Express and it appears as soon as you start Windows if a bill's awaiting payment. You can also launch Money Express any time by clicking the checkbook icon that Money places on your Windows taskbar. Then choose Open Events List from the pop-up menu that appears. (The icon's on the opposite end of the taskbar from the Start button, so you need to keep an eye out for it.) Click Money Express's Close button to dismiss the Bill Reminder. To disable reminders or change the advance warning period from its 10 days default value, choose Tools➪Options from the Money menu bar and then click the Bills and Deposits tab of the Options dialog box that appears.

If a bill is due (or overdue!), Money places a notice on the Money Home Page (in the Reminders section on the lower right corner). Click that notice to go directly to the Bills & Deposits window.

Scheduling an investment

For a scheduled investment, such as a regular investment in your retirement account, fill out the investment form in the Create New Scheduled Transaction Wizard as follows:

1. In the Purchase Date text box, enter the date for the next purchase.

2. Click `Inv. Account` to choose in which of your investment accounts you're making your investment.

3. Click `Investment` to type the stock or mutual fund or select from existing investments.

4. Enter values for the Number of Shares that you expect to buy, the Price Per Share that you expect to pay (you can change it at purchase time), and the Commission (in dollars).

5. Leave Check Number blank if you expect to pay by check; choose Print if you expect to print a check (and choose Epay for electronic payments).

6. Click Payee and enter the name of the organization you're paying for these shares.

7. Click Transfer Account and choose the account from which you're transferring funds or writing a check to buy the shares.

After filling out this form, click the Finish button in the Create New Scheduled Transaction Wizard. Money now keeps track of your scheduled investment.

Proceeding with scheduled transactions

After you pay a scheduled bill from your checkbook or carry out some other scheduled transaction, you want to record it in Money. To record the transaction as completed, follow these steps:

1. **Click Bills on Money's navigation bar.**

2. **Select the bill that you want to pay and then click the Record Payment button.**

   A Record Payment entry form appears.

3. **Click the Record Payment button that appears in the Record Payment form.**

Money draws a line through the transaction to mark it as recorded. Your account register now also shows this transaction.

Printing Checks

Actually, you can't print checks by using Money. You *can* print *on* checks, however, which means that you need to get blank, numbered checks. You probably already have checks — but you need special (and, naturally, more expensive) checks designed for Money to print on your printer. Money-compatible checks in different sizes and styles are available from several sources, including (no surprise) Microsoft. Consult a good office-supply store and bring your checkbook with you.

If you currently pay bills one at a time, you're going to find that printing checks in Money is more work than writing checks. But at least Money's checks are neatly printed, and if you're recording the check in Money anyway, printing is not *that* much additional work. If you pay several bills at once rather than singly, check printing is somewhat more worthwhile.

Setting up your printer for your checks

Windows already knows about your printer (assuming that you installed the printer correctly), but now you need to tell Money about your checks. Just follow these steps:

1. **Choose File⇨Print Setup⇨Check Setup from the Money menu bar.**

   The Check Setup dialog box appears.

2. **Review the printer selection information in the dialog box.**

   Money gets its information about what printer to use from Windows. If you have more than one printer installed on your PC and the one that you want to use doesn't appear in the Printer box, click that box to choose the correct printer.

3. **Review the check info in the Type box.**

   The Type box lists a check style and size. Compare that information to the label on your check package, and if the description differs, click the Type box to choose a description closer to the one on your package. The Laser Standard description is usually also okay for checks that you print on ink-jet printers. A picture to the right of the Type box shows how each style appears. Styles with white dots down the sides of the checks (representing holes) are only for printers that use sprockets to drive a continuous, perforated sheet of checks through the printer.

4. **Review the printer feed info in the Source box.**

   The Source box tells you where Money thinks you're going to feed the blank check sheets into your printer. Auto Sheet Feeder is where you normally put a stack of blank paper. Consulting your printer manual may help you figure out what Money is talking about. If you want to feed from a different place (say, a manual-feed slot), click Source and choose a new source.

Numbering your printed checks differently

You're probably not going to give up your checkbook. Your checkbook already contains numbered checks; unfortunately, you can't print on them. You probably don't want to drag sheets of Money's printable checks to the store with you to write on either, although you can. How, therefore, do you keep Money's check numbers in sync with your checkbook's number series and avoid duplicate or missing numbers? If you keep Money absolutely up to date by recording checkbook checks as you (and your spouse!) write them, Money uses the next check number in the series, and all you do is tear up any duplicate-numbered checks. But few humans are that organized. Instead, I suggest that you number your Money-printed checks very differently: Start at, say, check number 10,000.

5. **Decide whether you want the payee's address on the check.**

    Money normally prints the payee's address on the check, and if the payee's address isn't already on file in Money, it asks you for it at the time that you print a check. If you don't want the address printed, click to clear the Require Address For Payee When Printing Checks check box.

You can change the font that Money uses on the check by clicking the Font button and making selections in the Font dialog box. Click OK after you're done.

Actually printing checks

Before you can print a check, you must record the transaction (as a Print transaction) on your account register page or the bill payment page. See the earlier sections of this chapter for instructions on recording transactions in account registers and while paying bills. The transaction must have Print chosen in the Number drop-down list box if it's to result in a printed check.

After you record the transaction, the phrase Print Checks appears in a To Do area at the left side of the account's register page and the bill payment page or in the Reminders area of the Money Home Page. Then follow these steps:

1. **Click Print Checks in the To Do or Reminders area.**

    A Print Checks dialog box appears, telling you how many checks Money is ready to print at this time, as shown in Figure 15-3. If you want to print only certain checks, click the Selected Checks option button and, in the Select Checks dialog box that appears, click the checks that you *don't* want to print, which deselects them. (Deselected checks appear in white; checks that you intend to print appear in yellow.) Click OK after you finish.

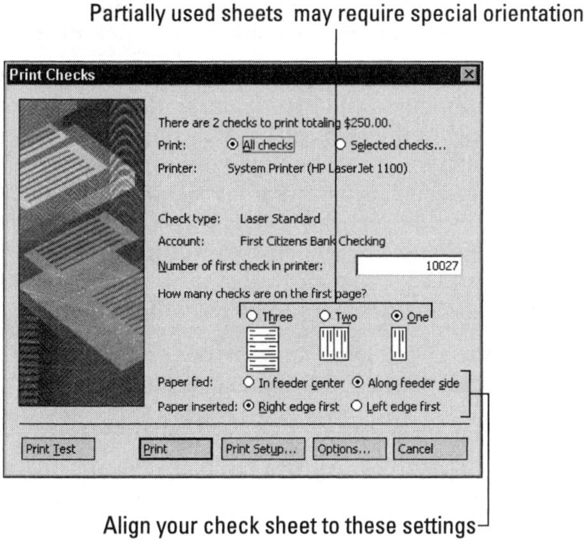

Partially used sheets may require special orientation

Figure 15-3:
The Print
Checks
dialog box.
(Notice that
sometimes
you must
print your
checks side
by side.)

Align your check sheet to these settings

2. **Examine your sheet of checks and type the lowest number on that page of checks in the Number of First Check in Printer text box.**

   If you're not printing on sheets of checks but on continuous-form paper, skip to Step 6. If you already used one or more of the checks on the first sheet of checks, you must tell the Print Checks dialog box how many checks remain on that sheet.

3. **Click the Three, Two, or One option button.**

   Each selection (Three, Two, or One) displays how to orient the first page of your check sheet in the printer.

4. **Place your checks in the printer feed area that you chose during setup.**

   Orient the top sheet the way that Money tells you in the preceding step. Align the edges as the Paper Fed and Paper Inserted buttons in the dialog box indicate or choose the orientation that your printer manual suggests and then click the buttons to match, as the following list describes:

   • **In Feeder Center:** Money expects you to center the checks in the feed area.

   • **Along Feeder Side:** Money expects you to align the edge of the page to the left (as you face the printer's front) in the feed area.

   • **Right Edge First/Left Edge First:** Choose which edge of the check, right or left (as you read the check), goes into the printer first.

5. **If you're not certain that everything is set up right, insert a plain piece of paper in place of the check sheet and Click Print Test.**

   Money prints a dummy check. Lay the dummy over the check sheet in the correct orientation and hold the two up to the light to see whether everything is printing in the right place. If you need to reposition, click the Options button. In the Printing Alignment area of the Options dialog box that appears, you can adjust the printing position by ¼-inch intervals. Money provides two separate controls for full-sheet and partial-sheet adjustment. Adding 1 to a horizontal setting moves the printing ¼ inch to the right. (Adding 1 to a vertical setting moves the printing ¼ inch down.) Use negative numbers to go the other direction.

6. **If you're certain the check is going to print correctly, click the Print button (at the bottom of the Print Checks dialog box).**

7. **If the check prints satisfactorily, click the Finish button.**

   Otherwise, click the Reprint button in the Print Checks dialog box and then, in the Select Checks to Reprint dialog box that appears, click the check that you want to reprint. You need to reinsert and possibly reorient the top check sheet (as I describe in Step 4) because you used one of the checks. Then click the OK button.

Reconciling Accounts

Do your records and the bank's records agree? You can find out by using Money's reconciliation feature. Personally, I hate *reconciling,* otherwise known as balancing one's checkbook, because I simply end up wasting hours tracking down some stupid typo I made. I prefer to enter data into Money directly from the bank statement so that the two must agree! I review for errors by comparing Money's register to my checkbook register. But then, I suspect I'm morally deficient in my banking practices.

If you feel morally bound to reconcile your account, begin by making sure that you entered all the transactions from your checkbook, ATM receipts, and other records into the Money register. Then take your monthly statement firmly by the hand and follow these steps:

1. **Open Money to the account register page by clicking Accounts on the navigation bar (clicking it again, if necessary, to see the list of all accounts) and then double-clicking your account.**

2. **Click <u>B</u>alance This Account on the left side of the screen.**

   The Balance Wizard strides onto your screen in a well-balanced fashion, as shown in Figure 15-4.

3. **Enter the statement date and ending balance from your bank statement in the appropriate drop-down list boxes.**

   Money obtains the starting balance from your last reconciliation.

4. **Enter any service charge(s) in the Service Charge drop-down list box and click its Category drop-down list box to categorize that expense.**

5. **Enter any interest earned in the Interest Earned drop-down list box, and click its Category drop-down list box to categorize that income.**

6. **Click Next to open a reconciliation window for your account.**

   The panel in the left side of the window describes the three steps you need to take next.

Reconciling an account with online reports from your bank

Money can (in theory) automatically reconcile your account with an online report that — if your bank offers this service — Money downloaded from your bank the last time that you went online. Click Tools⇨Connect to Online Services or click Accounts and then, in the left pane, click Get Online Statements.

Then choose your bank or other financial institution from the list that appears. If more than one account appears, click the account that you want.

Your bank's Internet Web page appears — probably a logon page requiring a password, your Social Security number, or whatever. Follow the instructions, which vary depending on how your bank set up its Web site.

7. **Take one of the following actions in the panel at the left side of the reconciliation window:**

   • Review each transaction listed and click the skinny C column for each transaction that matches the bank statement. (*C* stands for *Cleared.*)

   • To add or edit transactions (for example, your statement may show ATM fees), click the Click Here to Add or Edit Transactions check box. A data entry form appears, which works exactly like the one in your account register.

   • By clearing, adding, and editing transactions, you reduce the Difference figure (as shown in Step 2 of the instructions on the left panel of the window) to zero.

8. **Click Next.**

Types of Electronic Transactions

Money provides for a variety of electronic transactions, including the following:

- ✔ **Epays:** Electronic payments that you make, one at a time.

- ✔ **Apays:** Automatic payments of the same amount, which you need to make regularly, that you instruct your bank's computer to make.

- ✔ **Web payments:** Bill paying and other transactions such as statement downloading that use your bank's Web page.

- ✔ **Xfers:** Transfers between two accounts at the same bank or other institution.

- ✔ **E-bills:** Electronic bills that come to you through a Web site.

In the spirit of not belaboring the online part of Money in this book, I refer you to Money's Help files for full information about these types of transactions. Choose Help⇨Help Topics from the Money menu bar. In the Help panel that appears, click the area Ask Money at the bottom of the panel and type the following text: **Learn about Epays, Apays**. The Help panel displays the text `Learn about Epays, Apays, Web Payments, Xfers, E-bills, and automatic transactions`. Click that text to view the Help file. Click the X in the upper right-hand corner of the Help panel to remove the panel.

Chapter 16

Budgeting, Reporting, and Analyzing

*H*aving all your transactions neatly organized and displayed in Money is lovely, but it doesn't pay the bills. Well . . . actually, it *does* pay the bills, I guess, but what I mean is that neatness and organization aren't everything.

One of the benefits of entering all your transactions into a computer program and categorizing them is that the program can help you summarize and analyze your finances, and do some planning. It can also help you prepare reports and charts of financial information for the people nearest and dearest to you, like your spouse, your accountant, or the Internal Revenue Service.

Money does all this work with the aid of *planners* (in Money's Planners department) and with reports and charts (in Money's Reports department). In this chapter, I focus on the tools I think most people want to use: the Budget Planner, and the report and chart features. The report and chart features are particularly useful for that most popular pastime, paying taxes, where you need to separate the wheat from the chaff. (And pay taxes on the wheat.)

How to really clean up

Money's planning, reporting, and charting features need a clean set of categories to work well. (Oh — you thought I was going to give you my secret stock market tips to really clean up with? Given my financial expertise, you should be glad I'm not!) No, fortunately for you, I'm just suggesting that you clean up your categories so that using Money's planners and decision tools is easier.

Click More and then click Categories & Payees on Money's navigation bar, and make sure that your categories make sense. (See Chapter 15 for more details. You're okay if you haven't added any categories to Money's original set.) Problem spots are

✔ **Categories with different names but that mean the same thing.** Dividends, for instance, and Dividend Income. To fix the problem, click one (say, Dividend Income) and click the Delete button. Money asks you what category to reassign its transactions to. (Select Dividend in this example.)

✔ **Categories unassigned to groups.** Double-click the category and, in the window that appears, click to select a Category Group. Click the Back button on the navigation bar to return to the Categories window.

✔ **Categories that should be subcategories.** Fred's Dividend Income should be a subcategory of Fred's Income, for instance. To make Category X a subcategory under Category Y, click Category X, click the Move button at the bottom of the window, and enter Category Y in the Move Transactions dialog box that appears. The category can keep its old name.

Budgeting

Ugh. Budgeting. Nothing is more depressing than trying to stick to a budget. But I'm not talking about *sticking* to a budget, here; I'm talking about *making a budget!* Totally unrelated. Much more fun.

Money makes building a budget interesting by automatically adding up all the many picky details about your various types of income, savings, bills, and debts, and then showing you how well you can expect to do monthly or yearly. Money can also *autobudget:* create a budget for you based on previous transactions. The Budget Planner's reports and forecast chart can help you see where you may have budget problems, and how fast savings will increase under your plan.

Even with the raw, untamed excitement of using Money, budgeting can be a bit tedious, so get yourself a large box of cookies and a pot of coffee. Remember, budgets are good for you.

Getting started

1. **Click Planner on the Money navigation bar and then click Create a Budget on the screen that appears.**

   (If you've already created a budget, this option, intelligently, does not appear. However, you can repeat the process by clicking Update My Budget and then clicking Getting Started.)

   The Getting Started screen appears.

2. **Click the <u>Group</u> <u>Your</u> <u>Accounts</u> link to enter the Organize by Accounts dialog box.**

   Here you review and/or change how you want Money to think of your various accounts: Which ones are for day-to-day expenses, and which ones are for long-term savings, for instance. Click an account and then click a purpose. Money uses these purposes to help you plan.

   Click Close at the bottom of the dialog box when you're done.

3. **Click Next in the top-right corner of the Getting Started screen.**

   The Budget Planner begins to step you through a series of windows for each kind of budget item. This chapter has a subsection for each planner window.

You can move directly to any Budget Planner page by clicking its name (Debt, for instance) on the left-hand panel of the Budget Planner window.

Have a cookie.

Income

You know that as you record your deposits in Money, you associate them with categories, right? (Oh, come on. I'm sure you do. But, if not, check out Chapter 14.) Money uses the total deposits you have associated with each category to estimate an initial income budget. Figure 16-1 shows the Income window.

The task here is to include all important income categories in the plan and to establish a reasonable budget amount for each category. To remove a trivial, incorrect, or otherwise insufferable category, click it and then click the Remove button.

To add a category of income, click Add Category. A dialog box politely asks you to select the category (or subcategory). If you select a category and then click Next, a second screen appears. Despite its tedious explanation, it merely wants to know if you want to include all the category's subcategories. Click Yes if so, click No if not, and then click Finish.

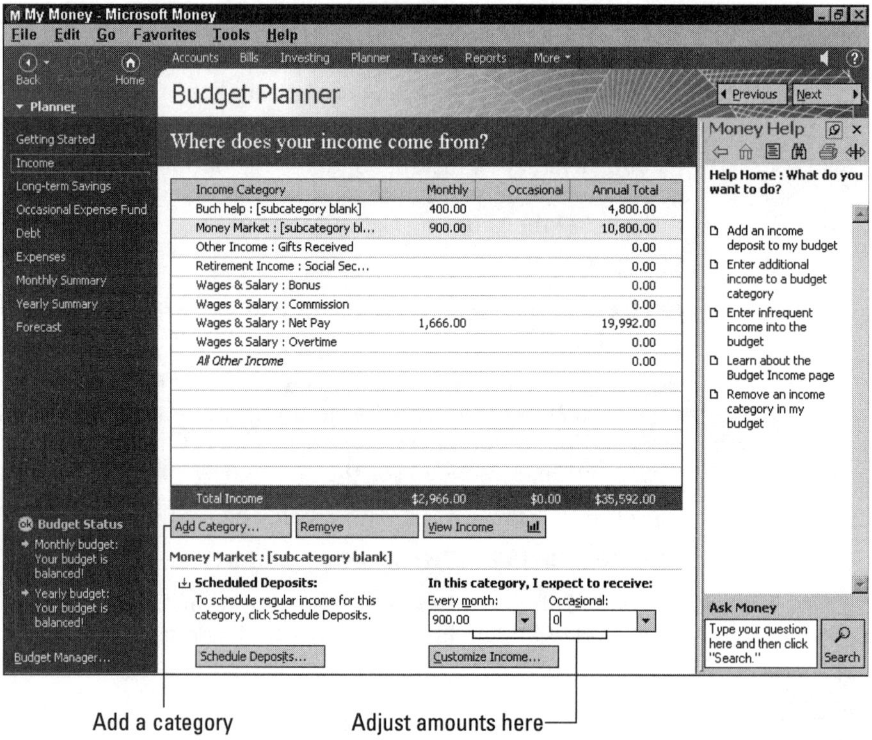

Figure 16-1:
Use income
categories
to budget
income.

Add a category

Adjust amounts here

You don't have to live with the amounts shown. Click the category, and you can adjust the amounts. Figure 16-1 shows you where. (*Occasional* income is added income, by the way, not an alternative to monthly income.)

Is your income seasonal? If you're a ski instructor or gardener, click Customize Income and click Custom in the dialog box that appears. You can then enter a separate figure for each month.

Click Next in the window's upper-right corner (or click Long-Term Savings in the window's left panel) to proceed to the Long-Term Savings window.

Have another cookie.

Long-term savings

The Money philosophy (if software can have a philosophy — a matter for philosophers to decide) is that you should consider saving money to be "paying yourself first," and give it an appropriately high priority compared to spending it (paying other people). That philosophy is why savings occurs before expenses in this planner, as I'm sure it does in your life.

In the Long-Term Savings window, you can enter an amount by double-clicking the highlighted line labeled `Contributions to Long-term Savings`. In the Customize Contribution dialog box that appears, either enter a monthly and (optional) occasional value, or (if your savings contributions will be seasonal) click Custom and enter a contribution for each month.

You can also add specific, scheduled deposits into any account to which you gave the purpose of long-term savings (back on the Getting Started screen with the Group Your Accounts feature). Click New Contribution, and a wizard-like series of dialog boxes asks you nosy questions, culminating in a data entry form. Fill out this form as you would for a transfer transaction in an account register (see Chapter 15 for details) and then click Finish.

Click Next in the window's upper-right corner (or click Occasional Expense Fund in the window's left panel) to proceed to the Occasional Expense Fund window.

Put a cookie under the sofa for long-term savings. Or for the dog. Whoever gets there first.

Occasional expenses

Money's occasional expenses are for those very special occasions, like a vacation, a romantic dinner, or your car's exhaust system falling off on the turnpike. Here you budget for a certain periodic contribution, to save for your muffler guy's kid's college education.

Use this page like you do the Long-Term Savings window.

Click Next in the window's upper-right corner (or click Debt in the window's left panel) to move on to the Debt and Loans window.

(Now, pour a cup from that pot of coffee I recommended at the start. I know *I* need a cup!)

Debt and loans

Whatever happened to "neither a borrower nor a lender be?" We're all in hock up to our ears! So much so, that Money provides a Debt Reduction Planner, a close neighbor to the Budget Planner.

The Debt window shows you the debts the Budget Planner is currently aware of. If the Debt window doesn't display a loan or other debt account that you set up, and you want to add that debt, you must make the debt part of a *debt plan,* by using the Debt Reduction Planner.

A quick trip to the Debt Reduction Planner

You find a link (underlined text) to the Debt Reduction Planner at the top of the Debt window of the Budget Planner. You can also find a Debt Reduction Planner link in the top-level Planner window: Click Planner on Money's navigation bar to go to that window and then, whichever way you get to it, click the link.

Using either link gets you to the Debt Reduction Planner. It displays a Debt Plan window like the one in Figure 16-2.

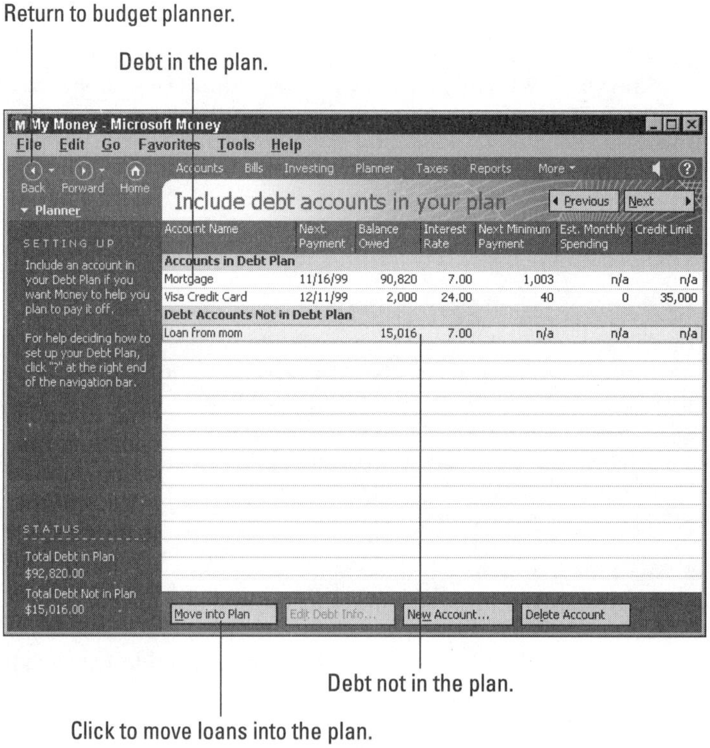

Return to budget planner.

Debt in the plan.

Figure 16-2:
You and Microsoft Money will feel better when your debt is in a plan.

Debt not in the plan.

Click to move loans into the plan.

Note: Figure 16-2 shows a mortgage in the plan, which is not really the high-interest kind of debt that the Debt Planner is normally concerned about. Mortgages are not usually high-interest debts. Remove such debt from your Debt Plan. Click the debt and then click the Move Out of Plan button (it takes the place of the Move into Plan button in Figure 16-2).

To bring a debt into the plan, click the debt in the lower portion of the window and then click the Move into Plan button at the bottom of the window. (The Debt Planner may ask you a few questions at this point.)

To edit anything about the debt, click the debt and then click the Edit Debt Info button. You can also add a new debt account by clicking the New Account button and following the instructions of the New Account Wizard.

Going back to the Budget Planner

To return to the Budget Planner, don't click the Next button in the Debt Reduction Planner, as you may do out of habit. Click the Back button on the Money navigation bar instead.

If debt reduction is a serious goal of yours, *do* click the Next button in the Debt Reduction Planner and continue in this tool until its end. I don't have the room in this book to do justice to this tool, but read the planner's instructions carefully, and you just may save some money in the end. To return to the Budget Planner, click Planner in Money's navigation bar and then click the link to the Budget Planner.

Have two cookies.

Click the Next button in the upper-right corner of the Budget Planner (or click Expenses in the window's left panel) to proceed to the Expenses window.

Expenses: Spending by category

In the Expenses window, the Budget Planner asks you to review each of your expense categories and set a monthly budget amount for each category. The Planner suggests amounts, and you can change them. Here's how to do it:

- ✔ **Autobudget:** If you already entered one month or more of categorized expenses into Money, click the Autobudget button to have the Budget Planner estimate a budget for you. In the Autobudget dialog box that appears, click to deselect the check boxes of categories that you want to omit from your budget and then click OK.

- ✔ **Enter budget amounts:** Click an expense category (one that doesn't have an amount of money specified), and two text boxes at the bottom right of the window appear. Click the Every Month box and enter whatever you think you'll spend monthly. If you think you may occasionally spend more (or if an expense is paid annually), click the Occasional box and type that amount, to be added to your monthly expense. Click Customize Spending to vary spending seasonally.

- ✔ **Add or remove categories:** To add a category not listed here or to create a new category, click the Add Category button to use the New Category dialog box described in Chapter 15. To remove a category from your budget, click it and then click the Remove button.

✓ **Budget for scheduled bills:** Categories that include scheduled bills display a red up-arrow icon, and if you click that category, you can review the bill summary in the lower-left corner of the window. Click the Edit Bills button there to display a dialog box where you can edit, delete, or add scheduled bills to the category. Click the Additional Spending button to add other monthly or seasonal expenses to this category.

✓ **Check your spending:** Click the View Spending button to see a report of your past six months' spending.

Now go to the Monthly Summary window. Click Next in the window's upper-right corner (or click Expenses in the window's left panel). Yawn. Have a cup of coffee.

Monthly or yearly summary

This is the moment of truth. The Budget Planner takes the monthly amounts that you budgeted for income and outgo, and puts them all together in the Monthly Summary window. If monthly savings, expenses, and debt payments exceed monthly income, the planner lets you know here. Have a nice, stiff cup of coffee and ponder whether you can rent out that spare room for extra income.

If you have income left over, choose whether to place the extra in your savings (click Save It in My Occasional Expense Fund) or spend it (click Spend the Money). Surprisingly, Money does not suggest where you should spend your money — an admirable show of restraint by Microsoft.

For a yearly summary, click the Next button in the upper-right corner of the window (or click Yearly Summary in the window's left panel). The yearly summary combines both monthly and occasional amounts into a single report. If you have a lot of once-a-year payments, this summary may hold some additional surprises for you. Consider having some more cookies.

Forecast

Click the Next button in the upper-right corner of the Yearly Summary window or click Forecast on the left side of the Budget Planner window, and you get a chart showing the gradual rise (or fall) of your fortunes.

Click the Interpret the Forecast link for tips on interpreting the graph. The tips appear in the Money Help panel. Click the X in its upper-right corner to remove the tips when you finish reading them.

Click the <u>Customize</u> link to change the chart. In the Customize Report dialog box that appears, you may make the following changes (click the Apply button to see the result of your choice, or click OK if you are done fiddling):

- Click in the Show Next selection box to select a time period for the forecast.
- Click Level of Detail to change the time interval on the bar from weeks to months — or to another time interval.
- To make your unscheduled expenses appear either at the beginning or end of the month, click in the Unscheduled Monthly Expenses Happen selection box and select one of those options.
- To do the same for annual expenses, click in the Unscheduled Annual Expenses Happen selection box.
- Click the Chart tab for chart options. By clicking to clear the Stacked check box, you can un-stack the Monthly Expense Fund (blue) from the Occasional Expense Fund (yellow). Select the Show in 3D check box for bars with depth, or deselect the Show Gridlines check box to eliminate the horizontal lines on the chart.

You're done! That's everything the Budget Planner can tell you, budget-wise. Click Finish in the upper-right corner of the window, and finish off that box of cookies!

Analyzing with Reports and Charts

Money's reports and charts help you summarize and visualize your expense and income categories. Or, in more practical terms, they can help you do the following

- Make gee-whiz color charts and reports to justify to your spouse, boss, or accountant all the time you're spending with this program.
- Find all your tax-related income and expenses by category.
- See who is getting all your money.
- Compare your current income to your current spending.
- Find out whether or not you are living within your budget.
- See your net worth or watch how your accounts change over time.
- Display price trends of your stocks and schedule your bankruptcy.

Choosing and using report and chart windows

To perform any or all of the marvelous Money chart and report functions, stroll through Money's fabulous gallery of reports and charts and pick one that fits right over the living room couch. Do the following:

1. **Click Reports on the Money navigation bar.**

   Money's Report and Chart Gallery rushes to your aid, listing various groups of charts down the left panel.

2. **On the left side of the window, click to select a category of reports and charts.**

3. **On the right side of the window, click to select a specific report or chart.**

4. **If any selection boxes appear at the bottom of the window, click them to make selections that adjust the focus of your report or chart.**

   Depending on the specific report or chart that you choose, you can click in a selection box and choose to focus on general categories (such as taxable transactions), specific income or expense categories, accounts, or date ranges.

5. **Click the Go to Report/Chart button to view your selected report or chart.**

   If you select a chart, it may appear in any of several forms: bar, line, or pie chart. Depending on what other forms of chart are available, you can change the form.

Pie charts are useful for seeing proportions: what portion of your spending is on dining out, for instance. Line charts are useful for trends or things that vary over time, like spending in a particular category. Bar charts are useful for comparing values.

Figure 16-3 shows a bar chart and the controls for changing to a different form of chart. If a form of chart is not available, that button is grayed out.

In Money, you can turn many charts into reports, and vice versa. Simply click the Report button or one of the Chart buttons shown in Figure 16-3 to make the transformation.

Here are a few tips for chart and report windows:

  ✔ Most charts and reports need some customization to be useful. For instance, I limited the chart in Figure 16-3 to high values to avoid squeezing dozens of bars illegibly into the chart. See "Customizing reports and charts," later in this chapter.

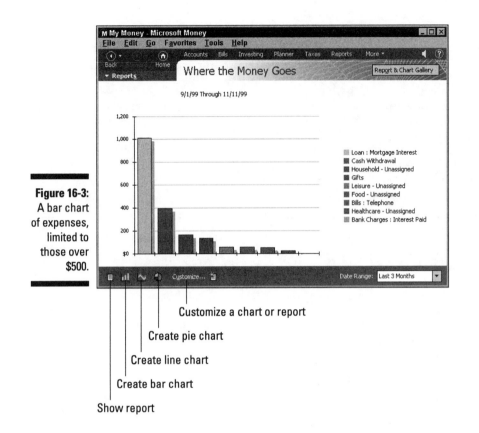

Figure 16-3:
A bar chart
of expenses,
limited to
those over
$500.

Customize a chart or report

Create pie chart

Create line chart

Create bar chart

Show report

✔ Pause your cursor over any bar, pie segment, line, or legend entry (in the list on the right side) to see the dollar value of that item. Double-click that item to see what categories, accounts, or transactions it includes.

✔ To choose new dates, either double-click the dates at the top of the chart or report, or click the Date Range list box at the lower right. Both take you to the Customization dialog box, which I discuss in the next section.

✔ To view the details of a transaction in a report, double-click it. To edit the transaction in the View Transaction dialog box that appears, double-click the transaction.

✔ To return to the gallery to select a different report or chart, click the <u>Report</u> & <u>Chart Gallery</u> link at the top right of the report or chart page.

✔ Reports tend to be long, and you generally need to print them to get the big picture. See "Printing your report or chart," later in this chapter.

Customizing reports and charts

Money's predesigned reports and charts are great, but most of them need some customization to be useful to you. You can customize a report before you display it by clicking the Customize button in the report and chart gallery (labeled Pick A Report Or Chart), or by clicking Customize at the bottom left of the chart or report window.

The Customize Report dialog box then appears, displaying several tabbed cards, like index cards. Click a tab to select it. Each of the most important tabs is described in the next eight sections. (The trivial tabs, Text and Font, I'm sure you can figure out on your own.)

To see your customizations applied to the chart or report currently displayed, click the Apply button in the dialog box. You probably need to drag the dialog box by its title bar to get it out of the way. Click the OK button after you make all the customizations you want.

One of the most useful customizations you can perform is to limit the amount of data displayed. Money has a tendency to show you too much: too many categories, too many accounts, too many payees, or too many transactions. To limit the data, use the tabs that I describe in the following sections. In particular, see how the Rows and Columns tab can create an *all other* category containing all the tiny, floor-sweepings data that you don't want to show separately.

Unfortunately, you can't undo changes. But you can use the Reset button to undo all your customizations and return to the predesigned, default settings that were in effect when you first chose this report or chart from the Gallery.

To save your customized chart or report, add it to Money's Favorites. Click Favorites on the Money menu bar, and in the Add to Favorites dialog box that appears, type a report name. Click OK, and your report is listed as a link on the Money Home Page. Click that link to return to the report or chart, or choose Favorites⇨Favorite Reports and then your report's name.

Date

The Date tab is pretty obvious, I think. It limits your display to data between certain dates. Click Range to select preset ranges, like Previous Year, or click in the From or To text boxes to enter custom dates.

Account

The Account tab limits your chart or report to certain accounts. Click to deselect an account's check box and remove it from the display. Click Select All to select all the accounts or click Clear All to remove all the accounts.

If you need to select just a handful of accounts, click Clear All first to deselect all check boxes. If some accounts are closed, you can limit the display to just the open ones by clicking All Open Accounts.

Category

The Category tab limits your chart or report to certain categories or subcategories. As in the Account tab, click to deselect a category's check box to remove it from the display. If you need to select just a handful of accounts, click Clear All first to deselect all check boxes. Click one of the Select buttons to select various types of categories: All Categories, Income, Expense, or Tax-Related.

Click to deselect the Show Subcategories check box to eliminate subcategories from the list.

Payee

The payee tab works just like the Account and Category tabs, but for payees! Deselect the check boxes for payees that you want to eliminate. (From the report/chart that is.)

Amount

The Amount tab lets you restrict the display to certain exact amounts (click Search on This Amount) or a range of amounts (click Search on This Range).

To specify a range of amounts, click the From box to enter the low end and then click the To box to enter the high end. For an open-ended range (say, above $500), leave the other value (To, in this example) blank.

Details

The Details tab enables you to limit the chart or report by type of transactions you want (click the Type box to select), and/or the transaction's reconciliation status (click the Status box to select), and/or the check number.

You can limit the display to a particular check number (click Find This Check Number and enter a check number in that box), or to a range of check numbers (click Find This Range, and enter the lowest and highest check numbers in the From and To boxes, respectively).

Rows & Columns

The Rows & Columns tab is intended to let you specify what appears in the rows and columns of reports (as its name implies), but it also affects charts. (Note that the following description applies only when you're customizing *some* of the reports or charts. For example, you'll see the following options if you've selected Net Worth from the What I Have reports option. However, if you select Tax-Related Transactions from the Taxes reports option, the following elements won't be visible on the Rows & Columns tab.)

A very useful option in this tab is to create an *all other* category into which you sweep stuff whose amounts are under a certain percentage of the total: all categories, for instance, where the amount is under 2 percent of the total. Click the Combine All Values Under __ % of Total box, and enter the percentage. This choice helps reduce clutter in your report or chart.

Click Rows to choose what each row of the report (or bar or pie slice of a chart) displays: a category, an account, a particular week, or a particular month.

Click Columns to select what each column of the report displays (or what the horizontal axis of a chart displays). You can have a column for each month, for instance, to create a spreadsheet-like report.

Select the Sort by Amount check box to have rows appear in descending order of amount. Otherwise, rows appear in alphabetical order.

Chart

The Chart tab lets you add features to charts, change the form of a chart (pie, bar, or line), or switch between chart and report form. Among the features that you can add are labels to pie segments in a pie chart, 3D-looking bars, lines, or pies, and horizontal gridlines. You can also position the chart's legend (the text that says what color means what) to the right or below the chart, or turn it off.

Printing your report or chart

Printing a report or chart is straightforward. In a report, you have the option of printing specific page numbers. In a report or chart, you can print vertically (Portrait) or sideways (Landscape). Choose File⇨Print.

If you're printing a report, the Print Report dialog box appears. To print the whole thing, just click OK. To print just certain pages, print the entire report once to find out where the page breaks are. Then choose File⇨Print again, click Pages, and enter the starting page and ending page numbers, respectively in the From and To text boxes. For multiple copies, double-click in the Copies text box and enter the number of copies you want. When printing multiple copies of multipage reports, click Collate Copies to avoid having to collate yourself.

If you're printing a chart, the Print Chart dialog box appears. Choose the number of copies and the print quality, and then click OK.

In either the Print Chart or Print Report dialog box, you have the setup options that nearly every Windows program provides. To use a different printer, sideways printing, funny-sized paper, or your printer's manual inser-tion slot, just click the Setup button. The Report and Chart Setup box appears. To select another printer installed on your PC, click the Printer selection box. For sideways printing (for reports with many columns, for instance), click Landscape. Select a new paper size by clicking Size, if neces-sary, or a manual feed slot by clicking Source. (Click Options to fiddle with printer settings, like quality of printing.) Click OK when you're done.

Chapter 17

Investing with Money

● ●

In This Chapter

▶ Starting your investment accounts

▶ Buy! Sell! Enter Data!

▶ Getting good and bad news online

▶ Figuring out what to buy or sell next

● ●

*I*nvesting with money is a good idea. Traders (despite the name) are notoriously unwilling to accept livestock and other hard goods.

Investing with Microsoft *Money* (Microsoft's software, not its cash) is a similarly good idea. (Investing with its cash would be an even better deal, if you could get it.) Not only does Money then include your investments in its reports and planners, but it also gives you useful graphs and views for comparing and evaluating your investments. It even offers a very simple way to obtain price histories and current trading online, so you can be up to date. Grab your portfolio's statements and prospectuses *(prospecti?)* and fire up Money. Even if you currently have no investments, Money lets you track whatever securities look attractive to you.

Setting Up Investment Accounts

Before you set up an investment account, make sure that you understand that an investment *account* is not the same as a specific *security:* a stock, a bond, a fund, or a certificate of deposit (CD). An investment *account* in Money matches your account with a broker, a bank, or an investment firm — it's a pool of money or value with your name attached to it. Some accounts involve only a single security; others involve many different securities. If you simply want data on a prospective security, see the tip in the later section, "Viewing Current and Prospective Investments."

You set up an investment account much the same as you set up a bank account. (Chapter 14 discusses setting up such accounts.) Here is a quick review:

- ✔ First, click Accounts on the navigation bar.

- ✔ Second, click the <u>Set</u> <u>Up</u> <u>Accounts</u> link on the left side of the page. Then click Add a New Account in the middle of the page. The New Account dialog box (a wizard) appears and takes you through the process of setting up an account. Fill out the forms and click the Next button to proceed.

You can use Money to get stock prices from the Internet *without* setting up private online services with your bank or investment firm. The phrase *online services* in Money refers to private account services that enable you to make transactions or download statements (topics that this book does not get into).

Recording Your Buying, Selling, and Dividends

Recording your investment transactions is very similar to recording bank and checking account transactions in Money (see Chapter 15). The procedure for investments goes like this:

1. **Click Investing on the navigation bar.**

   The Manage Your Investments and Savings window appears, displaying various options and features.

2. **Click the <u>See</u> <u>Investment</u> <u>Accounts</u> link.**

   The Portfolio page appears.

3. **Click an investment account.**

   The investment's register opens, as shown in Figure 17-1.

4. **Click the <u>Investment</u> <u>Transactions</u> link in the left panel of the screen.**

5. **Click in the Date drop-down list box and enter a date.**

   (If you don't see text boxes where you can enter new information, click the Edit button.)

6. **Click in the Investment drop-down list box and select an investment.**

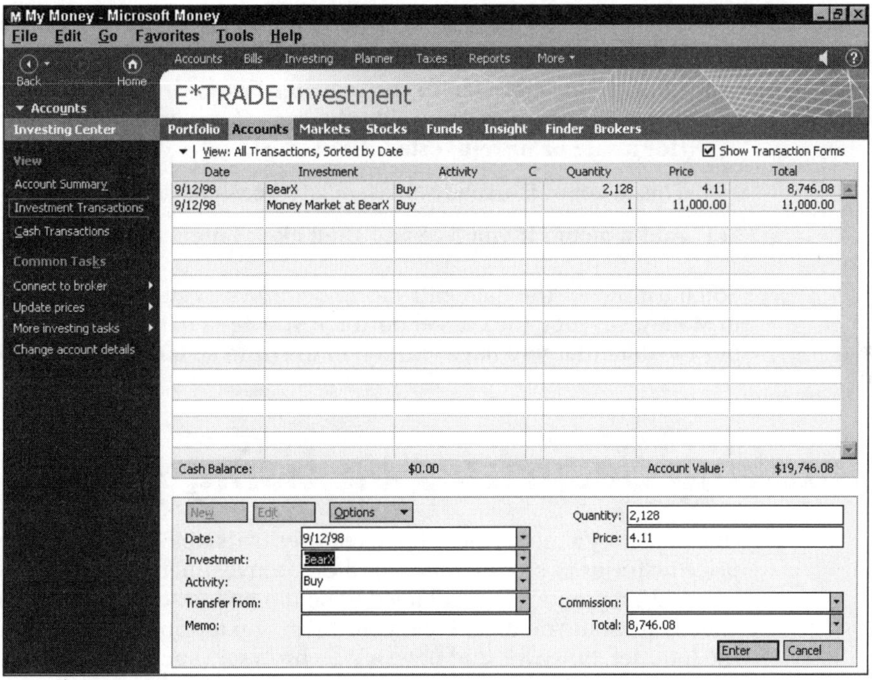

M My Money - Microsoft Money

File Edit Go Favorites Tools Help

Accounts Bills Investing Planner Taxes Reports More ▾

Back Home

▾ Accounts

Investing Center

E*TRADE Investment

Portfolio Accounts Markets Stocks Funds Insight Finder Brokers

▾ | View: All Transactions, Sorted by Date   ☑ Show Transaction Forms

View

Account Summary

Investment Transactions

Cash Transactions

Common Tasks

Connect to broker

Update prices

More investing tasks

Change account details

Date	Investment	Activity	C	Quantity	Price	Total
9/12/98	BearX	Buy		2,128	4.11	8,746.08
9/12/98	Money Market at BearX	Buy		1	11,000.00	11,000.00

| Cash Balance: | $0.00 | | Account Value: | $19,746.08 |

New	Edit	Options ▾		Quantity:	2,128
Date:	9/12/98	▾	Price:	4.11
Investment:	BearX	▾	
Activity:	Buy	▾	
Transfer from:		▾	Commission:	
Memo:			Total:	8,746.08

Enter   Cancel

Figure 17-1:
Recording
investment
transactions:
not a whole
lot different
than
recording
bank or
check
transactions.

If you haven't invested in this security before, Money launches an
inquisitive little wizard. The wizard's questions include what kind of
investment it is, its tax status, and its *ticker symbol* — the symbol that
represents it in the stock market. Refer to your broker or the security's
prospectus for this symbol. Only by entering the symbol can you get
online quotes and history for this security.

TIP

You can also find symbols online. Using Internet Explorer, go to the
address home.microsoft.com. (This is the page that IE, by default,
starts with unless you've used IE's Tools⇨Internet Options feature to
specify a different home page.) Look for the Personal Finance area and
click the Find Symbol link.

7. **Click in the Activity drop-down list box and select Buy, Sell, or
   another activity.**

8. **Click in and enter values into any two of the following text boxes:
   Price (price per share), Quantity (how many shares), or Total (how
   much money you spent or received).**

Money computes the third value that you leave blank. Check it against
your statement.

9. **Click in the Commission drop-down list box and enter a commission, if any.**

10. **Click in the Transfer To (or Transfer From) drop-down list box and select the account supplying the cash (for a buy) or receiving the cash (for a sale or unreinvested dividends).**

    This account is usually an associated cash account.

11. **Add a memo if you like and then click Enter.**

You must fill out the data entry form before you can go to any other window in Money. Or, click the Cancel button if you need to go to another window, but the data that you have entered in the form so far will be lost.

Tracking Securities by Using Online Data

One of Money's most solid online features is its ability to obtain prices and price histories of stocks, funds, and other investments online. The process is free and easy, and you don't need to set up online services with your financial institution. You must have your PC set up for online communications on the Internet, however, and have a Web browser (such as Internet Explorer, which comes with Works Suite) installed. (See Part IV of this book for instructions.) Then do the following:

1. **Click Investing on Money's navigation bar and then click Portfolio.**

   You're viewing the Portfolio page.

2. **Click the Update Prices option in the left panel.**

   A submenu pops out, offering you four ways to update the prices of your securities (online, manually, automatically, or "pick quotes to download").

3. **Choose Update Price Online.**

   You're connected to an online quotes site (though you don't see it displayed). Your stock prices and other investments in your portfolio are updated — as is the information about the Dow, the Nasdaq, and the S&P 500.

Money now knows the current value of all the securities you updated! It also downloaded the most recent day's high and low prices, and a history of the security's performance for the past 12 months. See the next section for instructions on viewing and making use of this information.

Viewing Current and Prospective Investments

Money gives you eight different ways to examine your investments, plus a price history graph for individual investments. The price history graph even lets you visually compare one investment to other investments.

Portfolio views

Click Investing on Money's navigation bar, then click Portfolio, and then click the See a Different View option in the left pane. Choose one of the eight different views from the submenu that pops out.

Money does not know the value of *anything,* right at this minute. All views showing *current* values, changes, or high/low figures can at best use only the most recently downloaded figures. Even the most recently downloaded market values are delayed from actual market values according to trading laws.

Here's where to look for what:

- ✔ **Standard View** is the one you see by default when you first request the Portfolio. It shows the current market value of your investments and the change in various indexes (the DJIA, Nasdaq, and S&P 500).

- ✔ **Performance View** shows how your investments have been doing: current price, most recent change in price, dividends, interest, and appreciation.

- ✔ **Return Calculations View** shows the percentage return on your investment (gain or loss) over several time frames ranging from one week to three years.

- ✔ **Valuation View** is similar to Performance view. You see a breakdown that includes commissions, reinvestments, and the total gain (or loss) for each investment.

- ✔ **Quotes View** shows recent trading history: last value, change, high/low values, and trading volume.

- ✔ **Holdings View** gives a current status report of all your accounts and holdings: how many shares you hold, their prices, and the total value.

- ✔ **Fundamental Data View** helps you review the basic economic statistics of a security: 52-week high and low, and current P/E (price/earnings) value.

- ✔ **My Custom View** is perhaps the most useful of all. You can choose from among 75 different items of financial data to create a personalized portfolio view. To do this, click See a Different View in the left pane and then choose Customize Any View from the pop-out submenu.

Graphically viewing and comparing security prices

Money's Price History view is a great way to see how a security's price has been doing. You can also compare a security to a standard index or another security. Here's how:

1. **Click Investing on Money's navigation bar.**

   You're viewing the Investments Center's Manage Your Investments and Savings page.

2. **Click Portfolio just under the navigation bar.**

   You see the Standard View of your investment holdings.

3. **Double-click any security listed to display the details of that security.**

   You now get a very nice graph of the past 52 weeks' prices, as Figure 17-2 shows.

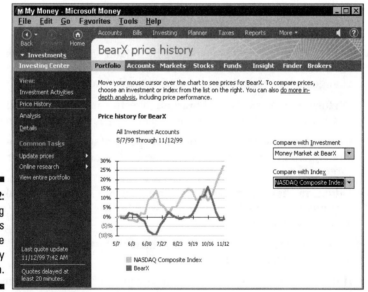

Figure 17-2:
Comparing investments in a Price History graph.

To compare a security's price history to that of other securities, click in the Compare with Investment list box and select a security. That security's price history is overlaid on the graph. Similarly, click in the Compare with Index list box and select Standard and Poor's, the NASDAQ, or the Dow Jones Industrial Average to overlay the graph.

Part IV

'Netting Ventured, 'Netting Gained

In this part . . .

If, to you, online is where the laundry goes after the clothes dryer breaks, take heart! No, Works Suite can't fix your dryer. But it can take your PC online — connecting you to the Internet. From there, you can go to your dryer manufacturer's online disclaimer of responsibility or even to a fellow launderer in Fort Lauderdale.

In this part, you see how Microsoft Internet Explorer can get you out of the laundry room and onto the Internet's World Wide Web — the ultimate online wilderness. A special Internet Connection Wizard ensures that you can get online without getting hung out to dry.

Also in this part, you find out how to use Microsoft Outlook Express to send and receive e-mail. This part also shows you how to use Outlook Express to get the latest news and gossip in your profession or hobby from Internet newsgroups — public forums on anything from raising aardvarks to touring Zanzibar.

Chapter 18

Gearing Up for the Internet

· ·

· ·

*O*kay, just what is all the noise about, anyway? What is "being online" and why has the whole world gone wild over the Internet? Good questions, pilgrim — questions best answered by plugging in and going online yourself. This chapter explains how and why to get yourself on the Internet.

Ways and Whys of Going Online

Being (or going) *online* means different things to different people, but the broadest definition of being online is that your PC is communicating in some way with another computer. To Windows and to most people, the word *online* means *connected to the Internet.* The Internet is a global network of comput-ers in which, if you connect your PC to one of those computers, your PC can talk to *any* of those computers.

But why on earth would you want your PC to talk to any other computer? Doesn't it get into enough mischief by itself? Read on to find out.

Things to do online and why

Here are the various online activities you can do, in order of popularity, and why you may want to do them:

✔ **E-mailing:** Exchange typed messages or files with other people. Often you can exchange pictures or other files (such as the Word, spreadsheet, database, or other files you create in Works Suite) with other people, too, by electronic mail. The Microsoft e-mail software that comes with Works is Outlook Express, covered in Chapter 20.

✔ **Web browsing (also known as *surfing*):** Look up something in the vast heaps of information publicly available on the World Wide Web (or just *Web*) on nearly any topic you can name. The Web is a collection of public electronic documents, with text, illustrations, animations, audio, and even video. Web documents are placed on a computer that runs a *Web server* program at a particular address on the Internet. A collection of such files is called a *Web site,* and each document (called a *Web page*) has its own address at that site. You tell your Web browser the address of the document you want, and it delivers the document to your screen. You can also click *hyperlinks* that automatically supply the address and then route you to the desired page. The Web browsing software that comes with Works is Microsoft Internet Explorer.

Some Web sites let you do e-mail through your web browser. Some are even free, although they attach advertisements to your e-mail. If you use one of them, you don't necessarily need to use or set up Outlook Express.

✔ **Downloading:** Obtain software and information from the Internet (usually from the Web). You can use Internet Explorer to download from the Internet.

✔ **Joining newsgroups:** Read and publicly exchange typed messages with a group of people about a particular topic. The newsgroup software that you get with Works is Outlook Express (which handles both e-mail and news).

✔ **Chatting:** Spend time exchanging messages in a live, but often sophomoric, public dialog on a subject. Groups form around subjects, and are thought of as being in a *chat room.* Everyone in the group types lines of text to each other, and the lines appear, one after the other, in a single window. Works Suite provides no specialized chat software, but chat groups increasingly use the Web, so you can chat through your Web browser (Internet Explorer).

Finding the best way to connect

To engage in any of the activities I mention, you need to be connected. No, I don't mean you need highly placed friends — although that always helps. What you need is a computer connection to the Internet.

You can get a connection to the Internet in any of three ways:

- ✔ Through your company's or university's network (often called an in*tra*net), which in turn connects you to the Internet.

- ✔ By joining a private network, such as America Online or CompuServe, that includes Internet service.

- ✔ By connecting directly to the Internet through an Internet service provider (ISP). Except for some kinds of corporate or university connections, your connection is through your phone line (usually of a variety called a a *dial-up* connection).

This chapter focuses on that last (and most common) way of connecting to the Internet: through an Internet service provider. If you connect through your company, a university, or an online service that supplies its own software, you must get special instructions — and perhaps, special hardware — from that organization.

Gathering What You Need

If you want to connect to the Internet, you need to get and do a few things. (Don't panic as you read these tasks — your PC has an Internet Connection Wizard that can help you do the hard stuff):

- ✔ **Get a modem, if you don't already have one.** A *modem* is an additional chunk of PC hardware that connects your PC to another computer (and its modem) via a phone line. If your PC has a modem, you can find a standard phone jack on the back of your PC (if your modem is internal) or on the modem case (if external) for you to connect your phone line. If you must buy a modem, I suggest buying one rated for 56,000 bits per second (often stated as *56 Kbps*), the fastest and now most commonly used modem for dial-up connections. Follow the installation instructions that come with your new modem.

- ✔ **Get an account with an Internet service provider (ISP).** An ISP has a big computer permanently connected to the Internet that your PC can connect to by calling on the phone line. The big computer "speaks Internet speak" (called *TCP/IP*) to your PC and the rest of the world. See the section "Finding an Internet Service Provider Yourself" for more info.

- ✔ **Set up your PC to go online.** Your PC needs software that works with your modem to call your ISP's computer by phone and "speak Internet-speak" to that computer. Windows comes with dial-up networking software, and in fact, your PC may already be set up to use the software. If not, the Internet Connection Wizard will set it up.

✔ **Set up your e-mail (or *mail*) and newsgroup (or *news*) service.** Your mail and news software, Outlook Express, must communicate with special computers called mail and news *servers,* managed by your ISP. You have to give your PC the names of those servers, plus your personal identification and password, before you can use those servers to get mail or news.

Whew! Sounds like a lot of effort, right? It would indeed be a lot of effort, except that the Internet Connection Wizard helps you get an ISP, sets up your PC to go online, and guides you through setting up e-mail and news. See "Running the Internet Connection Wizard" section later in this chapter.

Note: You may need the Windows installation diskettes or CD if your PC isn't set up for networking; the wizard lets you know. If you do need the Windows installation program and don't have it, you need to have a very forceful conversation with the person who supplied your PC.

Finding an Internet Service Provider Yourself

The Internet Connection Wizard can help you find an ISP, if you like, but it typically offers only major, nationwide companies. You can find local ISPs by looking in the yellow or commercial pages of phone books or in the business pages of your newspaper. Colleges and universities sometimes offer access for alumni or local people, as well.

What sort of ISP should you look for? Local ISPs sometimes offer more bang for your buck, with better help services, lower rates, or more local phone numbers for your PC to call. National ISPs are good if you travel, because your chances are good of getting a local number to call for access from wherever you are. Some smaller ISPs compete by offering reciprocal arrangements with other ISPs when you need remote access.

ISP attributes to look for include local phone numbers, a reputation for patient and accessible customer service, reliable dial-up access (few busy signals, lost line connections, or other connection problems), and low cost. You are better off if you ask other users before you sign up. Charges typically range from about $6 to $25 per month. If you discover that you don't like your ISP, switching to another is easy — until you start using e-mail. After you have e-mail, you have to notify all your friends about your e-mail address change if you change your ISP.

No matter how you connect your PC to the Internet, your ISP should give you the following information:

- ✔ The telephone number your PC should dial to go online. (Your ISP may list several numbers for you to choose from.)

- ✔ Your account name, also called your *user ID, login ID, logon ID,* or just *ID;* this name is typically derived from your first and last names, your initials, or both, such as `billgates` or `bgates`.

- ✔ A password (which you choose in consultation with your ISP, online, or on the phone). To create the most secure password, mix letters and numbers together, such as `i8newyork` (Godzilla's password).

- ✔ Your e-mail address, which typically looks something like `billgates@msn.net`.

- ✔ The names of things called *servers* for getting mail and newsgroup service, such as `mail.someISP.net`.

Your ISP may also give you other advanced stuff, such as IP addresses, DNS numbers, and so forth. Just write everything down for later use.

Running the Internet Connection Wizard

The easiest way to set up your PC to go online is to use the Microsoft Internet Connection Wizard. You should also run the wizard if you change ISPs (Internet service providers) or if your ISP tells you to use different settings.

The Internet Connection Wizard runs the first time you run Internet Explorer or Outlook Express. To run the wizard a second time to add or change your online settings, use whichever one of the following set of commands is available on the Start menu of your PC:

- ✔ Start➪Programs➪Accessories➪Communications➪ Internet Connection Wizard

- ✔ Start➪Programs➪Accessories➪Internet Tools➪ Internet Connection Wizard

Like all wizards, the Internet Connection Wizard is a series of dialog boxes that ask a lot of questions and ask you to fill out forms in response. After you fill out each form, click the Next button to advance to the next form. Click the Back button to return to an earlier screen or form. When you're done, click the Finish button.

When the Internet Connection Wizard first starts, it displays a screen that (when translated from technobabble) asks, "Do you need an Internet service provider?"

If you want Microsoft to help you choose an ISP, select the first option button (I want to sign up for a new Internet account). If you have already obtained your own ISP (or if you need to change information about your ISP), click the *third* option button (I want to set up my Internet connection manually). (The second option helps you change only to an ISP that Microsoft knows about.)

One or more additional screens follow, depending upon your choices, asking many questions and possibly requesting a method of payment. Here's where, if you obtained your own ISP, you need to enter some of the information (telephone numbers, account names, passwords, your shoe size) that your ISP gave you.

After the Internet Connection Wizard has set up your PC to talk to your Internet service provider (ISP), the wizard then usually offers to set up your PC so that it can send or receive electronic mail by using Outlook Express. If you have never set up e-mail on your PC, you "create a new e-mail account." Here is another place where you need the information from your ISP.

Going Online and Offline: The Dialing Process

When you launch an Internet program such as Internet Explorer or Outlook Express, Windows begins a process of *automatic dialing*. No, it's not surreptitiously dialing Bill Gates with your credit card number. Windows is dialing your Internet service provider (ISP) so that you can go online to the Internet.

When a Connect To or Dial-Up Connection dialog box appears, enter the account name (your *ID*) in the User Name box (unless it's already filled in). In the Password box, enter the password assigned to you by your ISP (unless that box is filled with ****). As you type the password, asterisks (****) appear in place of the characters you type, to thwart any spies who may be looking over your shoulder.

To avoid having to type the password in the future, select the Save Password check box if it's not grayed-out. (For strange and complicated security reasons, this check box is grayed out unless Windows is set up to request a Windows password when you start your computer.) If the dialog box that you're viewing is entitled Dial-Up Connection, you can avoid having to interact with it ever again by selecting its Connect Automatically check box.

If your PC succeeds in connecting, a connection icon (or button with an icon in Windows 95) appears on the Windows taskbar. The icon, shown at the left of this paragraph, features two PCs with a line (or a line and telephone) between them. (In Windows 98, the icon is tiny and lurks at the opposite end of the taskbar from the Start button.) You're now online! See Chapter 20 for details on using Internet Explorer and see Chapter 21 for the lowdown on Outlook Express.

To disconnect, scrutinize your Windows taskbar for that connection icon or button and then double-click it. In the dialog box that appears, click the Disconnect button. Some programs, when you close them, ask whether you want to disconnect.

 Internet Explorer and Outlook Express can both do certain work *offline* (not connected to the Internet), which saves you the cost of connection time to your ISP. Many people purchase unlimited Internet access for around $20 per month, but if you're on a less-expensive, hourly charge program, working offline can be a real money-saver. Offline, both Internet Explorer and Outlook Express can read documents and messages that you have downloaded or viewed previously. To work offline, click the Cancel button when the Dial-Up Connection dialog box appears, wait until the call is disconnected, and click the Work Offline button that now takes the place of the Cancel button. To return Internet Explorer or Outlook Express to online operation, choose File➪Work Offline from the menu bar of that program. This action toggles you back to Online status.

Chapter 19

Exploring with Internet Explorer

. . . .

In This Chapter
▶ Browsing

▶ Searching

▶ Printing

▶ Downloading

▶ E-mailing and other Internet activities

▶ Minimizing warning message

▶ Disconnecting

. . . .

*I*nternet Explorer is your Microsoft-built, Microsoft-tough sport-utility vehicle for a safari on the World Wide Web (also called just *the Web*). If you follow the instructions that I give you in Chapter 18, Internet Explorer is gassed up and ready to roll.

Internet Explorer isn't hard to drive, and this chapter gives you basic instructions and tips for navigating the Web. Double-click the Internet Explorer icon on your Windows desktop to start your Web-surfing safari. (The icon looks like a lower-case "e" with an orbiting satellite.) Your PC goes online (after some fooling around discussed in the preceding chapter), and you're ready to start browsing.

Note: Many computer writers (including me) tire of typing *Internet Explorer* all the time so use instead the abbreviation IE (or add the version number, such as IE 5.0). I use the abbreviation here so that you get used to seeing it elsewhere.

Ready to roll? You can also start IE running in a couple of other ways. In Works Task Launcher, click Programs near the top of the screen; then click Internet Explorer in the list of programs that appears on the left; finally, click the <u>Start</u> <u>Internet</u> <u>Explorer</u> link near the top-center of the Task Launcher. Or, in Windows 98, simply click the *e* icon on the Windows taskbar.

Home, Sweet Home Page

Each time you start Internet Explorer, it first displays a Web page from some-where on the Internet. The page that Internet Explorer turns to first (no matter where it is) is known as *Internet Explorer's home page. Home page* just means "starting page."

Microsoft initially sets IE's home page to the Microsoft Web site. If you prefer to have IE go initially to another page on the Internet, such as a search engine or your company's or university's home page, first browse to that page. Then, in IE, choose <u>T</u>ools⇨Internet <u>O</u>ptions from the menu bar, click the General tab on the Internet Options dialog box that appears, and click the Use Current button.

Browsing the Web

Browsing is the trendy activity of the day, whether you're into computers, shopping, or eating. If you apply the term to the Web, however, *browsing* means viewing the documents (together with their graphics and sounds) that you find at various Web addresses around the world.

Viewing a distant Web document isn't quite like viewing a distant mountain through a telescope; it's more like having someone ship a copy of the distant mountain to your doorstep piece by piece. The Web site transmits the entire document to your Web browser, and this transmission can take a while.

Browsing by typing an address

One way to browse the Web is to specify a document's address, which is known as an *URL* (and which you pronounce as either *earl* or *You Are Ell*). Addresses on the Web are a bit cryptic; you've undoubtedly seen them on TV and elsewhere. They typically look like the following addresses:

- ✔ http://www.snoggle.com
- ✔ www.snoggle.com
- ✔ home.snoggle.net/users/barney.html

Technically speaking, all Web addresses begin with http://, but you may omit it and just type the rest of the address: www.brightleaf.com/tracking, for example. A slash (/tracking) indicates folders under the main address (brightleaf.com). Individual Web documents typically end in .htm, .html, .shtml, or .asp.

If you know the URL of the Web site you want to see (for example, www
.dummies.com), you can type that address (or paste it by using Ctrl+V if you
copy it from elsewhere) in one of the following two places:

> ✔ **Click the white area (text box) on the Address Bar (as shown in
>   Figure 19-1) and start typing.** You replace the old address with what-
>   ever you type. As you type, IE displays a list of previously-visited
>   addresses that match your typing so far. You may click one to go there.
>   Press Enter after you finish typing or click the Go button at the right end
>   of the Address Bar.

> ✔ **Choose File➪Open (or press Ctrl+O) and type the address in the Open
>   dialog box that appears.** Press Enter after you finish or click OK.

After the Web page loads, its title appears in the title bar of the Internet
Explorer window, and its full address (URL) appears in the Address text box
(see Figure 19-1).

Graphics are often links also

Type an address

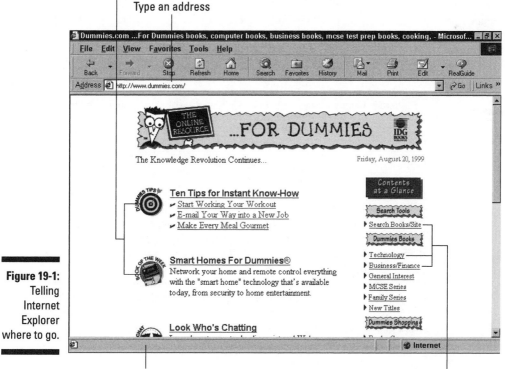

Figure 19-1:
Telling
Internet
Explorer
where to go.

Status bar shows a link's address

Links to click

Browsing with buttons

The IE toolbar gives you some helpful controls for browsing and other jobs. Figure 19-2 shows what each button does.

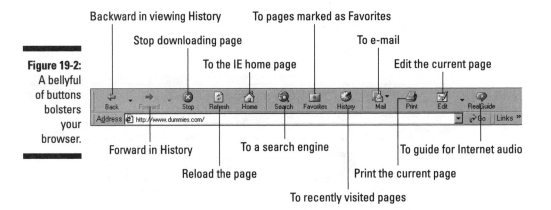

Figure 19-2:
A bellyful of buttons bolsters your browser.

Backward in viewing History — Stop downloading page — To the IE home page — To pages marked as Favorites — To e-mail — Edit the current page

Forward in History — Reload the page — To a search engine — To recently visited pages — Print the current page — To guide for Internet audio

Some of the features that I identify in the text in Figure 19-2 employ special terms, which I explain in following sections of this chapter. The button for editing a page takes you to a completely different program and is mainly useful for people who create and edit their own Web pages. Clicking the Mail button gives you a list of choices that cause Windows to run Outlook Express and do various things with it. RealGuide and Links may or may not appear on your browser. They're Microsoft guides to various things on the Web that Microsoft thinks are cool. (Exactly *why* Microsoft thinks highly of them I leave to your imagination, but I suspect the answer may involve the transfer of little green pieces of paper.)

Browsing by clicking links on Web pages

If you're currently viewing a Web document in Internet Explorer, you can view a different document by clicking a *link* on the current document. Links can take the form of buttons, specially marked text, or certain graphics on the page.

The best way to tell whether a word, a graphic, a button, or some other element on the page is a link is to move your cursor over that element without clicking. The cursor changes from an arrow to a little hand if the element's a link. The address to which the link takes you appears at the bottom-left margin (in the *status bar*) of the Internet Explorer window.

Text links are easy to spot. They're usually underlined and often appear in a distinctive color (by default, bright blue for unvisited pages, purple if you've already visited that page).

Clicking some links starts downloading a file instead of taking you directly to another Web page. If that happens unexpectedly, simply press the Esc key to exit from the File Download dialog box that appears. See the section "Downloading Programs and Other Files from the Web," later in this chapter, for more information.

Returning to a page in History

Don't know much about History? Well, Internet Explorer does. Each time you use IE, it keeps a record of the Web pages you visit so that you can return to them. Several buttons on the toolbar can help you travel through time, as the following list describes:

- ✔ **Back:** To return to the last Web page you visited, click the Back button on the toolbar. Keep clicking the Back button to move backward in History.

- ✔ **Forward:** After moving back in History, you can move forward again by clicking the Forward button.

- ✔ **Down arrows:** To jump back to any recently visited page in History, click the tiny down arrow adjoining the Back button and choose a page title off the list that appears. Similarly, to jump forward in History, click the tiny down arrow adjoining the Forward button. Click the down arrow at the far right of the Address bar and you can revisit a previously visited site by clicking its address in the drop-down list that appears.

- ✔ **History:** To revisit any Web page you visited in the past 20 days, click the History button. (You can change this time frame by choosing Tools⇨Internet Options and then, on the General tab of the Internet Options dialog box that appears, entering a new value less than 99 in the Days to Keep Pages in the History box.)

If you click the History button, a History menu appears at the left side of the IE window, as shown in Figure 19-3. IE organizes your browsing history by the day and week in which you visit a Web site. The Web sites you visit today, for example, appear in a Today category. IE groups earlier sites by the day of the week (such as Monday), or how many weeks ago you visited (such as 2 Weeks Ago). Any Web sites you visited appear as folder icons.

Change the way sites are listed.

Search for word in an address.

Remove History panel.

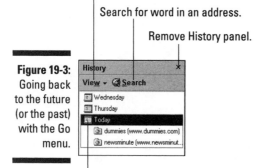

Figure 19-3: Going back to the future (or the past) with the Go menu.

Click to expand/collapse list.

Here's how to use the History panel:

✔ **To view sites visited earlier:** Click the icon for the day or week that you visited. (These icons look like tiny calendar pages. Really.) The icon spews forth (that is, it *expands* into) a list of folders for all the sites you visited. To *collapse* the list (or stuff it back into the icon, so to speak), click the icon again. IE keeps track of your browsing for the past 20 days (unless you increase or decrease that limit, as I describe in the entry for the History button in the bulleted list a few paragraphs back).

✔ **To open a folder for a given Web site:** Click it. Pages you visited on that site appear indented under the folder. (Click the folder again to close it.)

✔ **To return to any page listed in a folder:** Just click it. That page appears in the right pane of the IE window.

✔ **If the page name or week icon that you want isn't visible in the History panel:** Try clicking the tiny up or down arrows at the top and bottom right, to scroll the list.

✔ **To remove the History panel altogether:** Click the X in the upper-right corner of the panel.

How to treat panes in your window

Sometimes, Internet Explorer divides its window into multiple panes, known as *frames*. If a Web page uses frames, part of the page stays still while the other part changes after you click a link.

Depending on how the page designer creates the page, you can sometimes scroll the contents of a frame independently of the other frames. You can also often click and drag the borders that appear between the frames. You can also print frames independently of one another. (See the section "Printing Web Documents," later in this chapter.)

Sometimes, a new (usually small) window even appears on-screen! The new window may contain a special message or some controls for playing audio or video. It may even be a whole new IE window! To clear this window off your screen, click the X in the upper-right corner of the window.

Returning to your favorite pages

Now, just where was that recipe for tripe soufflé? The Web is so vast that you may never find that recipe again, much to the dismay (or joy) of your dinner guests. The Favorites feature helps you rise above absentmindedness.

Adding to Favorites

If you view a Web page that you think you may want to revisit, tell IE to add it to your list of favorites. Choose F̱avorites⇨A̱dd to Favorites from the menu bar. The Add Favorite dialog box appears, offering some nit-picky options.

Make sure that the text in the Name text box (which starts out as the title of the Web page) is descriptive enough that you can recognize the page by that text. If not, type new text. Then click OK or press Enter to enter the page in the basic Favorites list.

You can keep your favorite pages in various folders, too. The Favorites list already has several folders. Click to open a folder, or click New Folder to create your own folder. When you click OK, your favorite goes into that folder.

Returning to Favorites

To return to a favorite page, click F̱avorites on the menu bar. A list of your Favorites drops down. Click your favorite's name in that list. Click a folder to view additional favorites in that folder. (Alternatively, you can click the Favorites button on the toolbar, and a similar list appears in a pane at the left of the IE window.)

Organizing Favorites

After you have a dozen or so favorites in this list, you may want to add folders so that you can organize them or change the names of your existing favorites. Choose Favorites➪Organize Favorites to access the Organize Favorites dialog box.

To move a favorite to a folder, you can drag it. You can rename or delete favorites and folders or create new folders just as you can in an Open or Save As dialog box, as I describe in the appendix of this book. Or you can click the favorite or folder and then click the Move, Delete, or Rename button.

Searching the Web for Information

Don't know something? Check the Web. The Web is turning into a vast library of information. But unlike your town library (or so I hope), the librarians of the Web are computer programs, and the quality of information ranges from timeless and irrefutable truths to complete and utter Biscuit Sauce (BS). Only you can determine which is which.

What I call "librarians" are known as *search engines* to most people. These search engines all live at different addresses (URLs), and they all have different strengths and weaknesses. Two popular ones are AltaVista (at www.altavista.com) and Yahoo! (at www.yahoo.com). Although they differ in the details, in general they enable you to choose a subject, and then they present you with a page of links to various Web sites about that subject. In some engines, a brief excerpt from the page accompanies each link so that you can tell whether the page is of interest to you.

Because so many search engines are available, Microsoft designed Internet Explorer with a Search Assistant feature that enables you to search several of these engines at the same time. You can use this feature by clicking the Search button on the toolbar.

After you click the Search button on the toolbar, a Search panel opens on the left-hand side of the IE window. Unless you have been fooling with IE's settings, you see a group of search categories (Web page, address, business) and a text box in which you can type one or more search terms. After you finish typing the search terms, click the Search button. To try again with a new search, click the New button at the top left of the Search panel.

To see the Microsoft listing of search engines to use or to choose a different search engine, click the Customize button near the top of the Search panel. The Customize Search Settings dialog box maintains a list of engines that you're using and the order in which the Search Assistant uses them. You can select and deselect search engines by clicking their check boxes. You can set the order in which the Search Assistant uses them by selecting an engine and clicking the arrow buttons (Move Up and Move Down) below each list.

Printing Web Documents

You can print most Web documents just as easily as you print Works documents. In fact, the print command (File⇨Print) is the same in all those programs, and the associated Print dialog box is very similar. The printed page includes graphics and, if you have a color printer, color. (Colored backgrounds, however, don't print. Thank goodness, or you'd deplete your ink cartridge in about a minute.)

Some pages on the Web use frames, which complicate the printing process slightly. If you want to print a single frame, click inside that frame before giving the print command. If you want to print just selected text, drag your mouse cursor across that text. Then choose File⇨Print, as usual, and at the bottom of the Print dialog box, you see several choices for printing:

- **As Laid Out on Screen:** Your printout looks the same as your screen, except that the printout includes any documents in any frame that go below the screen as well.

- **Only the Selected Frame:** The entire document of the frame that you click in or in which you select text prints out.

- **All Frames Individually:** Each frame prints separately as a full document.

Click one of the preceding choices. If you want to print only selected text, choose Selection in the Print dialog box.

Copying from Web pages to other documents

You can copy any text or graphic from the IE window by using the Windows Clipboard. To copy a graphic, right-click the graphic and choose Copy from the drop-down menu. To copy text, select the text first (click and drag your mouse cursor across the text) and then right-click and choose Copy. To paste, open Word or another Windows program and choose Edit⇨Paste from its menu bar.

Downloading Programs and Other Files from the Web

A Web browser such as Internet Explorer enables you to acquire (download) all kinds of stuff. Many companies and individuals make programs available for free on the Web. From Microsoft, you can download enhancements to Windows or to Internet Explorer itself. Various companies offer add-on software or special viewers for special purposes. You can also download graphics files, music, audio, and video files that can play on PCs equipped to do so!

If you look around carefully, you can find one or more download areas on the Web sites of Microsoft and most other PC software vendors. Use search engines to find free graphics (also known as *clip art*), music, and video files. Follow the links and instructions, and eventually you click a link that causes Internet Explorer to download the file that you choose.

To avoid computer viruses, be careful that you download files only from reputable sources. If you have a virus-scanning program, run it after downloading.

After you click a link that starts a download, a File Download dialog box briefly appears and then an Internet Explorer dialog box asks what you want to do with the file: Depending on the type of file, you have two or more choices, as follow:

- **Open this file from its current location:** This choice isn't for downloading files — just for viewing them by using associated programs (programs that link to IE for viewing special kinds of files). This choice *can* be a dangerous one. It can introduce viruses into your computer — even DOC (Word document) files can contain viruses.

- **Save this file to disk:** Click this button and a Save As dialog box appears so that you can choose where you want to save the file. (See the appendix for details of using a Save As dialog box.) Click the Save button.

- **Run this file from its current location:** This choice is another risky one unless you trust the Web-site owner. This choice actually runs a program, which is typically an installation program of some sort — but it can be anything, including a virus-contaminated program.

The File Download box reappears after you make your choice, usually giving you an estimate of how long the downloading process can take. To stop the download, click the Cancel button or press the Esc key. You can browse to other locations while a file is downloading; you can also use other programs or do other Internet tasks such as checking for e-mail — but expect your PC's response to be slower.

The software that you download is typically in the form of a *compressed file* (a ZIP file, usually), which saves downloading time but adds a step to the normal Windows installation process. If you have virus-scanning software, use it now on the file that you downloaded (check the virus-scanner vendor's instructions). Then, to begin installing the software, double-click the downloaded file. Sometimes, double-clicking the downloaded file only decompresses the installation files. In that case, find the install.exe or setup.exe file, which you need to virus-scan first, and then double-click to install the software. You may also find that you can't unzip the file unless you use the official unzip utility *WinZip*. To obtain this utility, go to www.winzip.com or locate it in your local computer store.

Secure and Insecure Sites

What about doing business on the Internet? Increasingly, businesses that accept orders and credit-card numbers over the Web use secure sites. *Secure* sites work with Internet Explorer to encrypt the data between your PC and the site in a very secure way. The risk of doing business over a secure site is generally considered less than that of using a credit card in person.

If you're browsing a secure site, Internet Explorer displays a lock icon on the status bar at the bottom of its window. If you move from a secure site to an insecure site, Internet Explorer warns you.

Disconnecting and Quitting

If you finish your Web browsing — or you're simply reading a document and not planning to click any of its links — disconnect. (See Chapter 18 for instructions.)

To reconnect, click the Refresh button in Internet Explorer's toolbar. (Your PC goes online automatically if any program demands information from the Internet. The Refresh button demands fresh information.) Another easy way to refresh is to press F5.

To quit Internet Explorer, choose File⇨Close or click the button with the X in the upper-right corner of the Internet Explorer window.

Chapter 20

Reaching Out with Outlook Express

. . . .

In This Chapter

▶ Communicating by e-mail and newsgroups

▶ Starting Outlook Express

▶ Knowing when to connect to the Internet

▶ Using the Outlook Express window

▶ Creating outgoing mail

▶ Reading incoming mail

▶ Joining and enjoying newsgroups

. . . .

*H*ear that distant drumming? It's the sound of e-mail and news messages being pounded out on PCs and wafting their way across the Internet wilderness. Now it's your turn to join in the fun, by using Outlook Express.

Send e-mail to family members or fire off that irate e-mail to your editor. Subscribe to a newsgroup of fellow newt breeders (or whatever your vocation or hobby may be) and catch up on the latest news. You can do it all with Microsoft Outlook Express.

If you haven't yet set up your PC to cruise the Internet or deal with e-mail and newsgroups, you'll encounter a wizard when you first try to use Outlook Express. You may as well initiate the encounter yourself by following the instructions in Chapter 18 first.

Outlook Express is Microsoft's cheap version of its Outlook software for e-mail and news. Your copy of Outlook Express either came installed with Windows or was installed when you first installed Works from the Works 2000 CD. But just because it's free, don't assume that Outlook Express is inferior: Many reviewers consider it the best e-mail/news software available. And the price is sure right!

Launching Outlook Express

To start Outlook Express, do one of the following:

- On the Windows taskbar, choose Start➪Programs➪Outlook Express or click the "envelope with two twisted blue arrows" icon on the taskbar near the Start button.

- If an icon labeled Outlook Express is on your desktop, double-click that icon.

- In the Works Task Launcher, click Outlook Express near the bottom of the left pane, and then click Start Outlook Express near the top, center of the right pane.

When you first launch Outlook Express (OE), it may display a Browse for Folder dialog box and ask you to select a folder to keep your messages in. Just click OK and accept the default chosen by OE. It may also ask if you want Outlook Express to be your *default mail client*. That means, will OE be your main e-mail program? Click to deselect the check box labeled Always Perform This Check When Starting Outlook Express and then click Yes. (Click No if you usually use a different e-mail program.)

Going Online — or Not

When you launch Outlook Express, it displays an Outlook Express Dial-Up Connection dialog box. You don't have to be connected to the Internet (that is, be online) to read or compose messages — only to receive and send them.

After you're online, how do you go offline? Choose File➪Work Offline in Outlook Express. Outlook Express asks whether you want to hang up the modem; click the Yes button — otherwise, you're wasting your money on connection time (unless you have an unlimited-use account with your Internet service provider)! Outlook Express automatically goes online again when you ask to send or receive messages — or it at least displays a message box, asking if you do want to reconnect. (You can also go offline by right-clicking on the "two computers connected" icon on your taskbar and choosing Disconnect from the context menu that appears.)

What's What in the Outlook Express Window

Figure 20-1 shows the Outlook Express window. The window looks like this figure most of the time — except when you first start Outlook Express. When you start Outlook Express, the right-hand window contains icons for e-mail, news, and contacts. You can click these icons to do the same tasks as many of the buttons and menu choices described in this chapter. To see the initial window at any time, click Outlook Express at the top of the left-hand pane.

Various message boxes and folders are listed on the left side of the window. Click a box or folder to view its contents on the right side of the window. (In Figure 20-1, I clicked Inbox and then I clicked a message from me, Dave Kay, to myself.) The bold type indicates unread messages. The number two next to the Inbox icon (on the left pane) tells me that I have two unread messages.

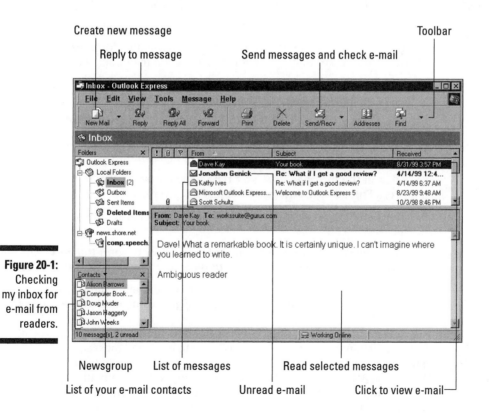

Figure 20-1: Checking my inbox for e-mail from readers.

Create new message

Reply to message

Send messages and check e-mail

Toolbar

Newsgroup

List of messages

Read selected messages

List of your e-mail contacts

Unread e-mail

Click to view e-mail

Creating E-Mail Messages

To send an e-mail message to someone, you need that person's address, in the form name@organization.com (or .edu, .net, or .org). Be careful to get all the characters *exactly* right, or your message probably won't go through. And remember, no spaces allowed.

To create an e-mail message, do the following:

1. **Click the New Mail button at the far left of the Outlook Express toolbar.**

   A New Message window then appears.

   If the New Mail button is not on the toolbar, choose Message⇨ New Message or just press Ctrl+N.

   If the New Mail button isn't visible, it may mean that you're currently viewing a newsgroup. For more on newsgroups, see the section "Downloading and Reading Newsgroup Messages," later in this chapter.

2. **Click in the To text box and type your recipient's e-mail address.**

   To send e-mail to several people, type their e-mail addresses one after the other, separating each address with a comma or semicolon.

3. **To send a copy of your message to someone else, click the Cc line and enter an address as you did in Step 2.**

4. **Click in the Subject text box and type a short description of your message subject.**

   That subject is now the title of your message window.

5. **Click in the message area and type your message. You don't need to press Enter at the end of a line, just keep typing.**

   You should press Enter only at the end of each paragraph in your message.

6. **Click the Send button in the message window to send the message now or choose File⇨Send Later to place the message in your Outbox.**

   The Outbox is one of the message boxes on the left-hand side of the window. It's the place where your messages reside until you send them.

You can send a file of any kind (an image, a document, a file from Microsoft Home Publishing, and so on) by *attaching it* to an e-mail message. To do that, in the message window, click the button with the paper-clip icon or choose Insert⇨File Attachment. In the Insert Attachment dialog box that appears, browse through your files, select the file you want to send, and then click the Attach button.

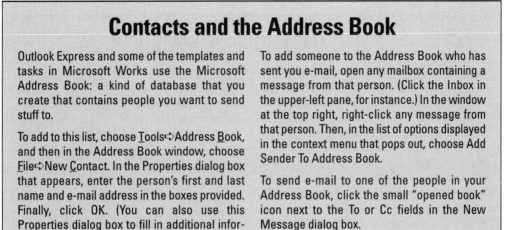

Contacts and the Address Book

Outlook Express and some of the templates and tasks in Microsoft Works use the Microsoft Address Book: a kind of database that you create that contains people you want to send stuff to.

To add to this list, choose Tools⇨Address Book, and then in the Address Book window, choose File⇨New Contact. In the Properties dialog box that appears, enter the person's first and last name and e-mail address in the boxes provided. Finally, click OK. (You can also use this Properties dialog box to fill in additional information about this person if you want.)

To add someone to the Address Book who has sent you e-mail, open any mailbox containing a message from that person. (Click the Inbox in the upper-left pane, for instance.) In the window at the top right, right-click any message from that person. Then, in the list of options displayed in the context menu that pops out, choose Add Sender To Address Book.

To send e-mail to one of the people in your Address Book, click the small "opened book" icon next to the To or Cc fields in the New Message dialog box.

Sending and Receiving E-Mail Messages

To check your e-mail — and, at the same time, send any messages you've written but not yet sent — click the Send/Receive button on the Outlook Express toolbar.

If you aren't already online, Outlook Express connects you now. If any dialog boxes appear, just click OK or the Connect button. If a Dial-Up Connection dialog box appears, select the Save Password check box and then click the Connect button. You remain online until you exit Outlook Express or until you choose File⇨Work Offline.

Messages are stored in boxes and folders, which are displayed in the left-hand pane; click a box or folder to open a message. Any messages that you receive go into the Inbox. Any messages that you have sent are stored in the Sent Items box. Your Outbox is empty at this point.

If someone sends you an attached file, a paper-clip icon appears at the top-right corner of the pane displaying the message text. Click that icon, and in the drop-down menu, choose Save Attachments. A Save Attachments dialog box appears that lets you select a folder for the file. Click the Save button to save the file in the folder displayed in the Save To box. (To select a different folder, click the Browse button at the bottom of the dialog box. Click to open a folder in the list displayed — preferably My Documents or a special folder you have created — and then click OK.)

Be afraid. Be very afraid!

Besides Save Attachments, another option appears on the menu that you see when you click the paper-clip icon: the name of the file. If you click the name of the file, you're telling Outlook Express to open that file — a bad idea, until you are sure the file is free of viruses. (Outlook Express opens the file by using a word processor, a graphics program, or some other application — based on the file's extension such as .doc or .bmp. If the file is *not* a document that your PC recognizes, a dialog box opens asking if you want to save this to disk or, more menacingly, *open* the file.)

Saving to the My Documents folder or a special folder that you have created is almost certainly safe; you can then run a virus-checking program (if it doesn't run automatically, as some do). But if you open a file, it immediately *runs* (executes) if it's an executable program. Be

afraid. Be very afraid of running a program before you have virus-checked it. Running an attached program is one way a virus can get into your computer.

If you are *expecting* a file attachment *created* by someone you know, it's probably safe to open it. But never open files sent from a stranger or forwarded by a friend (unless that friend has virus-checked it). Even if the file or document comes from a recognized source, don't assume that the addressee actually intended to send that document to you. Some viruses, such as the notorious Melissa, simply seize the Address Book and send themselves to all the people listed there. So to ensure your PC's safety, check an attachment with a good virus-checker program before opening it. You never know when Melissa or her evil cousins may be masquerading as your best friend in the world.

Reading, Deleting, and Replying to E-Mail Messages

To view the e-mail you've received, click Inbox in the left pane of the Outlook Express window. Outlook Express lists your new, unread messages (distinguished by bold type and a sealed-envelope icon) in the upper-right pane of the Outlook Express window, as shown in Figure 20-1. Click any listed message to view its contents in the lower-right pane.

To reply to a message, first click the message to view it. Then click the Reply button on the Outlook Express toolbar. The Reply button opens a message window just as if you were creating a new message, but with the text of the original message already included. Just type and send as you would any new message. (Most people leave the text from the original message as is — for reference — and just type their response above it in the window.)

To move a message to the Deleted Items box, click the message in the upper-right pane and then press the Delete key on your keyboard (or click the Delete button on the Outlook Express toolbar). To permanently delete the message, click the Deleted Items box, click the message (or Ctrl+click — that is, press the Ctrl key and click the mouse — to choose several messages) and then press the Delete key.

You can also move a message among the various boxes by dragging the message from the right pane onto a box in the left pane and then dropping the message by releasing your mouse button.

Setting Up Your News Account

Newsgroups are like giant bulletin boards where people with common interests post messages. The Internet has thousands of newsgroups; some of them are good, some are bad, and some are downright ugly. As with e-mail, newsgroup messages (called *postings*) can contain attachments such as pictures, sounds, programs, and other stuff. You can read postings without participating (called *lurking*), or you can contribute material yourself.

Many newsgroups contain extremely useful material from fellow enthusiasts on a given subject. Sometimes, experts are there — and they'll answer questions. Other newsgroups contain material that non-enthusiasts may find offensive. Also, postings can have computer viruses attached to them. Never open any files attached to a newsgroup posting without screening them with a virus checker first.

Avoiding spam

When you get to the page where the Internet Connection Wizard asks for your Internet News e-mail address, you can type your true e-mail address if you want it to appear on your postings. By including your e-mail address, other newsgroup readers can reply to your messages by sending e-mail instead of posting a reply on the newsgroup. However, I advise that you do not give out your e-mail address in public forums. This e-mail address can easily be picked up and used by people who send junk mail (they're referred to as *spammers*). If you give out your true e-mail address, you are likely to start receiving junk mail. You may want to give a fake e-mail address here. An *X* will do; the wizard will put up a warning message that the address seems bad but click Yes to continue

anyway. Spammers have automated robotic programs called *spiders* that continually roam newsgroups — harvesting e-mail addresses day and night. Spiders travel the Web, get it?

And spammers frequently say something like this in their messages: "If you do not want future mailings from us, reply to this address. . . ." Listen carefully: *Never ever* reply to any spam e-mail. Replying verifies you as a live, active e-mail account. Your address may then be transferred to a *preferred, verified* mass-mailing list — and you can expect your spam count to rise accordingly. Spammers seem to be considerate when offering to remove you from their mailings, but remember that spammers, like their telemarketing cousins, are, by definition, *in*considerate.

Before you can do any of this stuff, you need to set up Outlook Express to read newsgroups from your ISP's news server. Fortunately, the Internet Setup Wizard comes to your aid, as it did for setting up a mail account. Choose Tools➪Accounts from the Outlook Express menu bar. The Internet Accounts dialog box appears, listing all your e-mail and newsgroup (news) accounts. Click the Add button and choose News from the menu that pops up. From here on, the wizard prompts you to fill in information from your ISP about newsgroups and *servers*. You may need some help from your ISP for this!

Listing and Subscribing to Newsgroups

Newsgroups cover thousands of topics, so your first task is to decide which newsgroups to subscribe to. Choose Tools➪Newsgroups to begin the process. When you set up your news account (see the preceding section), you probably told Outlook Express to download a list of all the newsgroups available on your ISP's news server. If you didn't download the list then, Outlook Express now offers to do so. After gathering its list, you can then subscribe to some of the newsgroups. To quickly locate newsgroups that you may be interested in, try typing a word reflecting your interest (**dog**, for example) in the Display Newsgroups Which Contain text box.

To read or contribute to the messages in a newsgroup, you must first subscribe (notify OE that you want to view that newsgroup). Double-click newsgroup names and then subscribe to as many newsgroups as you like. To see which ones you are subscribed to, click the Subscribed tab at the bottom of the Newsgroups dialog box. To unsubscribe, just double-click the newsgroup.

To quit the Newsgroups dialog box, click its OK button. To return to the Newsgroups dialog box, choose Tools➪Newsgroups or click the Newsgroups button if it appears on the Outlook Express toolbar. (The button appears only when you are viewing news.) To update the list of newsgroups, click the Reset List button.

Downloading and Reading Newsgroup Messages

To download and read newsgroups, choose Tools➪Newsgroups or simply click the newsgroup's name in the left pane in the Outlook Express window. (In Figure 20-1, the newsgroup is entitled `news.shore.net`.) Here you see your subscribed newsgroups in a list and indented under your news account.

To download all the latest messages in a newsgroup, click the newsgroup. (In Figure 20-1, the newsgroup begins with `comp.speech`.)

In the same way that you click the e-mail Inbox to list mail messages, you click a newsgroup to list its messages in the upper-right pane. Click a newsgroup message to read its text in the lower-right pane.

Unlike e-mail messages, newsgroup messages are organized into *threads*. When someone *posts* a reply (sends a response) to a message, that reply is grouped with the original message, and a plus sign (+) appears to the left of the original message. Click the plus sign to display the replies, which are indented underneath the message.

Posting Newsgroup Messages

Posting (sending) a new newgroup message and posting a reply to an existing newsgroup message is very similar to sending and replying to e-mail — just click the magical buttons on the Outlook Express toolbar, as follows:

- ✔ **To create a message on a new topic for the newsgroup:** Click the newsgroup that you want to post to; then click the New Post button.

- ✔ **To post a reply to a previously received message:** View that message and then click the Reply Group button.

- ✔ **To reply by private e-mail to the author of a newsgroup message:** Click that message and then click the Reply button. Many posts do not include the correct return e-mail address in the From field, so the Reply button won't work. Sometimes, these people do give valid e-mail addresses elsewhere in the message, however; so you can compose an e-mail message to them the regular way. Their intention with this tactic is to make spammers work harder.

Fill out the message window that appears after you click any of the buttons just listed, just as you would for an e-mail message. Be sure to type a subject line for messages on new topics but not for replies. You don't need to fill out an address; the message is already addressed.

Click the Send button in the message window to send the message now or choose File➪Send Later to place the message in the Outbox. If you send the message now and you aren't already online, Outlook Express goes online. If you choose instead to send the message later, OE sends the message the next time that you go online.

Part V

Entertaining Enlightenment

The new desktop publishing software not only lets Rags produce a professional looking greeting card quickly and inexpensively, but it also allows him to say it his way.

In this part . . .

*1*f you've been falling asleep on your keyboard, suffering those nasty, rectangular, telltale head wrinkles, help is on the way. In this part, you'll see how to wake yourself up by researching caffeine in Microsoft Encarta Encyclopedia. Then take related links to articles on coffee, tea, India, the British Empire, General Montgomery, and the real meaning of the phrase "The Full Monty." (You may need to follow links to the Web to complete that particular trek!)

If that sort of random walk through geography, history, science, and culture doesn't get your neurons jingling, this part also shows you how to entertain your friends with cards, posters, banners, and other colorful projects that you can make by using Microsoft Home Publishing.

Still feeling lost? Tune in to Expedia Streets and Trips and see how to chart a path from San Diego to Las Vegas — and (if you have any money left) return!

Chapter 21

Encyclopedic Enlightenment: Encarta

. . . .

In This Chapter

▶ Starting up Encarta

▶ Understanding Encarta features

▶ Finding and reading articles

▶ Researching by using multimedia tools

▶ Controlling multimedia players

▶ Navigating between features

▶ Printing and copying to the Windows Clipboard

▶ Customizing the behavior of Encarta

. . . .

*T*he Microsoft Encarta 2000 Encyclopedia is ready to enlighten you in a most entertaining way. Although it's not clad in fine Corinthian leather like a good printed encyclopedia, the Encarta Encyclopedia CD-ROM has its advantages: interactive graphics and sound, the ability to search for topics and keywords, and availability right on your PC, where you are, perhaps, writing your research paper. Besides, Encarta sings and dances enchantingly. Try to get your fine-Corinthian-leather-bound encyclopedia to do *that!*

Launching Encarta and Gazing at the Home Page

You can start Encarta from the Windows Start button, the Works Task Launcher, or a program icon (if you have one on your desktop), just as you do for any other Windows program. But first, pop the Encarta CD in your PC's CD-ROM drive. Encarta doesn't work without the CD.

Encarta may start running all on its own, at this point; give it a few seconds to do so. If it doesn't start automatically, do one of the following:

- On the Windows taskbar, choose Start➪Programs➪Microsoft Encarta➪ Encarta Encyclopedia 2000.

- In the Works Task Launcher, click the Programs button; then select Encarta Encyclopedia in the left pane and Start Encarta Encyclopedia in the middle pane.

- If you see a Microsoft Encarta icon on your screen, double-click that icon.

Encarta swoops onto your screen and displays its *home page* (the starting screen). Here you have three main choices:

- **Encarta's search feature, the Pinpointer:** Use it to quickly locate all articles on a given feature, all audio or video clips, all maps, and other elements of Encarta. For more about the Pinpointer, see the section "Finding articles with the Pinpointer tool."

- **The Encarta Explorer:** A cool, animated, zooming table of contents — click subject categories and subcategories, zooming in on your subject until you get to the information you're looking for. Start this Explorer by clicking Encarta Explorer in the bulleted list just under Microsoft Encarta.

- **Media and Online Features:** *Media Features* include maps, interactive learning tools, and Mind Maze (an educational game). *Online features* offers links to Web sites on various topics and a Yearbook with recently added or updated articles.

Microsoft recognizes that, to a great extent, the Internet is a huge planet-wide encyclopedia. So Encarta gives you many ways to connect to the Internet from within Encarta itself. If you want additional information, updated articles, or special features, you need only click one of the many Internet links embedded within Encarta's articles. However, often when you do go to the Internet from Encarta, a warning notice pops up: "You have requested to open a World Wide Web site that is outside of Encarta Encyclopedia and is not under the control of Microsoft. Therefore. . . ." In other words: You're on your own, Buster! (I can only hope that this disclaimer doesn't become a legal requirement and start appearing every time you click a hyperlink — like those helpful warnings on every plastic bag: Don't put your head in this bag and hold it shut, or you could suffocate.)

Finding and Reading Articles

Most written information in Encarta appears as articles, as it does in a newspaper or a printed encyclopedia. You can get to any article by using the Encarta Pinpointer (or Find) tool. You can also get to a Microsoft-selected subset of these articles through the Explorer tool.

Finding articles with the Pinpointer tool

The Pinpointer is Encarta's name for its Find feature. It appears in a panel on the left side of the Encarta window when you first run Encarta or (if it is not present already) when you click Find on the menu bar. Here's how to use it:

✔ **To locate an article:** Type the name of the topic in the text box next to the Find button on the menu bar. As you type, Pinpointer looks for and lists subjects that match what you've typed so far. Typing *Bud* gets you to *Bud Fowler,* for instance; typing *Buda* gets you to *Budapest.*

✔ **To see an article:** Click any subject listed in the Pinpointer list box. For example, I clicked Bach in the Pinpointer window. After you've located an article, the screen looks like Figure 21-1, where callouts show you what's going on in a typical article page — and a lot is going on!

✔ **To see more subjects:** If the list is long, use the Pinpointer's scroll bar. (Click the down arrow at the bottom of the scroll bar.)

✔ **To limit the Pinpointer's list box to displaying only a particular category (such as maps):** Click the down arrow under the Choose a Type of Information drop-down list and then select one of the categories.

Reading articles

As you can see in Figure 21-1, a typical article's start page, called its Contents page, is divided into several zones. (You can force Encarta to skip the Contents page and go directly to the beginning of the article if you want. See "Printing, Copying, and Options" at the end of this chapter.) Not every topic includes the same number of zones, but roughly from left to right these zones can include the following:

Miscellany (maps, a game, and so on)

Go online, update articles

Forward

Behaviors, copying, viewing

Launch pinpointer   Home Page

Similar to Internet Explorer's
Favorites feature

Audio Multimedia   Back

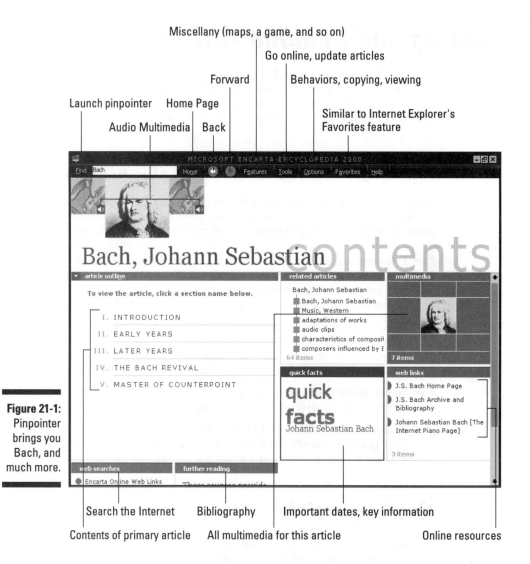

Figure 21-1:
Pinpointer
brings you
Bach, and
much more.

Search the Internet   Bibliography   Important dates, key information

Contents of primary article   All multimedia for this article   Online resources

> ✔ **Article Outline:** A mini–table of contents that divides an article into several logical sections so you can quickly skip to an area you're interested in. Just click the subject area of interest, and it appears. You see the Article Outline only with larger articles. Shorter articles are simply displayed directly, with a scroll bar along the right-hand edge of the Encarta window.

> ✔ **Audio or Video Clips:** If an article boasts associated audio or video, you may see a photo or drawing with a small speaker icon for audio (refer to Figure 21-1) or a small TV icon for video. Click one of these icons to move to a clip. To run a clip, click the right-arrow symbol underneath the symbol of the clip, as you can see in Figure 21-2.

Stop

Play (changes to Pause while playing)

Figure 21-2:
Use these
multimedia
tools to
control an
audio or
video clip.

Slider   Fast-forward

Rewind

- ✔ **Web Searches:** Break out of the limitations of a single Encarta CD-ROM and roam the Internet for additional information about your topic (assuming you have an Internet connection). You can find a collection of Encarta Online Links — revised every month, a search engine that checks recent news or magazine coverage of your topic, and an Internet-wide search feature.

- ✔ **Further Reading:** A list of books and reference materials for those interested in using an old-fashioned paper-based technology to expand their knowledge. Also included is a link to the Barnes & Noble online bookstore, for your convenience in ordering a title or two.

- ✔ **Related Articles:** Additional information on your topic. Click one of these links to move elsewhere in Encarta for further information.

- ✔ **Quick Facts:** Provides a brief overview of the essential information on a topic. It is usually a timeline, with the dates of important events in the subject's history.

- ✔ **Multimedia:** Photos, maps, audio, video, charts, and illustrations to enrich your research and learning.

- ✔ **Web Links:** Special sites on the Internet that pertain to the topic. For instance, for the Bach article, Encarta lists The J.S. Bach Home Page, The J.S. Bach Archive, and Johann Sebastian Bach (The Internet Piano Page), this last site containing several audio files of Bach's work.

Mucking with Media

Curmudgeonly writers like myself (who enjoy $10 words such as *curmudgeonly*) grumble at non-text forms of information (*and* at these forms of information co-opting the word *media*); nonetheless, Encarta is full of it. Media, I mean. Or, specifically, animations, videos, sound recordings, and other fun, lively stuff that's also called *multimedia*. Hmphh. Since when are encyclopedias supposed to be fun!?

Media in Encarta may refer to one of two different things:

✔ **Content,** which appears in media *players* — the boxes in articles and elsewhere that have buttons, sliders, and other controls.

✔ **Media Features,** which (for the most part) are tools for exploring the content in Encarta by geography, history, and topic.

Media content and players

The multimedia (non-text) content in Encarta includes illustrations, animations, slide shows, sounds, video, charts, maps, tables, and 360-degree views. These media may appear within an article, or you can view them on their own. (Click Find on the menu bar, delete any text in the Find text box, and in the Choose a Type of Information list box, select Videos, Sound, or whatever media you want. A list of all available media appears.) Wherever media appear, they're contained in a *player,* or a separate window with specialized controls.

These controls are so much like the ones on tape, CD, and videocassette players that I'm sure you can figure out which are the Play, Rewind, Stop, Fast-Forward, and other buttons. If you want to print a frame from a video, pause the video, right-click on the image, and choose Print from the context menu that appears. To copy an illustration to the Clipboard, right-click on the image and choose Copy from the context menu that appears.

Media features

The media *features* in Encarta are a mix of interactive presentations *(interactivities)* that stand alone from the articles, plus various aids for browsing through or expanding on articles (Encarta Explorer, World Maps, Yearbook, and Web Links). Choose Features and then select one of the following:

✔ **Encarta Explorer:** This feature is an animated tree directory — a way to quickly locate information by going down through categories. In Encarta Explorer, you start out with really general categories like History, Geography, Humanities, Science, and Social Science, as shown in Figure 21-3. Then you click one of them to get a list of categories within that big category.

Figure 21-3:
This is the outermost level of the Encarta Explorer — drill down until you find exactly what you're looking for.

✔ **World Maps:** The World Map window enables you to explore Encarta articles by geography or view maps. Click the map to zoom in, or get a map by clicking in the Find a Place text box in the lower left, typing a location, and clicking any place listed. Click the Zoom Out button at the top to move further and further out until you're seeing the whole world again. You can zoom many rivers, towns, and other features on the map (move your mouse and when you see the arrow mouse pointer change to a magnifying glass with a + in it — click to zoom). Sometimes the pointer changes to a hand with a pointing finger. In that case, you can click to get a description of the location, or go directly to an article about it.

✔ **Interactivities:** Click any subject listed. These interactive tools spring up in their own windows, and those windows create windows. All interactivities are different, so look for an Instructions button to click. Try bird identification or dinosaur structure.

✔ **Yearbook:** Click any of these topics to see the very latest revisions and additions to Encarta. These articles were written too recently to have been formally included in Encarta itself. Click the Downloads link in the upper-right corner of the Yearbook page and then click the Update Encarta button to download (from the Internet) all the current updates.

✔ **Web Links:** This is a huge list of what looks like thousands of Web sites that Encarta's busy researchers have compiled for your entertainment and edification. Everything from Aguirre to Zurich Tourism. Click any item in the immense list to see a brief description. In the Web Links Description dialog box, you can also choose to copy the address (URL) or be directly connected to the site.

✔ **Mind Maze:** Mind Maze is an adventure game in the form of a medieval castle. Wander around by clicking doors. Provoke characters and objects by clicking them. Get points for answering questions. Take naps. Press the F1 key for help.

Help, I've Moved, and I Can't Get Back!

Encarta sometimes leaves you on a screen without any apparent way to get anywhere else! Here are the secret controls:

✔ You can always go back to the previous page by clicking the back arrow button on the menu bar (or forward by clicking the forward arrow button). These buttons work something like the way the similar buttons work in Internet Explorer. Encarta is very literal about going back, so if you made many wrong turns in getting to the current screen, you'll go backward through them all again!

✔ Try pressing the Esc key to get out of whatever you're into.

✔ To exit a window, click the X in any window's upper-right corner. If two Xs are present, click the inner of the two. (The outer X is for Encarta itself; clicking that X exits the program.)

✔ To return to the starting screen (home page), click Home on the menu bar.

Printing, Copying, and Options

You can copy or print nearly any image or text in Encarta. By *copy,* I mean copy stuff to the hidden Windows Clipboard (discussed in the appendix), from which you can paste that stuff into documents in Word, Works, or other programs. (Click in that document and choose Edit⇨Paste.) Here's where to go in Encarta to copy or print:

✔ On the menu bar, choose Options and then (if not grayed out) choose either Print or Copy; then choose Text Selection, Whole Article, Image/Frame, or Caption. To print a chunk of text, drag across the text to highlight it before choosing Options⇨Print⇨Text Selection. An image or a frame of a moving image must be visible in order to print or copy it.

✔ In many windows displaying text or graphical content, right-click the item and then choose the appropriate Copy or Print option from the context menu. (To copy a frame of a video or animation, pause the presentation first.)

✔ You can choose Options⇨Text Size and modify the text size by choosing Small, Medium, or Large.

You can also choose Options⇨Settings, and by selecting or deselecting check boxes in the list of behaviors displayed, you can customize how Encarta behaves. Here are some of the customizations you may want to select:

✔ Deselect the Play Menu and Button Sounds check box to get rid of the sounds played when you click buttons or drop menus.

✔ Deselect the Display Home Screen When I Start Encarta Encyclopedia check box to display a different article, selected at random, each time you start Encarta. This is a pretty odd behavior, but seeing something unexpected can be exciting.

✔ If you use the Internet links frequently, deselect the Ask Me for Confirmation Before Jumping to the Internet check box.

Select the Skip Contents Page check box to avoid seeing the Contents page when you go to an article. I describe the Contents page in the section "Reading articles," earlier in this chapter.

Chapter 22

Entertaining Your Creativity

• •

In This Chapter

▶ Getting started with Home Publishing 2000

▶ Starting a new project

▶ Understanding the editing features

▶ Printing your creations

▶ Sending projects electronically

• •

*I*n today's business world, you never know what partnerships may form next, and what can result: Alcoa Aluminum and Fruit of the Loom? Disney and the Louvre? Hallmark and Microsoft? Well, wonder no more about the fruits of that last partnership. You've got it: Microsoft's Home Publishing 2000, one of the cutest chunks of clicking, whistling, clanking, and barking software to ever acquire real estate (and lots of it) on a disk drive.

With Home Publishing 2000, you can create cards, banners, certificates of achievement, calendars, business cards, crafts, envelopes, flyers, pamphlets, newsletters, party sets, postcards, posters, signs, framed photos, reports, presentations, stationery, and (with special paper) stickers and labels. Then you can print 'em, e-mail 'em, stick 'em, pass 'em out, or put 'em on the Internet for friends to see!

Getting Started

As with any Windows program, you can start Home Publishing by either double-clicking its icon on the desktop or by choosing it from the Start button of the Windows taskbar. Look for an icon on your screen labeled Home Publishing 2000; if you find it, double-click it. If you can't find the icon, go to the Windows taskbar (usually located across the bottom of your screen) and choose Start⇨Programs⇨Microsoft Home Publishing 2000.

After Home Publishing starts, you see the Paper Projects page, as shown in Figure 22-1.

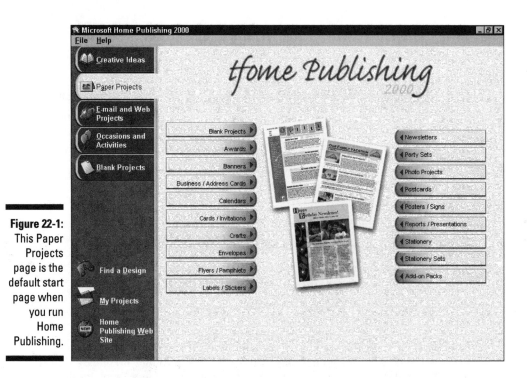

Figure 22-1:
This Paper Projects page is the default start page when you run Home Publishing.

As with all Works programs, you can also choose Home Publishing from the Works Task Launcher.

The opening screen of Home Publishing, shown in Figure 22-1, gives you an idea of the program's primary capabilities.

Keep the Home Publishing Images and Artwork CD (CD #5) handy. Home Publishing may ask for it!

Features on the opening screen

Here are the things that you can do from the opening screen:

- ✔ Start a new project by clicking one of the many types of projects displayed on the buttons: flyers, cards, invitations, and so on.

- ✔ Open a project that you've created before by choosing File⇨Open. Alternatively, you can click the My Projects button in the left pane. (Or look at the bottom of the File menu to see a list of the projects you've recently worked on.)

✔ View new projects you can use and materials you can order on the Home Publishing Web site by clicking the <u>Home</u> <u>Publishing</u> <u>Web</u> <u>Site</u> link on the left pane. Your Internet browser starts up and locates the site.

✔ Pause your mouse pointer over any of the buttons to see samples of the kinds of projects that button represents.

✔ Click any of the five tabs on the left pane to go to various additional features in Home Publishing. (These tabs are described in the next section, "The five launch tabs.")

✔ Locate a project by clicking the Find a Design button in the left pane. The Home Publishing Search page is displayed. If you type *Birthday* and click the Search button, you see thumbnail examples of 821 different birthday-related projects that you can choose from. Just use the scroll bar to view them and then double-click the one you want. The Home Publishing editing window then appears, where you can modify the design in many different ways. (See "Working on Your Own in the Editing Screen" later in this chapter.)

The five launch tabs

Click any of the five tabs on the left pane to go to a different window where you can try all kinds of projects. Here's what each of these tabs does:

✔ The **Creative Ideas** tab takes you to the Welcome Page. You can see the Welcome Page in Figure 22-2. Creative Ideas introduces you to the various kinds of projects that you can work on — it's actually an elaborate and attractive Help feature. Try clicking the Cards option, and then after the Cards help screen appears, click any of the pictures displayed to see suggestions and ideas to inspire you and tap into your creativity.

✔ The **Paper Projects** tab displays Home Publishing's initial screen, as shown in Figure 22-1. It's described in the preceding section, "Features on the opening screen."

✔ The **E-mail and Web Projects** tab shows you how to publish projects on a Web site or send them to your friends as e-mail.

✔ The **Occasions and Activities** tab works very much like the Creative Ideas tab, but Occasions and Activities organizes the project options by categories such as Mother's Day, School Activities, and the ever-popular *Just Because.*

✔ The **Blank Projects** tab is for those wild or brave people who don't need any design help. You build envelopes, cards, stationery, posters, or any other project *from the ground up.* You get a blank poster, for example, and you choose everything from the background color to the graphics and text. Remember, if you do start with a blank project, you can't blame anyone else if people open their eyes very, very wide and describe the final result as "hmmmm . . . ahh . . . interesting."

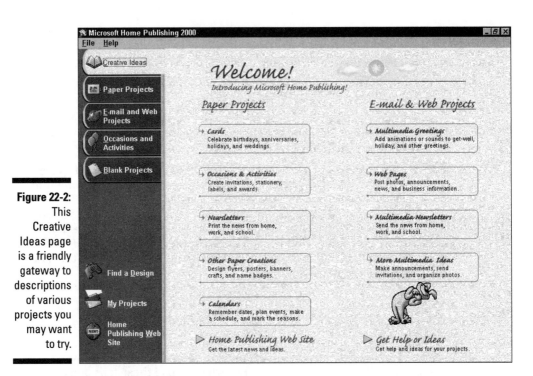

Figure 22-2:
This
Creative
Ideas page
is a friendly
gateway to
descriptions
of various
projects you
may want
to try.

Starting a New Project

You can start a new project from most locations in Home Publishing. The Creative Ideas, Paper Projects, E-mail and Web Projects, Occasions and Activities, and Blank Projects tabs are always visible unless you're in thumbnail or editing mode. And you can start projects by clicking any of these tabs and then double-clicking a design that you like to enter edit mode. In edit mode you customize the project and save the results.

You can also start blank projects by choosing File⇨New⇨Blank Paper Project *or* Blank E-mail *or* Web Project. But remember that with blank projects, you have to fill in the blanks — you have no professionally designed template to modify. And I do mean *professional.* Look on the back of the greeting cards, and you see that they were designed by Hallmark. Think you can compete with those guys? If so, go ahead and give it your best shot. Me, I'll stick with just modifying their excellent designs a little.

Another good way to begin a new project is to use the search feature. Click the Find a Design button in the left pane of any of the main tab pages; then type in the kind of project you're looking for and click the Search button. Scroll through the samples and double-click the one you want to work with.

Any time that you want to go back to the home page, press Ctrl+N or choose File⇨Close and Return to Opening Screen.

Working on Your Own in the Editing Screen

Home Publishing boasts a feature-packed editing mode. As soon as you double-click a thumbnail design, that design is opened in the edit screen, as shown in Figure 22-3.

You can also get to editing mode by choosing to start a blank project or by loading in an existing project you previously saved. However you get there, the editing suite is full of tools to let you get precisely the results you're after.

On the editing screen, you can customize the heck out of whatever project you're working on: Change, resize, rotate, or move images; add, move, and remove text; contour text to various shapes; and add borders and colors.

If you don't want to do any more work on your project, you can print it, send it electronically, or you can save it for later. (Home Publishing automatically prompts you to save your work before you exit the program, return to the opening screen, or start another project.) See the sections "Printing" and "Sending Projects Electronically," later in this chapter, for more information.

You edit your project by either clicking the buttons along the top of the editing screen or selecting from the menu choices in the left pane under Main Options. The editor offers more editing options than I can possibly discuss here, but here are some basics for editing your project:

- ✔ **To add text or graphics to another page of your project:** First view that page by clicking one of the view control buttons at the bottom of the left pane (refer to Figure 22-3). Click Inside Left, for instance, to view the inside-left page of a greeting card. Click Inside Spread to see both inside pages at once.

- ✔ **To get a hint about what a button does:** Pause your mouse cursor over the button until a description appears.

- ✔ **To select an object (text box or image) for editing:** Click it. The currently selected object has a rectangle around it. (The rectangle doesn't print.)

- ✔ **To add a block of text:** Click the Add New Text Block button (with *abc* on it). For a block of text in a swoopy, shaped outline, click the Add New Shaped Text button (with the capital *A* on it).

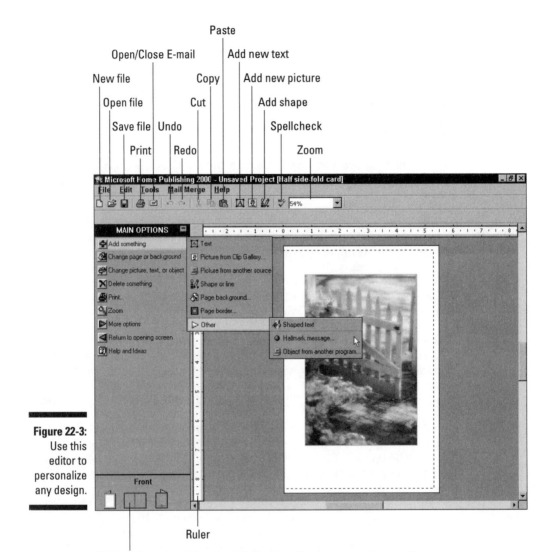

Paste

Open/Close E-mail

Add new text

New file

Copy

Add new picture

Open file

Cut

Add shape

Save file | Undo

Spellcheck

Print | Redo

Zoom

Figure 22-3:
Use this
editor to
personalize
any design.

Ruler

Click to view other sides of a folded project (such as a greeting card)

✔ **To add clip art (small images):** Click the Add New Picture button (with the face on it).

✔ **To replace text:** Click the text and type. Press the Backspace or Delete key to delete.

✔ **To change the appearance of a specific chunk of text:** First click and drag across that chunk to select it, and then click buttons or menu selections.

✔ **To move an object:** Slowly move your cursor over it until the cursor changes to a four-headed arrow. Then click and drag the object to where you want it.

✔ **To change an object's size:** Drag a side or corner of the object.

✔ **To undo a change:** Press Ctrl+Z; repeat to undo even earlier changes.

That was a list of the basics. Here's my list of some of the coolest special features:

✔ **Have Hallmark say it for you.** Are you tongue-tied? Puss, your aunt's favorite Siamese kitty, has collapsed. Auntie's devastated. What can possibly be said? Hallmark to the rescue. Click the Add Something option under Main Options in the left pane, select Other, and then select Hallmark Message (refer to Figure 22-3). Click Sympathy in the Select a Category list box and then select Loss of Pet. In the Messages For list box, select the option labeled `I know how much your cat meant . . .`, and there it is, the perfect message — click OK and substitute *Auntie* for *Margaret* in your card:

> ```
> I know how much your cat meant to you, Auntie, and how you
> must be feeling now. I hope it helps to know I care and
> I'll be thinking about you.
> ```

✔ **Use Shaped Text.** Choose from a couple of dozen different shapes into which you pour text. Do you want to say *I love you* with the message shaped like a stop sign? No problem. Click the Add Something option under Main Options in the left pane, select Other, and then select Shaped Text. Click the shape that you want and then type in the text you want shaped like that. Click OK, and your message looks like the Star Wars credits or some other special effect.

✔ **Shadow it.** Fewer special tricks make text look more three-dimensional and more attractive than a drop-shadow. To add shadowing, drag your mouse over some text to select it in your project and then click the Shadow button on the special Text-Modifying toolbar that appears when you select text. The Shadow button looks like a dark blue *O* with, appropriately, a shadow under it.

✔ **Add a Gradient Background.** If your printer is up to it, few backgrounds are more attractive than gradients. And Home Publishing offers a wide selection of different kinds of gradients to choose from, as shown in Figure 22-4. Click the Change Page or Background option under Main Options in the left pane and then select Page Background. Then click the Solid Color or Gradient option button. Click the down arrow next to the sample color and then click the Gradient button. You see the Gradient Fill dialog box, shown in Figure 22-4. (Don't forget to also try clicking the Reverse Colors button and changing the Type from Normal to Rainbow or Stripes to see many additional effects.)

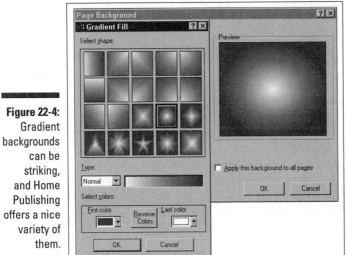

Figure 22-4:
Gradient
backgrounds
can be
striking,
and Home
Publishing
offers a nice
variety of
them.

Printing

Printing in Home Publishing is somewhat limited by a very non-electronic technology: paper. Check your printer manual, however; you may be pleasantly surprised to discover that you can print on heavier stock (nice for certificates) or continuous form paper (nice for banners). Some printers can even print iron-on templates so that you can create custom T-shirts, tote bags, or other fabric items.

To print your project, you must be viewing it in the editing screen. (See the preceding section, "Working on Your Own in the Editing Screen," for ways to get to that screen.) Then either click the Print button at the top of the screen or choose File⇨Print. Home Publishing initially runs a special printer test to make sure that it understands how paper goes through your printer. In that test, Home Publishing asks you to select a picture that looks most like your printer. Pictures can be misleading, so I suggest that after you click your choice of pictures, you also read the text description that appears. If the description doesn't sound correct, try another choice. After Home Publishing understands your printer, it won't need to run the test again.

Sending Projects Electronically

Microsoft gives you three ways to publish your projects electronically: by e-mail, by Web site, and to an Internet-ready file (.htm is the file extension) that you save on your hard drive (which you could later attach to e-mail if you want). To view your project in these various forms, your recipient must have e-mail software for e-mail, or a Web browser for Web site or .htm file viewing.

To send e-mail, click the E-mail and Web Projects tab (if you're not in the editor mode). If you're in the editor, choose File⇨Send by E-mail. In either case, the first time you try to send your document as an e-mail attachment, you see a dialog box asking you to select your preferred e-mail transmission method: AOL, Outlook Express, Hotmail, or as an attachment. Select your method and then select the Do Not Show This Again check box to avoid having to see this dialog box in the future. After you click OK, your e-mail transmission method appears. If you chose Outlook Express, you see its Send menus and text boxes. Fill in the To field and click the Send button. Home Publishing then translates your project into an .htm file, connects to your mail server, and e-mails the .htm file as an attachment.

To publish your document to a Web site that you *control* (can put documents on), choose File⇨Publish to Web⇨Publish to a Web Site. You then see a dialog box where you define where in your Web site you want this located (as the home page, or elsewhere), the name of your site's host, the address for uploading your document, and other details necessary to accomplish the job of posting the .htm file.

To save your document as an .htm file (Web document) on your hard drive, choose File⇨Publish to Web⇨Publish to a Folder on My Computer. The .htm file is created and then saved. By double-clicking it in Windows Explorer, your browser loads and displays it. You can also choose File⇨Open in your browser and locate the .htm file to load it and view it.

Chapter 23

Geographic Enlightenment: Expedia Streets & Trips 2000

● ●

In This Chapter

▶ Starting up Streets & Trips

▶ Locating an address

▶ Finding a place

▶ Planning a route

● ●

*B*affled? Lost in Yonkers? Never worry again about travel terrors such as sitting in a road construction traffic jam, trying to make sense of the streets of Pittsburgh, or finding your way back to a hotel after a walking tour of Boston. Streets & Trips 2000 to the rescue!

With its powerful mapping technology and immense database, Streets & Trips makes planning an excursion — whether it's for only two blocks or a round-trip jaunt of 6,000 miles — a piece of cake. The program contains many useful features, such as What's Nearby (which shows restaurants, lodging, shopping, and dozens of other categories). If you're stranded in St. Louis, you can even ask for a map showing the nearest ATM machine. Try that one with a paper map!

Launching Streets & Trips and Seeing the Big Picture

You can start Streets & Trips from the Windows Start button, the Works Task Launcher, or a program icon (if you have one on-screen), just as you can any other Windows program. But first, insert CD #7 from the Works Suite in your PC's CD-ROM drive. Streets & Trips refuses to assist you without that CD. In fact, if you wait a few seconds after inserting the CD, Streets & Trips may start on its own. If it doesn't start up right away, then perform one of the following actions:

✔ On the Windows Taskbar, choose Start➪Programs➪ Microsoft Streets & Trips 2000.

✔ In the Works Task Launcher, click the Programs button and then select Expedia Streets & Trips in the left pane and Start Expedia Streets & Trips in the middle pane.

✔ If you see a Microsoft Streets & Trips 2000 icon on-screen, double-click that icon.

Streets & Trips makes an appearance on your monitor and displays its Start Screen dialog box, as shown in Figure 23-1.

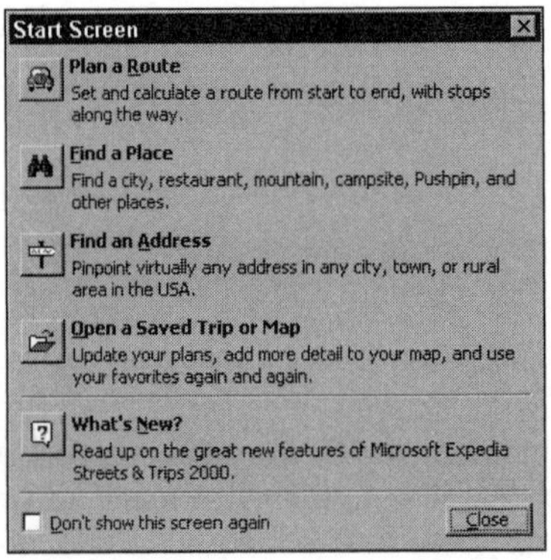

Figure 23-1: Click one of these buttons to start a common Streets & Trips feature.

Streets & Trips makes an appearance on your monitor and displays its Start Screen dialog box, as shown in Figure 23-1.

Click the Close button to shut down the Start Screen dialog box. You now see the default start-up view in Streets & Trips: a map of the United States, ready for you to zoom in on, paint, annotate, or otherwise manipulate. Figure 23-2 shows the main Streets & Trips tools and views.

This book doesn't allow enough space for me to cover all the features in Streets & Trips, but I can describe those that you're likely to use most — starting with the task of finding an address or a place.

Create a new pushpin

Highlight a location

Move Map

Draw a highlighted line

Drag a box to define zoom

Show scale and context windows

Specify where your trip ends

Connect to the Internet

Define where your trip begins

Show drawing toolbar

Type in a location to display it on the map

Trip directions view

Zoom slider

Show road, terrain, or political maps

Locate nearby attractions

Zoom buttons

Map view   Plan a trip

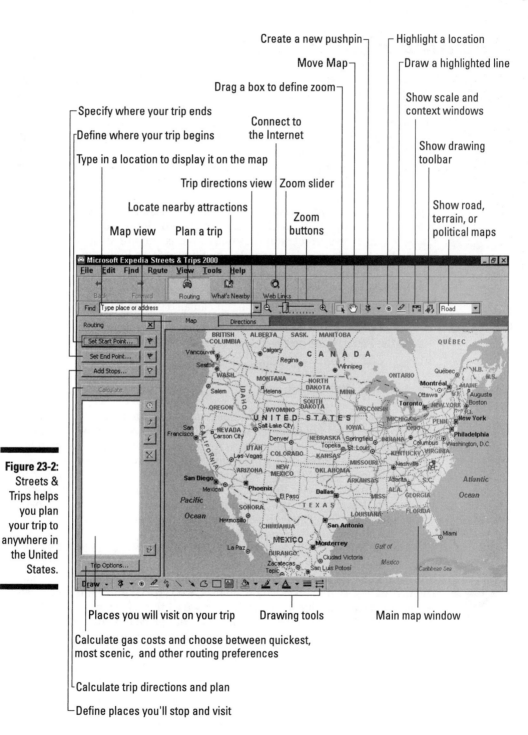

Figure 23-2:
Streets & Trips helps you plan your trip to anywhere in the United States.

Places you will visit on your trip   Drawing tools   Main map window

Calculate gas costs and choose between quickest, most scenic, and other routing preferences

Calculate trip directions and plan

Define places you'll stop and visit

Locating Nearly Anything

You can locate a specific address and have Streets & Trips display it on the map. Just choose Find➪Address or press Ctrl+A. The Find dialog box appears with its Address tab open. Fill in the street, city and state, and, optionally, the zip code, in the appropriate text boxes. Then click the Find button. But hey — addresses are easy! How about finding Billy Bob's Bowling Alley and Beer Palace or the location of your first romance — even if you don't know the address? By using Streets & Trips, finding nearly anything in the United States that's large enough to have a name is quick and easy.

Try searching for a place instead of an address. Assume, for example, that you don't know the address of the Empire State Building. You can search for cities, towns, rivers, and landmarks both famous and not-so-famous. Here's how to locate a place — for example, the Empire State Building:

1. **Choose Find➪Place.**

   The Find dialog box appears. (You can also press Ctrl+F to open the Find dialog box.)

2. **In the Place Name text box, type the name of the place you're looking for.**

   For this example, type **Empire State Building** in the Place Name text box.

3. **Click the Find button.**

A list of selections appears, with the best guess automatically appearing in the map window and highlighted in the Find dialog box, as shown in Figure 23-3. Click any other selection to view it in the map window. To zoom in and out on the map window, drag the sliding control between the – and + magnifying glass icons on the toolbar. Drag the control to the left to zoom out or to the right to zoom in (refer to Figure 23-2). To move the map around, move your cursor toward one edge of the map until the cursor becomes a broad arrow and then click. The map scrolls beneath your cursor.

You can use the Find a Place feature to zero in on any place in the Streets & Trips database. If an Izzy's exists in Boston, can Streets & Trips find it for you? You bet. (If you know the city, type a comma after the place name and then type the city name.) Hospitals, banks, ski resorts, museums, and even features such as bowling alleys and malls are all there for you to search. Go ahead and look up the location of some favorite place in your past, such as your high school or that great little bookstore with the free coffee.

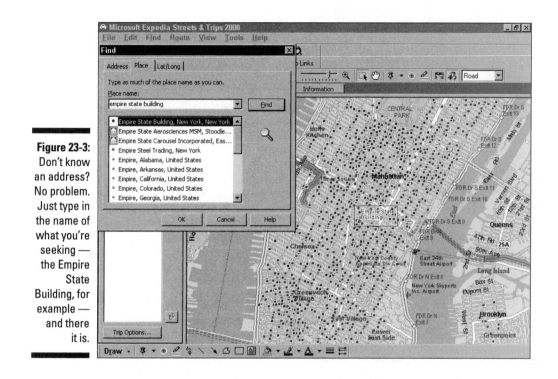

Figure 23-3:
Don't know
an address?
No problem.
Just type in
the name of
what you're
seeking —
the Empire
State
Building, for
example —
and there
it is.

Time to Plan a Trip

If you want details about the best route to take, including warnings about
areas to avoid because of construction delays, you can't do better than
Streets & Trips. To get a bit of experience with the trip-planner feature in
Streets & Trips, follow these steps to plan an imaginary four-day trip from
San Diego, California, to Las Vegas:

1. **Click the Routing button in the standard toolbar at the top of the
   Streets & Trips window.**

   The Routing window appears on the left side of the screen.

2. **Click the Set Start Point button.**

   The Find a Place to Start dialog box appears.

3. **Click the Address tab and, in the City text box, enter the name of the
   city from which you're starting your journey.**

   For your imaginary trip, type **San Diego** in the City text box.

4. **Click the Find button.**

   The list box fills with references to San Diego, but the first one is the correct one. The map displays San Diego.

5. **Click OK to accept this location as your start point.**

   The start location of your trip, San Diego in this example, appears in the Routing list box with a 1 next to it, indicating that it's the first location on your trip.

6. **Click the Add Stops button.**

   The Find a Place for a Stop dialog box appears.

7. **In the Place Name text box, type the name of the city where you want to stop and then click the Find button.**

   For this example, type **Las Vegas** in the Place Name text box. The map displays Las Vegas.

8. **Click OK to accept this destination as a stop on your trip.**

   Las Vegas appears in the Routing list box with a 2 next to it, indicating that it's the next stop on your trip.

9. **Click the Set End Point button.**

   The Find a Place to End dialog box appears.

10. **Click the Address tab of the Find a Place to End dialog box. From there, you have two options: 1) in the City text box, type the name of the city in which you intend to end your trip, or 2) click the down arrow next to the text box and select that city from the drop-down list that appears.**

    Type **San Diego** again or click its name in the drop-down list.

11. **Click the Find button.**

    The list box fills with references to San Diego and similar phrases, but the first one is the correct one.

12. **Click OK to accept this destination as the end point of your trip.**

    The name of your last stop — San Diego in this imaginary journey — appears in the Routing list box with a 3 next to it, indicating that it's the next (and final) location for your trip.

    Now all you need to do is specify how long you want to stay in Las Vegas. Say that you want to go for three days so that you have a chance to really wipe out your savings account in style.

13. **In the Routing list box, click to select the number and name of the city where you intend to spend some time.**

    For your imaginary journey, select the option labeled 2. Las Vegas in the Routing list box.

14. Click the Clock icon just to the right of the Routing list box.

The Clock icon is the top of the four icons to the right of the list box. The Edit Time dialog box now appears, where you can specify how long you want to stay at this stop on your trip and, optionally, when you want to arrive and depart.

15. Click in the Stop For check box to select it and click the down-arrow icon to change the setting from the default *hours/minutes* (Hrs:Mns) to *nights*.

16. Click the up-arrow icon until the text box gives you the correct number of nights.

For the example, you want it to read 3.

17. Click OK.

The Routing list box now displays 2. Las Vegas (3 nights).

18. Click the Calculate button on the Routing window (just above the Routing list box).

Streets & Trips mulls things over for a few seconds and then displays the following results:

- A list box appears showing you the details of your route. You see each street and highway that you must take on each leg of your trip, how much time you're on that leg, how many miles you travel on that leg, and what you're heading toward. Streets & Trips even warns you of any potential highway problems (as you can see in the example shown in Figure 23-4, where the program cautions you that a road is under construction in Riverside). If you have set up your PC to go online, you can get the latest construction tips. To update the construction tips, choose Tools⇨ Update Construction Information. Click Yes on the Microsoft Expedia Streets & Trips 2000 dialog box that appears, which ventures an opinion as to whether your data is already up to date or not. A Downloading Construction Data dialog box appears while your PC goes online and connects to some unspecified location on the Internet. Once the data has been downloaded, another Microsoft Expedia Streets & Trips 2000 dialog box appears, telling you that the data has been downloaded. Click OK.

- The map now displays your route, highlighted by a broad, green line.

- New tabs at the top of the list box offer pictures of places of interest on your trip and additional, useful information about your stopovers. Click those tabs and you may be surprised at the wealth of information that Streets & Trips offers. Try the various options under Driving Directions.

You can print directions or a map (or both combined) in a travel strip by choosing File⇨Print.

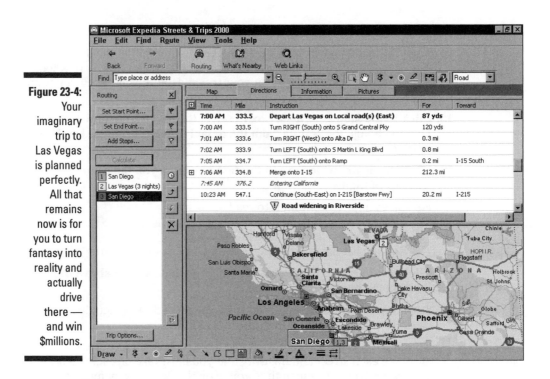

Figure 23-4:
Your imaginary trip to Las Vegas is planned perfectly. All that remains now is for you to turn fantasy into reality and actually drive there — and win $millions.

Part VI
The Part of Tens

The 5th Wave — By Rich Tennant

NO INTERNET ADDRESS

PLEASE

In this part . . .

As on *Sesame Street,* this part comes to you courtesy of the number ten — that is, ten nifty tricks and ten profound proscriptions (things not to do). If you don't find what you want in the rest of this book, you may just find it here.

If you don't find it here, I didn't have room to put it in this book. So visit `www.dummmies.com` on the Web and check out some of the following related titles from IDG Books Worldwide, Inc.:

- ✔ *Windows 98 For Dummies*
- ✔ *Microsoft Works 2000 For Windows For Dummies*
- ✔ *Word 2000 For Windows For Dummies*
- ✔ *Microsoft Money 2000 For Dummies*
- ✔ *Internet Explorer For Windows For Dummies*
- ✔ *Microsoft Outlook For Dummies*

Chapter 24

Ten Nifty Tricks

Remember those great ads for magic tricks in the back of comic books? Well, continuing in that tradition, here at the back of this book is a bunch of nifty, almost-magic tricks. You probably can't amaze your friends with these tricks, but you may actually enjoy your PC more, which is magic enough.

Cut, Copy, and Paste to or from E-Mail

The number-one, all-time most-frequently asked question I receive is, "How do I move text between an e-mail message and another program?" The secret is to use the invisible Windows Clipboard, which I describe in more detail in the appendix. Just click and drag your mouse across text in any window (even an e-mail message) to select that text and choose Edit⇨Copy from the menu bar of that window (or press Ctrl+C) to copy the text to the invisible Windows Clipboard. Then click at the point in the window where you want the text to appear (which can also be in an e-mail) and choose Edit⇨Paste from the menu bar of that window (or press Ctrl+V) to paste.

Clean Up Ragged Text

If text looks ragged, with some lines too long and others too short, you're probably looking at text with "hard" line breaks: invisible characters that force the line to wrap. (They occur either because of e-mail quirks or because someone pressed Enter at the end of a line instead of letting the line wrap.) You could remove these characters by clicking at the beginning of the line *after* each too-short line and then pressing the Backspace key on your keyboard.

If you have a big document, copy it into Word (see the preceding section) and take the following steps. Choose Edit⇨Replace. In Word's Find What text box, type the magic incantation ^p^p; in the Replace With text box, enter xxxxx, and then click Replace All. Delete one of the ^p's in the Find What box, delete all the xxxxx's in Replace With, and then click Replace All again. Finally, type xxxxx in the *Find What* box, type ^p in the *Replace With* box, and then click Replace All one more time.

Change Annoying Program Behaviors

The more modern and "full-featured" a program is, the more annoying behaviors it seems to exhibit. Contemporary word processors, in particular, feature many automatic behaviors that can drive you nuts. One secret to changing such behaviors is to figure out where the program's options, preferences, or auto-whatevers are hiding.

In most programs, look for a menu choice of Tools⇨Options, Tools⇨Customize, or Tools⇨Preferences to access key controls. In Microsoft Word, also check out Tools⇨AutoCorrect.

In any case, the dialog box that appears usually contains lots of check boxes for the various automatic options; if a check mark appears, that automatic option is on. Click it to clear any check mark and turn that option off. Click the various tabs in the dialog box to see additional options.

Drag and Drop Nearly Anything

This trick is one that nearly every Windows program can do. Open a My Computer window (or a Windows Explorer window). If you want to work on a document file, just drag that file from the My Computer/Explorer window over to the Word icon on your desktop. Release the mouse, and Word opens the file. Even if the file isn't a Word file, Word tries to import it. And don't forget that, in Outlook Express, you can drag messages and drop them into folders such as the Inbox. You also can select some text (drag your mouse over it) in Word and then drop it onto the Windows desktop. And you can drag a DOC or TXT file from Explorer and drop it onto the printer icon on your desktop to print that file. Drag desktop icons and drop them onto the Start button if you want to add them to the Start menu. My advice? Because you can drag and drop in hundreds of ways in Windows, just try it. If you can't drag, no harm's done. If you can, you now know a new trick.

Get Help in Dialog Boxes

If you're working in a dialog box, see whether a tiny ? symbol appears in the upper-right corner. If so, click the ?, and you see your mouse cursor transform from the usual arrow to an arrow-with-a-question mark-attached. Now move your mouse and click anything in the dialog box that puzzles you. You get an immediate answer. To close the Help box that appears, just click it. Click the ? again for additional Help. And don't forget that you can always print or copy the Help information for any option in a dialog box by right-clicking inside the Help box and then clicking Print or Copy from the pop-up menu that appears.

Import Documents

Many programs can read files from other programs. After you open a file by choosing File➪Open from the menu bar, the Open dialog box offers you a Files of Type list box. Click that box, and you open a list of file types that the program can read. Click one of those file types, and the File Name list box lists files of that type. Double-click a file to import, and your program converts it.

Export Documents

Exporting a file for a different program works a lot like importing: Choose the File➪Save As command from the menu bar and choose a file type in the Save As Type list box of the Save As dialog box that appears. If you don't see in the list the exact file type for the program to which you want to export a file, try either Text, Text & Tabs (also called *tab-delimited* in some programs), or Text & Commas (also called *comma-delimited*). Many programs can import those types of files.

Wrap Text in Small Windows

If you're working on a word-processor document in a tiny window, where lines extend beyond the window's edge, scrolling left and right so that you can read the text is a real pain. Instead, choose Tools⇨Options from the menu bar (or locate the Preferences or Options elsewhere; sometimes they're in the View menu). Click the Wordwrap or Wrap to Window check box in the dialog box that appears. The document doesn't word wrap this way if you print it; this trick just helps you read it.

Split a Word Window

In Word, you can split the window and thereby work on two different parts of a document simultaneously. At the very top of the vertical scroll bar, above the upward-pointing arrow, lies a microscopic, obscure, shy little rectangle. Click that guy and drag him downward. This action splits the document into two windows that you can scroll independently. You still have only one document, however, as both windows contain the same file. Click in either half to do your editing. To put the split away, drag the horizontal line that separates the two halves back up to the very top or bottom of the document window.

This feature enables you to view sections of your document that may lie far apart from one another. By using a split window, you can compare them, edit them at the same time, harmonize them, or otherwise reconcile them as necessary. It's all one document; you're just viewing two areas at once.

Try the Other Mouse Button

The *other* mouse button (the one on the right side of the mouse, unless you're a lefty and you reconfigured your mouse) has a surprising amount of power. In nearly any Windows program — or on the Windows desktop itself — try clicking something by using that right mouse button and see whether a pop-up menu appears. Or try highlighting (selecting) something — text or graphics — the usual way and then clicking the selected area with that other mouse button.

You often open a pop-up menu of editing commands such as Copy, Cut, and Paste; formatting commands; or other useful commands. If you right-click a toolbar, you usually get a list of additional available toolbars and perhaps a Customize option that enables you to add or remove buttons from the visible toolbars. Precisely what options appear on this pop-up menu depends on the context — that is, on what kind of window or other object you right-click. That's why the menu that pops up is also known as a *context menu*.

But wait — there's more! If a dialog box presents you with a thingy (a check box, a button, or whatever) that you don't understand, click the right mouse button on that thingy. In many programs, a brief explanation appears and occasionally is even helpful! (The explanation is the same one that appears if you click the ? symbol in the upper right-hand corner of the dialog box and then click the thingy; see the section "Get Help in Dialog Boxes," earlier in this chapter, for the lowdown.)

Chapter 25

Ten Things NOT to Do

*E*veryone has an idea about how things ought to work. Unfortunately, computers don't usually work that way. You can easily fall into old typewriter habits or form a mistaken impression that Works, Word, or some other program makes you do something that you don't really need to do. Here's my list of the top-ten errors, misconceptions, or just plain boo-boos that you want to avoid.

Don't Use Extra Spaces, Lines, or Tabs

If you're using multiple, consecutive spaces or tabs in a word-processing document, you're probably making your life difficult. If you're using multiple tabs in every line, you probably haven't set your tab stops or you've forgotten that you can indent a paragraph by using a toolbar button. (See Chapter 11.) If you're using blank lines to separate paragraphs, try pressing Ctrl+0 (that's a zero and not the letter O) to put a space above the paragraph instead. See Chapter 6 for additional better ways to do these sorts of things.

Don't Keep Pressing Enter to Begin a New Page

This trick may work nicely on your old Royal typewriter, but in word-processing documents, it creates a royal mess. Press Ctrl+Enter to start a new page or just keep typing and let the computer and printer worry about pagination. They do a good job of it, just as they handle line wrapping, the subject of the following tip.

Don't Press Enter at the End of Each Line

I know that I say this elsewhere, but seeing people fighting their word processor pains me greatly so I'm saying it again: If you press Enter at the end of every line in a word-processing document, Works can't word-wrap the lines for you. As a result, every time that you edit a line, you must manually readjust *every* line! AAAAARRRGGGHHH!! JUST DON'T DO IT — YOU HEAR ME?!! (Notice, too, how annoying text is if it's all in capital letters? If you want to know why adults shouldn't "shout" at each other this way, see the tenth section, "Don't Type in ALL CAPITALS," a bit later in this chapter.)

Don't Type Your Own File Extensions When Saving Files

To save a file, just type the file's name and not the DOC or any other extension in the File Name text box of the Save or Save As dialog box. Windows programs automatically add the correct extension to the file name. If you use your own special extension, Windows and your programs get very confused. Some programs, such as Word, are smart enough not to save a double extension, but others may save it as *Filename*.doc.doc!

Don't Number Your Pages Manually

Word can automagically number your word-processing pages, positioning the numbers where you want them. What more could you want? If you try to number your own pages by simply typing a number on each page, you must continually adjust them as you edit the document.

Don't Turn Off Your PC before Exiting

Hey! Time for dinner! But don't just flip the power switch on your PC. Exit your program and exit Windows first. (If your PC is one that suspends the state of all your programs — and of Windows — as you turn the PC off, you don't need to exit your program and Windows first. Some laptops also have a Suspend feature. Check your manual.) If you don't exit before you turn off your computer, Windows and your program can become confused after you restart your machine. At the very least, Windows will run a Scandisk program after you restart to make sure that you didn't damage any files by your action — and, if you did, your hard disk fills up with little Windows temporary files.

Don't Use Spaces for Blank Cells

If you want to remove an entry in your spreadsheet documents, don't type a space; press the Delete key instead. If you put a space in the cell and use a COUNT, AVG, or other statistical function, your program still counts that "blank" cell.

Don't Work in Tiny Windows Unnecessarily

Just because a program starts out with a smallish window doesn't mean that you must stay with it. Click and drag a corner or side of the Works window and enlarge Works. Do the same with your document windows. Better yet, maximize the Works or document window. See the appendix for a refresher on how to perform this action.

Do Not Stuff All Your Files in the Same Folder

See the appendix for ways to make new folders. As you save files, don't put too many of them in a single folder. If you stuff them all in the same folder, such as the Windows 98 My Documents folder, you eventually can become very confused. (Nothing's magical about the My Documents folder, by the way. Microsoft just decided to give you a folder with that name. You can put stuff in any folder you want; just stay away from the Windows folder.)

Don't Type in ALL CAPITALS

Don't type in all capital letters, particularly if you're using Outlook Express to send mail to somebody or post a message on a newsgroup. Most readers of such messages consider text in all caps the equivalent of your shouting at them. In other tools, using all capitals (uppercase letters) simply makes your documents harder to read. So do yourself *and* your readers a favor: Avoid 'em wherever possible.

Appendix

Clues for the Clueless: PC Basics

*I*f you ever open a computer magazine or a book about computing, you see it: lingo, arcana, gobbledygook, slang, mumbo-jumbo, gibberish, abbreviations, acronyms, jargon, cant, argot — in a word, lots of stuff that's really hard to understand unless you're one of the techno-elite.

The *For Dummies* books are for the rest of us: the few, the brave, and — in computer matters — the clueless; hence the appendix. If you're utterly new to the world of the PC, this appendix is your starting point. I can't do as complete a job of preparing you for Windows as, say, *Windows 98 For Dummies,* by Andy Rathbone (IDG Books Worldwide, Inc.), but I can try to keep you out of trouble.

So just what *is* Windows, and how is it different from Works Suite? Windows is the *foundation software* on which your programs (or *applications*), such as the programs of Works Suite, rely. It's the software that glues together all the parts of your computer into a working system and enables you to run one or more programs at a time. Windows not only serves as a foundation, but it also includes certain programs, known as *accessories* or *utilities,* that perform such basic jobs as displaying text or playing music. Programs that run under Windows all work in very much the same way — a behavior set that's part of what this appendix is about.

Cozying Up to Your Keyboard

PC keyboards differ from typewriter keyboards. Following are some of the keys you're likely to find on your PC keyboard:

- **Function keys:** These keys usually sit along the top of the keyboard and carry the labels F1 through F12. They perform different functions in different programs (except F1, which always displays a Help dialog box to answer your questions). Pressing a function key is one of many ways that a program enables you to give a command.

- **Typewriter keys:** Your old typewriter had most of the same character keys (*characters* being letters, numbers, and punctuation marks). The computer people added a few new ones, like a vertical bar and a tilde (~).

- **Navigation keys:** These keys lie to the right of the typewriter keys. You can use the four keys with arrows on them to move the *insertion point* (a typing cursor). The other navigation keys, Home, End, PgUp (or Page Up), and PgDn (or Page Down), move you around in a document in large gulps. Nearby is a Delete key, which deletes text following the insertion point or any item you *select.* (See the section "Selecting by Using the Mouse or Keyboard," later in this appendix.) The Backspace key deletes text preceding the insertion point. Also down near the Delete key is an Insert key that I recommend you avoid: If you press it, it makes you type over existing text. Press that key again to resume typing normally.

- **Numeric keypad:** This keypad at the far right of your keyboard duplicates the number keys and math symbols that appear across the top of your keyboard, plus adds another Enter key. If these keys don't appear to work correctly, press the NumLock key once.

- **Enter key:** This key generally bears the label *Enter* or displays an L-shaped arrow (or both). You use the Enter key to signal that you're through typing a paragraph or entering some data or instructions.

- **Esc key:** Known as the Escape key, this little guy enables you to back out of commands that you start but don't want to finish. Pressing Esc does the same thing as clicking the Cancel button that programs sometimes display (most often in dialog boxes).

> ✔ **Shift**, **Alt**, and **Ctrl (Control) keys:** These guys don't do anything by themselves: They work only if you press them at the same time you press other keys. The Shift key, if you use it as you're typing on the regular keyboard, produces the upper character on a key — just as the Shift key does on a typewriter. Otherwise, you use Shift and its fellow keys for *keyboard shortcuts*.

Keyboard shortcuts are alternative ways to give commands to programs, and appear in this book and in all Windows programs in a format similar to the following examples:

> ✔ Ctrl+S
>
> ✔ Alt+Shift+F1

These descriptions mean that you must press and hold the Ctrl (or Alt, or Shift) key and then press and release the other key shown. Ctrl+S, for example, means to press and hold the Ctrl key and then press and release the S key. If three keys appear in such a combination (as in the example of Alt+Shift+F1), you press and hold the first two keys together while you press and release the third key (F1 in this example).

Moseying Around with Your Mouse

The strange, rodent-shaped object with push buttons on top that plugs into your computer by its tail is know as a *mouse.* If you don't have such a thing, you may have some other kind of *pointing device,* all forms of which you wiggle side-to-side or front-to-back. One such device is a *trackball,* a device from which a ball sticks out for you to wiggle. On a laptop computer, you may have a tiny joysticklike lever to wiggle, somewhere near the G and H keys in the center of your keyboard. Or you may have a flat pad near your thumbs that you drag your finger across.

Your PC accommodates rodents and other wiggling critters so that you can point at control buttons and menus instead of needing always to type commands with your keyboard. Pointing also enables you to indicate what stuff you want to work on.

Mouse behavior

You can do two things with your mouse or other pointing device: wiggle it and click its buttons. (Well, you can do other things, I suppose, but that's up to you.) As you wiggle your pointing device it moves a *pointer.* (Typically, that pointer's an arrow, although that symbol changes depending on just what you're doing.)

Regardless of the type of pointing device you use, on either side of the device are *buttons*. Usually, a pointing device sports only two buttons (to the left and right); really snazzy dressers may have three. In most Windows programs, the left button is the most important one. The right button usually opens a pop-up menu of editing commands, such as Copy and Paste. But you can find the same commands elsewhere in the program (such as on the main menu bar); opening menus by right-clicking the mouse is simply a convenience. And you can do some specialized kinds of dragging with the right button. I discuss that skill in the section "Drag," coming up shortly.

Mouse skills

The first mouse skill that you need to control a Windows program is the capability to point and click. Here's exactly what this term and related terms mean:

- ✔ **To point:** Push your pointing device to move the mouse pointer. Position the pointer so that its tip is anywhere on top of or within the thing at which you're pointing.

- ✔ **To click:** Point to something and then press and release the left mouse button.

- ✔ **To double-click:** Similar to clicking, but you press and release the (left) mouse button twice in rapid succession.

- ✔ **To click and drag (also known simply as *dragging*):** Press the (left) button down and hold it down while moving the mouse. This action highlights (selects) something. And if you already selected something, this action *drags* the highlighted text or graphic around on-screen. After you're done dragging, release the button. Sometimes, as you drag, the object itself doesn't move; only an outline of it moves. The object itself moves after you finish dragging it and release the button. Releasing the button is known as *dropping* because the dragged item falls onto the screen wherever you drop it. The entire process is known as *dragging and dropping*.

Selecting by Using the Mouse or Keyboard

Pointing out something in a program is known as *selecting* it. To select something, drag across it (if it's text in a document) or click it (good for graphics, icons, or things in a list or menu). To select multiple things with a mouse, imagine a rectangle completely surrounding all those things and then drag from one corner of that rectangle (say, the upper left) to the opposite corner (lower right). You can also sometimes select multiple things by holding down the Shift or Ctrl key while you click each item that you want to include in the group of selected items. After you select something, it changes color, a frame appears around it, or black or some other contrasting color envelopes it.

In many programs, you can also select something by holding down either of the two Shift keys and pressing your navigation keys. Exactly how the selection occurs depends entirely on the program you use, so I can't describe the process precisely here.

Cutting, Copying, Pasting, and Dragging

Nearly all Windows programs offer a common set of features that make editing easy: the Cut, Copy, Paste, and Drag features. The Cut, Copy, and Paste features employ a Windows feature known as the *Clipboard*. The Windows Clipboard is a temporary and hidden storage area.

Copy or Cut and Paste

To move something, you can cut and paste it. This procedure is exactly like copying and pasting, except that you remove the original text or graphic from your document. Here's the procedure for copying or cutting and pasting:

1. **Select the text or illustration that you want to copy or move.**

2. **To copy something, press Ctrl+C, Choose Edit⇨Copy from the menu bar (or right-click and choose Copy from the pop-up menu), or Click the Copy button on the toolbar.**

   The Copy button normally displays two overlapping documents. To cut something instead of copying it, substitute any of the following: Press Ctrl+X, choose Edit⇨Cut from the menu bar, right-click and choose Cut from the pop-up menu, or click the Cut (scissors) button in the toolbar. This procedure copies (or moves) the selected stuff to the Windows Clipboard.

3. **Click where you want a copy (or the original) to appear.**

   This spot can be in the document on which you're working or in some other document. You can take your time opening documents, launching programs, or whatever you need to do. **Note:** Whatever you copy stays on the Clipboard only until you copy or cut something else or turn off your computer.

4. **Press Ctrl+V, Choose Edit⇨Paste from the menu bar (or right-click and choose Paste from the pop-up menu), or Click the Paste button in the toolbar.**

The Paste button displays a clipboard with a document. This procedure copies stuff from the Windows Clipboard and pastes it into the new location.

You can make as many copies as you want by repeating Steps 3 and 4 — until you put something new on the Clipboard.

Drag

Dragging is an easy way to move or copy text, an illustration, or a file to a different place within a window or even to another window. See the section "Controlling Program and Document Windows," later in this appendix, if windows are new to you.

Here's how to move or copy something by dragging it:

1. **Select the text, illustration, file, or other object that you want to move.**

2. **Place your mouse cursor over the highlighted area.**

3. **Press and hold the left mouse button (don't let go) and drag the selected text or illustration to where you want to move it.**

If you want to copy, not move, the selected text, press and hold the Ctrl key down at this point. If your destination isn't visible in the document window, drag to the window's edge in the direction you want to go. As your cursor hits the top or bottom edge of the window, the window scrolls. If your destination is in another window, just drag the object to the other window and then to your destination in that window.

4. **Release the mouse button at your final destination.**

You can also drag and drop by using the *right* mouse button. After you drop, you see a pop-up menu offering you the option of moving, copying, or possibly other choices. Click your choice in that menu.

Viewing the Windows Desktop

A short while after you turn on your PC, you should see something similar to what appears in Figure A-1: the Windows *desktop.* (Some PCs may first ask you for your name and a password. Try simply pressing the Enter key if the person who sold or gave you your PC didn't tell you what to do about this query.)

Folders

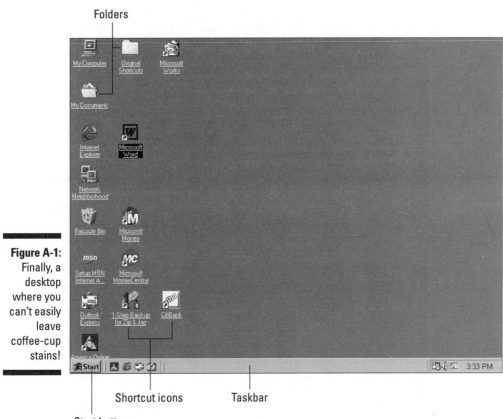

Figure A-1:
Finally, a
desktop
where you
can't easily
leave
coffee-cup
stains!

Shortcut icons   Taskbar

Start button

Following are a few tips for using the Windows desktop:

- **Icons** are small pictures, usually with a label. You double-click icons to do something (usually, to start a program). *Shortcuts* are icons displaying a tiny arrow in one corner. They start a program or open a window.

- **The taskbar**, that large gray band along the bottom (or side) of your screen, contains one or more items that look like buttons. You need to click a button only once to use it — don't double-click it. The Start button can help you run programs, as I describe in the following section.

- **The My Computer icon** enables you to open *windows* where you can view *folders* and *files* on your computer — all you do is double-click this icon. It also enables you to access the same standard Windows features (Setup, Help, Find) as does the Start button, which I describe in the following section.

✔ **The Recycle Bin icon** is a sort of trash can. Drag files or folders to this icon if you want to delete them. You don't actually delete the files and folders by dragging them here, just in case you change your mind. Double-click this icon to see what's in the bin. Then, to *really* delete files (which frees up additional disk space on your PC), choose File⇨ Empty Recycle Bin from the menu bar. To restore a file to its original folder, click that file (as it appears in the Recycle Bin window) and then choose File⇨Restore.

Finding, Starting, and Exiting Programs

Windows gives you several ways to start a program (also known as *launching, running,* or *executing* a program), as the following list describes:

✔ Click the Start button to browse through an extensive menu of programs and choose one to run. (Step-by-step instructions follow.)

✔ Double-click a *shortcut* — an icon (symbol) on the desktop displaying the program's name.

✔ Click a program icon on the Windows taskbar.

✔ In any *window* (a rectangle on-screen), double-click a file that displays a program's icon.

The fastest way to start (launch) a program is by using a shortcut or an icon on the taskbar. Not all programs have shortcuts sitting there on your desktop, but you can create shortcuts for them if you want. Just open Windows Explorer, My Computer, or click the Start button and follow its menus. After you see a program for which you want to make a shortcut, just drag and drop it onto the desktop. There it is — your new shortcut!

You can also always start any correctly installed program by using the Start button. Just follow these steps:

1. **Click the Start button on the Windows taskbar (refer to Figure A-1).**

2. **In the Start menu that appears, click Programs (or click one of the applications that you see in the list *above* the Programs option on the Start menu).**

   Another menu appears next to the first one.

3. **Move your cursor horizontally until it's on the new menu and then move the pointer vertically until it points to the program name that you want and click it.**

Sometimes yet another menu appears. At this point, your screen begins to resemble the one shown in Figure A-2. As Figure A-2 shows, a black rectangle envelopes (highlights) whatever you point to in a menu. If a triangular arrow appears to the right of a menu selection's title and a folder icon to the left, your pointer is on a folder. You aren't at your destination yet! Repeat Step 3 until your pointer highlights the program name that you want *and* a program icon (not a folder icon) appears to the left of that name, as shown for Microsoft Works Calendar in Figure A-2.

Now you're off and running. Your program appears in a window on-screen or fills the entire screen. You can run several programs at once if you want. If you need to copy something from your e-mail program to your word-processor program, for example, you can run both programs. To switch between running programs, press Alt+Tab.

To *exit* a program, choose File⊅Exit from the menu bar, press Alt+F4, or click the X in the upper right-hand corner of the program window. If you haven't yet saved your work as a file, the program may prompt you to do so.

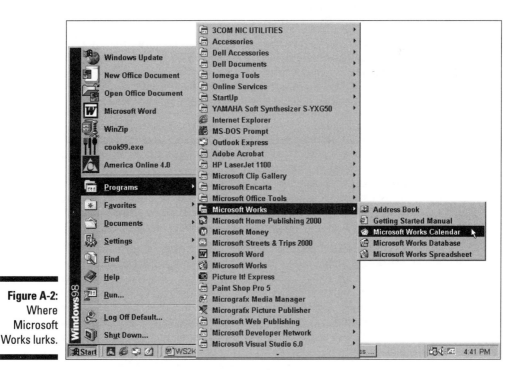

Figure A-2:
Where
Microsoft
Works lurks.

Understanding Disks, Folders, and Files

One subject that always confuses beginners is figuring out the basics about software: What and where is a program, a file, or a document? The following list provides you with an overview of what and where those things are:

- **Files:** Files are what a computer uses to store anything and everything: programs, documents, pictures — you name it. Files reside on a *disk* of some kind, and on most disks you can move, copy, or erase files. Each file has a *file name,* and whenever Windows lists files, it usually displays an *icon* (symbol) that tells you with what program the file associates (for example, Word).

- **File names:** Whenever you create anything on a PC (say, a document in Word), you save it as a file and give the file a name. The name can be up to 256 characters long and include spaces. Word, or whatever program you use, adds a period and three letters to the end to create an official Windows *file name.* These three letters are the file name *extension* and indicate with what program the file associates. (Files ending in .doc, for example, are Microsoft Word files.)

- **Folders:** *Folders* serve the same purpose as paper file folders in a file cabinet. (The "cabinet" in this case is a disk drive.) Folders (also known as *directories* or *subdirectories*) group and organize files. Folders may contain additional folders, and those additional folders can contain more folders, *ad nauseum.* You can make, move, copy, delete, and rename folders.

- **Disks and disk drives:** Disks have one job: to store files. *Hard disks* are disks that are permanently installed in your PC. Your programs — and Windows itself — are installed (stored) as files on a hard disk. *Disk drives* (the electronic boxes that contain, read, and write disks) you refer to by using letters with colons — for example, *C:* (which is the name of your main hard disk drive). You probably have additional disk drives of different kinds.

- **Diskettes and floppies:** *Diskettes* (most often simply referred to as disks) are floppy little plastic disks sealed within hard, flat plastic rectangles that you can insert into and remove from diskette drives on your PC. Windows calls a diskette a *3½-inch floppy.* You use diskettes for *backup* (keeping a copy of your files in case your hard disk breaks, or *crashes*) or to give files to other people. The disk drives for diskettes are nearly always known as *A:* (and, if you have a second one, *B:*). To insert a diskette into its drive, orient the disk's metal tab toward the drive and the disk label up. To remove the disk, press the button adjacent to the drive's slot. You must remove disks from the A: drive before you can start your PC running Windows.

✔ **CD and CD-ROMs:** *CDs* (also known as *CD-ROMs,* where *ROM* stands for *Read-Only Memory*) are disks that you can't alter or erase. Software vendors use CDs to distribute their programs. CDs go into special CD-ROM drives on your PC. To open a CD-ROM drive, press the button that protrudes from the drive, and a tray emerges. Place your disk label-side up on the tray and press the drive's button again. Some CDs automatically run a program as soon as you insert them. Some newer CD drives allow you to store your own files on CD's, too.

Viewing, browsing, and opening disk drives, folders, and files

The easiest way to view lists of your disk drives, folders, and files is to double-click the My Computer icon on your Windows desktop. A window opens. (See the section "Controlling Program and Document Windows," later in this appendix, if windows are new to you.) I call all windows that spring from the My Computer icon "My Computer windows."

In the first My Computer window, double-click any disk drive to display the files or folders on the disk in that drive. Double-click a folder to see what files or folders are within that folder.

To view the contents of any file that you create (which, in this book I call a *document file*), you need to start (launch) the program that made it and then open the file (by using, for example, the File➪Open command on that program's menu bar). An easy way to perform both actions at once is to double-click the document file.

The process of looking in various disk drives and folders for files is known as *browsing.* The technique for browsing is basically the same throughout Windows (including any My Computer windows and the Open and Save dialog boxes of all Windows programs). Following are the basic browsing techniques, using the Word Open dialog box as an example, as shown in Figure A-3:

✔ The window or dialog box shows only one folder's contents at a time. The folder's name appears at the top of the window or dialog box. (I call this folder the "currently displayed folder" in the following bullets.)

✔ To open a folder, double-click it (or click it and click the Open button if one is present).

✔ To open the folder in which the currently displayed folder resides, click the Up One Level button.

✔ To open other folders or other disk drives, click the down-arrow button to the right of the currently displayed folder's name. Double-click any folder or disk drive in the list that appears.

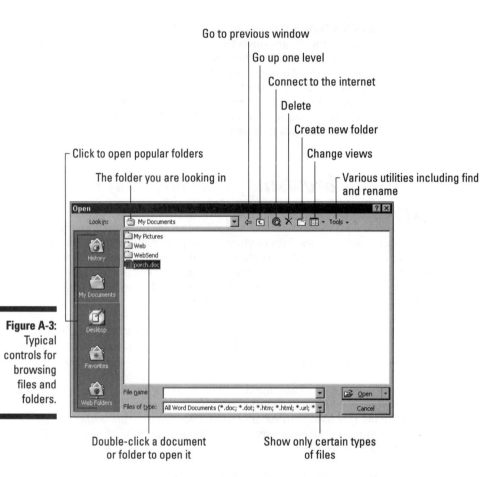

Go to previous window

Go up one level

Connect to the internet

Delete

Create new folder

Change views

Click to open popular folders

The folder you are looking in

Various utilities including find and rename

Figure A-3:
Typical controls for browsing files and folders.

Double-click a document or folder to open it

Show only certain types of files

✔ To see the kinds and sizes of files on display, click the Details button that some windows and dialog boxes provide. Or choose View➪Details from the menu bar.

✔ In Open or Save As dialog boxes, you see a Files of Type drop-down list box (below the File Name text box). Click that box to choose a new file type to import or export files from other programs.

Saving your work as a file

To return to a computer document that you created, you need to save your documents as a file on a disk. That disk can be either your permanent *hard disk* or a removable *diskette* (or *floppy disk*). Some programs, such as Microsoft Money, save everything automatically as you exit the program, so you don't need to think much about saving files.

Most Windows programs give you the following three ways to save your document as a file (choose your favorite):

- ✔ Choose File⇨Save from the menu bar.
- ✔ Press Ctrl+S.
- ✔ Click the floppy disk icon on the toolbar.

After you use these commands to save a document for the first time, your program opens a Save As dialog box so that you can give the file a name and a location. After you save the document for the first time, these commands no longer display a dialog box at all but simply save the document under the same name and in the same location.

To make a copy of the file and give it a different name, different location, or even a different *file type,* use the File⇨Save *As* command from the menu bar to open the Save As dialog box. This procedure is helpful if you need slightly different versions of the same file (for example, if you're sending the same letter to three different people).

The Save As dialog box is a close relative of the Open dialog box that you see in Figure A-3 — a twin, in fact. These two dialog boxes work in almost exactly the same way: You must enter the new file name, and you can also assign a folder and disk for your new file to go into by following these steps:

1. **Type a name in the File Name box of the Save As dialog box.**

   The suggested name is highlighted at first, so just type and your new name replaces the suggested one. Or click the File Name text box, press the Delete or Backspace key to delete the characters, and type new ones. (Omit the three-letter extension, .doc or whatever; your program supplies the extension automatically.) Use up to 256 characters, including spaces but not the \/"*?"<> or | characters.

2. **You may browse to open a folder on a disk drive, as I describe in the preceding section, or create a new folder as I describe in the following section.**

   If you do nothing else but type a name, your file simply goes into the folder that the program chooses for you.

3. **Click the Save button (or, in some programs, the OK button) in the Save As dialog box to close the dialog box and save your file.**

Managing files and folders

You're the boss concerning files and folders. You can move, copy, rename, or delete any file or folder on a hard or floppy disk. (Avoid moving or deleting anything in the Program Files or Windows folder, however, or you may damage programs.) Copying is especially useful: You want to save a copy of any important file or folder to a floppy in case your hard disk fails.

The following instructions work whenever you have a My Computer window open on your screen.

In some programs, such as Works or Word, the following actions also work in an Open or Save (or Save As) dialog box:

- **Copy a file:** Right-click the file's name or icon to select the file and choose Copy from the pop-up menu that appears. Double-click the My Computer icon and browse to view the contents of the disk drive or folder where you want to put the copy. Then right-click that window and choose Paste from the pop-up menu.

- **Move a file:** Do exactly as I describe in the preceding bullet for copying a file, except that, instead of choosing Copy, choose Cut.

- **Copy or move a file by dragging:** Begin with two windows open (or a window and a dialog box), one displaying the file that you want to move and the other displaying the folder where you want to put the file. To move a file, click the file's icon and drag the icon to its destination folder. To copy a file, press and hold the Ctrl key while dragging. Release the mouse button after you're done.

- **Rename a file:** Click the file's icon or name and then click its name. The text of the name now appears highlighted within a surrounding rectangle. Type a new name or click within the text to insert or delete text. Click anywhere outside the rectangle after you're done typing.

- **Delete or undelete a file:** Drag the file to the Recycle Bin icon on your screen to delete it. Or click the file and then press the Delete key on your keyboard; if a Confirm File Delete dialog box appears, click its Yes button. For instructions on restoring deleted files or emptying the Recycle Bin, see the discussion of the Recycle Bin icon in the section "Viewing the Windows Desktop," earlier in this appendix.

- **Manage folders:** You move, copy, rename, or delete a folder just as you do a file. If you copy, move, or delete a folder, you copy or move all its contents with it.

- **Create a folder:** In a My Computer window, choose File⇨New⇨Folder from the menu bar. In a Save or Save As dialog box, click the New Folder button if one is present. (Refer to Figure A-3.) The words new folder appear highlighted; type a new name for the folder. Press the Enter key after you're done typing.

Controlling Program and Document Windows

Windows is full of windows. No surprise, right? Everywhere you look on-screen, more and more of these rectangles appear, full of cryptic controls, exhibiting odd behaviors, and obstinately refusing to show you the parts of your document that you want to see. In this section, I show you how to take control of your windows.

Controlling program windows

Whenever you run a program, it does its thing entirely in a window: the *program window*. (*Sometimes* computer terms make sense!) You can run several programs simultaneously on your PC, each one in its own window, or you can *maximize* a program's window to fill your screen.

Here's what's what in the program window:

- Every program window has a bar at the top known as the *title bar*.
- Whenever you're working in a program window, that window is *active*, its title bar appears in color (usually blue), and it appears on top of all other windows. Otherwise (if, say, you switch to using another program), the title bar remains a dull, sleepy gray. Any keyboard commands that you use (such as Ctrl+S) apply only to the active program window.
- To select a program window (make it active and move it to the top of other windows), click its title bar.
- To move a program window, drag it by its title bar.
- To change the size of a program window, click any edge or corner (causing your cursor to turn into a double-headed arrow) and drag.

The title bar also contains buttons (in the right-hand corner) that are useful for controlling the size of your program window, as shown in the Works title bar in Figure A-4.

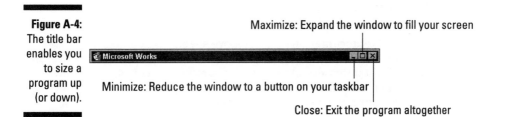

Figure A-4: The title bar enables you to size a program up (or down).

Maximize: Expand the window to fill your screen

Minimize: Reduce the window to a button on your taskbar

Close: Exit the program altogether

Figure A-4 shows you how to minimize, maximize, and close a program Window, and defines what those terms mean. After you minimize or maximize a window, here's how to restore it to its previous size:

✔ After you maximize a window, Windows replaces the maximize button with one that looks like two overlapping rectangles. Click this button to restore your program window to an intermediate size.

✔ To restore a window after you minimize it (shrink it to a button on the Windows taskbar), click its button on the taskbar.

Controlling document windows

Program windows often contain even more windows. In Works and Word, for example, whenever you create or open a document, that document gets its own Window. Document windows work very much as program windows do, with a few twists, as the following list describes:

✔ If Window is a selection on the program's menu bar, click Window to explore the various document-window controls the program provides. Two common choices in the Window menu are Cascade (make all document windows overlap neatly) and Tile (put windows side by side, like tiles). You can also make any window active by choosing it from a numbered list at the bottom of the Window menu.

✔ If you minimize a document window, it shrinks to an icon or rectangle at the bottom left of the program window. Click that icon or rectangle to reinflate the document window.

✔ If you maximize a document window, the tiny buttons that control that document window appear just below the title bar (but still on the right side).

Moving around in a document window

At the side (and perhaps at the bottom) of your document are scroll bars that enable you to move a document around within its document window, as the following list describes:

✔ **To slide the document up or down in little increments:** Click the arrows at the top and bottom.

✔ **To slide the document with a lot more speed:** Click and drag the box in the middle up or down. (Or click above or below the box.) The position of this box on the scroll bar gives you a rough idea of where you are in the document. If the box is large, nearly filling the scroll bar, that means most of your document is visible in the window.

✔ **To slide the document horizontally (in case your window isn't wide enough to display the entire width of the document):** A horizontal scroll bar at the bottom of the window works the same way as the vertical one.

An alternative to scrolling is to use the *navigation keys* on your keyboard: the arrow keys or the Page Up, Page Down, Home, and End keys. The arrow keys move one small step at a time, but the Page Up and Page Down keys move one window's worth at a time.

Ordering from the Menu Bar

If you're hungry for action, do as hungry people do everywhere: Use a menu to place your order. *Menus* are simply lists of words running horizontally (a *menu bar*) or vertically (a *drop-down menu*), from which you choose commands to give your program. Figure A-5 shows a Works menu bar. Nearly all Windows programs (and the Windows Start button, too) display menus and menu bars of some description.

Click any of the words in a menu bar, and a menu of commands drops down. Then click one of these commands to execute it. To perform the command File⇨Save, for example, you click File on the menu bar; then click Save on the menu that drops down. Yet another menu may appear, or if a menu selection ends in an ellipsis (those ... things), a *dialog box* springs up. (See the section "Dealing with Dialog Boxes," later in this appendix.)

Shortcut keys give you another way to make choices from menus. All those underlined letters in the menu bar that you see in Figure A-5 are known as *hot keys*. Press the Alt key *and* the hot key in any menu bar (Alt+F for File, for example). Then, in the menu that drops down, press the hot key for your next menu choice, such as *S* for Save. (You may either hold the Alt key down throughout all your choices or release it after the first choice and simply press hot keys alone.)

Toiling with Toolbars

Toolbars, such as the Works toolbar shown in Figure A-6, are rows of buttons appearing just below the menu bar. Some programs, such as Word, have many toolbars. Click View⇨Toolbar (or Toolbars) to enable or clear check marks that display toolbars.

Drop-down menu

Dots indicate that a dialog box follows

Underscores indicate Alt+key shortcut   Menu bar

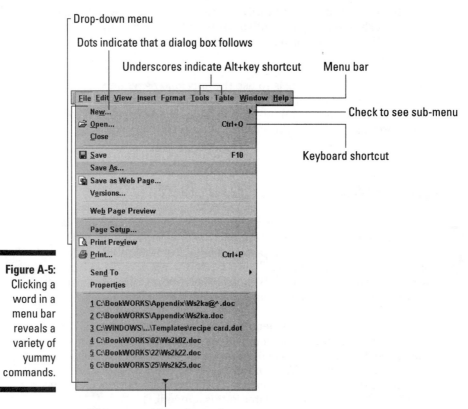

Check to see sub-menu

Keyboard shortcut

Figure A-5:
Clicking a
word in a
menu bar
reveals a
variety of
yummy
commands.

Click to see additional menu items

Change your typeface (font)

Start a new document

Save

See additional buttons

Print preview   Bold   Center

Copy   Underline

Figure A-6:
Buttons
commonly
found on the
Works
toolbar.

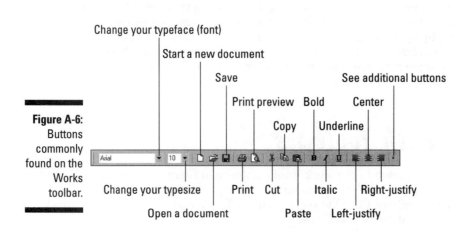

Change your typesize   Print   Cut   Italic   Right-justify

Open a document   Paste   Left-justify

Each button with an icon is a shortcut to some command in the menu bar. Click the button and stuff happens: You save your file, for example, or you print something out. The selection of buttons available in certain toolbars may change, depending on exactly what you're doing in a particular program.

If you forget what a button does, just move your mouse cursor over it (but don't click). In nearly all recent Windows programs, a tiny square appears containing a description of the button's function.

Dealing with Dialog Boxes

Dialog boxes crop up all over the place. In a menu, a command that ends in three dots (. . .) warns you that you're about to deal with a dialog box. The dialog box's purpose in life is to enable you to specify important details about the command — for example, what to name the file that you want to store and where to put it.

On the surface, dialog boxes look like windows, but you usually can't shrink or expand dialog boxes. (You can drag them around by their title bars, however, if they get in the way.) Internally, dialog boxes can look like darn near anything. Figure A-7 shows an example from Works.

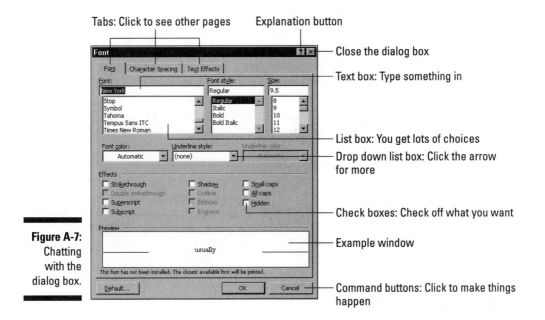

Figure A-7: Chatting with the dialog box.

Don't try to memorize all the names and distinctions of the thingies in a dialog box. I certainly don't use the names any more than I must. Just refer back here if you get confused. The following list describes how this dialog box stuff works:

- **Text box:** To fill in a text box, you type something in the box, or sometimes, you can click something in a *list box* immediately underneath the text box. After you open a dialog box, it usually lists some suggestion in the main text box. You can delete that suggestion by pressing the Delete key, or you can change the suggestion by clicking in the text box and typing in some text. Press the Backspace or Delete keys to erase single characters or text that you select. Do *not* press the Enter key after you're done typing; click the next item you want to set up in the dialog box. Click the OK button or press the Enter key after all items in the dialog box are as you want them.

- **List or scroll box:** List boxes or scroll boxes show you a list of choices. Click one of the choices, and that choice generally appears in a text box above the list. Double-click a choice, and the computer not only chooses that item, but it also tells the dialog box, "I'm done — go and do your thing!" If more text appears in the list than fits in the list box, a scroll bar appears alongside the list box. (Such scroll bars work the same as the scroll bars in your document window.)

- **Drop-down list box:** These guys will show you several choices, but to see them you have to click the down-arrow (tiny triangle) that is part of such a box. (Sometimes clicking the contents of the box also works.) A list of choices appears; click one.

- **Check boxes:** Check boxes are like tax forms but are more fun. Check off one or more items by clicking them or the boxes next to them. A check mark appears if an item is selected. Click the item (or the box next to it) again to deselect it.

- **Option (or "radio") buttons:** These buttons enable you to click only one thing in the list. The center of the button appears black after you select the button.

- **Command buttons:** The most important command button is the OK button (or Close button). Click the OK button if you're ready to proceed with the task the dialog box is about (for example, printing). Click Close if you make some changes but don't want to perform the task (printing) yet. If you want to back out of a command, click Cancel. Other command buttons may take you to yet more dialog boxes.

Finding Files

Sometimes, your files get lost in the enormous hard disk drives that most PCs have today. Windows provides a helpful feature for finding these files.

Click the Start button on the Windows taskbar and then choose Find⇨
Files or Folders. The Find dialog box appears, displaying multiple tabs; click a
tab name at the top of the dialog box to select a tab. Following are the most
useful things to know and their tabs:

- ✔ **Choose the Name & Location tab if you know part of the name.** First,
  press the Del key to delete any text in the Name text box and then type
  the part of the name that you remember in that text box. Substitute the
  * (asterisk) character for the part that you don't remember. If you're
  looking for an invoice, for example, and you know that the file begins
  with *inv,* type **inv***. To look only for Works documents, add a Works
  three-letter extension to the end: .wps for a word-processing file, .wks
  for a work-sheet file, .wdb for a database file, or .wcm for a communications file. For Word documents, end with .doc.

- ✔ **Choose the Date Modified tab if you know when you created or last
  modified the file or folder.** First, click Find All Files Created or Modified.
  Then specify the date, either by clicking between and then double-
  clicking and typing over the dates shown or by clicking During the
  Previous and typing a number of preceding months or days in the box
  provided.

- ✔ **Choose the Advanced tab if you know any text that the file or folder
  contains.** This selection is *really* useful because you don't need to
  remember anything about the document's name or location! If you wrote
  a letter to Mr. Smith about condominiums, just enter either **Smith** or
  condominium into the Containing Text text box. Try to choose a unique
  word or phrase.

After you specify something on any or all of the tabs, press the Enter key or
click Find Now. A list of documents appears at the bottom of the Find dialog
box — just double-click the document you want to open it!

Printing

Printing proceeds roughly the same way in each Works program. As in all
Windows programs, Microsoft quite unreasonably forces the commands that
have anything to do with printing to live in the File menu: File⇨Page Setup,
File⇨Print Preview, and File⇨Print.

Setting up the page

Ever since humankind moved from scrolls to pages, things have gone down-
hill. Now you must worry about top and bottom margins as well as side margins. Even worse, now you can print the darn pages sideways! Back to scrolls,
I say! Meanwhile. . . .

You don't need to set up the page every time you print — just set up the page once for each document. In fact, if you like a program's normal settings, you don't need to set up the page at all. If you want to create custom settings and use them for other documents, create a custom template. See Chapter 8 for details.

Making marginal decisions

Page margins in Works are the spaces between the edge of the page and the regular body text (including any footnotes) of the document. *Headers* and *footers* (text, including page numbers, that appears on the top or bottom of every page) go within these page margins.

Choose File⇨Page Setup to open a Page Setup dialog box; then click the Margins tab. The Margins tab then graces you with its presence, where you can change margins for the text, for headers, and for footers.

Setting source, size, and orientation

At least 99 percent of the work you probably will print is on standard-sized paper in the normal, or *portrait,* orientation. But for spreadsheets, flyers, and other work, you may want your printer to print sideways, in the *landscape* orientation. (Do *not* put the paper sideways into your printer!)

To set up a Works Suite program for a different size or orientation of paper, choose File⇨Page Setup to open a Page Setup dialog box; then click the Source, Size & Orientation tab in that dialog box. (In Word, click the Paper Size or Paper Source tab.) You'll find the controls you need there.

If you're using an envelope or special paper and you need to use a special paper-feeding place (or *source*) on your printer, click the Source drop-down list box and select that source from the list that appears. If that source is a manual-feed slot, Works prompts you at the right time to put the paper in.

Options for printing and displaying

Each type of document has certain special quirks, or *options,* for page setup. With spreadsheets and databases, for example, you may or may not want gridlines separating lines and columns of data. See the individual tool chapters in this book for more information on those options.

Previewing coming attractiveness

You've formatted your document, and you think that it's going to look quite attractive on paper. But how do you know? Time for a preview of coming attractiveness! Specifically, time for *Print Preview.* Print Preview shows you how Works thinks your document is going to look in print, without wasting paper.

Most Windows applications provide a Print Preview feature similar to the one you find in Works. Read about Word's Print Preview feature in Chapter 11, for instance.

You can access Print Preview in one of the following three ways:

- ✔ Choose File⇨Print Preview from the menu bar.
- ✔ Click the button in the menu bar that looks like a document with a monocle.

  (To determine whether you're on the right button, place your mouse cursor over the button without clicking; if you're on the money, Works shows you a tiny label reading *Print Preview.*)

- ✔ Choose File⇨Print and then click the Preview button in the Print dialog box that appears.

To view maximum or minimum magnifications of the document, click the Zoom In or Zoom Out buttons respectively, or click the document itself. Three clicks on the document take you through all available magnifications. After magnifying the view, use the vertical and horizontal scroll bars to check out any parts of the document that extend beyond the window.

Printing on actual paper!

What next? Imagine — printing on paper instead of on a computer screen! (Beats printing on an empty stomach!) Printing is a little different for each program in Works Suite. For the most important printing variations within each tool, see the chapters on that tool. In general, however, printing is pretty simple if things go right. Simply perform the following steps:

1. **Turn on your printer and wait until it comes on-line. (With some of the latest printers, this step isn't required! As soon as a print job moves to them, they power up all by themselves.)**

   Most printers have an indicator light somewhere to tell you that the printer has had its morning coffee, done its exercises, and is ready to roll. See your printer manual.

2. **To print the entire document without further ado, click the Print button on the Works toolbar (the button with a picture of a printer on it).**

   At this point, you're essentially done. Read the following section "Terminating printing," if you change your mind about printing the document.

If you want to print only a part of the document, print multiple copies, change to another printer (or fax modem), or adjust the quality of printing, follow these steps instead:

1. **Choose File⇨Print from the menu bar or press Ctrl+P.**

   The Print dialog box comes to your aid.

2. **Make any of the following choices in that dialog box:**

   • For multiple copies, click the Number of Copies box and type the number of copies that you want (but don't press the Enter key yet). You can also click the up or down arrows next to that box to change the page count.

   • To print a specific group of pages, click in the Pages box and type the starting and ending page numbers.

   • To print faster but with less quality, click the Draft Quality Printing check box to select it.

   • To change to another printer (or *print* to a fax modem to send a fax), click in the Name drop-down list box and select a printer (or fax modem) from the list that appears.

   • To use any of the special options your printer provides, click the Options button.

     A printer-specific dialog box appears. You need to check your printer manual for instructions.

3. **Click OK (or press Enter).**

   If all goes well, you can now just close your eyes and wait for your document to print. If you change your mind about printing — quick, read the following section, "Terminating printing." If you're *printing* to a fax modem, your fax software now takes over.

Terminating printing

Don't just turn off the printer to stop printing. Your paper may get stuck halfway, or your PC may become confused and send you error messages. Don't just turn off the PC, either, or it may become confused after you restart it.

Depending upon what printer you use, a dialog box for your printer may appear on your screen as soon as you click OK in the Print dialog box (Step 3 of the preceding section). If such a dialog box appears, click the stop button (sometimes marked with a black square). I can't tell you exactly what to click because the dialog box comes from your printer's manufacturer. Check your manual for details.

If no dialog box for your printer appears on your screen, Windows provides a quick emergency stop procedure for terminating a printing job. Follow these steps:

1. **Click the printer icon on the Windows taskbar, over to the right near the clock.**

2. **In the dialog box that appears, right-click on your file's name and then choose Cancel Printing from the menu that appears.**

   Printing may continue for a page or so, depending on how many pages have already downloaded to your printer's memory. If it keeps up too long, turn your printer off and then back on to clear its memory.

Hollering for Help

This book covers so many topics that I can focus on only the basics. If you need help with a topic — especially a more advanced feature of a program — and this book or another *For Dummies* book just doesn't answer it, your best alternative is to read the Help files.

If you need help *while using any program,* you can perform any of the following actions to read the Help files:

- **Press the F1 key.** The exact results of pressing F1 vary from program to program. In Word, for example, pressing F1 wakes up a cartoon helper known as the Office Assistant.

- **Choose Help⇨Contents from the menu bar.** This action enables you to browse topics from a table of contents. Choose Help⇨Index to use an alphabetical index to locate topics. Some programs, such as Word, combine these choices: Choose Help⇨Contents and Index.

For help on Windows itself (not one of your programs), click the Start button on the Windows taskbar and then choose Help.

After you choose Help⇨Contents and/or Index from a program's menu bar (or choose Start⇨Help from the Windows taskbar), you see a Help Topics dialog box containing three tabs sticking up like index cards. Each tab gives you a different way to access the same Help documentation. Click a tab to use that method, as the following list describes:

- **Contents:** Organizes information by topic, similar to a table of contents. Double-click any subject with a book icon to view a list of documents about that subject. Double-click any subject (or single-click it and then click the Display button) to view the documentation, which appears in a Help dialog box. Click the Help Topics button in that dialog box to return to the Help Contents dialog box.

✔ **Index:** Organizes subjects alphabetically, similar to a book's index. Click the text box at the top (marked 1) and type the first few letters of a word or phrase describing what you want Help on. As you type, Help looks at what you've typed so far and scrolls the list of subjects in the lower box (marked 2) to match your typing, if it can. Press the Backspace key to change your typing.

If a subject displays a folder icon, click the folder to reveal subtopics. After you see the subject you want, double-click that subject. Click the Help Topics button in that dialog box to return to the Help Contents dialog box.

✔ **Search (in Windows 98) or Find (in Windows 95):** These options search exhaustively for every occurrence of whatever text you type (say, **disk**) in the text box at the top of the tab. Box 2 of this tab displays words that begin similarly to whatever you type (say, disk and disks); click one and then double-click any topic in box 3. (The first time that you use this tab, your program may ask permission to take a moment to build an index. Press the Enter key if your program does ask.)

As you're reading a Help document in a Help dialog box, you can get more information in several ways, as follow:

- Click any green, underlined text to get an explanation of that text.

- Click any Related Topics button.

- Click a button displaying a tiny arrow (a *shortcut* indicator) to actually perform the activity that Help describes.

- Click the Back button to return to previous panels.

To clear your screen of Help, click the X in the upper right-hand corner of the dialog box.

Shutting Down

To shut down your PC, click the Start button; the Shut Down Windows dialog box appears. The choice Shut Down the Computer is currently chosen in that dialog box; click the Yes button. Wait until your PC screen indicates that you may now turn off the power to your computer and then (what else?) turn off the power.

If a program gets stuck (doesn't respond to you) or your PC otherwise seems to go haywire, try the same procedure but click the Restart the Computer option before clicking the Yes button. An emergency way to free your PC from a stuck program is to press Ctrl+Alt+Delete. A Close Program dialog box appears with a list of running programs; click the name of the stuck program and then click the End Task button. Wait a minute and, if the program's still stuck, repeat. You then may need to restart your PC before running that program again.

If you shut down your PC, any programs currently running also shut down. If you've performed any work in those programs that you haven't saved as a file, the programs prompt you to do so.

Index

• X •

• Y •

• Z •

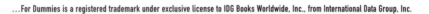

Discover Dummies Online!

The Dummies Web Site is your fun and friendly online resource for the latest information about ...For Dummies® books and your favorite topics. The Web site is the place to communicate with us, exchange ideas with other ...For Dummies readers, chat with authors, and have fun!

Ten Fun and Useful Things You Can Do at www.dummies.com

1. Win free ...For Dummies books and more!
2. Register your book and be entered in a prize drawing.
3. Meet your favorite authors through the IDG Books Author Chat Series.
4. Exchange helpful information with other ...For Dummies readers.
5. Discover other great ...For Dummies books you must have!
6. Purchase Dummieswear™ exclusively from our Web site.
7. Buy ...For Dummies books online.
8. Talk to us. Make comments, ask questions, get answers!
9. Download free software.
10. Find additional useful resources from authors.

Link directly to these ten fun and useful things at **http://www.dummies.com/10useful**

For other technology titles from IDG Books Worldwide, go to
www.idgbooks.com

Not on the Web yet? It's easy to get started with *Dummies 101®: The Internet For Windows® 98* or *The Internet For Dummies*, 6th Edition, at local retailers everywhere.

Find other ...*For Dummies* books on these topics:
Business • Career • Databases • Food & Beverage • Games • Gardening • Graphics • Hardware
Health & Fitness • Internet and the World Wide Web • Networking • Office Suites
Operating Systems • Personal Finance • Pets • Programming • Recreation • Sports
Spreadsheets • Teacher Resources • Test Prep • Word Processing

IDG BOOKS WORLDWIDE
BOOK REGISTRATION

Register This Book and Win!

We want to hear from you!

Visit **http://my2cents.dummies.com** to register this book and tell us how you liked it!

- ✔ Get entered in our monthly prize giveaway.

- ✔ Give us feedback about this book — tell us what you like best, what you like least, or maybe what you'd like to ask the author and us to change!

- ✔ Let us know any other *...For Dummies*® topics that interest you.

Your feedback helps us determine what books to publish, tells us what coverage to add as we revise our books, and lets us know whether we're meeting your needs as a *...For Dummies* reader. You're our most valuable resource, and what you have to say is important to us!

Not on the Web yet? It's easy to get started with *Dummies 101*®*: The Internet For Windows*® *98* or *The Internet For Dummies*,® 6th Edition, at local retailers everywhere.

Or let us know what you think by sending us a letter at the following address:

...For Dummies Book Registration
Dummies Press
10475 Crosspoint Blvd.
Indianapolis, IN 46256

™

**BESTSELLING
BOOK SERIES**